Wandering Through Mysterious Labyrinths

Reflections on a Life of Adventure, Pilgrimage and Chronic Disease

Bob Scheidt

Copyright © 2023 by Bob Scheidt

All rights reserved, including the right to reproduce this book or portions thereof of in any form whatsoever without prior written permission from the author. This includes storage in a retrieval system or transmission in any form. For information, contact the author.

Dedication

*This book is dedicated to my mother, Anna,
my wife, Nancy, and my daughters, Adrienne and Amberly.
Four strong women who made me who I am today.*

"Yours is a bright light
A soul on fire
My inspiration
You take my spirit higher."

— Mindy Smith, "Please Stay"

CONTENTS

Prologue IX
1. Remembering The Future 1
2. Teenage Daydreams 9
3. A Descent Into Darkness 17
4. Finding My Way Out Of The Darkness 25
5. Following In The Spirit Of Kerouac 37
6. Running And Being 51
7. Angels Appear Among Us 63
8. The Immeasurable Calculus Of Distance 69
9. I Take To The Open Road 85
10. The Call Of The Sirens Of California 103
11. Walking The Bulge And Bulk Of The American Continent 113
12. Among The Cathedral Towers Of The Alpine Deities 127
13. The Divinity Of The American Landscape 141
14. Walking My Way Back Home And On To The Ocean 165
15. Circumambulation 185
16. The Enchantments Of The Empire By The Sea 201
17. The Deserts Stark And Holy 217
18. Texas Radio And The Big Beat 231
19. Chasing Autumn Along The Atlantic Ocean 247
20. Islands, Keys, And The Ghost Of Ernest Hemingway 253
21. The Poisons And The Panaceas 261
22. An Awakening On The Way To Santiago 269
23. Across France In Search Of Jeanne D'arc 289
24. Camino Portuguese And The Most Fascinating City In The World ...309
25. Death And Beauty On The Camino Del Norte 325
26. A Return To The Way Of The North 339
27. Obrigado, Merci, And Gracias 353

28. Following In The Footsteps Of Myself 365
29. The Camino Of The Imagination — The Covid-19 Pandemic 373
30. My Magnum Opus — From The Black Madonnas Of Southern France To The End Of The Earth 381
31. Walking My Way Into The Next World 385

Prologue

*"I recall the wonder of it all,
Each dream of life I'll share with you."*

— Patti Smith, "Dream of Life"

Each and every year is a gift bestowed to me. Whether by a sky god, a benevolent creator, or just good fortune. I am here once again, on the surface of the earth, still breathing and moving forward, and still searching for something I'm not sure I'm ever going to find.

It took me until my 50s to begin to understand that it is the search, and not necessarily the finding, that is important. So now, after 67 years of living on the precipice of life, with three near-death experiences, surviving countless broken bones, and contracting three serious and dangerous health issues, I'm just glad to be alive. And not just alive but overjoyed to be able to continue adventuring in the mountains, through the forests, and along the oceans of the world.

From age 18 on, I led a dualistic life. My journeys left me in a state of awe, and yet dealing every day with life-threatening Type 1 diabetes was wearying to the bone. I experienced times of darkness and dread in my adventuresome life, as well as times of exhilaration and illumination while surviving disease and injury. At times, they blended seamlessly. In a way, they became my life, and sometimes they defined me. Of course, there were other aspects of my life journey: my wonderful childhood, my marriage, the births of my children, the operations of my business. But the dual nature of my lust for adventure and my obsession-like concentration on my health problems affected even those.

    This rendering of my life's adventure combines those defining aspects of my nature and how I rolled with the punches and stayed in the fight to create a life of epic proportions. I hope to inspire all kinds of readers, with all kinds of problems, who also have the all-encompassing gift of the human spirit to help them work through their troubles. Turn the page, and let the stories begin.

Chapter 1

Remembering the Future

*"I've been telling my dreams to the scarecrow,
About the places that I'd like to see.
I say, 'Friend do you think I'll ever get there?'
Aw, but he just stands there smiling back at me."*

— Sara Evans, "Born to Fly"

My idyllic childhood experience took place in a semi-rural stretch of heaven in Berks County, Pennsylvania, surrounded on three sides by uninhabited woodlands, rippling creeks, and fields with boundaries made by old-fashioned stonewall fences. On the other side of the house lay an empty plot of land on which my dad, my two brothers, and I built our own athletic field, a place to play baseball, soccer, and football with an outdoor basketball court one house down.

I was the oldest son, and my brother, Scott, came along three and a half years later, with my youngest brother, Craig, arriving a year later. Other than minor fights and disagreements, we got along quite well and would to this day fiercely stand up for each other. We went to a small middle and high school five miles away with a competitive nature when it came to sports. My brothers and the neighborhood kids excelled on the athletic fields, but I found that competitiveness wasn't important to me. My dad would come home from a hard job in an iron foundry, take off his back brace, and pitch hardball to us, trying to mold us into excellent baseball players. But often he would tell me, no matter what sport we played, "You aren't driven enough. You lack aggressiveness. All you seem to want to do is walk around in the woods all the time." He was right, and I sometimes felt that it was a fault of mine. Years later, though, I slowly came to understand that meandering was my greatest talent.

The backcountry represented freedom to me, a place that had no coaches, teachers, or referees, at least not in the traditional sense. It still had laws — the law of nature — plus heat and humidity in the summer, bitter cold and deep snows in the winter, not to mention poisonous leaves and berries. Though I rarely saw any, a few black bears, bobcats, and coyotes roamed the lands. I saw plenty of snakes, mostly water snakes, ringnecks, garter snakes, and black snakes, which I'd catch occasionally and keep in cages in the basement. I would take them out and play with them while watching television at night, and one time, a big, scary-looking hognose escaped its poorly built cage and snuggled under my mom's folded wash in the laundry basket. While the hognose is known for being gentle and serene, my mom didn't know that, so it was lucky I was home and able to pacify the writhing snake and my screaming mother.

Looking back, I realize how cruel it was to keep those snakes from the freedom of the creeks and wildlands. I guess I rationalized it because I occasionally found snakes crushed on the road in front of the house, and it taught me lessons about vulnerability versus free rein. If I wanted my freedom with all the dangers that came with it, then those snakes should have had their freedom, too. (One of those dangers I accepted was rattlesnakes, thick black-and-yellow creatures that abounded in the stone fences and the abandoned rock quarry where I climbed. You learned early on to place your hands carefully.)

The first of many close calls with death I would have in my life came in childhood. I sometimes slept in a lean-to I'd build in the woods near the house, and one night a nasty thunderstorm came upon me. My mom came out to bring me in, and a bolt of lightning split a tree in half very close to us.

Other adventures filled the years. The summer after I turned 14, I dammed up a creek in a holler and created a little ice-cold swimming hole. That winter, to my mom's trepidation, I shouldered my pack and walked — and sometimes crawled — out behind the house and over huge snow drifts during a full-on blizzard. Upon reaching my campground, I stamped out a tent platform just like Sir Edmund Hillary did when he became the first man to climb Mount Everest, made a small fire using twigs and dead branches, and fell into a state of total contentment. The wind roared through the night, and at times I shivered in my cheap cotton sleeping bag, but I felt like a mountaineer on a high peak in a remote corner of the world. The blizzard closed school for a week, so I had several nights of play acting like I was in the Himalayas.

I took a hunter safety course at school taught by a legendary outdoorsman, and I enjoyed learning about guns and ballistics and hearing stories about epic hunting adventures. My dad was so proud because he felt this combined both our interests, my love of walking and his love of hunting. On the first Saturday of small-game hunting, we woke at five in the morning to a cold, frosty day and consumed a hearty breakfast before heading out on foot through my familiar woodlands. Even though I always felt at home out here, something felt different, uncomfortable even, that day. My dad sensed it, too, and grumbled a bit.

As we walked through a harvested corn field, a rabbit ran out from the brush. He told me to shoot it, but I paused, and as the rabbit zig-zagged in a wide circle around us, I raised my shotgun and followed it. This eventually put my dad into the line of fire, and he started to yell, "Don't shoot! Don't shoot!" He didn't have to worry, though, as I wasn't going to shoot anyway. It angered him when I said I really wasn't into hunting, but we tried over a few more weekends, even going to a deer-hunting camp with his brothers and buddies at a cabin up north. I liked driving the deer through the mountains by walking fast toward a group of waiting hunters, but that only drove it deeper into my mind that I could walk fast in the woods during every season of the year.

And I realized my dad didn't understand me.

"You don't like hunting 'cause you are lazy and don't want to get up early in the morning to go out into the cold," he told me.

But that was hardly the case.

"I want to get up every morning early and head out into whatever the weather is, and walk forever," I countered. "I just don't need to carry a gun or shoot anything."

To add insult to injury, I told him I wanted to sell my gun for a camera, for that was how I would shoot wildlife. Thus ended my hunting career.

My dad was not a tyrant — he just wanted us to spend time together. In fact, he later went on hikes with me, sometimes using the excuse that he was scouting for deer. He even joined me, many years later, for some of my greatest hiking adventures.

***

My family was not into traveling. Sure, we occasionally took bus trips to Philadelphia or New York City to catch a baseball game, or traveled with the Boy Scouts or our local church to the World's Fair in New York or the Smithsonian Institution in Washington, D.C. But we never planned and set off on week-long, adventurous wanderings across states to lakes or national parks. Instead, I went to three one-week camps, one after the other, during the summer.

The first took place in a nerdy state Grange camp in central Pennsylvania, with some recreation, a pool, lots of Grange stuff, and arts and crafts. A lot of girls hung out at our cabin of six boys because the governor's son was our bunkmate. Good-looking, popular, and talkative, he also had grown out of that awkward phase early teens go through, both bodily and in terms of self-confidence. Little did I know I would lag for a few more years.

From day one, we knew the camp held a big dance on Thursday night, and each boy was supposed to ask a girl to be his dance partner. Some kids were scared to jump in the lake or to climb the mountain among the huge timber rattlesnakes. I liked those things — it was asking a girl to be my dance partner that terrified me. My plan was to let the other four guys in our cabin pick from Mr. Confidence's leftovers, and I'd try to convince one of the last of the bunch to at least make it look like we were having a good time. It turned out she was just as shy as I was. We danced a few times, and the rest of the night we sat in a corner, barely talking, the definition of wallflowers. But we survived and never saw or heard from each other again.

The next camp, run by the Lutheran Church, sat by the Delaware River at the base of the Pocono Mountains. I barely remember any details of my time there other than that I got a little uncharacteristically homesick, which my mom loved to hear because she felt I was trying to escape home life. (I always thought she was glad to have a vacation from my neuroses.) There was one major highlight, though: the rocky beach crawling with poisonous copperhead snakes.

The third week of my summer travels took me to Boy Scout camp, held just south of the ridge the Appalachian Trail passed over. There were no girls at this camp, which was both good and bad. With the morning oatmeal cooked in 10-gallon pots and scooped onto plates with a small shovel, it's no surprise the food wasn't very good. I mostly loved some of the Native American lore we learned, although the teacher may have been a fake Native American. He seemed genuine, however, and this began my lifetime of interest in the history and culture of all the tribes I eventually encountered on my wanderings.

One highlight of Scout Camp was seeing huge rattlesnakes on our daily hikes. Kids and leaders got bit regularly, and we learned what to do if it happened to us or a hiking partner. One day, our leader even caught a snake and carried it one mile back to camp as it writhed and rattled so we could milk the venom and display it for all to see in a glass cage. It was a fantastic specimen.

The big sendoff on the last night was a performance of off-key songs and low-rated skits. The feature of the evening was the sisters of the scouts, whose parents had dragged them along to watch their lame brothers try to sing and act. I enjoyed watching the displeasure on their faces.

My favorite part of the summer, though, was hanging out with my maternal grandparents for two weeks. The eight miles of travel put me far enough away from home to make it seem like a different world. It was different from spending time with my paternal grandmother, who lived just down the street from us, though I did love sleeping over at her house, too. In Hancock, where my grandfather and grandmother Reinhard lived, there were new kids to hang out with, trains running all day and night a block away, and cows in a meadow behind the house. My grandfather also was a great baseball manager and coach, so of course we built a playing field in his side yard, with one bonus: there was an electric fence in the outfield, which became the home-run boundary. On the other side of that fence, along with the regular cows, was a huge bull chained to a telephone pole. If someone hit a home run, the outfielder had to roll under the fence, grab the ball, and run like hell because the ornery bull would stomp, snort, and strain to break the chain. He never got loose, but we were all terrified of the possibility. It did liven up the game.

I adored just hanging out with my grandfather, partly because he was a storyteller, a prankster, and a man about town. Everyone called him Monroe even though his name was Manrow, which I never understood. He took me with him on his daily trips to town, where he included me in his pranks, happy to have a foil along. At the bigger grocery store, where everyone knew him, he would have me distract the older women shoppers so he could put tampons and menstrual pads in their carts. Then we would watch when they checked out and were surprised to find something they didn't need. Soon, a voice would come over the loudspeaker: "Will Monroe Reinhard please refrain from putting things in other shopper's carts."

He had nicknames for everybody, including the one-armed grocer at the smaller store just across the railroad tracks. My grandfather called him lefty, even though he only had a right arm. I was always asking the man how he lost his arm, but he never told me because he said it was too gruesome to describe. We always stopped in at the town barber, who my grandfather called "the butcher," and then we went to the meat market, where the actual butcher asked him if he wanted the usual two-pound slab of ham. My grandfather would say, "Yes, you know how I like it: fresh, but could you make sure it's dead this time. Last week it was still snorting." Once again it was an old routine followed by raucous laughter.

My wife and kids have always noticed that to this day I display many characteristics of my grandfather Reinhard, especially the pranks and humor. I am honored by any comparison to him. Whenever I hear a distant train whistle, I immediately am transported back to those days sleeping in Hancock. My three grandparents all passed on to the next world in the 1990s, and I still miss them. All of them make me want to play a huge role in my own grandchildren's lives.

Whenever I was back home, I continued spending vast amounts of time wandering the woods and fields, among the creeks, rock crags, and rolling hills. There was so much variety that it never got old for me. I reveled in this freedom, thinking I would never want to leave. But then something subtle started calling me. Some of the further vistas showed me other worlds. The field across the street took me over many of those fabled stone fences, built almost 150 years earlier. After crossing four fields and several fences, I ascended a mild grade where, at the top, I could look north toward a high ridge, probably 30 miles away, that ran from west to east.

I had known about the strangeness of that range, how it appeared a bright dark blue from a distance but looked wrapped in a green canopy when you got closer. It was called the Blue Mountain ridge, and on top of it ran a series of paths and dirt roads for 2,000 miles. At the prominent point I looked at, known as the Pinnacle, the highest point in my county, you could walk 1,100 miles south through six states to Georgia, or north 900 miles to Maine. You would end up on the highest peaks east of the Mississippi River. The pull of that visionary trail would never leave me. Though it took two more years for me to get there, the sight and idea of it formed the beginning of my slow emergence into the rest of the world — into a life of adventure.

Other features of the landscape drew me further beyond. A bouldered spot called Ginter's Peak sat to the northeast of our house, about a two-mile hike and scramble away. I liked climbing it on cold, clear, late-autumn evenings as the dark gathered around the dusk. You could watch the lights blink on in the houses spread out below and in the stars spread out above. Though I felt content about where I was in that space and time, a nagging voice called me in a language I didn't yet understand: "ultreia" — "go beyond." As I descended the peak by flashlight and hiked back to the house, I mused on where exactly "beyond" was. I had no idea, but I knew I had to go.

Then one day, the visions and dreams began. I saw jagged, snow-covered peaks above sky-blue glacial lakes. The Great Plains stretched out to the horizon, populated by many tribes. A vast ocean and rocky cliffs. Places of big medicine amid canyons and seismic rifts in the earth. Years later, I read that astrophysicist Stephen Hawking called this "remembering the future" And that writer Joseph Campbell spoke of it as "the calling." I felt it in my mind and gut, but most of all, I felt it in my heart and soul. It was soon time to leave those provincial landscapes that had so nourished my youth, strengthened my body, sharpened my instincts, and set my mind a-wondering. The world was calling, and I felt I had no choice — I had to answer that call.

Chapter 2

Teenage Daydreams

*"The dogs on Main Street howl 'cause they understand
If I could take one moment into my hands
Mister I ain't a boy, no I'm a man
And I believe in a promised land."*

— Bruce Springsteen, "The Promised Land"

Back in early high school, they tried to put me in a box. But then in eleventh grade, I experienced a rapid growth spurt, both in body and mind, and I became too big for the box. It took a lot of hard work in my junior year for that to happen. Academically, I had to accept the fact that math and science, at least the higher-echelon courses like calculus and trigonometry, were too difficult for my right-brain way of thinking. I knew I needed good grades to get into college, so I dropped back to general math and brought my dismal grade point average up a few points.

While I did okay in biology, chemistry and physics confounded me. A buddy of mine, the local school drug dealer, tutored me. He never studied or handed in homework, but he aced all the tests, saying it came naturally to him. He said he spent his spare time reading about quantum physics and quantum mechanics, and he learned chemistry by operating his own drug lab. With his help, I squeaked by with a C.

One month before graduation, he told me he was dropping out. I told him that was crazy, that no one drops out this close to the end.

"That's exactly why I'm doing it," he said. "Nobody else does it. My work here is done!"

I never heard from him again, but his work tutoring me helped me through some difficult times. And then a few years later, I forgot everything I learned from math and science.

***

I wasn't the sharpest tool in the shed, but I was sharp enough to know I had to come out of my shell. My shy disposition, especially around girls, had me wrapped in a neurotic bundle of nerves. To break out, I figured I had to throw myself into a bunch of uncomfortable situations. In a debate class, I led my group to a huge win by arguing against sex ed by ending my rant with, "Experience is the best teacher!" I, of course, had absolutely no sexual experience at the time. I took a speech class and joined drama club, and though it was late in the year, I got to learn all of Romeo's dialogue for "Romeo and Juliet." (I still remember about a third of it.) I joined the school newspaper as the cub sports reporter and started to find a groove for writing, using my access to some of the jocks to get the inside locker room news. That got me in trouble with my senior sportswriter superior because I scooped him even though he was a jock. He had even more access than I did but was not as good of a writer. I was not afraid to submit controversial articles either, some which got turned down, although others squeaked through the sensors. I butted heads with the faculty adviser at times, but I did learn the craft of writing from her. I also had her for English class during those two years, where I was exposed to the classics of literature.

Around this time, my body also changed. I had always lagged the other kids physically. I didn't shave until I was 25, while other kids started in 10th grade. (One of my buddies had full facial hair in eighth grade, but that's because he flunked three times and was actually 16.) I had a huge growth spurt the summer before eleventh grade and eventually grew to be six-feet, one-inch tall. I joined an after-school weightlifting club and became good friends with the meatheads there. I found out that most of them were very educated in sports nutrition and body mechanics, with some philosophy thrown in. Some days, I rode my bicycle to school solo, and other times my buddy Kurt rode with me. Back in elementary school, Kurt and I had made a path through the woods and along a creek to walk the one mile to school. Years later, on the six-mile ride back home from high school, we had a choice of a straight-up steep climb, called Carls Hill, or a slightly longer but less-steep climb called Smoketown Hill. Either way, I became very fit, which would bode well for the difficult future ahead of me.

I joined the track team during my senior year after an unsuccessful time on the baseball team. Baseball was in the Scheidt blood; both my brothers were excellent players, but it somehow missed me. Scott was a great catcher, known for his skilled handling of pitchers. Craig was the best hitter out of the three of us, and he also had a sizzling fastball as a pitcher. Both went on to become wonderful coaches for their own sons.

I thought track would suit me, but I still had a problem with structure and eventually dropped out. I headed back to the after-school gym, where one day a guy suggested we walk six miles to a soda machine, have a drink or two, and then walk back. He said it would be good for defining our muscles. Only a few miles in, I was already totally in a groove. The other guys got tired and a bit grumpy on the way back, saying, "What the heck did we get ourselves into?" But I felt on top of the world, my beta endorphins pumping, and upon arrival, I knew I could have gone on for many more miles. I had inadvertently found what would become my most towering of talents.

My favorite class during high school was a mini course taught by a history teacher in which we read "The Lord of the Rings" trilogy, which encompassed over a thousand pages. A lot of the roughneck kids whined and moaned; they had probably never read a book before. I was skeptical that even I, an avid reader, could pull this off. The teacher was enthralled with these books, though, and his enthusiasm rubbed off on us. He even got into the history of Middle Earth, and we debated the decisions the lead characters made. Even now, I like to think about what parents and school boards would have to say about a history teacher teaching the history of a fictional kingdom. I loved the subversive nature of that fact. Everybody got so hooked on the story that I think that teacher may have turned most of those kids into lifelong readers. At the very least, he made one out of me. I still reread Tolkien to this day.

I graduated from high school in June 1973, having greatly improved my grades from the year before, and just missed out on the

"Most Improved Student Award." My SAT scores totally reflected the disparity of my strengths and weaknesses, though. I got a 380 out of 800 on the math portion and a 700 out of 800 on the verbal. That put me somewhere in the lower-middle range of kids taking the test. I applied to Penn State to study journalism with low hopes of getting accepted.

Around this time, I noticed a red light on a distant hill almost five miles due east of my house. At night, I would go out in the front yard and gaze at this flashing beacon that called to me. Though it was a television transmission tower and the red light a warning for low-flying planes, for me, it acted as part of the alchemical process that began to lead me somewhere else.

One day, I put on my pack and followed a power line in that direction. It was May, and the noonday sun was heating things up. I scrambled for an hour and a half, mostly uphill through high grass and thorn bushes. I came out onto a clearing, and there before me stood the tower. I immediately got goosebumps all over my body. The process was working. Something important was happening. It was another step, of many, that took me into the wider world.

After viewing the distant Appalachian Trail from my rock perch in the field across from my house, I decided to finally plan to hike some of it. I researched it at the library and started eyeing some equipment in the local sporting goods store. I also had learned some survival skills in Boy Scouts. I figured I would end up going alone, but a few days before our graduation ceremony, some of my fellow classmates got the idea that to celebrate we would take a three-day backpacking trip on the A.T. Eighteen classmates were interested. Slowly, that number dwindled to two: one of my best buds and an engaging art chick I had only gotten to know during the last few weeks of school. I felt overjoyed as I anticipated my first far-afield adventure, but the hike turned out to be a bit of a debacle. The Appalachian Trail in Pennsylvania, we soon found out, is a mass of rock piles set on a ridge and surrounded by a canopy of deciduous trees on which were painted white marks for us to follow. We started walking from the top of the mountain at the Route 309 crossing. Immediately, we grew hot, got bug bites, saw our first rattlesnake, and got lost. It turned out we were following the State Game Lands boundary markers, which resembled the trail markers. No one, including the guidebook, mentioned that.

My buddy, Einar, wore an old pack basket, and as the sweat increased, it rubbed his shirtless back raw. When he took it off to rest, his back looked like he had the wounds of stigmata. The girl, Nita, carried a Duluth Trading Co. pack, the kind trappers carried in the great north woods. It hung down too far on her back, and we tried to adjust it to no avail. We carried a cast iron frying pan that weighed a ton and wore all-cotton clothes that never dried. Most of our food was canned and heavy because we would not pass by any stores during the three days. Our three-person tent weighed 10 pounds and leaked like a sieve, which we found out on the first night during a thunderstorm.

Day two brought more rocks and heat and bugs, and then we ran out of water. The map showed a road crossing ahead, and we anticipated finding a soda machine. No such luck, though, as the hamlet of Eckville consisted of a few boarded-up seasonal cabins. We were so thirsty that we thought of hitchhiking home. I talked them out of it by telling them there was water ahead, though I wasn't sure. As the sun started setting, I followed my instincts and went off-trail to find a small, moss-covered spring that had cold, sweet water bubbling out of it. We were saved, though we guzzled so much so fast that we all got gut aches. The next day was better: not as hot, and more than half the day we walked on a dirt road. We got to the parking lot in Port Clinton where we were to be picked up, giddy just to have survived.

But the biggest lesson I learned from those not-very-fun three days was that, days later, I only remembered the high points: the camaraderie with my mates and how we pulled each other up during the many rough times, forging friendships that are harder to attain in civilized life; the peace and quiet of the woodlands; the feeling of accomplishment in my tired muscles; and, finally, the wonder we felt at the four vistas. Tri-county Lookout, Dan's Pulpit, Pulpit Rock, and the Pinnacle — all those peaks had a cool breeze blowing across them and views of thirty or more miles in several directions. But the most truly transformational aspect of those vistas is that I was now looking at a band of hills to the south where I had stood two years ago, gazing north to these mountains. My vision from back then had now been accomplished, and I wanted to return again and again and then go further. I had expanded my world once more, and the path led on forever.

***

Every summer at the end of June and into the beginning of July, the eastern Pennsylvania area where I grew up hosts the Kutztown Folk Festival to celebrate our culture. My ancestors emigrated to this area from southern Germany. The landscapes here were similar, and the distinct four seasons of weather were comparable. A bunch of us are Lutherans, following the Christianity of Martin Luther, so while our festival is a bit like Oktoberfest because we do have a beer garden, it's hardly Oktoberfest because we only have one beer garden. Instead, it's more about how our culture has evolved over four-hundred or so years into its own uniqueness, with its own traditions, foods, crafts, games, music, and dances. Most people in my neck of the woods grew up at the folk festival, tagging along with their parents when they took time off from their regular jobs to work at or donate their time at the annual event. As we grew into teenagers, some of us found the folk festival to be an introduction into the working world, as it gave us our first paychecks.

For me, the festival had three prominent parts: intriguing, haunting, and marvelous. The intriguing aspect was how I was made assistant to the herpetologist at the snake lore tent. I felt at home among the various specimens, and while I did not get to handle any poisonous snakes, or milk them for antivenom, I did get to display all of the others. My favorites were the big black snakes that took skill to handle; you need to place your hand on the back of their heads since they might be prone to bite. I decided that I wanted to be a herpetologist when I grew up. My mom wasn't pleased, not because of my future career choice but rather because of my present financial situation. At the end of the week, my wages consisted of the choice of two snakes to take home with me. She finally agreed, saying, "Okay, you can continue to be the son that God has sent to test me." And then she added, "But no poisonous snakes!"

The haunting part of the festival was how, year after year, a couple of times a day, a reenactment of a historical hanging took place with an executioner, a real gallows, and the stuffed dummy of a young woman. As the story goes, unmarried Susanna Cox was arrested and tried for the ax murder of her newborn baby in 1809. She was sentenced to death by hanging. Amid a clear blue and cloudless sky, the hangman fixed the noose around her neck and asked if she had any last words for the gathered crowd. She proclaimed her innocence, and when her heart stopped beating, a great black storm cloud rose on the horizon, advancing toward the gallows, producing torrents of rain mixed with deadly lightning strikes. Later, they found out she had been unfairly accused and the possibility existed that a prominent member of the town parliament had raped her and then killed the baby to cover it up. I still get chills watching all this play out many, many years later, and occasionally I dream of the sound the trap door makes as the executioner releases it and her body falls, her neck snapping as the noose tightens, squeezing the life from her unfairly accused body. A tale as old as time.

During the 1973 festival, my brothers and I volunteered at the Topton Grange tent. They served cafeteria-style meals, and we operated a beverage stand. We also served as night watchmen, which meant we got very little sleep. One hot evening, a few of our gang of ne'er-do-wells snuck in and stole an ice-cold watermelon from a neighboring stand. As we cut it up, the police walked in. We all thought we were going to be in huge trouble, but one of our gang offered a slice to each of the cops, and they were very grateful. It turned out they were just making rounds. We seemed to be avoiding trouble, barely, during the entire festival.

The marvelous event happened mid-week. I had noticed a cute girl working at a hex-sign jewelry stand in the building next to our beverage stand. By then I had conquered my fear of girls, at least to a point. But I was still a little scared to just go in and chat with her cold, so I devised a plan. The first day, I sent my younger brother over to her with an iced tea and straw and followed up the next day by sending my middle brother with another tea.

"Look for beautiful, brown pig-tailed braids sticking out of a colorful bonnet, big expressive green eyes, short of stature but possessing a mighty presence," I told them, knowing they'd need a detailed description of the right girl or they would mess it up.

I instructed them not to say a word. Finally, on the third day, I strolled in, less nerdy looking than my brothers, though not by much, and handed her the tea and straw and told her I had sent the drinks because I was worried about her hydration. She didn't seem repulsed by me or my stupid scheme, and I managed to use complete sentences as we talked a bit. She took a quick break, we took a short stroll around the festival, I asked her on a date, and she accepted. I felt on top of the world, and the rest is history.

Chapter 3

A Descent into Darkness

*" 'Twas in another lifetime, one of toil and blood
When blackness was a virtue and the road was full of mud
I came in from the wilderness, a creature void of form
'Come in,' she said, 'I'll give you shelter from the storm.'"*

— Bob Dylan, "Shelter from the Storm"

The girl, Nancy, and I continued dating through the summer. We were now committed to each other. I worked at a car dealership in town, washing cars, and Nancy would occasionally drop by to bring me lunch on her way to the pool. She was a fearless woman and wore a white string bikini. I would take a lot of crap from my co-workers for the rest of the day after her visits, mainly about, "How does a guy like you date a girl like that?" So I would turn it around on them and ask the same question: "How does a loser like you end up with the nice wife you married?" None of us had any game, though we all thought we did.

I received a letter from Penn State advising me to attend a community college for my first year. If I could prove worthy of Penn State's journalism program, then I could transfer my credits there for my sophomore year. I prepared myself mentally for attending Reading Area Community College, then only in its second year of existence and located near the foundry where my dad worked.

In the meantime, I quit the car-washing job with two weeks to go. I needed one big adventure before the summer ended. The Boy Scouts were taking a week-long backpacking trip on the Appalachian Trail, part of the 50-mile award they gave out. I had no interest in awards or having to obey leaders for that length of time. Of course, I was very interested in adventure, so two buddies, Rickie and Randy, and I devised a plan: we would tell our parents that we were going on the Boy Scout hike but instead follow our own route, on foot, to trails, mountains, campsites, and swimming pools of girls whose parents were out of town and had well-stocked, unlocked liquor cabinets. It seemed like a great plan until my dad wanted to drive us the one mile to the church where the Boy Scouts were meeting. I managed to deflect him by saying, "It's only one more mile, which is nothing if you are walking fifty."

We left the house mid-morning on foot, using lightly travelled blacktop, dirt, and wooded roads to reach the mighty Blue Mountains. Under a clear blue sky, those mountains beckoned to us, representing freedom, fun, and feats of imagination. I felt a few small pangs of guilt for misleading my parents, but I rationalized it by thinking that I would leave home in the near future anyway and be out of their hair for the rest of my life. Sure, we would keep in touch, as I would send them dispatches from far-flung frontiers of the world, and they would be proud of the great and famous explorer I had become.

My two buddies did not have girlfriends. I was committed, so the plan was for me to call from payphones so Nancy could try and find us when we were at road crossings. I started to question her sanity for wasting her time trying to find a rogue like me. I had yet to understand the insanity of love.

That first day took us through the village of New Smithville. We were hot and tired and needed to find a place to camp. As we looked to the hills, we noticed a trail to the west and followed it one mile to a clearing in the forest. Here we established our base camp. We had hiked fifteen miles and were centrally located to the many exciting possibilities that existed around the village. Girl No. 1's house and swimming pool was right across the street. A general store was a mile away, and a pool and recreation center belonging to a trailer park sat a mile to the west. Girl No. 2's house and pool were just over two miles to the east, with a truck stop diner along Interstate 78 just north of that. Our idyllic campsite became our end-of-summer slice of heaven.

We established a routine while waking the second day: turn on the tiny, tinny-sounding transistor radio, which only picked up one Top 40 station out of Allentown; start a fire; cook breakfast or eat cereal and milk; take a long hike; eat lunch either from our supplies or go to the store; walk to the trailer park swimming pool; take another hike, ending at the diner; go swimming at either of the girls' swimming pools; and then walk home to sleep. Repeat for five days.

I was adamant about hiking a certain number of miles each day. We were, after all, supposed to be on a 50-mile hike. I was overjoyed to determine we'd walked a total of 73 miles. We lorded that over the Scouts who waved their 50-mile award badges in our faces weeks later. Plus, we mentioned three other factors we had that week that they didn't have: swimming pools, girls, and alcohol. What we didn't have was Scout leaders and badges. ("We don't need no stinkin' badges.")

We ran short of money toward the end of the week and were finally kicked out of the diner for barely leaving any tips for the burned-out, middle-aged waitresses. We also wore out our welcome at the trailer park and at both girls' houses. Their parents were due home soon, and we had gone a bit hard on the liquor supplies. Plus, when my buddies drank too much, they made unwanted passes at the girls.

Nancy stopped at our campground one night, which was a good test for our future. If she saw how much I reveled in the grubbiness and freedom of adventures, she might not be so keen on a future with a tramp like me. But I detected no bad vibes from her. I seemed to pass the test. When I walked her down the rocky descent to her car, I warned her to take it slow since she had clogs on. I thought they were sexy but also bad for hiking. She didn't heed my advice and instead went jogging down the trail. Halfway down, she overtread her ankle and scraped her legs. I ran back to camp and grabbed the first-aid kit, proceeding to clean and patch her wounds. I distinctly remember getting very excited about touching her smooth, tanned legs, though I forced myself to concentrate on the doctoring at hand. I also had to realize that this girl was a rebel, and if we stayed together, she wouldn't always take my advice. I actually liked that about her, so she also passed a major test.

We left our hallowed campsite early on Friday afternoon. Once again, the hot August sun beat down and slowed our pace. During the late afternoon, we realized that we would not make it back to my house, so we detoured a mile to the farm where Nancy lived with her parents and where we could sleep hidden in the tall cornfields. It got dark right as we arrived. Our adventure wasn't over yet though. The next morning, we were greeted by the sun and a jolly farmer. He got a laugh out of the idea that someone would sleep in a cornfield and invited us in for a big breakfast. I figured he must be the hired hand. He looked too young to be Nancy's father, plus she always mentioned that her dad was grumpy and they didn't often see eye to eye. We were indeed famished, having exhausted the last of our camp food, so we nervously followed him in. I wondered what kind of mood the grumpy dad would be in when we met. As we entered the big kitchen, I saw Nancy looking gorgeous as usual, making my heart skip a few beats. Her mom was very cordial as Nancy introduced us.

"I see you already met my dad," Nancy said.

Since that time, I have always gotten along with him. He always got out his pocket atlas to see where I was going to adventure next.

And so I passed another test. I learned on this amazing, week-long walk that adventures can be tests, in both obvious and subtle ways. Adventures were never easy, but they helped you grow mentally, physically, and spiritually. I looked forward to a life full of adventures — a life, even back home, lived like an adventure.

***

I began my college life in September 1973. Even though I was not academically inclined, I enjoyed the challenge, which also included a job in another car dealership washing cars for five hours every morning. Then I had classes from 1 p.m. until 9 p.m., after which I went home to the farm where I lived with Nancy and her parents, as she was completing her senior year of high school. I had to do my homework late into the night, writing papers on an old Royal manual typewriter. I can still hear those keys hitting the ribbon. I finally fell asleep for three hours, rising at five in the morning to pick up my mom and take her to her job in a sewing machine factory so I could use her car to go to my job and classes. It was exhausting yet exhilarating. I felt like I was slowly becoming the journalist I wanted to be, practicing to be a sleep-deprived foreign correspondent. I took the one math course I needed for four years of college, general math, from 5 to 9 every Monday night. I aced it, which for me was a solid C. That meant no more math.

I managed a B in world cultures, which I did enjoy. I especially excelled in communications, which included learning to speed read on a screen. My professor had me tutor other students for extra cash. During vacations, I also watched his old Victorian mansion in Wyomissing while he went to Florida. Nancy and I moved in for a week during each break and played house. The mansion turned out to be haunted, and male students, some of whom I knew, constantly stopped by. We soon deduced that the professor was gay and hadn't notified his favorite students that he was vacationing.

Another class I thrived in was literature. That was in the second semester and also a Monday night class. It was a difficult and grueling learning experience in which we had to read a novel every week and then write a 2,000-word paper due the next week. I read all week and banged out the papers during the weekend. Nancy was very accommodating, as were her parents, always hearing the tap of those typewriter keys. She and I didn't have a lot of free time together because we were both extremely busy, with her working at a sandwich shop and excelling in all her subjects during her senior year.

My literature class required a few students to read their essays each week in front of the other students and then get critiqued viciously by both the professor and the rest of the class. The professor was extra hard on my papers and readings, and I started to get a complex. She was a hard-boiled, attractive, sports car-driving character who I imagined probably got fired from a few good colleges for drinking or having affairs with students. We read a bunch of Shakespeare, which I was familiar with; some Russian authors I was somewhat familiar with; and a couple Hemingway novels I was experiencing for the first time. I think the professor was in love with Hemingway and wanted to be one of his mistresses. I fell in love with his terse, concise writing style. I also loved that he was an adventurer, and I hoped to one day follow in his footsteps throughout the world.

As we approached the end of the semester, I felt very nervous about my grade in this class. In the end, I received an A+, and after questioning her harsh criticisms, she told me it was tough love and that she felt I had something worth striving for. I needed revisions and read-throughs, but the time I put into it would be worth the finished project. I felt like I was slowly becoming a real writer.

Another plus at college was the access it provided to a library, not only for schoolwork but also books by famous adventurers, climbers, and travelers. It even had some how-to books on equipment and packing lists. I would skip a class now and then and sit by Lake Ontelaunee reading and re-reading these lists and accounts. Yes, I wanted to be a writer, but only to write about my real love: adventure.

***

Everything seemed to be following an upward trajectory: my relationship with Nancy, college, the adventures I was engaging in, and the future adventures that were still in the planning stage. But as I was to learn many times in my life, fate appears and rears her head like the hydra, full of venomous snakes instead of hair, and threatens to poison all those carefully laid plans. As Indiana Jones said, "Why did it have to be snakes?"

In the autumn of 1973, my energy lagged. I had a lot going on in my life, things that could drain the vitality of an average person. But when it came to energy, I had never been lacking. I started to feel a creeping sense of mortality. Then more symptoms appeared. Constant thirst, constant urination, weight loss, and, while driving, traffic signs became blurry. Nancy's mother was caring for a crippled aunt who suffered from diabetes, and she recognized my symptoms. I went to the doctor, and a blood test revealed I had a blood glucose reading of 670, which immediately led to a diagnosis of what was then known as juvenile diabetes and now is called Type 1 insulin-dependent diabetes. The idea confounded me. The diabetics I knew of were all elderly, and when I reported to the doctor's office every Saturday morning at 6 for a blood test, the long line stretching onto the sidewalk was full of elderly people. I think even the doctor was confused. I was his only young patient.

I threw myself into research, which in 1973 was quite limited. I needed to be reassured that my goals of adventure, and indeed my entire adventurous life, could be met and carried onward. I did not allow myself any self-pity or negativity. I indulged instead in all the usual sports psychology tropes. I used the analogy of climbing a mountain. This would be a slight setback, akin to having to cross a wide crevasse in order to continue to the summit.

But my doctor did not help. He told me I would need to take a daily shot of insulin for the rest of my life, though I would probably only live another 30 to 35 years. I did the math in my head as he continued to talk. If I was lucky, I'd live to be 53. A life diminished. My optimism kicked in and told me I'd have plenty of time to reach my goals, but then the doctor knocked me down again, telling me I'd have to take it easy. Any wounds would have a good chance of becoming gangrenous, which would result in amputations. I would be constantly dogged by the threat of blindness and the loss of a kidney or two. All of that was confirmed by Nancy's doctor, who advised her to think about our relationship. Was she willing to live a life caring for an invalid, and the possibility of her being a young widow? She never flinched. In the years since, she has sometimes thought about what a so-called "normal" life would have been like, but she is still here in my life, and so am I.

Diabetes as a way of life became our reality, and it was only the beginning of a series of troubles. A terrible, debilitating car accident; occasional seizures; a mauling by a huge dog; and a broken arm all followed in the next three years. The darkness swirled around us, then descended, dragging us down with it. How would we ever find a way out, back into the light?

Chapter 4

Finding My Way Out of the Darkness

"Wake up to find out that you are the eyes of the world."

— The Grateful Dead, "Eyes of the World"

Younger, fitter, newly diagnosed diabetics go through what's called a "honeymoon" phase soon after the diagnosis. I still felt good physically, before and after learning I had the disease. Mentally, I drew strength from my positive attitude, but I still had a lot of questions and maybe a trace of anxiety and depression gurgling around in my psyche. I had to make a lot of adjustments in my daily life, and my spiritual worldview took a major punch to the gut. Once again, thoughts of a life diminished crept in.

Probably the two strongest weapons in my arsenal were my yearning and calling to explore the world. I knew what it would take — mind, body, and spirit — to answer the call to a lifetime of adventure. I had read some of the diaries, stories, and accounts of explorers who had gone before me, including Lewis and Clark, Sir Richard Francis Burton, Ernest Shackleton, and Reinhold Messner, who'd mounted Himalayan expeditions. I vowed early on to research deeper, learn extensively, train my body even harder, and remember what I had heard in those solo journeys in the woods and fields of my adolescence: "go further; the world awaits."

In the early 1970s, we had no personal blood glucose meters, and in fact, I didn't get my first one until 1982. Instead, I calculated my blood glucose on how I felt and that weekly Saturday blood test. For many years after my diagnosis, I gave myself a disposable syringe of long-acting NPH insulin. It had four peaks and valleys, about every five hours. I had to plan my meals around those peaks; I had to eat when I wasn't hungry, and I couldn't eat when I was starving. Starting in 1982, I began taking short-acting mealtime boluses of R insulin. I had always had a good nutritional way of life thanks to my mom, though I did cut way back on sugar. I didn't think in terms of counting carbohydrates until 1982 as well.

***

Nancy graduated from high school in June 1974. Our commitment to each other was solid, and with that in mind, she also applied to and was accepted by Penn State. The next week, we drove to campus to check out the lay of the land and inquire about apartments and jobs. We both had student loans, so we figured we'd live spartan-like, working hard at both our studies and jobs. There would not be much time for extracurricular activities. It would be tough, but we had each other for support.

We left campus that weekend excited that our future was taking shape, committing once again to working hard for the rest of the summer and saving our money by living on love. In less than two months, our real life together would commence in a glorious fairytale, a story that would be retold over and over again, a saga for the ages.

We were three-hundred miles into the return journey with only eight miles to go until we reached home. Nancy was driving, and I was navigating. There was a traffic light ahead where we wanted to make a left-hand turn onto a rural road. We saw an ice cream shoppe on the corner as Nancy flicked on her turn signal. The traffic light gave us a green arrow to turn, and then a huge Cadillac seemed to appear out of nowhere, barreling head-on toward us. Nancy never saw it. I saw the end of my life on earth.

Then came a huge crunch of metal, right into my door. The initial impact threw me onto Nancy's lap, with my elbow knocking her out cold with a massive concussion. I realized we should get out quickly before we became engulfed in flames. While fumbling for the driver's-side door, I heard the continuous sound of metal crunching mixed with screaming. The Cadillac had spun around after hitting us, and the driver, distraught after returning from the hospital where her father had been admitted with a heart attack, had hit the gas instead of the brake and then continued into the ice cream shop. She hit two more cars in the parking lot before crashing into the glass front of the building where people waited to order. Six more people were injured, three in cars and three inside the shop. One of them was pregnant, and it was a miracle she did not lose the baby.

On the other side of the road, I managed to get the door open and started to crawl out. When I touched the ground, I fell. I hadn't noticed that my lower right leg was badly mangled. I felt like passing out, but I realized Nancy was still in the car. I grabbed the door handle and pulled myself up onto my good leg and started dragging Nancy out of the car. People came to help drag her, and now me, away from it. I lay there a bit, noticing the arrival of the first responders. I passed out to the sight of blinking red lights and the sound of someone yelling that it looked like the aftermath of war.

I woke up in the ambulance on the way to the hospital. The woman on the gurney next to me was thrashing about, screaming wildly. One of the emergency medical technicians asked me, "Could you please comfort your wife?" I looked over and saw the face I had glimpsed through the windshield of the speeding Cadillac as it crashed into us.

"That's not my wife," I replied. "That's the woman that caused this carnage!" Then I passed out again.

I stayed awake most of that night as the surgeons pieced my leg together and casted it all the way from my toes to my hip. I begged the nurses to find out if Nancy was okay. Half an hour later, they told me she had a bad concussion but was stable in a different hospital. I breathed a sigh of relief and then felt a searing pain in my left elbow, the one that had given Nancy the concussion.

***

I convalesced at my parents' house, and Nancy did the same at her parents' farm. We had no money, and finding a job would be difficult, especially since I had no idea when I would be able to walk again. Some hard cold facts were staring us in the face. Financially, we would not be able to begin our life at Penn State, at least for the fall semester. There would be no adventures that summer, and maybe not even during the rest of the year.

I had to dig deep to find my way through this setback. Type 1 diabetes works best when you are active for at least an hour a day, so I started taking two-mile hikes on dirt roads, through my hallowed woods, on crutches, in the heat and humidity of a Pennsylvania summer. I sweated so much that I got blisters in my armpits despite the rubber padding. I passed the time by reading adventure tales of long hikes by Colin Fletcher and Eric Ryback. I watched the Watergate trials every afternoon, learning all the major and minor characters, then talked about it like it was the greatest soap opera on television. Friends would stop by to borrow my tent or backpacks or technical clothing and talk with anticipation of their coming adventures, some I would have been on if life hadn't intervened. When they returned, they regaled me with stories of the hijinks that ensued, how it always turned into a misadventure because they were still finding their way, and how, at times, they wished I was out there with them, where they could tap into my experience and levelheadedness to balance the stress. This gave me a feeling of being there, but it also broke my heart. At least my equipment was going on adventures.

I made some money by selling homemade corn-cob pipes outside the folk festival grounds, where the busloads of tourists from New York and New Jersey were dropped off and picked up. It was a strategic location because my buddies would walk between the rows of seats with trays of pipes, pitching it to the grandmothers as the "last chance to buy your grandkids a souvenir for only 25 cents." Then they would point out the window to me sitting on a lawn chair, crafting pipes with my leg cast propped up on a table, and add, "Our friend is trying to make money to pay his way through college after breaking his leg in a car accident." Those damn pipes sold like hotcakes.

My bulldog Dutchess hung out with me all day long, following me on my crutch walks and occasionally sprinting after squirrels and rabbits. She was a loyal companion and helped me heal, though the sad fact was that, once healed, I would be so busy I would have less time to hang out with her.

A girl who was working on her grandfather's farm just down the street would stop by some afternoons with freshly picked strawberries. She claimed they were medicinal. We would sit on the porch for an hour or so, her doing most of the talking, as she took to vocal flights of fancy, stories that would zig and zag, one thread leading to another, and none of the elements relating to each other. And then like a mad genius, she would bring it together at the end. She was goofy and flighty and quite sweet, helping me pass my downtime. Both my mom and Nancy got a little nervous about her spending so much time with me, but this girl knew I was in a relationship, and in fact had graduated from high school with Nancy. I just think she needed someone to talk to, someone who actually seemed to be entertained by her wackiness, and of course someone with a broken leg who couldn't run away in the middle of a story.

One day, Nancy's father pulled into the driveway. It was not quite a year since he had invited me and my dirtbag friends into his kitchen for breakfast when he discovered us camping in his cornfield. I was touched that he had come to visit me. As a farmer, he didn't have a lot of time. He presented a bag to me, saying that he wanted to get me something to listen to while healing. He had stopped at the record store on Main Street in Kutztown, knowing I bought music there. He asked the owner to pick out something that would appeal to me that I didn't already own. I opened the bag and found a bright yellow double album by Elton John called "Goodbye Yellow Brick Road." I listened to it repeatedly during those long days of recovery, and it's still one of my favorite albums. It was a big deal that he did this for me, and I thought that maybe he really did want me as a son-in-law. If that was the case, he would get his wish granted two and a half years later.

***

I finally healed through the winter of 1974-75, and then it was time to get back in shape. That spring, I joined the Allentown Hiking Club, and in no time, only one day-hike in, I knew I had found my tribe. I liked the idea of having a quarterly listing of hikes and backpacking trips planned for every weekend. They also occasionally listed caving and rock-climbing trips. The variety was delicious, a virtual smorgasbord in which almost every weekend you could choose from a short day-hike, a long day-hike, or a two-day backpacking trip, with three- or four-day backpacking trips planned for holiday weekends.

The northeast winters can be brutal, so the action always slowed down a bit that time of year, but even then, the diehards would slog through storms or switch to cross-country skis, snowshoes, or even ice climbing. After joining a few different kinds of hikes, I started noticing a unique dynamic. These fellow hikers were extremely friendly and could exist comfortably in the wilderness on long solo trips, but the next week they would be totally gregarious during group events. Competitiveness seemed to be missing; everyone pulled together during strenuous outings. Another observation caught my eye: most of these hikers did not have athletic builds. All kinds of bodies were represented. Lots of older, even elderly walkers participated, but it was a mistake to take them lightly, even though I was one of the youngest members. Out on the trails, they could glide through the mountains at a steady pace with a pack on, day after day, in all kinds of weather and terrain. They could suffer, with joy and a sense of humor, through the worst of conditions. Many of the regulars soon became my kindred spirits and mentors.

I was extremely interested in the longer backpacking trips. I had lived in Pennsylvania all my life but had no idea of the wilderness trails in the north-central areas of the state. I had always dreamed of faraway, exotic mountains, rivers, forests, and lakes. But now my new tribe introduced me to a vast area of all those things, wild beyond belief, only a few hours away. I started going on extended backpacking hikes every long weekend. One of my favorites was the Black Forest Trail in Lycoming County, a 42-mile loop that had 13 major climbs and steep descents in and out of creek hollows, with vistas that looked out over hemlock forests all the way to the horizon. At night, if you sat on a ledge and watched the sun set, waiting for the lights to come on in the valleys, you would be shocked to discover there were no habitations below other than a few wilderness cabins that were only seasonally occupied. You could be out there for three or four days and rarely run into another human. You were more likely to see a black bear, a bobcat, or a fat timber rattlesnake. I had found God's country.

About 10 miles to the west of the Black Forest was the Susquehannock Trail in Potter County. It was an 85-mile inverted oval, and though it was connected to the Black Forest Trail by two links —

an eight-mile north link and a six-mile south link — the two big trails differed greatly. The Susquehannock was less steep, having only half the major climbs in double the mileage. It made up for having less elevation with a multitude of gently flowing streams, both large and small, which you sometimes could follow along the banks for miles and miles. One such spot is the Hammersley Wild Area, which lies 10 miles from any human area. You follow Hammersley Fork for almost eight miles through beautiful meadows until you come to a huge rock that blocks the stream, causing a six-foot-deep pool that is great to swim in during hot weather. It is a shock, though, as the water is icy cold.

If you start at the northern terminus to hike the entire trail in one week, you will reach a very small town at the southern terminus where you can resupply, called Cross Fork. The trail passes through a few state parks, including Cherry Springs, which bills itself as one of the darkest places east of the Mississippi River. Some of the open mountaintop meadows host star-watching parties in summer, and back in the '70s and '80s you could climb the Cherry Springs fire tower, which gave you unimpeded vistas in all directions. One of the hiking club members described the rolling forested mountains as "looking like someone kicked a bunched-up carpet into a corner." One of my dreams was to hike the Black Forest Trail, take the north link over to the Susquehannock, hike the entire oval, then take the south link back to the Black Forest for the end. That would cover 140 miles — almost two weeks' worth of pure isolation and adventure.

In Sullivan County, another exciting trail existed, one totally unique from any of the other trails. The Loyalsock Trail, named after the Loyalsock Creek, which snakes through the canyons, was named by Native Americans and means "fast water." The trail ran in a west-to-east line of 55 miles. The vistas were epic, and walking through the misty forests at dawn was like something out of the books of J.R.R. Tolkien. What set this trail apart was the many waterfalls, including a 90-foot ribbon called Angel Falls. One waterfall had a ladder made of wooden logs that you climbed right alongside the gushing water. Near the completion of the Loyalsock Trail was a magical spot known as the Haystacks, where the creek flowed in and around huge mounds of rock, creating a sparkling show of bright, sunlit water. Northcentral Pennsylvania turned out to be my Shangri La.

Some lesser used trails were the Mid State Trail in Centre County, the Donut Hole Trail in northern Clinton County, and the

Chuck Keiper Trail in southern Clinton County. I hiked them all, some multiple times, some on my own, but most of them amid the antics of the revolving cast of characters from the Allentown Hiking Club. When I wasn't backpacking, I was refining my equipment, testing it, reviewing maps and guidebooks, dreaming of past hikes, and daydreaming about future ones. It was a time of high adventure, and it consumed my life.

Many are the stories of the wild bunch that comprised most of the long-distance backpackers of the club. Jim was the unchosen leader. He was a bachelor, lived in a small second-floor apartment in the city, and went out hiking almost every weekend. At five-foot-six with a prominent beer belly, he didn't look like a long-distance wilderness trekker. He carried a pint bottle of Southern Comfort in the water bottle section of his pack, nipping at it throughout the hike. If he ran out of booze, he would hitchhike into town when we crossed a road. It could take a while since most of the trails were remote.

On the weekend of the 200th anniversary of the United States in 1976, a group of us set out to walk for four days on the Susquehannock Trail. In the late afternoon on the Fourth of July, Jim hiked two miles from our campsite to the nearest road and then hitchhiked into Coudersport to buy two six-packs of Genesee Cream Ale. We took bets on whether he would return, but sure enough, he made it back to camp as dusk darkened into night. We sat on a high clearing drinking beer, and off in the distance, fireworks began to light up the sky. It turned out to be an epic celebration for five tired adventurers, and it set the bar high for many years of adventures to come. After that, we never doubted leader Jim's ability to conjure a good time over and over again. He had some obvious problems, but when it came to hiking, he was fully functioning, out-hiking everyone else in our lively band of eccentric adventurers.

Joe was the opposite of Jim. Tall and gangly, skinny as a rail, Joe didn't have an alcohol problem. His obsession was snakes, especially poisonous ones. He would bring a snake-catching stick on hikes and put specimens into a bag to take home to his myriad glass cages. He lived with his mom in the suburbs, and she put up with his obsession, figuring it was better than drugs or drink. On one backpacking trip on the Mid State Trail, he tied the sleeves and collar of his spare T-shirt and dropped a huge yellow phase rattlesnake he had caught into this improvised bag. It fascinated me, but I felt glad to have my own tent that night.

The night before, as we camped on a ridge overlooking the distant lights of Penn State University, about a half-mile in from the road, a group of frat boys encountered us while walking back to a party. After they got drunk, they started bothering us. Joe normally was a mild-mannered guy, but he threatened to beat the bullies with his pointed snake sticks and to empty his bags of rattlesnakes into their cars. They decided to head back to campus after that, and we moved further into the woods.

In the '70s, you could buy freeze-dried dinners. They were lightweight, and all you had to do was boil water, pour it into the bag of food, and wait ten minutes until it reconstituted, and you could have a grand dinner. The meals never tasted that great, and you got bad, smelly gas from too much of it, probably because we didn't wait long enough for the reconstituting process to happen. We were too damn hungry. But all those bad memories of freeze-dried food don't stop me from getting goosebumps when I happen to see a packet in an old picture.

Another hiker, nicknamed Suds, tried his damnedest to figure out how to make freeze-dried beer. Every weekend, somewhere deep into a wilderness backpacking trip, he would pour cold spring water into a bottle filled with his newest magic powder, and soon we could have all the beer we wanted. It tasted terrible every time and never got better. Eventually, Suds just calculated the mileage to the next road where he and Jim could hitchhike into a town to get real beer. And just like Jim, Suds could hike rough, rugged trails and never break a sweat.

The Allentown Hiking Club wasn't exclusively an old-boys club and was in fact balanced pretty evenly with some hard-hiking sisters who came out regularly. One woman, Kathy, was a nurse and had just moved to the area from Colorado. The first couple of weeks she was in town, she joined the gang for a few backpacking forays. One weekend on the Loyalsock Trail, I slipped on a steep descent during a downpour. Kathy had to wrap my wrist twice a day. I enjoyed watching and feeling her skilled hands fix my injury. The other guys got jealous and would claim they too were hurting. I thought that was low of them, trying to feign injury just to have Kathy take care of them. My injury healed by the last day, and when Kathy asked if she should wrap it one more time, I said yes even though it no longer hurt. So who was I to judge the other scalawags in the club? When I returned home and Nancy heard the story, she wasn't happy, but she felt grateful that someone who knew what she was doing could take care of another one of my many injuries.

The other woman, Janet, was a very fit blonde who also was a long-distance athlete. She went on to run a couple of 50-mile trail races years later. She hiked with our gang as part of her training. It was hard to hold a conversation with Janet. She didn't have a lot going on in her life, and she didn't want conversation to slow her down. As I got to know her better, I was impressed by her detailed knowledge of all the trails we hiked.

By 1976, I had grown so close to these kindred spirits, who I hiked with multiple times each year, that I invited them all to my wedding to Nancy. Jim, Suds, Joe, and Janet all attended. Their wedding present to us was to outfit my wife with hiking and backpacking gear, including boots, a backpack, a sleeping bag, and a GORE-TEX raincoat. They knew how important that would be to our future. Nancy and I thought that was very endearing of them, and she would go on to get a lot of use out of it. Maybe more so than most of the other wedding presents.

***

There were times my optimistic thinking faded to the background and I thought I might be living an accursed life, if such a thing exists. I started to have seizures every couple of months. They were dangerous in that I could be driving, climbing a rock wall, or trekking into a remote region when they happened. They would manifest without warning, knock me to the ground, and leave me bathed in a pool of sweat and blood. It would take a day or two to recover, with all my leg muscles sore from cramping. The doctors initially thought I might have epilepsy since my father had grand mal seizures since he was eight years old. He took medication all his life and did not drink alcohol because of the diagnosis.

I went through rigorous testing, brain scans, and electroencephalograms after each episode, but no results were conclusive. I stopped driving and going on extensive hikes, replacing them with running shorter distances but faster and sticking close to home. Before all this began, I had gotten a Siberian husky puppy, and as he grew bigger and stronger, he ran with me. I named him Telemachus after the son of Odysseus, the hero of Greek mythology, as I was fascinated at the time by the book "The Odyssey." Telemachus was my trusted sidekick, and I figured that after solving the mystery of my seizure problem we could go on to longer overnight adventures, especially in the winter.

Tragedy now reared its ugly head once again. Telemachus also started having seizures, even at night, where we would wake up and find him so worn out it looked like he was dead. We took him to the vet, and after trying several medications to no avail, they advised euthanasia. After having him as my buddy for less than a year and a half, I held him as he died and then buried him in a field behind the barn on Nancy's parents' farm. I had picked him out because he seemed to be the runt of the litter, smaller and less lively than the rest of his brothers and sisters. I was always rooting for the underdog. He had overcome being the runt and become a strong, healthy compatriot. Now the inevitable comparison started to take form. I, too, was strong and healthy but also medically compromised. I, too, had the same kind of seizures. Though it doesn't make sense, I started to think, "Why shouldn't I also be put down?"

My seizures eventually were found to be the result of low blood sugar — not enough glucose reaching the brain and therefore causing it to seize. This is quite common among diabetics. People knew a lot less about the disease back then, especially since I only had Tes-Tape urine strips to test my blood glucose, and they were almost two hours behind the actual real-time blood glucose level.

I didn't feel the seizures coming on because I had always taught myself to ignore weakness and push through it. The valuable lesson I learned was to listen to my body. Feel, chart, evaluate, and compensate. To this day, low blood glucose seizures are always in the back of my mind, especially when traveling, training, and adventuring, and even more so when I go out alone. I went on to have a few nasty episodes, but with technology and further training and testing, I have been able to minimize them.

***

And the hits just kept on coming. While descending a steep mountainside in the mid-'70s, I slipped on piles of small acorns and fell, breaking my right arm. This was the second time I broke that arm

(I also broke the left arm when I was in eighth grade). I couldn't afford downtime, so I learned to use my left hand and thus became ambidextrous. I always tried to find the positive in every situation and every person.

Then, three months after the broken arm healed, I was attacked by a huge St. Bernard. Nancy and I were visiting her aunt's farm, and as we left, I bent down to pet the dog, which reared up and attacked my face, lion-like. He dragged both sharp-nailed paws down the sides of my face and tore off my lower lip with his teeth. I wrapped my face in towels and went to the hospital, losing a ton of blood, getting 70 plastic surgery stitches and having my lower lip re-attached. I looked like a mummy for three weeks and still have a few bad facial scars. The fun was never ending, and I would have laughed out loud if I hadn't been afraid of the stitches popping out.

Chapter 5

Following in the Spirit of Kerouac

*"These are the clouds of Michelangelo
Muscular with gods and sungold
Shine on your witness in the refuge of the roads."*

— Joni Mitchell, "Refuge of the Roads"

I'm not a great fighter, but I can take a punch. I get knocked down, and I get right back up off the mat before the count hits five. I've always been a fast healer. So I took a few punches, got back up, and healed my many wounds. But the biggest punch I took had come three years earlier when I fell in love with Nancy Lee Miller. I was still fuzzy in the head and reeling when I came off the mat after taking that hit. We'd been living together, off and on, for two years at this point in our story, but you can't live in sin forever. The time had come to make a commitment. We got married during an actual hurricane on October 9, 1976. That hurricane spawned a round of tornadoes and torrential rainstorms. True love cannot be stopped by weather. To this day, after being together for 47 years, my wife says, "Our life together has always been stormy." But I qualify that with, "But it's never been boring!"

Our wedding ceremony was fairly common except for the weather histrionics. We wrote our own vows. They were heartfelt but not wildly creative. Because of the foul weather, we could not take outdoor photos. The wedding reception, however, was a party for the ages. Both of us, and all our friends and relatives, knew how to celebrate and have a rousing good time. The weather once again played a role, though this time in the positive. Months before the wedding, we began receiving responses to the invitations. A hundred guests were sorry they couldn't attend because the Topton Halloween parade was being held the same night. Their kids were in the various school marching bands, driving fire trucks, or on organizational floats. But the hurricane caused the parade to be postponed. With an extra 100 guests now suddenly attending, the ranks of partygoers swelled to 600.

Luckily the venue was big and had two floors, with a dance floor upstairs where three buddies of ours, in a band called Trey, performed raucous rock 'n' roll tunes at full volume. It was hard to believe that guitar, organ, and drums could make that much noise. Even though the downstairs was where you could eat, drink, and talk, the music and dancing penetrated the ceiling, causing the lights to dim and sway. There was a no-alcohol policy on the upper floor, but people had flasks and pint bottles in their pockets, so there was nowhere you could escape the imbibing and inebriation. The polished wooden floors soon swarmed in sweat thanks to the jungle-like humidity the hurricane left in its wake. The wild dancing almost caused injuries, especially during the limbo.

Outside, the shrubbery alongside the building was baptized by volumes of vomit spewed by old high school classmates and my brother Scott, who had consumed way too much Champagne. Later, he crashed a few steps up the staircase, where he lay for the rest of the party, a goofy smile permanently plastered on his face. The party was supposed to end at midnight, but my father-in-law pulled a few strings with his fellow Grange Hall buddies. Trey kept up a relentless, driving rhythm, and the dancing reached a fevered pitch. Dancers started singing along, slurring the words to songs they could barely remember in their drunken, sweat-soaked state of mind.

At two in the morning, it started winding down. Drunks, including my middle brother, were carried to cars, driven home, and thrown onto front lawns. Others stumbled to their cars, where they slept until the sun crept over the roof. The members of Trey packed up their instruments, and upon waking the next day found they had lost 10 pounds each. Nancy and I drove to a motel honeymoon suite where we immediately fell into a deep slumber. The consummation had happened years ago!

***

Financially, times were still pretty rough for us. Nancy had just finished two years at Lehigh County Community College in May 1976, receiving an associate degree in computer programming. She then started working at Blue Cross/Blue Shield Lehigh Valley, while I began apprenticing as a painter/decorator specializing in both the exterior and interior of churches. Some had steeples as high as 80 feet tall, so my rock-climbing and mountain-climbing skills came in handy.

Now that Nancy had graduated and begun to work, the plan was that we would save money to pay off our student loans and eventually I would go back to college. Our apartment rent and food bills, though, left our bank account at an anemic level. We had to be economically creative with planning our honeymoon. It wasn't that I was a cheapskate — I just basically had no money. We decided to backpack along the Appalachian Trail in Shenandoah National Park in Virginia. There is no better way for young newlyweds to get to know each other than by taking a cheap adventure together. We splurged on a night each at Skyland Lodge and Big Meadows Lodge right on the trail, then camped in the tent for the rest of the trip. The costs of the resorts were negligible, but to us, they seemed the height of high couture. We also splurged on two nights of fine dining at both lodges and cooked food we brought from home on our Svea backpacking stove for the rest of our meals.

Our car got 32 miles to the gallon, so the drive south and back would be very cheap. Nancy packed the wedding gifts from the members of the Allentown Hiking Club, items that spoke to the wonderfulness of these kindred spirits of mine. They made sure Nancy and I could meet the challenge of the terrain and weather with trail-tested gear.

This was our first big adventure together, and we felt the high that goes with the planning, packing, picking of music, and finally the setting off down the road, rolling into the mountains of Virginia. We left on the Monday after the wedding, heading down Interstate 81 toward Luray Caverns. That's where a road took us up to the top of the

Appalachian ridge, where we then bisected the Appalachian Trail. Virginia has the most miles of the trail, with more than 500. If you planned to hike the entire trail from Georgia north to Maine, you would be a third of the way to completion at the point where we started.

The fall colors were at their peak with yellows, reds, and oranges in abundance and in equal measure. The Appalachian Trail in northern Virginia is one of the easiest sections of the entire 2,100 miles. It consists of mostly ridge walking with vistas to the west of the snake-like Shenandoah River and beyond into West Virginia's rugged Massanutten range. To the east, you are witness to the alluvial plains that roll and flatten to the Atlantic Ocean, except for a few monadnocks that stand out in bold relief from that plain, the most prominent of which is Old Rag. The lone peak of Old Rag has an allure to it; it calls out to be climbed. It is not easy, though, with a few tricky leaps of faith from boulder to boulder with nasty gaps in between, made even trickier in the rain or snow. For many years, Suds led the Allentown Hiking Club on a New Year's Eve/Day overnight trip where they slept in the shelter on the summit. Some years I heard it was brutally cold with substantial snow. I was not going to lead Nancy to Old Rag on this trip. She had to get used to carrying her new pack on the flatter Appalachian Trail ridge.

Starting out the first morning, we had overcast skies and drizzle most of the day. Nancy was not happy. One had to take the bad weather, and any discomfort caused by weather or adversity, in stride as part of the overall adventure. The low points always accentuate the high points. I learned this a few years before, but Nancy, still new to the journey, was on a learning curve. And everyone is an individual. Some handle adversity better than others. Nancy would hopefully get used to this as a part of our life together.

The next day, the rising sun started drying out the Shenandoah ridge. With yesterday's wind, leaves started falling and littered the trail with a carpet of vibrant colors. Soon they would turn brown and eventually crackle into dust. The balancing high points were in play that day. Vistas abounded every couple of miles, and there were places to rest in the series of shelters called "bird nests." We spent that night at Skyland Resort and the following evening at Big Meadows Resort.

The last days of our honeymoon led us over the Pinnacles, Stony Man, and Little Stony Man. At this time of year, there was little chance that we would meet a through-hiker, someone hiking the entire

2,100 miles in one go. Most of them start at the southern terminus in the spring and finish five to seven months later at the northern terminus on Maine's Mount Katahdin. However, a smaller number start in the summer in Maine and finish in Georgia in late autumn. We only saw one south-bounder, and after a quick hello, the hiker moved on fast. It was getting very late in the season, and that person would have to climb a few 6,000-foot peaks on which snow could be expected.

The short meeting was enough to create a sense of wonderment in my psyche and set me to planning a through hike sometime in the future. This was a fault of mine: instead of enjoying where I was, especially here on my honeymoon, I would drift off excitedly. It was a part of me I would have to learn to balance, one in which I would concentrate on what Ram Dass called "Be here now," with the creative vision of moving forward with a sense of wonder. I also was learning, even though Nancy and I had been together for over three years, that your future plans intersect with that of your significant other. Some of those "others" we would create together in the future. Time in the mountains, deserts, and along bodies of water expose you to deep, laser-sharp thinking. It keeps you both grounded and sends your imagination soaring. That is made even better when sharing the wonderment with someone you love.

The drizzle returned on our last day, obscuring some of the vistas, but we had plenty of magic to take home with us. Some of the most spirited moments of adventures happen on the drive home, when the feeling of accomplishment meets that of gratitude that the rigors of those days pushing oneself onward are now complete. Nancy had survived, our wedded bliss had survived, and now the challenge of returning to the real world lurked ahead. Together, we arose to that challenge and looked forward to beginning our married life together. I'm a big believer in the power of adventures to guide you.

***

We moved into a small apartment in a complex in the town of Topton, about six or seven miles from each of the places where we had grown up and where I had gone to school. In fact, the building where I went to kindergarten had been demolished to build our apartment building. Life was tough, but we were extremely happy. I worked outside for long hours in the heat and humidity of summer and the bitter cold of winter, sometimes high off the ground on ladders or scaffolds. Nancy worked at Blue Cross, which meant driving almost an hour to and from each day. My diabetes seemed to be in control, though the tools to check oneself were not yet available in the late 1970s. At least once a month I backpacked with the hiking club for three or four days at a time. We started adding new trails and new locations. We hiked the Appalachian Trail in New Jersey and New York. We tried a new trail in south-central Pennsylvania called the Tuscarora Trail, which paralleled the Appalachian Trail, sometimes 50 miles apart, and eventually ran into Maryland and northern Virginia. Rarely used and rugged, with a lack of water sources, it followed the ridge line with a descent and ascent into a gap every ten miles or so. Further north, we backpacked on the Quehanna Trail, an oval of 60 miles that started and finished in Parker Dam State Park. This trail was very remote.

Around this time, I became enamored with the writings of Jack Kerouac. I had read "On the Road" in 1975 and was blown away by how his writing made me feel like I was in the vehicle and moving across America. I wanted to recreate Kerouac's journeys and write about them. But what really rearranged my molecules was his follow-up book, "The Dharma Bums." Now his gang of holy fools was not only driving around America but also walking, hiking, and climbing. He spoke my language. One of my favorite sections was when his new mentor, Japhy Ryder (poet Gary Snyder in real life), takes Jack to an Army-Navy store so Jack can procure a wilderness kit. Under Japhy's guidance, he buys a rucksack, boots, cooking pots, a sleeping bag, and some wool clothing. After using the gear in the High Sierra, Jack dreams of future trips in America and beyond. He called it a "rucksack revolution," wherein everybody would be travelling and hiking, and there would be a network of like-minded souls with whom you could crash between trips to rejuvenate and get new ideas.

I had started to adventure locally with those same ideas, but the magical western part of the country called me to come and explore what Kerouac called "the broad bulge and bulk of the American continent." "The Dharma Bums" also introduced me to Buddhism, since Japhy Ryder travels to Japan to study and then brings that way of life with him back to the states. I found that meditation was useful to help me through all my health problems. I even found that meditating while walking really grounded me. With new knowledge and Kerouac's inspiration, Nancy, my cousin Mike (who was my best man in my wedding), and I got out the maps, reviewed our equipment, and started training for the altitude, approaching it all with an exuberant spirit beyond anything I had experienced before. Little did I know that I would duplicate that feeling many more times during the rest of my life.

We headed out of the driveway one August morning in 1977. Our plan was to follow Interstate 70 through Pennsylvania, Ohio, Indiana, Illinois, Missouri, Kansas, and on into Colorado and Utah. At 22, I had only been in a few eastern states since my parents were not really travelers, so driving through the Midwest to the mountains and deserts of the West was a big deal. We dug deep into our sparse cash supply to procure a cheap hotel room in Oakley, Kansas, where a nasty storm brewed with possible severe tornadoes in the forecast. The storm came on like a runaway freight train and lashed the tiny, exposed motel for a few hours. The roof remained intact, and we were so glad not to have been in our tent.

The next day brought what became one of my greatest memories. After driving across the plains from Kansas into Colorado for a few hours, we saw what looked like a mighty band of clouds rising from the prairie. It looked nothing like the thunderclouds we had witnessed the night before. These were majestic. After a few more miles of driving, we realized what we had been looking at through the dirty windshield: the front range of the mighty Rocky Mountains. A little nervousness and fear, or maybe it was respect, hit me. We would be climbing some of those formidable heights. The alpine world had been revealed to me, and it opened my mind to possibilities for the present but also to a future of gazing upon and climbing the mountains of the world.

We camped just west of Denver, hoping to start slowly acclimatizing to the elevation by starting 6,000 feet above sea level. The next day, we took a side trip back a long dirt road, hoping to find singer/songwriter Dan Fogelberg's ranch and recording studio. As we got closer, I had a change of heart, thinking that we shouldn't arrive unannounced and interrupt his day of work. We turned around, eventually finding Interstate 70, and headed up toward Loveland Pass, where the interstate goes through a tunnel. There was a long string of backed-up traffic, so we pulled onto the shoulder and Mike and I ran up to the mouth of the tunnel. Halfway up, we were wheezing and out of breath, realizing how much of a challenge the altitude would be for us lowlanders. Finally, as we drew closer to the entrance, ambulances started screaming by us, in the other direction, and we knew something nasty had happened. We saw a lot of wreckage scattered on the highway, some barely recognizable, then got word from other bystanders that a small motorhome driven by an elderly couple had lost control coming out of the tunnel and crashed head-on into a tractor-trailer. It was hard to believe that the couple could have survived. It chilled us to the bone and caused us to double-down on awareness while driving.

The car we were in was a boat-like Plymouth Fury III with a 440 engine that easily handled the ascents and going 80 miles per hour for hours at a time on the wide-open highway. It sucked gallons of gas, but the price was only 45 cents per gallon. Nancy's dad loaned us this deus ex machina that was so wide I could lay my six-foot frame on the back seat and sleep without bending my knees.

We stopped for a bit in overpriced Vail and skipped Aspen since it was off the beaten path. Our goal was to reach the point where Colorado drops off into the desert and eventually blends into Utah. We had followed the Colorado River for hours, and it continued after we crossed the state line. This was a landscape unlike anything I had ever seen, even in photos. Jagged towers rose across the river with mountains beyond. Arches appeared in the distance to the west. Nancy got a little freaked out by the remote landscapes and lack of any civilization, but I drank it all in. To me, the sparseness of the desert was holy, the place where religions were born. I would walk and bicycle many miles across deserts and plains in the future, but for now, we turned around and headed back to Grand Junction, Colorado, where my cousin Debbie and her husband lived. She was a nurse at a hospital in an area where few medical services were available. We stayed there for a few days and climbed some buttes and mesas, the 5,000- to 11,000-foot elevation a gradual acclimation to the eventual peaks we encountered at 14,000 feet further on in our adventure.

I thought of Kerouac most days, reading passages from cheap, beat-up paperbacks before falling asleep. My copies were stained with sweat and rain from being carried in my backpack and bore marks from coffee and beer as well. His books had a biblical hold on me, and now I wasn't just reading them — I was living them, too.

***

I had asked Mike to be my best man in my wedding mainly because of the adventures we had taken together, including a couple of three-day excursions on the Appalachian Trail heading west toward Harrisburg and east toward New Jersey. One December, we froze through the night in Kirkridge Shelter, seven miles from the Delaware Water Gap. Every time we fell asleep, we would wake up thinking that hours had passed and that it would soon be morning, when we could warm up by hiking fast. We would soon realize only ten minutes had passed. This happened all through the night.

After that test, the fact that he wanted to keep backpacking with me meant that he was the one who earned the best man title. Now here we were among the high peaks of the West, for which we had trained together through the Pennsylvania heat and humidity, running bleachers at the soccer field with packs on, climbing to the Pinnacle, and running up the mountain to the Port Clinton fire tower, then continuing up the 250 steps to its top. We ate rusty nails for breakfast and shit out digested specks of metal. By August, my buddy and I were ready for the Colorado Alpine summits.

We drove out of the desert surrounding Grand Junction and headed south to the San Juan Mountain range. Our main goal was to climb up to 12,000 feet on two 14,000-foot peaks, Mount Sneffels and Red Mountain. The day before the climbs, we visited the abyss-like canyon of the Gunnison River and stopped for lunch in Ouray, billed as "The Switzerland of America."

The varieties of off-brand beers you could find in Colorado amazed me. I wanted to try them all but also had to be reminded by my wife that there is inherent danger for Type 1 diabetics to indulge beyond a certain point. That danger comes from loss of judgment if your blood glucose starts dropping, and the alcohol in a strong beer actually causes the drop-off. At the very least, the simple carbs of alcohol and grains could cause extremely high blood glucose, which would make me dehydrated and nauseated — not a great situation for mountain climbs up to altitude. I still had no way of testing my own blood sugar except for urine test tape and its delayed results. Although I felt that Nancy was nagging me, in reality, she was playing the smart wife. After yelling at each other for a few minutes, we stopped, looked around, and realized how ridiculous it was that we were arguing in one of the most beautiful places on earth. How could anyone be mad here? And soon we weren't.

After climbing up both peaks as far as we felt was necessary, we headed further south to the Four Corners, where the borders of Colorado, Utah, Arizona, and New Mexico butt up against each other. That night, we stayed in a shabby, cheap hotel in Cortez, where we heard what sounded like drug deals and fighting happening in the parking lot overnight. It woke us up a few times, including once when someone pounded on the door. I tried calling the front desk, but they only spoke Spanish. Our only weapon was a Bowie knife I kept under my pillow. Eventually, it ended around three in the morning.

More travails awaited us. We had tickets to the Durango and Silverton Narrow Gauge Railroad, which takes you into the heart of the San Juans. During the drive to the train station, though, the old Plymouth's water pump gave out. We dropped the car at a garage, where they said they could fix it while we rode the train to Silverton and back.

The alpine scenery was the wildest we had seen since arriving in Colorado. Snow-covered spires towered above the swift-flowing Animas River. Windom Peak, Mount Wilson, and Sunlight Peak made themselves known as I checked my map to call them out. Every half hour, the train stopped and left off a few backpackers, who would hike into the wilderness areas for a week and then get picked up as the train came back the following week. I took notice of the excitement on the faces of those leaving and a sense of peace and effort on those getting picked up. It made me want to put on my backpack and head out on the trails, and in a few days I would.

The train took a two-hour break in the mining town of Silverton, where we ate lunch and hiked around. We were in the middle of nowhere; the town's few streets were dirt. As we headed back to Durango, we came across a powerful thunderstorm, and the accompanying downpour caused a landslide on the tracks in front of us. Mike and I actually grabbed shovels and helped the engineer and two ticket-takers remove rocks and mud. It took a while, and the strenuousness of the effort caused me to have a low blood sugar reaction, which I arrested by eating two peanut butter cups from the train snack bar.

The long delay brought us back into Durango three hours late, which meant the garage our car was in had closed for the evening. Luckily, we had left the tent and sleeping bags at a campground five miles on the outskirts of the city. We hitchhiked to the campground with a father and son from California, and the next morning I ran back to the garage and retrieved the repaired Fury lll. Our southern Colorado adventures were complete, and it was time to head back north to Rocky Mountain National Park, where our hopefully acclimatized bodies were ready to make an assault on Longs Peak.

Longs Peak is one of the highest summits in the lower 48 states. To climb it, we would have to wake up at 4:30 and start climbing at 5. It would take all day, and we would need to keep a brisk pace to beat the darkness of the coming night as we descended. Mike, his brother-in-law Willard, and I said goodbye to Nancy and my cousin Debbie, as they opted to shop in nearby Estes Park.

The campground we camped at sat at 9,000 feet elevation, leaving us 5,259 feet to ascend and then descend. The faint light of dawn brightened the gorgeous scenery of stunted pines surrounded by mountains of all sizes. Before long, we were above the tree line, and the newly risen sun guided us upward.

During our research ahead of the trip, we had read and heard from prodigious climbers that a good diet during the day of the climb consisted of bran flakes with watered-down milk for breakfast, figs and bananas during the climb, and peanut butter and jelly sandwiches for lunch. We didn't have access to energy bars or gels back then, but we did have a powdered form of Gatorade to which we added double the recommended amount of water. I had no idea what my blood glucose was, but I did know that I was fit, acclimatized, and feeling great. In fact, I was practically swooning with the whole idea of climbing a difficult mountain in crystal-clear air with the camaraderie of kindred spirits. This would eventually become a lifelong pursuit: to find and duplicate the same buzz mentally, physically, and spiritually. Adventure was presenting itself as a drug to me. Throughout my life, I would go looking for that fix.

We ate lunch at the base of the Diamond Route, which takes you up the big wall, a technical climb with rope, carabiners, and harnesses. We weren't ready for that kind of climbing yet. I was surprised by Mike's brother-in-law, who thought our diet was overblown hokum and instead packed two egg salad sandwiches. He also thought that living and running in Grand Junction at 5,000 feet was enough acclimatization for climbing in higher altitudes. When we got to the keyhole to climb the backside to the summit, he had a rumbling stomach and nausea. Add to that the thousand-foot drop from the narrow trail from that point on, and he decided to wait for us to return. Every year, a few people fall to their death along this stretch.

It now became a matter of Zen-like concentration, with each footfall coming down on solid earth, inhaling and exhaling in measured amounts, expending energy in a way that ensured we'd have a bit left for the final push. That push came with a hard left turn and to a hand-over-hand balancing movement upward for a thousand feet. I noticed I was gasping a bit more amid the adrenalized excitement. I stopped to snack lightly a few times to make sure my blood glucose kept up with me.

After another hour of climbing, it seemed like the summit materialized from a dream. Suddenly there was no more mountain to climb. I got down on my stomach and crawled to the drop-off, where I could look down and see the big wall climbers hammering pitons, placing, protecting, belaying — the rock jock boys living a dream of high exposure. We, too, were living it, in a less exposed way, but as flatlanders we felt the same degree of exuberance.

Then it suddenly got dark. Black clouds moved in, and it started snowing. Lightning flashed — thankfully off in the distance — a normal weather show on summer afternoons there in the high Rockies. We shot photos of each other with little piles of snow on our heads and shoulders, proof to the unbelievers who would think our story of August snowfall melodramatic.

There was no lingering on the summit even with the sunshine returning, as fractured, resplendent light prisms danced all around us. We, of course, had to return the same way we had come and now even more conscientiously since we would be fighting gravity. Back through the keyhole, Willard was waiting for us.

"What the hell took you guys so long," he joked.

After we regaled him with tales of our heightened experience, he vowed to return one day properly prepared. From there, we navigated the boulder field and cruised the long stretch of trail back into the tree line and onward to the campground. It wasn't until we sat down at the picnic table that the weariness and hunger hit us hard. But nothing could diminish the glow surrounding us two crazy climbers, who had summited the highest peak in Rocky Mountain National Park.

***

You might think that a three-day backpacking trip would be a letdown after the all-day climb of the day before, but you would be wrong. We were still in the heart of the Colorado Rockies, and two beautiful lakes awaited us. Bluebird and Ouzel lakes lay at 9,000-feet elevation, so the trails were fairly flat and followed the in-and-out effluence of creeks that raged all around us. Luckily, the trails were well maintained, with wooden bridges at the widest crossings. And Nancy felt more attuned to her backpack, which she had carried, off and on, for almost a year now.

During the first night, we saw a sublime show of constellations and falling stars. Being from the East Coast made the celestial display even more sublime, since during most summer evenings back home, the night sky usually was lost in a thickness of humid clouds. I woke up at sunrise and decided to bushwhack to the other side of the lake, where I sat on a rock peacefully meditating on the beauty of the West. When Nancy and Mike spotted me, they started pointing to a spot a few yards away to the right of me. When I stood up, I saw the towering antlers of a bull elk, a truly magnificent sight, as it ambled toward the meadows surrounding us.

After breakfast, we hiked on to Ouzel Lake, slightly smaller than Bluebird. The days and nights played out in a pattern, as they probably had since the beginning of time, and we got lost like Alice, down the rabbit hole. The beauty was almost surreal, and we soaked it all in. Home and the other world, our lives back east, had to be returned to. But I knew that I would be back, if not sooner, then definitely later.

We powered our way north to Cheyenne, Wyoming, adding another new state to our list. I remained in the dream of Kerouac's novels but also now lived them. Jack, too, had stopped in Cheyenne during his first trip west, riding on the back of a flatbed truck with a cast of characters and two young cowboys for drivers. I looked for his ghost while walking the dusty streets. Parts of it were still a frontier town in 1977 but probably already different from the 1940s of Kerouac's travels. Now it was time to summon the ghost of Neal Cassady, Kerouac's driver and protagonist, one of the greatest drivers in history, and unleash the heavy RPMs of the old Plymouth 440, heading east on Interstate 80 on a last chance power drive, back through the Midwest and on to home, to a life of continuous adventures.

Chapter 6

Running and Being

"Now I been out in the desert, just doin' my time
Searchin' through the dust, lookin' for a sign
If there's a light up ahead well brother I don't know
But I got this fever burnin' in my soul."

— Johnny Cash, "Further on up the Road"

The backpacking and hiking continued through the late 1970s, the only break coming in 1979 when Nancy and I bought a fixer-upper house in the borough of Kutztown, Pennsylvania. We did most of the work ourselves, which took some time and energy, so I looked to add a new way of keeping fit in a shorter amount of time. Right across the street from our new house was a Saucony running shoe factory. The shoes took their name from the creek that splits Kutztown in two, a waterway named by the Leni Lenape tribe ("Saucony" means "fast water"). One afternoon, I took a break and walked down the street, where I saw fliers on telephone poles advertising a 10K road run that would start and finish right in front of our new house. I had to look up the distance of what 10K translated to in miles: 6.2. I figured that I hiked 15 miles up and down mountains each day, with a pack on, and thus could knock off a few quick miles for a race. I entered and then trained for the next month.

On the day of the race, I was amazed at the number of runners who showed up, most of them looking like they'd been running races for a few years. My brother Scott joined me, and we looked out of place in our hiking clothes, though we both had bought a pair of Saucony shoes. What I really noticed was the camaraderie among all levels and ages of runners. I had always felt that among my hiking buddies, but this was on another level. There was a palpable energy buzzing among the runners.

When the starting gun went off, we headed south on the road paralleling the creek, then out past the elementary school and up a slight hill, which led past the borough line. After a steep climb, we hit the halfway point, 3.1 miles, where there was a water and snack stand. I gulped down some fruit juice to keep my blood glucose up for the big finish. The runners then turned around and headed back into town. I felt pretty good crossing the finish line, which meant I probably didn't run fast enough. I figured I needed to preserve some energy for working on my house late into the night and then getting up early the next day for a 12-mile hike, and I finished somewhere in the middle of the pack of 300 or so runners. The racing was fun, but on that day, I had no idea how much of a hold it would have on me during the next few years.

As with any addiction, it started slow and then soon escalated. Scott and I figured we'd run a race every month. Quite a few of the "in-deep" runners did a race, sometimes two, almost every weekend. Our distances started to climb, and soon we were running 15Ks, then ten-milers, and eventually a half marathon (13.1 miles). We figured that was the upper limit, at least for now.

We approached the racing with a lackadaisical attitude. We were not fast at all, and never did speed work. We continued finishing races with some fuel left in our tanks. We both seemed happy with that, still loving the great vibes among all the runners.

***

I was way more serious about my backpacking than I was about running, though. Nancy was getting psyched about some upcoming trips, or at least she did a good job at feigning interest. Sometimes I pushed her a little too hard, like on one backpacking trip to the Loyalsock Trail in Sullivan County over a Memorial Day weekend. I so wanted to introduce her to this part of the world. My youngest brother, Craig, also decided to tag along, as he, too, needed to escape normalcy for a few days. The plan was to hike in from the eastern terminus of the 59-mile trail along Loyalsock Creek, surrounded by otherworldly stone formations rising from the swirling waters, called the Haystacks. Then, we'd move on to Sones Pond, where we could camp for the night and watch the deer, birds, beavers, owls, and maybe even a black bear. It would be way better than anything you could watch on television. The next day, we would hike back to the car. A simple six miles in and six miles back.

The problem was that we were in the midst of a rare spring drought. The disappearance of the inflow and outflow of the feeder streams caused the level of Sones Pond to drop. That caused clouds of mosquitoes to swarm the pond's banks. I came up with an alternate plan: we would continue on to Tom's Run Creek, another three miles, where I knew we would find a beautiful waterfall. The total mileage was edging toward 10 for the day, a bit much for Nancy, and we also were running low on water. Nancy didn't complain, but I could tell she would be glad to find our camp soon. The good thing was that we would only have to do five miles the next day to reach Worlds End State Park. Then came the next test for Nancy: we would have to hitchhike to get back to our car, which was 20 miles away by road. As soon as I told her that, her nerve ends started buzzing, and not in a good way. Because of the low water situation, Alpine Falls was a thin thread, but camping next to it still was pretty awesome. My brother kept waking up thinking he forgot to turn off the faucet.

With years of backpacking behind me, I was in a groove of eating a nourishing, diabetes-friendly diet without having to carry a lot of weight in my pack. Oatmeal packets with peanut butter and seeds dumped in while cooking made up breakfast. Then I would nibble throughout the day instead of having a big lunch, which consisted of dried fruits, Fig Newtons, Slim Jims, and mini cans of Vienna sausages. For dinner, I would have cheese added to cooked rice or noodles with freeze-dried veggies and some form of cake. The night would end with a cup or two of sugar-free hot chocolate around the campfire.

Worlds End State Park has the best name of any of Pennsylvania's state parks. Though it's not that big, it might be my favorite. On that trip, we reached the last lookout, High Rock Vista, a thousand feet above the park, and beheld a true wonderland. The creek undulated like a snake, and where it was dammed up a swimming hole formed. Mountains covered in a mix of deciduous and pine trees rose as far as the eye could see.

From that lookout, a drama of humanity played out below us. It was Memorial Day, and the park was full, so we would have no problem getting a ride back to the car. Right before we descended, a loud roar of engines cut the silence. A motorcycle gang of 16 Harleys rolled through the park, followed by two shaggin' wagons. They even staged some races in the parking lots.

"We better be sure to stay away from those dudes," Nancy told us.

After we descended the mountain on the last mile of our trip, we checked in at the ranger station and told them of our need for a lift.

"No problem," a young ranger told us. "There's plenty of people in the park."

We took a dip in the swimming area in Loyalsock Creek, water that stays icy cold even in the middle of a heat wave. As our hunger kicked in, the ranger appeared and told us to follow him. He had found us a ride, but it was Nancy's worst nightmare. Of course, it was with the motorcycle gang. The leader shook our hands and told us to throw our packs in the van hauling their repair tools along with two dudes and two motorcycle mamas. Nancy resisted.

"I'm not getting in there," she said. "What if they have drugs and we get stopped?"

I took her aside and gently talked her down until she reluctantly agreed. Off we went, sitting on our packs among shag-carpeted walls and ceiling, with two of the gang sitting in the back on coolers. The stories began to be told, though we had to shout over the loud music of Bonnie Raitt on the tape deck and the van driver continually yelling, "Sweet Bonnie."

It turned out the group was from western Pennsylvania and was taking a long road trip around America, stopping next in Watkins Glen, New York, for an Allman Brothers concert. They were curious about the whole backpacking thing and listened intently while serving us beer and ham sandwiches. That may have been the best ham sandwich I ever ate.

When they dropped us off at our car, the rest of the gang wanted in on the storytelling and story listening. Then they loaded us up with more sandwiches and beer for the ride home, and I tried to give them gas money which they kindly refused. Sweaty hugs ensued, and then we headed in opposite directions, but not before I gave them my address and asked them to send me dispatches from their continuing road trip.

So Nancy was wrong (there was no danger) and right (there were plenty of drugs to choose from) and wrong again (we did not get stopped by law enforcement). We were in Sullivan County — outlaw country — and we were with the outlaws!

***

My brother Scott and I were on the path of developing a serious running obsession. The great American running boom was in full swing, and though we were late to the party, the movement fascinated us. Backpacking was still a big part of my life, but running was making inroads. With lots of physical labor, going up and down ladders and scaffoldings at work and continuing to fix up my own house, I had to summon loads of energy. To add to that, Nancy and I started a serious discussion about having children in the next few years. My Type 1 diabetes still demanded concentration and a supreme balancing act 24/7. But even with all that stuff circulating in my head, my brother dropped an enticing bomb: "Let's run a marathon!" I said, sure, let's do it, and in no time the planning and training began.

I still yearned to see and backpack through certain places, though, especially New England. I figured the easiest place in those states Nancy and I could backpack through would be on the Appalachian Trail in southern Vermont. The drive north through western Connecticut and Massachusetts was gorgeous, but when we crossed into Vermont, we both felt a palpable sense of welcome, somehow knowing this would be our new favorite place. We hiked north to Stratton Pond and climbed the fire tower, which gave us our first above-the-trees lay of the land of the Green Mountains. One night, we set up our tent on the north side of South Bourne Pond. There, we made our first observation of the community of long-distance hikers on the Appalachian Trail, who were now seasoned after walking 1,600 miles to this point (that left 500 rugged miles to go to the terminus on Mount Katahdin in Maine). A group was right behind us, bearded, dirty, and smelly, and they stripped down nude and dove into the pond. The ponds of Vermont would serve as their bathtubs. Nancy was not yet fully integrated into the through-hiker dirtbag culture and had to overcome a learning curve. She was a quick study, though, because when we approached North Bourne Pond the next day, she and I stripped down and cleansed our sins in the holy waters of the Appalachian Trail.

Right after dinner on our second night on the trail, I hiked over to the south side of the pond to talk with the through-hikers staying at the shelter. They had found a large pot, and all eight of them threw what they were going to cook that evening into it, creating a potluck stew. Even though I had nothing to contribute since I had already eaten, they offered me a bowl (typical long-distance behavior). Then the stories began. I got lost in their world and forgot about mine. It got dark, and the stories were not ebbing, but I had to get back to Nancy and our campsite, and now I had to do it in the dark. I finally stumbled my way back, using Nancy's yells as a guide, though I was curious about what or who she was yelling at. It turned out she was fighting off several porcupines who were trying to get our food, while also getting bitten by clouds of mosquitoes. She was not happy with me and still gives me shit about my abandonment of her and my ability to get carried away by fantasy, in this case that of being a long-distance through-hiker. Later, we finished the hike in the village of Manchester Center, a trail resupply spot. It was such a quaint but also utilitarian town, and it became one of our favorite places in Vermont.

The following year we tried backpacking in the White Mountains of New Hampshire. We never got to the trails, though, since the pouring rain caused small-stream flooding for an entire week. My judgment was becoming better, as I decided not to push Nancy to slog through a damp, soggy, and even dangerous mess. We hung out in North Conway, near where the Appalachian Trail passed, and also took a day trip into Maine. The highlight for me was meeting a couple who were bicycling from Seattle, Washington, to Portland, Maine. I also had done some bicycling, and after asking them a million questions, even to the point of watching them unpack their gear for the night, they gave me a bunch of new ideas that I added to my expanding list.

The next summer, we backpacked in a completely new neck of the northern woods: the Adirondack Mountains of upstate New York. As I got the packs ready back home, Nancy questioned why I would add long underwear, wool hats, and mittens. I had been advised by some of my Allentown Hiking Club buddies. After hiking all day, we set up camp at the base of Big Slide Mountain. That night, the temps went down to 39 degrees — in August. We wore all the clothing in our packs. It warmed up fast as we climbed to the top of Big Slide in a thick fog, which obscured the vista, and in the next few days we climbed several 4,000-footers. This was a thickly forested landscape with lakes everywhere, different from Vermont, which was right across Lake Champlain.

We came back to Vermont the next year to hike the Long Trail north to Canada. It was a much more rugged trail compared with southern Vermont — rockier, with thick roots and steeper climbs. It included a climb of Mount Mansfield, Vermont's highest point at 4,395 feet above sea level. Nancy and I climbed it with a nasty storm approaching, but luckily it blew over. We stayed in the ski town of Stowe on our last night, and something happened in that motel that would change our lives forever.

***

The first marathon my brother Scott and I chose to run was the God's Country Marathon in upstate Potter County. I chose this one because I was familiar with the area from hiking on the Susquehannock Trail. We would run on the shoulder of Route 6 for most of the way, east to west, Galeton to Coudersport, passing by the northern gateway of the Susquehannock Trail about halfway through the race. That meant a long, steady climb of 1,000 feet up Denton Hill.

In my mind, I thought running straight for almost four hours would be excruciating. I could hike all day with a heavy pack and just glide through the day, but running was harder for me. I was 6-foot-1 with a lot of my 170 pounds in my tree-trunk legs, and most of the runners were very thin. But I realized that if you trained adequately and paced yourself, and ran your own race, you could finish, usually in the middle of the pack.

The weather that day was sunny and humid — typical Pennsylvania conditions. Scott and I made sure to keep hydrated, and we glided up the climb at a steady pace. The finish was exciting, as we entered the high school stadium and ran the last quarter mile on the track. There weren't a lot of spectators since this was a lightly populated part of the state. We finished a few minutes under four hours with 250 total finishers and could now cross off our list completing one of the longest-distance challenges in the running world. We could go on to something else. Been there, done that. The hook, however, had entered our psyche. We wanted more — not immediately while recovering, but soon after.

Training for and running races and going on multi-day backpacking trips integrated well for me. I went on two major trips in 1980. In the spring, a buddy from high school, Bill, was hiking the entire Appalachian Trail. He started on Georgia's Springer Mountain in March. I sent his weekly food supplies to towns along the way, along with batteries, socks, and other miscellanea. I was living a bit vicariously through him while helping him out logistically, but I did get to join him for four days in May in Shenandoah National Park, the same area where Nancy and I had backpacked for our honeymoon. It was never a problem for me to repeat an adventure. The season, weather, and fellow hikers could all be different. In a space of years, you yourself could be different. All these factors came into play for this trip. My brother Scott decided to do his first backpacking trip, a friend from the Allentown Hiking Club named Ellen jumped in, and another high school friend, Einar, joined, too. He had joined me on my first backpacking trip in 1973 and also knew Bill.

After a seven-hour drive, we arrived at the trailhead in central Virginia, and Bill soon walked right to the parking lot. His transformation amazed me. He had shed his small beer belly, and tree trunks much like my own had replaced his skinny legs.

We hiked to the first shelter, where we camped for the first night. Bill had lots of stories, which always took on a dramatic, animated quality when told in the middle of an adventure. In fact, it was one of my favorite things about adventures. The next day was very humid, with the feel of ominous storms in the air. We arrived at a shelter as the storm hit. With seven miles still to go for the day, we decided to eat lunch in the shelter. Lightning crackled, followed by rolling thunder, but the storm soon passed to the north.

The shelter was full of through-hikers, and we were all witnesses to the antics of Einar. He was always an off-the-wall personality, so why should it be any different out there? He milled about outside the shelters while the lighting split trees near him. Then, after a downpour, he realized he had left his pack out in the rain. His huge box of macaroni was now spilling out of the wet packaging and expanding, filling his pack with warm, uncooked pasta. He shrugged his shoulders and started eating it and offering it all around to everyone.

Bill said he had met a lot of characters on his hike north but none were like Einar. The other hikers asked us if we knew this character. We admitted that, yes, we did, and said we expected more antics to ensue throughout the trip. And, of course, they did.

One day, we awoke to a dripping, all-encompassing fog that lasted through most of the morning, making the air damp and chilly. We decided to grab lunch inside the Skyland's window-lined dining room to warm up. Einar, who was still eating soggy macaroni, said he didn't have any money. We offered to pay for a bowl of soup, but he decided to sit outside around a charred campfire ring. We could barely see him through the fog. While eating our hearty and steaming French onion soup, the fog began lifting. Everyone in the dining room could now watch Einar warming up his macaroni on a roaring fire he had just started. And right above him was a big metal sign that read: "No campfires or cooking allowed!"

On our last day on the trail, we skimmed the edges of the ridge and looked out from the same vistas Nancy and I had viewed four years earlier after our wedding. Scott picked up some nasty blisters since he wasn't used to wearing boots all day and walking up and down mountains. I encouraged him by saying that this experience would make our next marathon feel easier. We said goodbye to Bill as he headed north on the trail to Maine. He was now a bit more than a third of the way with several more months of trekking to go. We drove north on Interstate 81 and back to our homes in Pennsylvania. While it was nice to return to the comforts of home, there was no doubt in my mind which method I would have liked to use to get there.

***

In the fall I longed to be tested on a solo adventure of maybe a week or so in length. Nancy was extremely nervous about this because of my health problems. I researched and found a linear 70-mile trail in southwestern Pennsylvania called the Laurel Highlands Trail, which consisted of a bunch of state parks stacked against each other. The rangers could arrange transport from one end of the trail to the other, and I could leave the car in a protected place for the entire eight days. The trail also was unique in that it had shelter areas every 10 miles or so with six three-sided shelters in each area. It cost $1 per night and had to be reserved in advance, and the ranger would check in each night. I even arranged to have the ranger call my wife each night. It was perfect for my independence while also maintaining a measure of safety. Nancy reluctantly agreed I could give it a whirl.

I was excited beyond measure, packing and repacking. I would need food for all eight days, since I couldn't count on the lone bar a mile off the middle of the trail being open. Seventy miles in eight days was a bit short for my daily goals, but I figured I would do a short day at the beginning and end, both of which included driving five hours. Plus, there were lots of side trails taking you to ponds, ski areas, and Frank Lloyd Wright's Fallingwater.

The weather that late September was superb, with the leaves starting to change color. The trek involved mostly ridge walking except for a massive climb out of Ohiopyle State Park at the beginning and a descent into Johnstown at the end. The Laurel Highlands are a gorgeous range, with pulse-quickening vistas.

I knew there was a chance I would feel lonely, especially since the trails were empty that time of year, and I did hardly see any other hikers. The rangers checking in didn't have time for trail talk, though they were very friendly and glad to keep my wife updated. I also worried about being hungry, but I got used to having less food a few days in. I needed to lower my insulin intake because of ingesting fewer carbs and the taxing hiking. The bar happened to be open and worth the mile out and back. I had a burger and an ice-cold Rolling Rock.

The trip was sunny and temperate except for day seven, on which it rained lightly most of the day. Each shelter had a fireplace and cut wood, though, so it was easy to dry your clothes. I had a wonderful experience, was never lonely, and came home fit, tan, and with a new sense of independence. In fact, Nancy said I was glowing. Most times, I would rather hike with Nancy, my brothers, and hiking club members, but this was a true test of my solo capabilities.

***

Scott and I continued training and ran a marathon or two each year. We did one in Harrisburg, which started and finished by the state Capitol and crossed several bridges over the Susquehanna River. We finished in three hours, 49 minutes. Then came the Philadelphia marathon on a raw, late-November day with icy rain coming down. I ran faster because of the cold and finished in three hours, 37 minutes.

My fastest marathon time, though, came in my hometown at the Dolphin Marathon, sponsored by an athletic clothing company. It took place in early spring, and a wild storm blew through that morning but cleared up fast, leaving a raw wind in its place. At the finish, I was down to a tank top and shorts, though I still had on mittens since my hands were damn cold. I knew I had to run fast because of the hometown crowds and, once again, the windy cold. It all came together for me as I finished in my fastest time ever to this day: three hours, 31 minutes. I would go on to run a total of 20 marathons, some with brother Scott and some with brother Craig. To this day, I honor my brothers and revel in the time we spent training and competing.

We were in deep with running, and now distances beyond the marathon called us. We started with a few 50Ks (31 miles) and then the Dannon Two Bridges 36-miler in Washington, D.C. It started in Alexandria, traveled to the home of George Washington, then headed back north into D.C., over the Potomac, and then by all of the monuments. At the finish line in front of the Lincoln Memorial, the organizers had backed in a tractor-trailer filled with Dannon yogurt, and runners could eat all they wanted. Scott and I ate seven each.

Next up was the Lake Waramaug 50-miler in Connecticut, which consisted of seven laps around a 7.15-mile lake. This was the big time. Some of the best ultra-runners in the country were competing, like Park Barner, Dieter Dauberman, Stu Middleman, and Ray Kroelewitz. Leslie Welch from England set a new women's world record for the 50-mile run at six hours, two minutes. I finished my first 50-miler with my best time of eight hours, one minute. Even though Scott and I had no chance in hell to win, we had gone toe to toe with the best in the world. What distance would be too far? The world went on from there, rolling ahead of us to dizzying heights and ridiculous distances.

Chapter 7

Angels Appear Among Us

"For you there might be a brighter star
But through my eyes the light of you is all I see
For you there might be another song
But all my heart can hear is your melody."

— Stevie Wonder, "Another Star"

Two months after returning from our adventure on the Long Trail in Vermont, and our dalliance in a motel room in Stowe, came the news of a celestial being who would appear to us in seven months' time. We were both enthusiastic and terrified. Our lives would change forever. My wife, being practical and pragmatic, went to questions: "Are we truly ready for this?" "Will we be good enough parents?" "Will this baby still love us as they grow up when we inevitably screw up?" My thoughts were of how this creature would be raised in a life of adventure in all aspects of his or her life. My hope was that our children would become our kindred spirits in the everyday adventure of our lives together. They may not be adventurers in the narrow sense, but they would be raised to treat everything they do as a wonderful adventure.

Nancy loved her pregnancy. For her, it was a revelation, the week-to-week growth and changes to her body as we walked and hiked right up to delivery. She nurtured the forming fetus (and herself) with nutrition, music (both recorded and played on the piano), reading to the baby bump, and, of course, walking, walking, walking. Our first ultrasound looked great. We didn't want to know the gender of the child; we wanted it to be a mystery, a surprise after the long journey of pregnancy.

Nancy continued to work at Blue Cross of Lehigh Valley until her due date. I didn't like the long, 18-mile drive she had to take to get there, but she was always a good driver, and traffic in the 1980s wasn't that heavy. Her only setback came one day at lunch, when during a walk she stopped for a bite to eat at the Brass Rail Bar. She had a slight dizzy spell and slumped off her barstool onto the floor. Most workers and patrons thought she was drunk because this was still early on in her pregnancy. Luckily, no harm to future mom or fetus.

The delivery day drew closer, but the baby was not quite ready for her entrance into the world. A few false hints at delivery came up, but nothing strong enough to send us racing to the hospital. Not quite three weeks past her due date, Nancy did a 5K race held on the Lehigh Parkway trails. It was a women's race, but they allowed me to accompany Nancy because of her now huge baby bump (another plus was that our hospital was only two miles away).

It was a well-attended race with elite runners and fast times. Nancy did not challenge for the win. In fact, she finished in last place, her protruding baby bump leading the way. I was never so proud of Nancy as I was that day, and the excitement and motion finally stirred the baby into action. With a little help from an inducement, Adrienne Rebecca Scheidt was born the next day, May 16, 1983. I think she finally decided to make her entrance after realizing that an awesome mother was waiting to nurture her on the outside.

The delivery was fast and furious. That's easy for me to say — I wasn't doing the pushing. Nancy's miles of walking paid off. In fact, maybe a bit too much. Her final push sent Adrienne shooting out so fast the doctors had to catch her. She immediately cried, but I swear she was half smirking, like she was saying, "I guess you guys thought I'd never exit the womb!" It was an over-the-top, cinematic entrance into the world. Little did we know then that drama and pizzaz would continue to inform her life.

I had added long-distance bicycling to my training regimen and did a few citizen races and some fundraising events, too. It was a good way to keep up my fitness while taking me away from the constant pounding of the pavement. I went to sleep at home the night after the birth figuring I'd bicycle the 20 miles to the hospital, spend the day with my two girls, then bike home, arriving just before dark. On the way in, I stopped a mile before the hospital at a flower shop and got two yellow roses. For that last mile, I was so excited, carrying the flowers in one hand, steering and braking with the other, and shouting "Buongiorno, bellissima giornata," to all the people I passed like the kid in the movie "Breaking Away."

Both Nancy and Adrienne had had a semi-restful night. Upon seeing my little girl's face again, for the first time now in the daylight, my thoughts immediately went to Greek mythology. Her beauty shone like that of Helen of Troy, "the face that launched a thousand ships." Helen's beauty was so stunning that it started the Trojan War. I wondered how many figurative wars that little face I was looking at would start, a launching of another thousand ships.

A day later, the three of us arrived home, and immediately I put Adrienne in the snugli front carrier while Nancy rested. I wanted to introduce Adrienne to the town she would grow up in and its people. She mostly slept, then cried all night. Adrienne was what they called "colicky," crying for a big portion of each evening. I started taking long walks with her in the middle of the night so Nancy could sleep. I was beginning to train for ultramarathon events, so the extra mileage was welcome and, at the same time, gave me time to bond with my daughter.

Soon summer arrived, and the weather became perfect for walking. We would stop for a beverage halfway at the Turkey Hill Mini Market. Soon the workers began to expect to see us every night. Adrienne would always sleep during most of the walk; maybe she felt like she was back in the comfort of the womb. It was the closest I would ever come to feeling pregnant.

Adrienne grew up with sky-blue eyes and a big head of curly blonde locks, her signature look already at age two. We took lots of hikes on the nearby Appalachian Trail, to Hawk Mountain Bird Sanctuary, and of course around town. She soon graduated to a back carrier. I was calculating at what age she would be able to go backpacking in the carrier, and at what age she could carry her own pack. We also started riding around with her on the back of the bicycle in a blue Cookie Monster-themed child carrier. She would call out to people we'd pass, saying, "I want Cookie."

Then one long weekend, the three of us, along with our friend Ann and my brother Craig, drove north to Boston so Craig and I could run the Sri Chinmoy 12-hour race. It took place on a quarter-mile track in a stadium, which worked out well for Adrienne since she could see us every two- to three-minute lap and even pretend she was running in the race. It was hot, and my diabetes does not love the heat, but we kept hydrated, and Craig and I finished tied for 27th place with 53 miles completed. Some big guns in the ultra world were competing, including Marcy Schwam, who won the women's race, and Stu Mittleman and Trischul Chearns in the men's race. All the way home, we listened to "Sesame Street" songs and plays, all of us singing along at high volume with the windows rolled down. We got a lot of stares as we drove through the campus of Yale University in New Haven, Connecticut.

I completed a few bike races on a five-mile loop near Rodale Farms. It was 35 miles, so you had to complete seven laps at a pretty good pace. Then I rode in a few long two-day rides for the MS Foundation. They consisted of 75 miles each day from the Lehigh County velodrome to Lancaster and back. The same ride was duplicated, but this time for cancer research. My brother Craig was now my partner in crime, as Scott was recently married and was never as much a fan of bicycling as he was of running.

At four, Adrienne ran her first race, if you don't count the one she did while in the womb. It was a one-mile fun run in our hometown, and judging by the look on Adrienne's face, she wasn't having any fun. Nancy ran the 5K, and I ran a 10K. In the fall, it was back to marathons in Harrisburg and Philadelphia. Then, the next seismic shift happened in our family. Nancy was pregnant again, due sometime in late winter. Adrienne had had a sleepover at my parents' house, so child No. 2 was probably conceived in one of the rooms of our house. Not as exciting as Stowe, Vermont, but it produced the same outcome. All of us were excited, but especially Adrienne, who looked forward to having a baby sister or brother.

By this point, Nancy had started a new job at Kutztown University. Once again, she loved being pregnant, and once again we did not want to know the sex of the child until he or she arrived. Nancy worked right up to delivery, and both of us scrambled home from our jobs and rushed to the hospital when the time came. Only hours later, on February 24, 1988, another baby girl made her entrance into the world. We named her Amberly Joelle. Still dabbling in mythology, I thought of Circe, the fierce goddess who bewitches Odysseus in Homer's epic telling. Amberly's face was full of fascination, with huge bright eyes of deep soul, and I imagined her growing up and conjuring spells. In fact, she had already cast her spell on us and especially on her big sister, who visited her in the hospital in big-eyed wonderment. The two sisters were different in appearance and temperament, plus there was now almost five years between them. But as they grew up, they would always remain close. Their bond would always be strong. There was no mythology in that at all. They would always have each other's backs.

Since Amberly was born in February, it was harder to take her for long walks in the snugli, as it was often bitter cold and icy in the long Pennsylvanian winter. Slowly it turned to spring, and the mileage increased. Eventually, Amberly followed her sister, transitioning from front carrier to back carrier and also onto her own rear bike seat, though hers was Big Bird-themed. One big difference between the two girls was that Amberly talked to me while in the snugli, making baby sounds instead of sleeping. As she got older and transitioned to the back carrier, she continued telling stories, now in advancing language. Adrienne sang; Amberly talked.

Since Nancy could walk to work even in the worst weather and I was now running my own painting and decorating business, I would stay home with the kids on snow cancellation days when they were in daycare and school. Some of our favorite memories are of those days. Things could get pretty wild as we played games like hide and seek, put on snowsuits to sled and have snowball battles, came back in to warm up, went back out again, then walked uptown over huge snowdrifts to eat lunch at the Fancy Pantry. I'd let the girls order whatever they wanted on the menu, and they loved that freedom. It seemed like half the day consisted of putting on and taking off snow clothes, and the basement wash line ended up strung with drying winter clothes. We set up our tent in the living room, and the girls would watch cartoons out of the mesh back window. By the end of the day, the house would look like a tornado had touched down, so 20 minutes before Nancy was due to come home we would scramble to clean up. One time, she came home early and was appalled at the wreckage, but what she really missed was the fun.

One constant during those days of revelry was music. It was always on, the soundtrack for my kids growing up. A lot of the time I played crooners such as Frank Sinatra and Tony Bennett backed by a big band. I would sing along with Frank or Tony, and the girls would laugh and say, "Dad, you can't sing!" Of course, how could I match those guys? I would tell the girls that one day I would sing to each of them at their weddings. I was setting myself up for embarrassment but also figured they would forget that many years later. They just laughed, as much at the thought of their far-off weddings as my promise to sing to them.

Chapter 8

The Immeasurable Calculus of Distance

"You know the day destroys the night
Night divides the day
Tried to run
Tried to hide
Break on through to the other side."

— The Doors, "Break on Through (To the Other Side)"

As the distances got longer and longer, I came to a revelation. I never really liked running. It was great for fitness and a quick option for keeping in shape, but I could never get in a real groove. I took notice of this at races where elite runners seemed as if they never touched the ground, almost as if they floated. I never felt that way. It felt like I was plodding like the big, old Budweiser Clydesdales. But the strange thing was that I still loved going to races. It definitely was the camaraderie among other runners that I craved — the shared pain and misery that results in a shared completion.

The revelation was thus: I am a walker. Fast, steady, energy-conserving, almost metronome like. When I am totally in it, I can glide like the elite runners. Obviously, there is a gap in the time it takes. I ran at an eight-minute mile pace for marathons and only walked at a pace of 12 to 14 minutes per mile. However, in the ultramarathon, even the elite runners walk a portion, especially as the distances get longer. On steep ascents during races, I have passed runners while walking fast. Then, during long, mountainous bicycle races, I also noticed that if I got off the bike to push at the steepest section, I would pass slower cyclists who were still peddling their bikes. What I could do in a lengthy footrace is sustain that walking pace all day, and even, as I would find out later, into the night.

The switch from running to walking happened gradually through a systematic process. But knowing it was happening was enlightening and freeing. I knew now that I was always a walker, powerful but smooth and not intimidated by extreme terrain or distance. What better way to transition than a trail 50-miler, and one in my own backyard? The Rocky One 50-Miler was billed as "the toughest 50-miler east of the Mississippi", and in the 1980s, it was. Taking place on the Appalachian Trail with a start and finish in the town of Hamburg, Pennsylvania, a 20-minute drive from my house, this race sounded right up my alley. Forty runners signed up from a bunch of eastern states, some with Western States 100-Miler credentials, including race director Mike Ranck. He was a Hamburg High School science teacher who had finished sixth in the previous year's Western States.

My goal was to finish without hurting myself. I knew from experience that the path was extremely rocky, and there was always the chance of stepping on a rattlesnake and getting bitten. Those dangers would slow down the runners whereas I, as a fast walker, could power my way through at my normal walking pace. I trained as I usually would, race or no race, by hiking on the Appalachian Trail sections of the course.

The race began on a cold, late-November morning. That cold would at least keep down the rattlesnake threat. Everyone shot off at the start, leaving only myself to entertain me. I treated the entire day as a long 50-mile hike. The course included four major climbs passing near to the Hawk Mountain Sanctuary at mile 30, the Port Clinton fire tower at mile 33, the Pinnacle overlook at mile 39, and the Pulpit Rock vista at mile 41. After a quick descent to the last aid station, there were eight miles to go. The race required all runners to have a pacer and two flashlights for those final eight miles. Being in last place was disheartening; the volunteers packed up the aid stations every time I walked away. The darkness was now settling in, and it started snowing.

My brother Scott was the unlucky guy to be asked to walk those last snowy, dark, rocky miles back to Hamburg with his crazy brother. At least I now had someone to talk to, and he had done his homework and memorized a bunch of bad jokes, which he parceled off, one every quarter mile.

Even the finish was underwhelming as most everyone had gone home. But then I found out that though I finished in last place, I was the seventh finisher. Of the 40 entries, a bunch had not even started, some had gotten injured along the way, and others just dropped out. I had controlled my blood glucose with no highs or lows, kept my pace at a steady but safe rate, and finished laughing at my brother's stupid jokes, even the ones he started repeating. As in life, I had survived and thrived once again

I walked the Rocky One 50-Miler two more times. The next year I again finished last, but this time I caught up to two guys from Ohio at mile 30, and the three of us finished in tenth, eleventh, and twelfth out of a field of 36. The race had been moved to September, which meant no snow or darkness, but an addition was a wet Schuylkill River crossing at mile 49.5 using a bull rope stretched from tree to tree.

Then, the final year I entered, I dropped out at mile 33 after a fat bee stung me on the back of my neck during the ascent at mile three and the poison caused my blood glucose to spike. By the time I dragged myself to the Port Clinton fire tower aid station, my blood glucose, (which I now had a personal meter to check) registered 380, causing dehydration and nausea. My brother Craig and my buddy Joe, who were running the 50 miles with me, went on to the finish.

My brothers and I did some more trail events, some of our own making. We did a bunch of fast one-day attempts on trails in Potter and Lycoming counties. Scott and I did some big mileage on the very remote Donut Hole Trail. Craig, another buddy named Louie, and I tried to speed walk the entire 42 miles of the Black Forest Trail in one day. Alas, it was the middle of summer, very hot and humid, and there were 13 steep climbs and descents and numerous rushing stream crossings. We started at daybreak, but it was very tough going. Fourteen hours later, we were only at mile 35, dehydrated and with darkness encroaching, and we had an outlet at a highway crossing, so we bailed. It was one of the toughest challenges I faced. Craig told me he doesn't want to talk about it ever again.

Another difficult race Craig and I participated in two years in a row was called the Overlook Overload. It took place in the Catskill Mountains of New York and started at the base of Overlook Mountain. It required you to climb 1,300 feet up a steep dirt road to the top of the mountain, 2.25 miles up and 2.25 miles down, as many times as possible in six hours. The road was rocky and rugged with lots of grooves from water runoff. You had to concentrate constantly. There was a nice vista on top, looking south to New York City and north to the rest of the gorgeous Catskills, but nobody dallied since it was a race. Craig and I ended up climbing and descending six laps, which gave us 27 miles. The following year it was much the same, but Craig sprained his ankle on lap three and had to hobble back to the car. Both years we had to keep stopping on the New York State Thruway to stretch on the way home because our legs cramped. This was another of these events we shook our heads at years later, saying, "What the hell were we thinking?"

We created our own race one Memorial Day weekend at my parents' house. I wanted to honor the trails and woodlands of my youth, so I marked off a loop of just under a mile, which started in the front lawn and used the porch as an aid station. Various friends stopped in to do a few miles, some came to party, and a few showed up to do both. Both of my brothers, Louie, and a new friend, Mary, did between 20 and 30 miles. We were all helping Mary train for her first marathon. I managed to glide through 40 miles of heaven, dredging up many memories and visions from coming of age on these same trails.

I went back to running again for a short spell to prepare for a 24-hour relay race on the Millersville University track. The premise was to gather a team of 10 runners, with each one running a fast mile and then handing off a baton to the next runner. Depending on how fast your team ran, your turn would come up every hour to hour and a half. Of course, those times would slow down as we cruised into nighttime and then into hours 20 to 24. It was hard to rally after running fast, taking a short nap, then running fast again for 24 hours, but we had fun, as there was a party atmosphere throughout what could have been a rather grim ordeal. What made it really tough, though, were the humid 100-degree temperatures of July. Thank God they had a cold, outdoor shower set up in which you could douse yourself right after your laps with your running clothes on. However, if you fell asleep between your laps, you would always wake up chilled. Our team included my two brothers; Neal, one of the top ultramarathoners in the United States; and two new friends, Linette and Tina, who later would become some of my biggest supporters at adventures and beyond. I felt good throughout the event, running some of my fastest miles ever, including one six-minute mile. But that was it for the running for me. I was about to enter the upper limits of distance, and my body told me to slow down and find that smooth walking groove again. The next 24-hour race would not be a relay. It would be a continuous 24 hours around a track, like a hamster in a cage on a wheel.

The Dawn to Dusk 24-Hour Race took place on a high school track in the suburbs of West Philadelphia. Our goal (Louie, Craig, and I) was 80 miles. The weather turned hot, an early-season May heat with some humidity thrown in. I have always struggled during hot weather, trying to balance the amount of liquid I take in with electrolytes, (potassium, magnesium, and sodium) and also trying not to overflow with liquid. When I get dehydrated, my blood glucose level goes up. It's a bad road to go down. On top of all that, I woke up in the morning with a bad sinus infection. The presence of infection in the body makes the blood glucose go up. There I went again with a battle of multiple fronts. I struggled throughout the race. On a track there is very little if any shade. It helps a lot when the sun goes down, but then the sleep deprivation kicks in. The midnight hour is when your handlers, the few spectators, and the other competitors become your saviors. Once again, camaraderie is everything. I got into an early groove, which always helps to draw attention away from any negative discomfort unrelated to the rigors of the race. As the heat kicked in and the nausea caused by the infection resulted in high blood glucose, even that groove didn't help. I gutted it out, finishing with 57 miles. Craig and Louie walked 72 miles. While this seemed like a loss to me, I realized that with all the troubles I had encountered, including Type 1 diabetes, I had just walked 57 miles in 24 hours. I had notions of even further challenges with time and distance in the near future. Those challenges, though even further, were in the realm of possibility because I had suffered so mightily today and still eked out 57 miles!

The next step up was a 48-hour race. This time, we had to look west to find such a beast. The Across the Years 48-Hour Race happened annually in Phoenix, Arizona. The premise was that the gun to start the race went off on the morning of December 31 and ended on the morning of January 2nd. You were running/walking across the years.

Every 10 years it was called Across the Decades, and then in 1999 to 2000, they named it Across the Centuries.

Training for such massive distances took energy, planning, and ingenuity. I had just started my own business and was enjoying the wonderfulness of a growing family. Ultra training involves big mileage, so I took on a newspaper route, which involved delivering 55 papers around Kutztown every morning. This entailed arising at 5 a.m., walking five miles, climbing lots of hills and staircases, and carrying two sacks of papers, one over each shoulder. It was a form of resistance training, and it came with a sense of completion, as it got easier having less weight the further I walked along the route. For more distance, I could add a few miles at the end and/or walk or bike in the evening, sometimes with the family. Plus, it helped by adding cash to our budget. On the weekends, I added even more mileage, increasing every other weekend.

I now also had more tools for controlling my diabetes. In 1982, I started using a meter, in which I inserted a strip into a slot, pricked a fingertip with a lancet device, then applied the blood to the strip, which in eight seconds gave me a blood glucose reading. I then adjusted the blood glucose by eating something if I was low, giving a syringe dosage of insulin if my glucose reading was high, or walking it down if it was slightly high. I started seeing an endocrinologist who took my control to a higher level by combining short- and long-acting insulins, which meant I would now administer four to five shots a day. This also lessened the chance for low blood sugar reactions and possible seizures. For a severe low, I also carried a syringe of emergency glucose. All these new innovations were paramount in helping me with my workday and the increasing mileage — basically my everyday life.

The location of the 48-hour race was a bonus since it was winter. We escaped into 70-degree daytime temps on the edge of the desert in Phoenix. As a prelude, Craig and I flew into Los Angeles, rented a car, and did a few days of light training in the San Gabriel Mountains and Joshua Tree National Park. We picked up a buddy of mine, John, who we had met at another race. John was a prolific ultramarathoner, running one almost every month. He lived in Monrovia, and on the drive to Phoenix, we stopped to see his brother Damian, who lived in a remote shack on the edge of the California desert. I asked Damian if I could have a glass of water, and he said, "Sure, help yourself." I noticed a pistol laying in the drying rack and asked him if it was loaded. He said, "Of course it's loaded. What good is a gun if it's not loaded?" That wasn't the first or last time I would hear that in America.

The drive to Phoenix took us through the gap of the two highest peaks in southern California, San Gregorio and San Jacinto. A few more hours of driving took us to the start of the race just north of Phoenix, with the prominent peak of Camelback Mountain rising above the high school track we would be walking around. The weather was tricky. At the morning start it was still cool — perfect walking weather. Later, though, it grew warm, no more than 70 degrees, but an unobstructed desert sun just baked us. Light breezes stirred into the late afternoon. By early evening, it went back to being almost perfect. Then at night, as it does in most desert climates, it got cold — the kind of cold that doesn't bother you while you move but which chills you when you slow down, rest, or even sleep. We had a tent set up in the infield plus good sleeping bags and backpacker mattresses. I actually felt warm and cozy, but Craig shivered, at times uncontrollably, through the one- or two-hour nap we took each night.

When you spend 40 hours out of 48 circling a track, sometimes the dumbest things can set you off laughing like a loon. Occasionally those things happen almost as if on a continual loop. You are so tired in mind and body that each time it happens, it kills you again and again. Two such instances stay in both my and my brother's memories. A small airstream trailer parked on the side of the straightaway served as the home for the volunteers who took turns manning the aid station table. They looked like kids from high school. To get in and out there, you passed through a screen door that was so translucent you could barely see it. Many times, a kid going in or out walked right into it and swore, causing fits of laughter from Craig and I. Part of the fun was seeing the kid try to act like nothing happened or hoping no one saw it. But we always saw it. It got to the point that even if it didn't happen for a while, we could break out in laughter just anticipating it.

Incident two involved a stray dog and León, who, like John, was an inveterate ultra-distance competitor from California. He could really space out; someone thought he may have been shell-shocked from a stint in the Army. During the race, a stray dog made its way onto the track. León tried to pet it, but it growled at and almost bit him. Once again, we giggled uncontrollably, but León continued to try and pet the dog, which reacted the same way each time, leaving us laughing every time. Just as the act finally got old, León started to growl and bark at the dog instead. León never laughed or thought of it as an act, but it cracked up Craig and I every time. And just like with the other incident, we laughed at just the memory of it.

The race had been one hell of a party. Craig and I walked every step together, finishing with 116 miles. John ran 140 miles, and León made it 110 miles. The winner — from British Columbia, Canada — finished with 186 miles. We had no time to rest, though; our flight home left in two hours. We had to drive to the airport and boarded the plane in the same clothes we had been walking in for the full 48 hours. Then, during the flight, we both kept getting leg spasms from the terrible leg room. The final straw was having to land in St. Louis because of an ice storm. We waited on the plane for three hours, but the freezing rain didn't let up.

The airline eventually got everyone a hotel room for the night, which worked out well for us. We could finally shower, stretch, and sleep in a bed, though we did have to walk a mile into a rough section of St. Louis to eat. The only place open that late at night was Popeyes, and it ended up being one of the best meals we ever ate.

After arriving at home the next day, my wife said, "Why does everything have to be an exhausting, over-the-top adventure with you? Can't you just take a relaxing vacation on a beach sometime?" Craig agreed with her to a point and then admitted, "With Bob, there is rarely, if ever, a dull moment."

***

Some say the extreme ultra distances are 10 percent physical and 90 percent mental. The average question I get from someone who has never participated in one is, "What the hell do you think about all the time you are out there?" We would soon find out the answer to that question, to the utmost degree. Craig and I now entered the Edward Payson Weston Six-Day Race.

In the second half of the 19th century, long-distance racing became a glamour sport. Let that sink in for a while. Now, let's go further into this alternate universe. Madison Square Garden would routinely sell out for races that would take 144 hours, in which runners and walkers would circle a short wooden plank track while spectators made bets about who would fall over first and eventually be the last man standing. Imagine that happening in today's hyperbolic world. But then again, think in terms of a modern-day reality show, of how mind-numbingly stupid most reality shows are, and how in America millions watch them. The six-day races of the late 1800s and early 1900s were raw, emotional, and precise, and attracted some of the best athletes in the world.

Edward Payson Weston, namesake of the race Craig and I were about to suffer through, was a showman of the highest caliber. He wore strange clothing more suited to an English countryman rancher enroute to church on horseback, including fancy gloves, and he carried a walking stick. He walked at a steady pace and didn't look like the one to bet on, at least early on. But as the race wore on, and as further races were staged, he became the favorite and he won several. In the late 1980s, he became my patron saint.

The six-day races were revived in the 1970s in different parts of the world, and a couple remain even today. The modern races are not betted on and have few, if any, spectators. But the idea of such a race seared my brain synapses. The entire premise sucked me in. Plus, in 1987, I figured there was no one in the world, or at least no one in the United States, with Type 1 diabetes who had finished one. I was willing to be the guinea pig. I could be studied under the microscope of a quarter-mile, black cinder track for six days and six nights, returning once more to my life as a hamster in a cage on a wheel.

The race took place in the heat and humidity of late June in Pennsauken, New Jersey, where you could have seen the skyscrapers of downtown Philadelphia if not for the thick, stagnant air. The track was located on the tree-lined banks of the Cooper River, but even that pleasant pastoral scene became gruesomely monotonous after the first 100 laps, with anywhere from 900 to 2,000 laps to go.

I had a long discussion with my endocrinologist and his staff months before the race. They were cautious but supportive. We obviously figured out a game plan, even setting up some possible situations that I role-played through. Most people I talked to felt it was dangerous, suggesting maybe I had gone too far, gotten too full of myself. That group was a minority. My supporters said if anyone could complete it, I could. Some of those supporters became actual supporters, acting as handlers during the race, and included Mary, Louie, Ann, Susan, and Tina. My friend Linette was well-versed in the act of mixing my special sugar-free electrolyte drink, giving me injections of insulin or glucose in an emergency, checking for signs of instability or inconsistency, and providing comic relief with a fat joke book she brought along. Craig was quite capable of performing all these duties too, as he planned to walk every step with me. I was hyper aware of all the hazards that were likely to be encountered and constantly self-monitored my situation. But once we got into the thick of it, especially at night when we walked half asleep or even hallucinating, it was good to have all these wonderful guardian friends checking in on me.

One very real threat was foot problems. We aimed to walk 250 to 300 miles in six days, sometimes in soaking rain. Surely, foot problems could arise. The Pennsylvania College of Podiatric Medicine came to the rescue, setting up a trailer in the middle of the track that was staffed by doctors, instructors, and interns. They saw some gruesome extremes of foot problems, a war zone of overused leg injuries, and falls onto the black cinders. They were especially intrigued at the challenge of having to treat Type 1 diabetic foot problems in these extreme conditions. Everything was in place to help me "survive and thrive." That was my old mantra, and it's close to my new mantra: "The goal is the path." I became a monk unto that path, and thus that path became my monastery.

On Sunday, June 21, 1987, at noon, the gun went off. It would not be fired again until six days and six nights, or 144 hours later. Three women and 15 men set out on a journey. For me, that journey was to prove what a Type 1 diabetic is capable of. If I could pull this off, then other people with diabetes would hopefully be inspired to walk a couple miles every other day, thus helping to control the day-to-day of living with a chronic disease.

What does one think about while walking for six days and nights?:

- If we do x number of miles per hour and times that by 144, then that is how many miles we end up with.
- We are slowing down, tired, hurting. At this rate, we will only end up with a lot less miles.
- Wow, we are on a roll. A surge of sorts. If we keep that up, we will exceed our expectations.
- During that last rainstorm, my soaked feet began to develop bad blisters. If they get infected, I'm dropping out, followed by a sigh of relief.

- My feet hurt like hell but are not infected. I'm going to finish this bastard of a race.
- For the next hour, I'm going to concentrate on illuminating performances by actors and actresses in works of cinematic art.
- Philadelphia is just over the Ben Franklin Bridge. Man, I am craving a cheesesteak.
- Damn, all we have left to eat is Power Bars and soup-in-a-cup.
- I miss my family. Why am I putting myself through this?
- That last joke that Linette told was hilarious.
- The bad jokes that Linette tells us actually stick in the brain longer than the good ones.
- What would I be doing if I was home right now?
- Back to performances of cinematic art.

Actually, there was no need to just live in your head. There was a virtual carnival happening all around you, even on some nights. One of the great moments that happened twice a day was when the Park Service came to empty and clean the portable toilets. They baked in the sun all day and got very full right before emptying, plus most of the entrants had some form of digestive distress happening deep within. A collective cheer emanated from around the track when the shit wagon showed up.

We slept twice a night in the back of my mom's old Dodge Caravan. At most, it counted as one hour of a restless, peripatetic sleep because it still felt like we were walking. It takes almost half an hour to prepare for sleep and to settle into it. Then, it takes another half-hour to get ready to head back to the track, especially for me to check and adjust my blood glucose with an insulin syringe shot or food. Even if you count the hours we slept as restful, we had a total of 12 hours of sleep in six nights. For other rest breaks, we had lawn chairs under the overhanging tailgate, where we could sit out of the sun or rain. Any kind of break felt so good, but it was so hard to get rolling again. You stiffen up fast, and your feet hurt the worst during the first mile or so after a break. Then, I guess the feet and the brain become numb to the pain.

Since the atmosphere was humid, chafing also started to bother me. I think it was Napoleon who said that chafing can halt the greatest of marching armies. All kinds of powders, creams, and salves are used to keep going round and round. Napoleon's armies had access to French herbal remedies, but they didn't have to pass by two smelly porta potties more than 2,000 times in six days.

As in any great adventure, the people you meet along the way turn into some of your favorite memories. Existing, in effect, within an enclosed, repeating landscape, the other participants become your family. Don Choi, from San Francisco was another of those amazing athletes, having won many ultra-distance races, but he displayed a very gracious nature. Two days into the race, he gave us some advice. His girlfriend was feeding him won-ton soup laced with soy sauce and bagels also soaked with soy sauce. The key ingredient was the sodium content. He actually asked his handler to prepare and feed us some of these potions. It blew our minds that he would be helpful to our journey.

The middle two days are the hardest, as you are no longer fresh and yet far away from the finish. On the fourth evening, when most of us were at a low point in the race, my brother turned on his big transistor radio and carried it on his shoulder. The San Francisco Giants were playing the Phillies, right across the Delaware River, and Craig was a lifelong Giants fan. As the game progressed, other participants fell in line behind us to hear the game. We soon had a conga line moving at a good clip in semi-circles. It had to be one of the strangest sights of a race in which the whole premise was strange. Don Choi was right behind us, as he was also a big Giants fan, but he and my brother were surrounded by an army of Phillies fans. I took turns carrying the radio, and Don even did a stint, and he was the current leader of the race! Then the game went into extra innings, providing us with even more entertainment. Later, Don thanked us for giving him a lift during what was a bad stretch for him. Like a lot of the other competitive runners, his fast walking pace allowed him to recover, still pad his lead, and take his mind off the gnawing pain. It led us into the last two days, allowing us to see the light at the end of the tunnel. The Giants won the game, and it seemed like we were all winning our own races within.

Bill Schultz, the race director of the Dawn to Dusk ultras, which we had participated in for three years now, was another talented athlete. He had won this six-day race two years earlier. During an interview with a newspaper, he told the reporter that "ultra-marathoners are not freaks. There is nothing freakish about the sport. People pushing themselves to find out where their outer limits are. How far the mind and body can extend themselves."

Clarence Ritchey, a professor out of Texas, was one of the best 60-or-older ultra runners in the world. However, he did exhibit a few idiosyncrasies. Clarence liked to drink beer during the race — hot beer. He kept a case in the infield by his tent, where it cooked in the summer sun. He also wore a clear, plastic raincoat during a few of the storms we walked through. But when the sun came back out, he kept it on, making the rest of us hot just watching him. He was so lost in his groove that he was cooking just like the beer he was drinking.

John Radich, the California Mountain Man, would go on to be a close buddy of mine long after the race ended. John was known for competing and training on mountain trails on the West Coast. He had finished multiple Badwater races, which went from the lowest point in the states, Death Valley, to the highest point in the lower 48 states, Mount Whitney. One year, he carried a backpack and continued on another 200 miles on the John Muir Trail, part of the Pacific Crest Trail, to Yosemite. He possessed one of the smoothest strides I have ever seen. Yet, John was equally at home on multi-day track races. If you look up the word "prolific" in the dictionary, you will find a picture of John Radich.

Neil Weygant was Buddha-like on the track, one of the nicest people you could meet at any race. But underneath all that serenity, Neil possessed the fire of the dragon. He was a threat to win any of the many ultras he did each year. And he pushed Choi through the entirety of this six-day race.

Wes Emmons was another of those names that popped up during East Coast ultras. He was in his 50s with a laid-back demeanor that belied his ability to churn out miles. He really came to life while listening to classical music, becoming quite animated by actually conducting the orchestra while walking around the track, especially when listening to Russian composer Dimitri Shastakovich. Instead of using up dwindling reserves of energy to mimic conducting, Wes produced more energy, and it rubbed off on the rest of the competitors.

The driving force of music compelled most entrants in the six-day race. We used cassette tapes in Walkmans with earphones. Every once in a while, someone would sing really badly along to whatever they were listening to, and Craig and I would try to guess what song it was, make our bets, and then ask the singer. Sometimes we were way off in our guesses, owing to their off-tune singing. We, too, were as guilty as any of the runners of singing off-tune, quite loudly at times. It was hard to expect good pitch and even the right lyrics from anyone while running 40 to 70 miles a day. Craig and I listened to mixed tapes we had made specifically for the race, mostly high-octane stuff with a driving beat. We both shared some Springsteen, Tears for Fears, and classic rock. I liked to listen to Coltrane's "Love Supreme" in the morning as a form of monastic prayer. That entire monastic way of life had a lot of shared elements with walking day and night, at least for me. I also listened to the frenzied energy of Miles Davis' "Bitches Brew" when I needed a real kick in the butt.

But one of the biggest remembrances for both Craig and I of the entire race was a bootleg tape from U2 that Craig procured from an unnamed source. It was just weeks before the Irish rock band unleashed a torrent of an album called "The Joshua Tree" onto the world. We took turns listening to it twice daily, which meant 12 listens each over six days. That spiritual desert music seared into our heart and souls, always picking us up when we faltered. The impact of that music was profound, even more so because of the desert-like heat and simulated remoteness we walked through. It helped us survive and thrive, and it still does to this day.

Three times during the race we had a bad thunderstorm accompanied by torrential rains. Most entrants retired to the safety of their vehicles, figuring it would pass quickly. Clarence always continued through it, almost as if that plastic raincoat he wore could deflect the lightning. We nervously waited for him to get struck, but he lucked out, and soon we were back out on the track. Now we had a dilemma. The rainwater pooled on the inside lane of the track. Your choice was to do the shortest distance possible in that lane in three inches of rainwater or walk further out, which added distance to each lap. Most of us took the shorter distance, though Wes went wide, calling it "the scenic route."

I controlled my diabetes with precision except for a few highs right before the storms hit and a few minor highs from dehydration. All my lows were minor and were arrested immediately. I didn't have to worry about going low while sleeping, since we barely slept. Another big help for surviving the heat was two buckets of ice water that sat at each end of the track with sponges you could use to squeeze the water onto your head. In an iconic photo in "Walking Magazine," I am walking wearing only shoes, flowered running shorts, and white-framed sunglasses while squeezing a sponge of ice water onto my head.

The long-awaited finish finally came within reach. There was a huge breach in the space/time continuum surrounding the race. It felt like we were walking for months and yet simultaneously like we were just starting out. This is a common occurrence that happens during adventures, as I would learn over and over again. For the last lap, all 18 finishers joined hands, with much laughter mixed with salty tears and, of course, a huge sigh of relief. A crowd of about 30 onlookers, mostly our families – including my wife, daughters and mother — cheered us on. My daughters were way too young to remember, except being told by both my wife and mom that their dad and uncle had a few loose screws in their head for doing something so ridiculous as walking around in a circle for six days and nights, receiving only a paper certificate, a small trophy, and a T-shirt. However, Craig and I each lost 10 pounds, which left our muscles cut and defined and, while laughing, we could then say that because of that, the pain and misery of the last six days was all worthwhile.

Some of the final mileage totals:

- 1st place: Don Choi, 447 miles
- 2nd: Neil Weygandt, 441 miles
- 3rd: Bill Schultz, 417 miles
- 5th: Clarence Ritchey, 400 miles
- 6th: John Radich, 351 miles
- 8th: Wes Emmons, 314 miles
- 9th: Susan Johnson, 313 miles
- 11th: Myra Linden, 304 miles
- Tied for 13th place and the only pure walkers: Bob and Craig Scheidt, 274 miles

In that same article in "Walking Magazine" that carried my photo, I told the author, Sally Moore, "I feel a kindred spirit with the early pioneers and adventurers. Once there was so much to explore, but now we're limited to space and far reaches of the earth, out of the financial range of most people. What's left is the mind, pushing yourself to extremes with problems to solve."

This event was both one of the most horrendous and one of the most illuminating things I have ever done. Craig was right by my side every step of the long way, my guardian angel, sharing with me the accomplishment of a lifetime. I proved to the world that a Type 1 diabetic could reach the outer limits of extreme mileage, could survive and thrive, could recover just two days later and jump right back into a physically demanding job, and could find that the goal truly is the path.

Chapter 9

I Take to the Open Road

*"There is a road, no simple highway,
Between the dawn and the dark of night,
And if you go no one may follow,
That path is for your steps alone."*

— The Grateful Dead, "Ripple"

At the end of my obsession with running/walking in long-distance events, I had accumulated 20 full marathons and 30 ultramarathons. After the full-on intensity of competing in some of those toughest challenges of my life, I felt the call of another re-invention of myself. The challenges would remain but now would come in adventures that I would conjure, research, plan, and execute. They would still involve long-distance walking but not in organized events. Just like Edward Payson Weston, I would walk across states and hold informational rallies about the link between walking and maintaining a healthy mind, body, and spirit. Once again, the re-invention was gradual, happening over years, and mostly occurring in the spring, with the rest of the year a mix of backpacking adventures, bicycle racing, and ultramarathons. I would speak to people in towns and cities, almost as if on a soap box, just like Weston did, though my talks were in borough halls, school auditoriums, grange halls, and hospitals. I would get to meet the people of the areas I walked through. Again, I felt a mixture of excitement and freedom of forward motion during events of my own creation.

The first such challenge was built upon another organized event, the Super Cities Walk for MS, a 15-mile walk from Allentown to Bethlehem, Muhlenberg College to Lehigh University. To promote this event, I planned to walk 85 miles in three days from Lancaster County to the start of the MS walk and then complete that 15-mile route along with hundreds of other walkers, making my grand total 100 miles in three days. Craig was back to join in the challenge and my buddy Louie, now in his 60s, was ready to roll. As they say in the movies, "The usual suspects."

My wife, who sometimes was an unwitting accomplice, drove us to a cheap motel on the northern outskirts of Lancaster. Day one dawned overcast with wisps of moisture in the air. We mostly followed back roads through Ephrata, Adamstown, Gouglersville, and Mohnton. The scenery was quite drab, but the conversation and hilarity did, as expected, make the miles fly by. Some of the talk came from Louie, who grew up outside Budapest in Hungary, and he regaled us with many stories.

As the day wore on and the weariness ensued, we walked along the edges of the city of Reading, a bit of clamor to dull our reverie. But soon we were following smooth trails along Tulpehocken Creek, heading out of the city toward Blue Marsh Lake Recreation Area. To finish our 40 miles, we passed the Berks County Prison, role-playing the part of escaped convicts, and then moved on to Leesport, where Nancy and the kids picked us up. Adrienne, now 8, was old enough to question why her father was always walking. Amberly, 3, just giggled at how her mother jokingly called her father "mentally unbalanced." As they grew up, they would come to understand that walking long distances" while seeming crazy, was what made their father who he was.

Day two was sunnier and started along the banks of Ontelaunee Dam, following wonderful trails toward Kutztown. Then, backroads took us past my friend Linette's house, where we were greeted with a banner in the front yard to encourage us onward. Louie had some back problems and walks a bit crooked, but he hung in there until we wound our way to the Lehigh Valley Velodrome. We did some interviews and soaked in the accomplishment of another 35 miles for the day. My kids curiously said, "Are you still walking? When will you get there?" They would have to understand that I would never actually get there. I would always be walking.

On day three, it was a quick, straight-shot 10 miles to Allentown. Upon arrival, we sought out the event coordinator, Dona, whom the three of us had a little crush on. She was far too busy to listen to the proclamations of quixotic wanderers in the throes of a walker's high. My mother, now 63, and Craig's wife, Tracy, joined us for the final 15 miles to Bethlehem. A huge crowd had gathered, ready to walk to raise money for research to find relief and a cure for victims of multiple sclerosis. My neighbor, Ginny, suffered from the effects of long-term MS and was relegated to a wheelchair for the rest of her life. This was why we chose this organization and did our 100-mile walk to help promote the Super Cities Walk.

The final 15 miles was a festive affair with long throngs of walkers stretching out ahead and behind us, especially on the bridges over the Lehigh River. There were food stands all along the route plus bands playing live music every mile. Then a dramatic entry over a huge bridge brought us onto the campus of Lehigh University, where we celebrated with a big party. We found Dona and congratulated her for organizing a very successful event and regaled her with stories of our hijinks from the last three days of walking. She even seemed genuinely interested, but we kept it to a minimum, which for us took a lot of constraint. These days of walking with my two buddies and then with the big crowd was magical. I had once again, in this reimagining, found my new path forward.

***

The idea of doing another promotional walk for the Super Cities Walk for MS percolated in my head for most of the next year. I decided, as a challenge, to double it. I would walk 200 miles in six days, and this time travel to Allentown from the north, starting just south of the Pennsylvania/New York state line below Elmira, New York. I would walk in familiar territory, traveling over a lot of the first two days through the mountains I hiked during the last 15 years. As a family, we also had vacationed every year nearby in a charming town called Wellsboro in Tioga County. It reminded us of New England, with gas streetlights separated in the middle by swaths of green and a fountain with statues of Wynken, Blynken, and Nod. The motels were cheap, and the town had an old-fashioned movie theater and a diner inside a train car. Every year, Wellsboro held a Dickens festival right before Christmas and a mountain laurel festival in the late spring. The hotel we always stayed at was run by a family, and their kids and our kids grew up together. It seemed to be the perfect place for me to start my next endurance adventure.

My dad and Craig drove me north for four hours to our friend's motel in downtown Wellsboro. Craig was not joining me for that year's walk. Maybe the ludicrousness of it all was getting to him. I would cover 35 to 40 miles a day on foot once again. I did have a new partner in crime, someone equally crazy enough to endure the distance and actually revel in it. John Knabb had trained with me a few times, but his life was a whirlwind of work, family, and travel. He is one of the few people for whom the phrase "burning the candle at both ends" was not hyperbole. He was known for throwing himself into extraneous situations and somehow swimming his way through, coming out on the other side with the whole endeavor becoming a learning experience. Funny thing is even he didn't always know that, sometimes not even in retrospect. Two examples show this side of John. He attended high school with Nancy, and after the school day ended, he left to work on his family's hay farm. One day, he decided to stay and run with the cross-country team on its three-mile course. Being very friendly and knowing almost everyone, he fit right in. One of the best runners in the state lived near John in Maxatawny Township. As the lead runners shot out ahead at the beginning of the run, John hung right with them, barely breathing hard, making small talk, joking around, and yet comfortably running with the best of them. He was possessed of an amazing cardiovascular system, honed by long hours of hard work on the farm. Then, two miles into it, he peeled away, telling the gang, "I have to get to work. My dad's probably wondering where I am." After this happened a few times, the coach tried to recruit him, and while John would have liked to join the team, he honored his commitment to the farm.

Years later, my wife and I were at an outdoor party at John's farm. He was a legendary party animal. I knew of him but not well at that point. He approached me and asked what I had been up to lately. I enthusiastically went on about the 50-mile race I was going to run the next day in Allentown. I may have been too enthusiastic, and John picked right up on it and said he'd like to give it a shot. A little caught off guard, I told him I'd pick him up at five o'clock in the morning and left the party early to rest. When I pulled into the farm the next morning, the scene looked like a battlefield — hungover bodies lying about in the grass, with empty and half-filled bottles strewn around. John bounded out the door primed and ready. He had an entire pizza with him and proceeded to practically inhale it on the drive to the start of the race. He said he heard that you should carbo load for a run of such distance. He also mentioned that he had barely slept but was used to that.

The race was held on a two-mile blacktop square surrounded by dismal fields just north of the Lehigh Valley Airport. Planes landed and took off all day, and sometimes they were the only thing to take our minds off our discomfort. John shot off with the leaders, some of the best ultra-runners in the tri-state area. They were trying to figure out who this upstart was amongst them. Twenty miles in, he was still just behind them, having lapped me once. I wondered if he was going to pull it off and challenge them for the lead. He kept it up till mile 25 and then started fading. On the second lapping of me, he said he was shot but had to finish the lap to get back to the car. He guessed that the lack of sleep and alcohol were getting to him, but he was proud of having finished his first marathon with hardly any training. He immediately fell asleep in the front seat of my station wagon. Every two-mile lap I completed, I stopped for a break by opening the tailgate, waking him up, and sending him into spasms of leg cramps mixed with fear from his ongoing nightmares. The rest of the runners' families and handlers thought I was committing murder every time I opened that damn tailgate. I deduced that maybe John's only real misstep was not having drunk enough liquid and electrolytes.

When I finally completed the race, I dropped off John at his house. He looked like death warmed over. John's dad came out onto the porch and exclaimed, "What the hell happened, son"? John, in a thin, worn-out voice, proudly stated that he had just run 26 miles. His dad said, "Who the hell does that?" and John replied, "Bob just ran 50!"

It was the start of a crazy, mad, yet ultimately energizing friendship that would endure for many miles, on foot and vehicle, through the heart and soul of America.

***

The first day of the walk from Wellsboro to Allentown chilled us with a biting wind and temps in the low 20s. Snow showers appeared briefly in between periods of sunshine and a deep blue sky. Luckily, we were heading south and east with the wind pushing us. John had been up half the night with a bad respiratory virus. He took sips from a bottle of NyQuil even as we walked. This was my kind of country: bunched up mountains, water systems everywhere, a sort of western landscape yet uniquely Pennsylvanian. Twelve miles brought us to the town of Morris, where you could see the pits used for the annual Rattlesnake Roundup held in the summer. During spring, summer, and fall, the hills crawled with thick dark and gold rattlers living on the rim of Pine Creek Gorge, also called the Grand Canyon of Pennsylvania. We stopped for a snack at the general store, then headed east. It warmed a bit but barely. At 24 miles in, at the town of Liberty, John started hurting. He may have ingested too much NyQuil and not enough water. We headed south again, toward Williamsport, on Route 15. PennDOT was widening the road that took big trucks north into New York state. At the 30-mile mark John hitched a ride with one of the road workers to our motel just north of the city. He had once again proven his mettle. Even though he was very sick, he had managed 30 miles, the longest he had walked in one day, and with very little training. For the last 10 miles of the 40 total for the day, I had nice wide shoulders and continuing mountain vistas to enjoy.

Day two entailed 35 miles of walking at a brisk pace because we had a diabetes presentation to give at a university in Lewisburg. John was still sick, so he slept in and then hitched a ride to the halfway point of the day at Clyde Peeling's Reptiland. I knew of Clyde and figured that both of these fascinating characters would have a lot to talk about until I got there. I came out of the mountains into Williamsport, crossed the west branch of the Susquehanna River on a long bridge, then ascended a mountain that gave me a stunning vista of the city. I had stopped there many times while driving at night to backpacking adventures. Seeing the lights of the city spread out below always made my pulse race, knowing this was the gateway to the northern wilderness. Now I was on foot heading south toward home with four and a half long days to go.

John seemed to have recovered a bit, though Clyde was not around; he was hunting specimens somewhere in the jungles of the southern hemisphere. The landscapes now flattened as we followed the mighty Susquehanna River into Lewisburg. The only blip on the radar being Federal Correctional Complex, Allenwood, a so called "country-club prison," where Nixon's boys were incarcerated in the '70s. John started experiencing nausea and muscle aches during the last five miles. Our motel was right next to a hospital, very near the campus of Bucknell University, where I would speak later that evening. John immediately crawled into bed with the chills. I advised him to drink as much water as he could stomach and then left to walk to the hospital to inquire about John's condition. They told me to bring him in. In the meantime, he had drunk six glasses of water. He shivered during the quarter-mile walk to the emergency room. After a thorough examination, they put an IV into him and told me he was extremely dehydrated and would be kept overnight. The next day, John's wife picked him up and scolded me for pushing him too much. She should have known that no one pushes John harder than John himself.

I was alone for a few days as the difficult terrain turned mountainous again and the weather turned to a three-day icy rain. I now walked through the western section of the anthracite coal region, including the towns of Shamokin, Mount Carmel, Ashland, and Frackville, where huge slab coal heaps were spaced among the mountains. I was lonely, soaked, and shivering. My only rescue was a young reporter who walked a few miles with me every day and valiantly tried to interview me. But even on those days I would not have traded my life with anyone else. This is truly what I was put on this earth to do, and knowing that always carried me through.

My good Hungarian buddy Louie joined me in Pottsville for the last two days of walking into Allentown. That night, we presented at a banquet in Pottsville and raised money for MS research and aid. I was again promoting the MS Super Cities Walks held all over the country. The second to last day, Louie and I walked home to Kutztown over the Blue Mountains, crossing the Appalachian Trail perpendicularly. Then, using back roads through a few old, wooden covered bridges on roads I was very familiar with from bicycling and hiking with my wife, I cruised home. The last day, Louie and I walked 20 miles to Allentown and then walked the last of my 200 total miles with thousands of other walkers at the Super Cities Walk. It was the culmination of another challenging and soul-enriching experience. As I would duplicate for many years to come, I was already planning the next year's adventure, and beyond, before the one I was on ended. This kept me in a wonderful, perpetual loop of high spirits and drunk-like wonder, with the only drug being movement across the landscape.

***

Throughout the years that I walked for the Multiple Sclerosis Society, my family and I engaged in many summer and fall adventures. My children were growing up with this lifestyle. Adventures included backpacking trips, camping trips with lots of hiking and swimming, and bicycling, most of them taking place in our backyard Appalachian Mountains and the wilderness of northcentral Pennsylvania.

I first introduced Adrienne, then 8 years old, to backpacking at the lean-to shelters at the Hawk Mountain Sanctuary. The trail in from the parking lot was only half a mile, pacifying my worrisome wife, who stayed home with little Amberly. Adrienne and I left home for an easy 18-mile drive north to those omnipresent mountains that rose from the surrounding farm fields. You will encounter a rocky path almost anywhere you walk on the Blue Mountain ridge. It was fortuitous to arrive with some daylight remaining. After setting up camp in the shelters, we climbed to the top of the mountain to a vista called South Lookout. There, we watched the sun set in the mountains behind us and the moon rise in the valley in front of us. Then, the lights in the farmhouses blinked on below us, and the stars in the sky blinked on above us. It was quiet all around, but soon we heard the faint stirrings of the nocturnal forest animals. The magic enveloped all our senses. Then, we made a slow descent by headlamps down the stony trail and over our water-source creek, the shine of the aluminum shelter roof from our lights letting us know that we were home. We cooked dinner on a small stove, started a fire, then ate dessert while watching the crackle and pop of burning logs.

During the evening, we snuggled in our sleeping bags, Adrienne with the one stuffed animal she was allowed to carry in. Amid the chilly air, the night forest noises became louder. Deer, porcupines, squirrels, chipmunks, and even an occasional bear could have passed by at any time. In the morning, we donned our headlamps and followed the same trail back up to the lookout. This time, we watched the sun rise to the east and the lights in the valley disappear as night became day, the tilting of the earth since time immemorial. We cooked breakfast while feeling the warmth of the fully risen sun.

We were so lucky to have this available to us, a gift that we took advantage of countless times. Eventually, Amberly and my wife joined in. It was the perfect introduction to longer backpacking trips on the horizon, and it was way more enriching than anything we could have watched on television.

The next few years took Adrienne and I on many backpacking trips further north, replicating many of those trails I hiked on with the Allentown Hiking Club ten years prior. I now felt a surge of excitement to be able to introduce her to these storybook landscapes, though I had to tamp down the urge to tell stories about the old days ("Well, when I last came through here..."). It was better to live in the glorious moments, of which there were many. Adrienne and I backpacked the entire length of the Loyalsock Trail on four trips. We camped above and below cascading waterfalls, one which required you to climb a log ladder along it, and the enveloping spray made it feel as if it was raining. While perching on our campsite on high but gentle mountaintops, we watched the moon rise out of the hollows. Stopping for rest breaks in meadows and reading "The Lord of the Rings," we realized that the wooded glade we just walked through looked exactly like what Tolkien described. We giggled while waiting for hobbits, elves, and Gandalf to emerge from the trees. Once, we came upon a troop of young Boy Scouts struggling up a rise, their poorly packed gear dangling by fraying ropes outside their knapsacks. I felt bad for them as a much smaller Adrienne passed them singing showtunes and theme songs, making it seem way too easy. Saying some of the names of cascades, like Rode Falls and Angel Falls, and of vistas – Smith's Knob, Kettle Creek, and more — still gives me a warm, pleasant feeling, bringing back wonderful memories of bonding with my daughter.

Next up was the Black Forest Trail, which we did by dividing the 44 miles into two three-day backpacking treks. On the first one, we saw a huge black bear crossing the creek on top of Naval Run Falls. Adrienne will always remember the early October snow flurry that enveloped us on top of what may be the best vista in all of Pennsylvania, on top of Hemlock Mountain. The view to the south featured Pine Creek, as deep and wide as a river, cutting out a gorge among giant, hemlock-clad mountains. Another of my friends, Steve, a city boy on his first time in the wilds, joined us for this one. The temperatures dropped fast, so we got out our sleeping bags to eat lunch, which consisted of canned Vienna sausages we wrapped with potato rolls. The jellied substance the sausages came in gave us some fat we needed to burn to keep warm. Adrienne was always a trouper and rarely complained.

The next fall, we did the second half with my friends Megan and Josh. Both were outdoors people; Megan's parents owned a clothing and equipment store in Kutztown called Take a Hike. They were impressed with Adrienne's far-beyond-10-years maturity. In turn, Adrienne thought it was cool that Megan and Josh let her smoke a cigar on our last evening on top of Quarry Vista, from which it was so dark that we saw no lights of human presence. Then on the way home, they let her drink half a can of beer, confirming what she thought initially: that those two were the coolest people in the world.

***

My next big endurance challenge was to walk from Luray, Virginia, to Allentown, a trip of 300 miles in nine days. I was still walking for the Multiple Sclerosis Society and had always thought that it would be self-serving to walk to raise money for an organization that does research for my chronic disease: diabetes. But somewhere along those 300 miles, my ideas about my involvement with charities evolved. Part of the reason for so much inner dialogue during this walk was that I was alone for most of it. It started with a huge crowd and ended with one also. But in between, I was mostly alone.

My first mile happened underground in Luray Caverns, a big feature of the town. Before exiting the cave, there is a pool of water, a glacial cave fountain, that people throw coins into for good luck. Every year, they donate all the money to a cause. I chose to start walking at the caverns because they donated $32,000 dollars from the coins in the pool to the Multiple Sclerosis Society. As I exited the cave, a huge crowd waited for me. I gave a short speech on how the simple act of walking can have all kinds of influences on chronic disease. Then, mile two took me east on Main Street as part of a parade accompanied by the Luray High School band, gospel singers, the police, and fire companies. It started to snow as the crowds lining the streets cheered me on my way. It was exhilarating to say the least.

I crossed a bridge over the Shenandoah River at the foot of the Appalachian Ridge, turned, and followed the riverbank. Looking to the top of the peaks brought back memories of backpacking trips from almost 20 years earlier. I encountered a stiff headwind for most of the long, 36-mile day, with snow squalls appearing off and on all day. The scenery was quite exquisite, the river bending and curling, the forest a blend of evergreens and leafless deciduous trees. Toward the end of the day, I walked into the Civil War battlefield town of Front Royal, where I slept in an empty jail cell at the local police station. I was happy to get out of the brutal wind. The next morning, I exited the mountains and river. I was still on a high and grooving on it right on into Inwood, West Virginia, where I stayed at a small fire company and the town hosted me for a big meal. I gave a speech and went to sleep early in the firefighters' quarters. That north wind had again worn me out toward the end of the day, and I felt glad that there were no fire sirens that evening to startle me from my deep slumber.

I was only in West Virginia for a few miles, grabbing a second breakfast at a diner where a sign behind the counter proclaimed, "General Lee surrendered, but we didn't." I walked a mile on the Patsy Cline Memorial Highway with her songs playing in my head well after crossing into Maryland. At that point, I was just east of Harpers Ferry as I walked over a bridge across the Potomac River. The rest of the day was uneventful, though the wind persisted. I was interviewed by both a Hagerstown newspaper and the local television station, followed by a banquet and speech at the Best Western Venice Inn.

On day four, I woke up feeling a little rundown. My blood glucose was elevated a bit, maybe indicating the start of a respiratory infection. But I kept the pace before taking a nap in the woods in Catoctin State Park. The steep hill out of the park was a bit of drudgery, but the landscape was scenic, and that always rallied me. I felt better as I crossed into Pennsylvania, where a reporter waited for me as I approached Gettysburg. She explained that it was two miles to my motel, but instead, she would drive me to the battlefields, where we would walk two miles and she would interview me. It was an exciting end to another hard day with a bit of Civil War history thrown in.

On day five, I walked through York, an industrial city that looked like and was probably named after its sister city in England. The weather got very warm, and I had to be even more aware of hydration. The respiratory problem returned along with the high glucose readings. I had to dig deep to keep the mileage flowing. After being lonely for most of the walk, I looked forward to staying at my good friend Mary's house in Hallam on the west bank of the mighty Susquehanna River.

Mary was the perfect person to end my loneliness and lift my spirits a bit. She always displayed an upbeat attitude and had helped me out as a handler at some of my track ultramarathons in the past. Then, a few years earlier, she asked me to train her for her first marathon. The longest Mary had run at that point was five miles. By using a combination of running one mile and walking one mile in training and in the race, and gradually increasing the training miles in weekly increments, my brother and I helped Mary get to the finish line at the Philadelphia Marathon. Mary had what it takes, which is mostly attitude, and that attitude is what I needed after being mostly alone in my long miles of walking from central Virginia.

Mary and her baby daughter joined me for the first five miles of day six. We took turns pushing the stroller up, through, and back down Samuel B. Lewis State Park with vistas of the wide Susquehanna River. Then, Mary and Emma headed home, and I crossed the river on a mile-long bridge into the town of Columbia. I would not be alone for long, as my family was meeting me to spend the night just north of Lancaster. The rest of the walk that day was full of traffic, which continued all the way until after the city of Reading. My kids were growing up fast, and though they understood a lot more now, they still asked, "Where is dad walking now? Where will he walk next? Will he ever be done walking?" The older they got, the more they understood: I would never be done with walking.

The last three days were a duplicate of the three-day 100-mile walk I did two years earlier. This time, I was all alone until Allentown, when I encountered the biggest crowd to ever walk with me for the Super Cities Walk for MS. During those last three days, I came up with a new plan. My next walk would be a fundraiser for diabetes education and research. Maybe the next one would be 400 miles and cross the entire commonwealth of Pennsylvania.

As a leadup to that transition, I decided to do my first walk for the Juvenile Diabetes Foundation as a model and a planning vehicle for the "big one" the following year. My buddy Butch accompanied me, and since he was also interested in next year's "big one," we could plan it while walking 106 miles from Sullivan County south to Reading.

There was never a dull moment when walking with Butch. We started from his deer-hunting cabin on a mountain just south of Worlds End State Park. The first day took us to Bloomsburg, where sorority and fraternity students from the university took us out to the famous Bloomsburg Fair and then on a bar crawl to every drinking establishment in town. We followed for a stretch but then finally backed off because we had 30 miles of mountainous terrain to walk the next day. At our last bar for the evening, a local roughneck was so moved by what we were doing that he offered to pay some "ladies of the night' to go back to our hotel rooms with us. Butch and I quickly got out our wallets to show everyone pictures of our families.

We spent a jovial hour-long lunch break the next day sitting on a huge rock along the highway in a remote part of Northumberland County. Traffic was steady as everyone headed north to the fair. As we sat on that rock, we got the weirdest stares, especially when it was someone from back home. We laughed our asses off as to what was going through the heads of those people doing double takes. We could almost hear them saying, "What the hell are Butch and Scheidty doing causally sitting on a rock in the middle of nowhere?"

On the fourth day, we reached Reading and then took part in the JDF 6-mile walkathon. My family; my friend Linette, who was now Miss Pennsylvania; and my buddy DeLight Breidegam, the owner and CEO of East Penn Manufacturing-Deka Batteries, joined us. Since we had now roughly planned the next year's cross-Pennsylvania walk, we pitched it to DeLight, and he agreed to sponsor us. Then, Kathy, the president of JDF Reading, along with Jim from Lions Club International agreed to set us up with a speaking engagement for every night on the route. Everything started to fall into place. I told my kids on the way home that, yes, daddy would still be walking next year, on his longest walk yet.

***

Picture this: At 40, a man agrees to go on a road trip for 13 days with his parents, who are in their middle 60s. Add in the fact that this family never really travelled on multi-day trips together before this one. Then, mix in the challenge of walking 30 miles a day, presenting a diabetes program every night, and trying not to get lost (both me walking and them driving). Tempers could flare, old family squabbles could be dredged up and beg to be confronted, and tiredness would surely exacerbate the situation. With all these challenges before us, we drove to Wheeling, West Virginia, where the next day we would begin the Trans-Pennsylvania Ultra Walk for Diabetes.

Day one began in a warm, humid atmosphere. The hills rolled all the way toward Pittsburgh, but the pace was quick thanks to both excitement and uncertainty. My mom was by my side for the first five miles and in fact had pledged to walk the first five miles every day. That caused a bit of worry, as my dad did not have a keen sense of direction and was not too good at following maps. We had been given a new Plymouth van by Mente Chevrolet to use for the two-week walk. One hour after we started walking, my dad passed us and headed down to the five-mile mark to wait for us. At that point each morning, we had a snack break, and mom would take care of the logistics for the rest of the day. Luckily, I had inherited my sense of direction from my mom. Toward the end of the day, I started to understand the value of having a moving refreshment station, meaning I would have to carry very little weight. And even the companionship of my parents became an asset. Loneliness would not be a big factor in this adventure.

Day two began on the west side of Pittsburgh. It rained lightly as I started, but as I walked down into the city proper and began to cross bridges over the Monongahela, Ohio, and Allegheny rivers, the rain started to come down in buckets. The impressive view of the city, with its hills, skyscrapers, and stadiums, spread out before me, begging to be photographed. I had to be very careful since I had a fairly new Nikon camera shooting slide film for future presentations. I tried holding the camera under my raincoat hood while taking a few representative shots, but alas the water worked its way in and ruined it. I hoped we could find a shop that might be able to salvage it. My parents also struggled in the deluge, with my dad joking that he swore he saw an ark being built.

The rest of the day took me through the beautiful park system and university campuses. The rain never let up, and I was glad when I saw the van parked in the motel lot near Greenville. Mom and dad both talked wildly as they described the heavy traffic, tunnels, and poor visibility. They made it sound like they had it harder than I did. I was tired, soaked, and chilled and in no mood to listen to their complaining, but the more I thought about it, the more I realized that maybe they did have it harder. I was so used to walking through all kinds of conditions that the weather and terrain became just another element of any adventure.

The rain lingered into day three but eventually dried up, though the sun refused to shine. It was an uneventful walk into Johnstown. I took all my breaks while sitting in the backseat of the van. We had a presentation that night for the Lions Club, which was preceded by a banquet. That night I added a new act to my presentation, which normally consisted of a slide show of previous adventures with a diabetes section followed by a period of questions and answers. That night, they asked my dad to say a few words. I thought he was going to bomb because he started out by making a few observations about what he saw in Johnston. He specifically mentioned that there seemed to be a lot of elderly injured people on the sidewalks. People limping, on crutches, in wheelchairs. The crowd laughed, and he kept going, eventually making light of the fact that he never understood my obsession with walking. Yet here he was on my walking adventure. I don't think he knew that he was being funny. He expanded on his act the next night in Altoona, where we gave two presentations. I think the Lions Clubs phoned ahead and raved about this comedy act.

On day five, I walked a rural course on Route 45, and the next day, I diverted off the road at Colerain Picnic Area onto some of the Mid State Trail, taking rocky side trails back to Route 45 to meet my road vehicle. These trails were some of the same I backpacked on in the 1970s. I also passed the entrance to Camp Kanesatake, where I spent a week at Grange Camp in the late 1960s. The memories came at me fast and furiously, further enhanced by the discussions with my parents at breaks. It was becoming a rich experience for me and hopefully for my parents as well.

That afternoon, we rolled and walked into State College, home of the Penn State Nittany Lions. At the Lions Club banquet and presentation that evening, my dad took it to another level with his comedy act. When asked to give his view of this journey we were on, he got out a roadmap, the crowd waiting in anticipation. They didn't know what my mom and I knew well: my dad was bad at reading maps. Just like I struggled with higher math and reading music, my dad struggled with geography. He pinned the map on a corkboard and started to explain how our route south to Lewistown would be an easy one, since, in his mind, it was all downhill. The place erupted in laughter. They all knew, as did I, that we would have our biggest climb of the entire walk a few miles into starting out in the morning. He got it half right, though, because after attaining the summit at a roadside picnic area, it was mostly downhill into Lewistown.

The many switchbacks ascending and then descending were exhilarating to my spirit. I walked on a decent shoulder through waves of wooded ridges, part of the Bald Eagle State Forest, eventually crossing over the Mid State Trail again. It was so clear that I was able to tick off the names of familiar state parks east and west: Poe Valley, Penn-Roosevelt, Poe Paddy, and Greenwood Furnace, among others. The walk existed simultaneously as a journey into the past and a rich tapestry of the present. I somehow also knew I would return here in the future, though I had no idea then that it would be many, many times.

We progressed eastward at an average of 30 miles a day, walking and presenting programs, with my mom continuing to meet her challenge of walking the first five miles each morning. The adventure took on a unique quality, a splendid blend of getting to know the lives of new people while also getting to further know the lives of my parents. My dad had survived 44 years of backbreaking work in an iron foundry, wearing a dirtied black back brace each day, never complaining yet also bearing the brunt of the battering. My mom also worked 34 years as a sewing machine operator in a shirt factory. Both woke up early and came home late because they were involved in their respective unions, each of them doing a spell as union stewards. We had plenty while growing up and were never in want, but we also lived simply, knowing full well that we had what we had in part because of the left-leaning politics of unions. Their hard work was rewarded because of unions.

From Lewistown, we headed east again to Selinsgrove and Lewisburg, where we had a program at a hospital. As we rolled on toward, the anthracite region, we now retraced part of the route I had walked two years before. Another development started to happen each morning during my mom's five-mile portion. I was being covered by various news outlets, mostly newspapers but also some local television stations. They usually showed up in the morning, and when they found out my 66-year-old mother was walking with me, they wanted to interview her, too. She had a bit of a more sophisticated style and approach than my dad did during his evening standup. I had to chuckle to myself many times while walking alone about how my parents had become parts two and three in the three-ring circus that was the Trans-Pennsylvania Ultra Walk for the Cure.

We found ourselves traveling in some roughed-up places in the middle of nowhere through Schuylkill and Carbon counties on days 11 and 12. There was the hellish smoke of the underground mine fires of deserted Centralia and then Lost Creek, where half of the houses in town were partially burned down from different fires.

For a few days now, my dad had started stopping at cemeteries and wandering among the tombstones. My mom was worried that he had a death wish, and when we confronted him about it, he said, "I'm just looking for material for my comedy act."

"Why would you think that would be funny?" she asked.

"I didn't think the other stuff I've been saying was funny either," he countered.

East we continued through Shenandoah, Mahanoy City, and Barnesville, a spot that used to have a famous Oktoberfest. In Tamaqua, my friend and lawyer, Bob, joined me. He figured that by now my parents and I surely would have been in some form of legal trouble, but other than a few family disagreements, no one had succumbed to fisticuffs yet. On night 11, our presentation took place in the county hospital, where they put us up for the night in the maternity ward. That wing was closed for renovations, but it still felt strange sleeping in beds with foot stirrups. Since it was late September, the air had cooled, and the forested mountainsides erupted with leaves of blazing autumn reds, yellows, and oranges as we angled south-east through Tamaqua and Lehigh Gap. For our final night of the adventure, we presented for the Lions Club in a church in Slatington. The club got us lodging on the fourth floor of a run-down apartment complex. All night long fights and arguments went on, possibly related to drug trafficking. My mom and dad were so scared that the place was going to burn down that they slept in their clothes with their suitcases packed, ready to run.

My final day of walking took me through Nazareth by the speedway, home of the famous Andretti family, and then on into Easton. There, I crossed the bridge over the Delaware River into New Jersey, which marked the end of the walk. We were met there by the media and Jim, a representative of Lions Clubs International, and we toasted with a bottle of Champagne. Mom and dad said they were thrilled and so glad that they decided to join me on this adventure. But from now on, they were going to stick to normal vacations. They were getting too old to engage in such high jinks!

My parents also told me that I should continue to do more of this, what I truly loved. They said once I got to their ages, I would not be able to enjoy it as much. I understood where they were coming from but figured I'd wait and see if that deep love for adventure and long-distance walking would last into my 60s and 70s. But for right now, I was already looking toward the next year and California.

Chapter 10

The Call of the Sirens of California

*"My love's like the warmth of the sun
It won't ever die."*

— The Beach Boys, "The Warmth of the Sun"

The Black Forest Trail will always have a place in my heart. I will return again and again. But that region of the world was never a nice, laid-back vacation, or even an easy backpacking trip. It would continually challenge me and the suckers and souls who would accompany me. My youngest brother, Craig, had taken the dare to try and cover the 42 miles in one day with me years earlier. I promised him it would be easy this time. We would take three and a half days to backpack the entire trail.

Craig should have known better by now. Maybe he wasn't a sucker. Maybe instead he was a glutton for punishment. Maybe he was atoning for his sins. Whatever it was, he signed up again, and as usual, I delivered.

We drove north after work, our spirits running high, and camped at one of the trailheads. The Black Forest Trail casts a spell on hikers; it truly is a magnificent piece of outdoor art from a benevolent creator. Mighty hemlock trees and smaller groves of pine create a tunnel of soft paths and spooky passageways. All the beauty was earned with switchback climbs into and out of deep creek hollows, with lots of blowdowns to crawl over and around.

This time, we were in no hurry, and the May weather was superb. And for the first two days, it was. On our third and final night, we camped along Baldwin Creek. Only a mile earlier, we had crossed over the barrens, a section badly burned from a lightning storm, leaving a wide-open mountain lookout into Young Womans Creek drainages. It truly was a wild country, close to where three counties — Lycoming, Clinton, and Potter — came together. Near dusk, we were cooking dinner on our stove when a small yearling black bear strolled into camp. He had a red tag in his ear, which meant he was considered a nuisance bear. We shooed him off by yelling and throwing stones, but he kept returning. Finally, he went right to the hot chicken and noodles in the pot and cleaned it out. Then, he went to the pudding that was cooling in a pot in the creek and ate all that. As a final act of defiance, he chewed my sweaty, salty boots to shreds before leveling the tent, breaking its poles and clawing the rainfly. Then, he took off up the hollow. Craig was shaking, and though I was used to bears, even I was weirded out. We packed up the ruined bits of what was left. Luckily, I had trail sneakers with me, and we hiked out by headlamps on a shortcut to the car. Every time we heard rustling in the woods, which was a lot, we were startled.

I parked the old station wagon at the foot of the mountain, along Pine creek. We slept in the back, hoping to climb the Ravens Horn on a seven-mile hike the next day. I knew we had parked along a lightly used logging set of railroad tracks, but Craig didn't. In the middle of the night, a train flew by with its whistle blasting, leaving Craig screaming at the top of his lungs. He thought I had unknowingly parked on the tracks. During the hike the next day, Craig kept seeing bears around every corner. I reminded him to keep his eyes on the trail since we were more likely to see fat timber rattlesnakes than bears. His nerves were truly shot, mine a little less so. Most of my adventures, it seemed, would always have an element of fear. I guess that's why they called them adventures.

***

In September of that year, I got a call from an American Diabetes Association Chapter in Pittsburgh. Every year, a few disc jockeys from a downtown radio station did a three-day, 100-mile walk north to Lake Erie. They invited me to join them as a special guest star walker. I was honored to be considered, so I signed on, knowing that at least the beginning in Pittsburgh and the end on the lake would be scenic. The walk sort of spiraled downward from there. First, a late-summer heat wave hit for all three days. I've never liked the heat and humidity, but I can get through it. The mileages were tough, too: 40, 35, and 25 miles, but I was used to that. The problem was that the landscape in the middle 90 miles was so repetitive, with no shoulders on a heavily traveled road, that you could never get in a groove. It was back and forth into the gutter. The traffic never slowed down, either; it seemed like they were gunning for us. There was no shade and no scenery.

What saved me was the wonderful spirit of the other 10 walkers, a mix of radio personalities and ADA officials, most of whom had children with Type 1 diabetes. They had been doing this for 15 years at that point. They said all the negatives made it that much more rewarding, including the cheap, humid, airless motels and the crappy diner food. When we hit the Lake Erie shoreline at Presque Isle State Park, we found cooling breezes. My negativity readily dropped away, and I thought back on the fun times I had talking to the other walkers and doing live radio interviews as we pulled each other along.

They kindly invited me back for the following year, but this time I had a plan. I got out my map and showed them my idea: "How about next year we walk along Lake Erie's shoreline to Cleveland, about 100 miles? Then the next year, we'll walk along the shoreline of Lake Ontario to Buffalo, also about 100 miles?" But once again, they said the drudgery of the Pittsburgh-to-Erie route is what made it a challenge. It was now a 16-year tradition. I thanked them from the bottom of my heart for the invitations, but I would never walk that route again. It was the worst walk I have ever done. My disillusionment with the eastern part of America made me realize that it was time to head west. Possibly, all the way west, to another shoreline, the Pacific Ocean. There I would have maybe the walk of a lifetime with no problems, no hassles.

Be careful what you wish for!

***

In March 1996, I escaped the remnants of a brutal winter on the East Coast and flew to San Francisco. My plan was to walk 400 miles down the coast to Los Angeles. I would be out west for 18 days, the longest I had ever been away from my family. Upon landing, I was to spend the rest of the day wandering the streets of San Fran, which became my favorite city in the United States. I climbed Coit Tower, wandered the bay, ascended the hills, and descended the many staircases. Then, I bought a few lightweight books at City Lights Bookstore and started reading them while drinking a beer at Vesuvio's Bar across an alley named Jack Kerouac Street. It was a magnet for beat writers from around the world, and really for writers in general. Toward evening, my friend Bob picked me up and drove us across the Bay Bridge to his house high up in the Oakland Hills.

Bob Blackburn was a legend to me when I was growing up and feeling the first pangs of wanderlust. Bob's dad and mom lived on a farm down a lane behind our house, so when Bob came to visit his parents, we spent a few days walking in the woods, swimming in ponds, and chatting about travel. They were pretty one-sided since I had not traveled at all at that point. Bob, however, once brought a native family home with him from Somalia, and then an actual young cheetah. Whenever he described an exotic place he had visited, I pulled out my notebook and exclaimed, "I'm putting that on my list!" That list started to grow to multiple pages.

Bob had worked for the Peace Corps in the '60s, and his father, Hal, was a TWA pilot. Hal recognized me as a future explorer and presented me with a pith helmet from Africa for my sixth birthday. My mom always reminded me that I wanted to wear it everywhere. I looked up to both Hal and Bob as examples of a worldly life. Bob eventually moved with his family to Oakland, where he worked as a superintendent in the school district. One night after a late meeting, Bob and his co-workers were leaving a building when a hail of gunfire met them — an attack by the Symbionese Liberation Army. Some of them died, and Bob barely survived, losing a lot of blood. For the rest of his life, he had a slight limp. Later, the SLA would kidnap Patty Hearst, the daughter of newspaper magnate Randall Hearst.

Bob and I always stayed in touch by letters — long messages that were comical, compelling, and fascinating. This was a man who was a character straight out of the pages of some of the novels I read. It was an honor to now get to walk a few days with him as he led me out of the city and down the coast toward Santa Cruz.

In my mind I had always thought of California, and especially the coast, as the proverbial "land of milk and honey" — the promised land. My expectations were high. It is okay to have expectations, but as I would learn, it also was good to have those expectations shattered sometimes. This was part of life. I was about to learn that lesson during my walk down the California yellow brick road.

I still had a bit of jet lag upon arriving at Bob's house high up in the Oakland hills. I could feel something brewing in the atmosphere. Normally, you can see over the bay to the lights of San Francisco, a sublime panorama anytime during the day or night. But the clouds and mist were closing in. Slowly, storm clouds enveloped the early evening lights below. Bob's wife, Barb, noted that the weather service was warning of a huge frontal system coming off the Pacific from up north in Alaska. There was a chance of strong storms and low temperatures, at least by California standards, and the chance of flooding. Bob said I could hole up a day or two in his house and then we could start a day or two further south. That night, the powerhouse storm hit the Bay Area with high winds and torrential rains. No walking would happen for the next two days.

Though I initially felt restless and a bit let down, I once again rolled with the punches. This would give me time to see my mentor in action. Bob was a professor at the University of California, Berkeley. He also mentored students at Cal State in Hayward. I got to see both campuses and how beloved Bob was by all his students. His classes were some of the first that filled up. He taught school administration to students who would go on to become principals and superintendents. The students he mentored were those working on their master's degrees or doctorates.

In our downtime, we listened to Bob's huge collection of jazz records. We found out we were both fans of jazz and took turns playing our favorites and breaking them down. It was a master class for me and hopefully for Bob, too. We also watched a few classic movies from his collection.

On night two of the storm, we drove into downtown Oakland to attend a dinner party and saw the flooding on the way was getting rather deep. Professors and a few students, some of the sharpest minds in

America, attended the party. When Bob entered, he immediately controlled the table with a mix of pointed observations and off-the-wall jokes, heaping praise yet bringing his friends down to earth to populist ideas. It was pure genius. He was beloved by all. The next morning, I realized the storm actually had been a gift because I got to spend more time with Bob, his family, and his friends.

Bob and I started our walk just south of San Francisco. I was a little disappointed at missing 40 miles of Golden Gate Park and Ocean Beach, but the city was flooded. We hoped it would be less so up on the cliffs above Half Moon Bay and San Gregorio. We also cut inland a bit to see some of the huge redwood trees at Big Basin State Park, though we had to walk through some ankle-high water. I'd probably walk through waist-high water to feel the majesty of those trees.

The second day brought us into Santa Cruz. I wasn't prepared for the sensual feast this city would display. As you entered from the north, you came right onto the edge of the cliffs being pounded by the Pacific. We hugged the cliffs while walking downtown. There were a few big wave surfers challenging the dangerous monster waves. The boardwalk and pier were old-time Californian, with an amusement park, promenade, and cheap motels. Occasionally, there were shacks where the surfers pooled their money and slept on floors while training for the pro circuit.

We talked about the time Bob taught for a year in London. One of my favorite explorers was the Englishman Sir Richard Francis Burton, whose expedition into central Africa in the middle 1800s, discovered Lake Victoria as the source of the River Nile. I had read all his books and journals, and one of my favorite movies, "The Mountains of the Moon," was about Burton. I knew Burton was buried in a cement recreation of an Arab tent in a cemetery called Mortlake outside London. Burton had walked the pilgrimage to Mecca disguised as an Arab and spoke Arabic among 20 other languages.

I had sent a letter to Bob in London asking if he could find and photograph the grave for me. It turned out that he had only two days left before flying home, but he promised to hustle. He liked these kinds of treasure hunts. We came to realize there are three Mortlake Cemeteries, and of course it took him all three tries till he found the one Burton was buried in. He shot it, sent me the photos, and caught his plane home. He was also fascinated with Burton because of the time

Burton spent on the Red Sea coast and the fabled and dangerous city of Harar.

The next morning, Bob headed back to teaching while I was ready to walk to Monterey. People started telling me that the farm fields and Highway 1 were flooded north of Castroville. I decided to take the day to walk every inch of Santa Cruz and let the floods drain. It has been sunny for the last two days. I even took in a French movie in an art theater and bought a one-pound sleeping bag from a new company called Moonstone. I was worried I might have to sleep outside if I got thrown off course walking the 90 miles of wilderness in Big Sur. I had come to California for a nice walk, but once again it was becoming an adventure.

I walked south through the vegetable fields, and once again I had a feast for my eyes upon entering Monterey. I walked through the golf course, where no one was playing because of the flooding. There were new water traps everywhere. The next morning, at the front desk of the motel, I learned that a raging river had washed the bridge into Big Sur at Carmel to the ocean. Mud slides onto Route 1 also had happened every couple of miles. If I would have crossed that bridge the day prior, I would have been stuck inside the Big Sur wilderness. I called my ultra buddy John in southern California, who told me to stay put. Bridges were out, and there were mudslides all the way down into Malibu. It was one of the worst winter storms in California history.

John had run the 48-hour and six-day races with me and was self-employed, so he could take the week off and drive inland on the interstate to try and pick me up. Then, we would drive back down to the southern end of Big Sur, which was less mountainous and therefore had fewer mudslides. We could walk north to where the first bad slide occurred, then return south back to the car. It wasn't what I had envisaged when planning this walk, but it definitely was a way to salvage it. I spent the rest of the day walking every inch of Carmel and Monterey in the gorgeous California sun. Not a bad alternative. Help was on the way.

What a great buddy John was. An old Marine, he was trained to get things done in whatever means necessary. My continuing walk was his next deployment. John was a quiet man, but when people walk long distances, stories bubble up from the past, float to the brain, and spill out anyone's spirit. That is true even for introverts. And John had a deep well of stories to draw from. He had lost count of all the ultramarathons he had run. He would go on to run across America and Europe.

After picking me up, John said the normal four-hour drive would be almost doubled. Washed-out bridges were everywhere, even a huge Interstate 5 bridge that, after washing away, had cars continuing to just speed off the end into the flooding river.

"You sure picked the damnedest spring ever to come to Cal," he said.

We slept in a cheap motel near Coalinga, continuing the next day back out to the Pacific at San Simeon and Hearst Castle. For the next couple of days, we walked up into Big Sur, passing Ragged Point and Cape San Martin to just beyond Gorda, where we turned around and headed back. The whole alternative route took us four days to walk.

Big Sur is one of the most beautiful places in the world. It radiates power vibes and big medicine. There were vistas that stopped us in our tracks and took our breath away. Supposedly, this was the less-scenic half. I can't even fathom what the upper half would have been like then. I hoped to come back one day and see.

We continued trekking down the coast toward Morro Bay and San Luis Obispo. We hit continuing mudslides and bridge washouts every day. It was like trying to solve a puzzle, and we never really got into a walking groove. But the beauty abounded, especially at Pismo Beach, where we saw two women sunbathing in the nude. Another big highlight was the Refugio and El Capitan state beaches, where we camped on the cliffs and walked on a bicycle trail with staircases leading us down onto the beach. Even there some of the bike trail was freshly washed away. Then, it was onward toward Santa Barbara.

Bicycle trails, promenades, and piers were in play now that we were in southern California. Those features served as walking surfaces for almost half of a normal day. Santa Barbara was resplendent with its beaches and red-tiled roofs on hillsides for miles on end, all with mountain peaks for a backdrop. Once again, some of those hillsides were sliding down, taking houses along with them. Further south, we camped at Carpinteria State Beach and then rolled into one of the surfing capitals of the world in Ventura. The sun shone every day, but the remnants of the storm were everywhere. Twice we had to detour because of bridges being out. Oxnard, Point Mugu, and Malibu fell to our swift pace. Then the walk ended at the pier in Santa Monica. John and I had two days left, so we did two climbs of peaks in the San

Gabriel and the San Bernardino mountains, places the Pacific Crest Trail passed over. I flew home after being on the Golden Coast for three weeks.

My expectations were once again shattered. California was not a place of only sun, fun, and high times. Sometimes storms blew through, invading your idealized, halcyon notions of a place. Walking usually gets you high with the brain chemistry stew of beta-endorphins, serotonin, and dopamine. However, that can be interrupted when confronted with constant decisions and problems to solve. The maintenance of my diabetes also can slow down that upbeat flow. But the result is an even higher high because you have made it through the storms, both literal and figurative, bona fide and embellished.

Chapter 11

Walking the Bulge and Bulk of the American Continent

*"Desert sky
Dream beneath a desert sky
The rivers run but soon run dry
We need new dreams tonight."*

— U-2, "In God's Country"

In the autumn of 1996, my two daughters and I used the simple framework of an overnight backpacking trip to Hawk Mountain to plan a proposal for the biggest adventure to ever cross our imagination. The proposal, planning, and execution were not simple, however. This grand undertaking would entail lots of people, financial backing, and extensive logistics.

The planning began around the campfire that night. Adrienne was 13, and Amberly had turned 8 back in late winter. Adrienne got out a tablet from her pack and made a pro/con list. I started a cost analysis proposal. Amberly drew pictures of campsite critters. It continued the next morning at sunrise on top of South Lookout, on the trails of the birds of prey sanctuary. Buzzing with excitement but tempered with a bit of fear, we headed home to begin selling the proposal to my wife. At first, she seemed blindsided. We pushed on because we had the passion of conviction.

The Walk Across America for Diabetes was born the next day. It took a monumental day of negotiating, bargaining, and, in the end, an agreeable compromise. The original idea was to take six months, starting in June, right as the school year ended. My kids would then have almost three months off. Then came the many-tiered hard sell. For all of September, October, and November, we would have to first go in front of the school board and ask them to allow us to homeschool the girls on the road during that time. It would be tough with me walking 25 miles a day and presenting diabetes programs to hospitals, schools, camps, and service organizations. They would be booked months in advance, which also meant that we had to keep to a tight schedule. But then again, this kind of adventure would be a constant learning process. The girls would be required to walk three to five miles a day, up and down mountains, thus providing them with physical education. Next came the obvious, geography. Also, History. Math would prove a little more difficult, but at least the simple math of calculating daily, weekly, and entire-trip mileages would be worth something. The girls were not quite into the higher maths yet. Journal-keeping would work for English composition, and helping with my presentations would work for public speaking. Since we would be using a small motorhome, they would have access to a kitchen table to work at, plus picnic tables at campgrounds. That should take care of school. Both girls were on board for this. The school board would maybe be the second-hardest test. Mom would be the hardest.

Though my wife would have loved the six months of being together and was used to the physicality of effort, she still liked her routine at home, along with her friends. I actually would not miss my friends, as a bunch of them would join me. But for my wife, as well as for all of us, the biggest impediment would be health insurance. She carried the benefits at her job doing payroll at Kutztown University. I thought we would be able to procure a six-month sabbatical of sorts in which the benefits would hold over. Surely, I could present a passionate case for what this grand adventure would be worth to the university to have one of its own out there making our great nation even better. But my wife came up with her own version.

Nancy did not like the six-months-straight idea at all. But as a loving wife, she knew how much this adventure meant to me. She also acknowledged the merits of such a grand undertaking, so she brought us to a compromise: I would walk a third of America for two months, then return home and work for 10 months, even adding in some six- and seven-day workweeks, and the family would join me for a week each year, or at least the girls would. Nancy didn't relish spending her vacation with the madman bums and holy fools who would be on board to drive and walk with me. I would return for the second year for another two months and again for two months in the third year. I didn't mind the compromise. I was just thrilled beyond belief that I was finally going to be witness to the reality of those visions I had in the sacred forests and fields of my boyhood wanderings.

***

My running and walking buddy John and I left home on a soft summer evening on May 31, 1997. It was a tear-stained, gut-wrenching goodbye for my family and I, as we all hugged, crying our hearts out. I had been gone for weeks at a time before, but never for the two months that were looking at us right now. It was especially hard on my youngest daughter, sweet Amberly, who would surely miss her daddy. Adrienne would join me in a month in Montana in one of the most spectacular places in the world, Glacier National Park. For John, leaving his home was a time of complete chaos, as his life was a flurry of work commitments for months leading up to this point, giving him no time to prepare. He was still packing as I pulled into his driveway. We finally hit the road together in the heavily laden, 19-foot 1974 motorhome plastered with the logos of our many sponsors applied by Kurt, my school adventure buddy from Rockland Signs. Some of them were local, and others were national brands concerning diabetes products.

We turned west toward the sunset. As my hometown faded into the distance, I thought of a line from Kerouac's "On the Road": "What is that feeling when you're driving away from people and they recede on the plain till you see their specks dispersing? It's the too-huge world vaulting us, and it's goodbye. But we lean forward to the next crazy adventure beneath the skies."

We stopped in Reading to pick up our fellow pilgrim, Kathie. She was joining us for the first three days and then would fly home from Billings, Montana. As president of our local chapter of the Juvenile Diabetes Foundation, she wanted to see us off. Some of the funds raised during our adventure would benefit that charity. Kathie's daughter Kaitlin has had Type 1 diabetes since she was a little girl. I seriously doubt if Kathie was prepared for the sheer mania that would ensue as we raced across America just so we could turn around and slowly walk back. John and Kathie soon entered into a verbal sparring match that would last not only through this trip but for years to come. Most of their arguments concerned the importance of intellectual life versus physical life, all done with shouting over the omnipresent music from the tape deck, and me acting as referee.

A light rain materialized out of the fog as we crossed from Pennsylvania into Ohio. Once again the words of Kerouac came to me: "It was drizzling and mysterious at the beginning of our journey. I could see that it was going to be one big saga of the mist ... and this was really the way that my whole road experience began and the things that were to come are too fantastic not to tell."

We rolled right through Indiana, then north along the edges of Chicago and Madison, Wisconsin, with Louis Armstrong singing and blowing his trumpet out of our vehicle's loudspeakers. Soon we turned west once more through Minnesota and South Dakota. Our goal was the Pine Ridge Indian Reservation, where we would present our first diabetes program at the medical center. Pine Ridge was the first of many wake-up calls on this odyssey we were just beginning. Driving onto the reservation, we immediately went from pleasant prairies to poverty, homelessness, and abandoned rusted shells of cars. It was more akin to entering the poorer parts of a major city. At the medical center where we gave our presentation, there was a line of mostly elderly Sioux tribal members waiting to see someone about their diabetes care. The only two caretakers were a nurse helping on her day off and the tribal dentist, also working on his day off. The care these diabetics needed was crushing the system. After spending a few hours with them, we were taken to the site of the Wounded Knee Massacre. Then, we drove north through the Black Hills, the rich lands that were stolen from the Lakota. Over the next three years, we would see so much more of this tragedy.

It was late afternoon when we crossed into Wyoming, figuring we would camp near Devils Tower National Monument. As we turned onto a dirt road that would lead us to Keyhole State Park, we were flagged down by a cowboy who needed a lift to his ranch to get tools for fixing his broken-down truck. He introduced himself as Marshall and his buddy leaning against a fence post as Homer. Homer was a short, pudgy cowboy, and he gave a wave as Marshall asked us a few questions in a hard western twang. Marshall was the real stuff, a living legend who 30 years earlier probably looked like the Marlboro Man.

"What do you boys think of Wyomin'?" he asked.

We had only been in Wyoming for 70 miles but noticed that it was practically devoid of humans, even on the vehicle-less interstate, so John now adapted a western twang and answered with complete irony, "Well, Marshall, it's a fine-looking state, but there's too damn many people."

Marshall removed his cowboy hat, scratched his head, thought to himself, then offered another question, "If this is too many people, then where the hell are you boys from?"

"We're from Pennsyltucky," John replied.

Again, Marshall scratched his head and admitted he'd missed the union of the two states, also noting he'd lived here most of his life. He then pointed out his prize bull, which was snorting and pawing in a fenced-off field. It was a fine specimen, one Hemingway would have raved about. Marshall now took notice that there was a female with us, and he tipped his hat to her, with a "Howdy, ma'am." In only a few minutes of time and one mile of driving, the real west had presented itself to us in one of the last of the mythological cowboys of the plains. For the rest of the trip, John called me Marshall and I called him Homer in tribute to these men, and the next day we crossed into Montana.

We dropped off Kathie at the airport in Billings to fly home. She was just starting to get into the vibe of the journey but also was a bit relieved she wouldn't have to put up with the ensuing shenanigans. I suspected that Kathie would return on a future segment of this grand three-year adventure.

John gunned the motorhome west past the snow-capped Bighorn mountains, which lay to the south, rolling past Bozeman and Butte, now deep into the Rocky Mountain range. We arrived in Missoula right before dark. Our goal for the night was a parking lot somewhere near Spokane, Washington. That would leave us a two-hour drive to arrive at the Colville Indian Reservation, where we would present a diabetes presentation at 10 a.m. But first, we had to battle the elements up and down a mountain pass in Idaho. John was a truck driver and accustomed to long drives through the night. He did 90 percent of the driving in the motorhome.

I felt totally confident in his abilities. In fact, I idolized him as the embodiment of Kerouac's driver, Dean Moriarty, the real-life Neal Cassady. It was spooky at times how their lives and personalities were similar. We gassed up in Missoula and prepped ourselves for the long, dark night of the soul. John never ingested caffeine. His wired brain kept him awake, but tonight he was faltering just ever so slightly. He bought a two-liter bottle of caffeinated Coca-Cola, guzzled it, and then in the cold, pouring rain, sprinted seven times around the motorhome while asking me to play Rage Against the Machine at high volume. He was now satiated and alert for, hopefully, the rest of the drive.

On the ramp onto Interstate 90, an image materialized out of the mist. It was an old Native American drifter, maybe Kerouac's "Saint Theresa bum." We stopped to offer him a ride, but he was heading north to Whitefish, looking peacefully content disappearing into the fog and blackness of the Montana wilderness, almost like a ghost. On top of Lookout Pass, Idaho, the rain turned to snow. At a highway rest stop, John and I, clad only in sweaty T-shirts and shorts, jumped out of the motorhome to use the facilities. A freezing wind howled down out of Canada. That splash of cold snow in the face further woke us up to help us reach Washington by morning.

The next day, we arrived right on time, and after my presentation, we met an Okanagan Native American named Dan who invited us to attend a northwest tribal powwow two weeks later. That would be right around the time I would be walking through central Washington. A couple more hours of driving brought us into downtown Seattle. We were both burned out from the hectic ride. John pulled into a parking lot, crawled into the upper bunk, and fell into a deep, lengthy sleep. I grumbled a bit about having to do the chores we had neglected, including a sink full of dirty dishes. In a bad mood I flung open the back window curtain to reveal the otherworldly neon of the Space Needle, and immediately I snapped out of that mood. I cleaned up everything and went on walkabout, past open-door bars with grunge music pouring out, down along the docks of Puget Sound, taking in all the magic of one of the most beautiful cities of the world. Other than a short drive north in the morning to Anacortes, the start of my walk across America, we had come to the end of the continent. It had been an epic road trip, and once again Kerouac's words spoke to me: "Mad road driving men ahead. Pencil traceries of our faintest wish in the travel of the horizon merged ... the crazed voyager of the lone automobile presses forth his eager insignificance in nose plates and licenses into the vast promise of life."

***

I was shaking uncontrollably as I checked my blood glucose and gave myself a dose of insulin from my MiniMed pump. Then I ate my morning oatmeal sitting on the sofa of the motorhome in Bayview State Park. I hoped this weird case of the shakes would ease off once I started walking. Stepping out the back door, I found my way to the edge of the bay looking beyond to where the mighty Pacific washed up onto the shore. A thousand different thoughts and emotions ran through my brain. A dream that came to me when I was 14 was now about to be acted out in real time. That dream grew as the years flew by, and its metamorphosis was to be a shining example to anyone who suffered the daily grind of living with diabetes: to prove to anyone battling a chronic disease that effort could lead you to transcend that disease. I offered prayers to the Creator/Great Mystery, spread an offering of twigs, leaves, and earth from my woods back home, where this walk had been conjured up. I dipped my walking staff into the salty water, turned east to face the entire continent that lay before me, and took the first steps. The Walk Across America for Diabetes has officially begun.

I walked fast on a nicely shouldered Route 20 through the hamlet of Burlington. John described my excited pace in his journal as "a furious ground-gobbling stride." Most of our walking discussions and our rest stop conversations centered on our just-completed drive across the continent. Later, it would turn to the walking mileage and stories we had just witnessed and the walking that lay ahead of us.

We lived inside that bubble of 10 to 50 miles of real estate. Our first walking partners met us for the last five miles of the day. Pat was a transplanted Chippewa Tribe member, and Gwen worked for the Northwestern Affiliated Tribes. They held a party that night in honor of our journey. The stories continued to flow through the night from both sides. Eventually, I had to get some rest. I had another 25 miles to walk the next day. John stayed up late, quite capable of storytelling for the both of us.

Soon, the North Cascades appeared before us, beginning with Mount Baker. I thought of a passage from Tolkein's "The Fellowship of the Ring": "Eastward the Barrowdowns rose, ridge behind ridge into the morning, and vanished out of eyesight into a guess; it was no more than a guess of blue and a remote white glimmer blending with the hem of the sky, but it spoke to them, out of memory and old tales, of the high and distant mountains."

Gwen and her husband acted as our guides for the day, leading us onto soft rail trails paralleling Route 20. It took a while to walk past Mount Baker. It stood to the north and with a mighty glacial expanse, rising to 10,775 feet of elevation. We were alert to a danger discussed at the party the night before. A mountain lion had attacked an 11-year-old girl as she rode an ATV on our trail. My walking pole had a rubber tip on it that screwed off by hand to reveal a one-inch spike. That would be our only weapon.

Giant cedar-sequoias trees, some reaching to 200 feet, populated our route for the next two days. We began to reach a state of enchantment as we worked our way, at four miles an hour, into North Cascades National Park.

The Skagit River soon became our companion as it flowed in the opposite direction. I tried washing our clothes in it that night in camp, but my hands went numb in the glacial iciness. There would be no towns or services for the next 68 miles, and I would be alone for part of that stretch as John left to pick up his son, Justin, at Seattle-Tacoma International Airport. That night, however, a couple rode in on a tandem bicycle, pulling a trailer with their gear and a little dog named Penny. I was walking the route of a trans-continental bike trail, so I had met a few cyclists over the last two days. But Skip and Kelly from the coast range of Oregon were something else altogether.

They turned out to be some of the most interesting and truly alive people I have ever met. Their unique bicycle had a personality of its own. The front of the bike was a recumbent where Kelly sat and provided 30% of the pedal power. Behind her sat Skip on a somewhat normally set-up bike with big rear drum brakes. Skip produced 70% of the pedal power, and that left Penny the dog in the trailer, along with the gear, where she provided 0% of the pedal power but much barking moral support. Penny was as intrepid as her owners. Skip had crossed the United States by bike many times and also had ridden across Australia. This was their first big trip together. When we first saw each other in the campground, we all knew that we had to get to know each other. To not try surely would have been a crime.

The first of my alone days I spent walking the park's trails in a drizzle, heading up peaks I had gazed upon days before. Today, a veil of mist and the fog on the lenses of my glasses hid them. It didn't matter; I knew they were there. I could feel them as they imparted their ancient wisdom to me.

I traversed the Panther Creek Trail and the Fourth of July Pass. Two of the many mountains encircling me were Gabriel Peak and Mesahchie Peak. I came onto deep patches of the lingering spring snow and then took side trails back down to my campsite. That evening was the first of many stimulating fireside conversations I would have with the Oregonian gang of three: man, woman, and dog.

Soon John and his son Justin, who was 12, returned from their hitch-hiking adventure. As usual, John had many wild stories. He never had to look for them — they found him. I had prepared Skip and Kelly for meeting John with what may have, in most cases, been hyperbole. After meeting him, though, they thought I had been understated in my explanation.

The next morning, I headed east on the beautiful, wide shoulders of North Cascades Highway. Skip and Kelly biked past me and stopped above on a vista parking lot overlooking Diablo Lake. Skip took a picture of me climbing the switchbacks at a nice, even clip, and it remains one of my favorite photographs. I've never been photogenic, so Skip had a mastery with the camera to capture me well enough that even I liked it.

When I reached the parking lot, the cerulean blue of the lake surrounded by ice-tinged peaks was a scene rarely duplicated anywhere in the world. The North Cascades continued to dazzle, and I realized that I definitely had chosen the best route for the Washington portion of the walk. Skip reminded me that one of the peaks ahead was named Desolation, where Kerouac had spent a summer as a fire lookout. I noticed the peak of Hozomeen Mountain, the beautiful terror that would drive Jack crazy. He wrote a poem from that time in the late 1950s:

Aurora Borealis
Over Hozomeen—
The void is stiller

The next big point in the walk was Rainy Pass, where the famed Pacific Crest Trail crosses the road I was walking on. The Canadian border was just a few days' walk north. John had the motorhome parked in a slot surrounded by seven-foot snowdrifts as he and Justin walked back to meet me. We had a few more miles of climbing to get to the highest peak of the road at Washington Pass. The prominent mountain points were Kangaroo Ridge, Liberty Bell Mountain (with a crack in its side), and Silver Star Mountain. We engaged in a snowball fight as we reached the ledge overlooking, to the east, what seemed like the rest of Washington state. It was all downhill from there, unlike my life which, at this moment, was truly at one of its many peaks.

At our camp that night in the valley, we met Pat the alligator hunter from Florida. After his wife died two years prior, he bought an Airstream trailer and was traveling to every national park. The next day, he would head north to Alaska. He asked if we had ever stared into the mouth of a live gator in the wild. We admitted we had not, and Pat replied, "You haven't lived unless you've stared into the jaws of a live gator." Pat told us a million stories that night around a campfire. It would take an entire book to retell them all. We finally fell asleep to the song of a coyote singing.

***

In central Washington, I walked to Lake Chelan, the site of the big gathering of northern tribes for a powwow that Dan had invited us to during our drive west. Skip and Kelly also went off-route to attend the powwow. They had no idea what they were getting into. The festival grounds were packed with Native dancers and spectators from as far away as northern Canada. Many bands accompanied the dancers. The viewing bleachers were packed, as were the campgrounds. It felt like a Native Woodstock. I usually do not get nervous about speaking in front of crowds, and I had 20 miles of walking under my belt for the day, which always inspires me instead of tiring me. But this was the biggest crowd I had ever addressed. Between a round of dances, Dan brought me up to the microphone. I did my usual message mix of facts, biography, storytelling, and inspiration, which lasts about 10 minutes. In this setting I could not access my slides, which are a mix of past adventures, me performing my diabetes routine, an introduction to my family, and slides of my homeland. Every year I added more slides and culled a few from the presentation. The slides add something, but in a situation like this dance performance, they are not necessary.

After I spoke, Dan announced that he and his new friend were going to dance. Now I'm nervous. Dan was one of the best dancers competing. I tried my best to put some spirit into it and mostly tried to mimic Dan. John laughed from the bleachers until Dan called him up to dance. Then Skip, Kelly, and Justin laughed until Dan called them up to dance. Now there were five white people dancing badly with one of the best in the Pacific Northwest. Then the bleachers emptied, and the football field filled with movement as the drummers turned up the volume. It truly was one of the highlights of my life. As the inspiration level reached its peak, everyone on the field formed a line and personally shook my hand or gave me a hug. It took over an hour. I wished I could have heard every story of every person, especially the tribal elders. My gang of five fellow travelers was so full of revelation that we had trouble sleeping that night. This wonderful encounter would remain in my heart and carry me across the rest of Washington and on into northern Idaho.

The remainder of Washington flew by in a flurry of hills, orchards, evergreens, and the high passes of Wauconda and Sherman. John and Justin flew home from Spokane, and Skip and Kelly decided to take the train back to Oregon, as Kelly had taken a pregnancy test that morning that came up positive. Next up as my driver was my good buddy Dave, who flew into Spokane. Dave, like I, also had his own painting and decorating business. He was not a long-distant walker but instead a prodigious climber who had summited Devils Tower; parts of the City of Rocks area of Idaho; and numerous climbs in West Virginia, Kentucky, and Tennessee. Dave and his son, Kyle, were looking to climb the big walls in Yosemite one day. There would be no letdown in this changing of the guard for the Walk Across America for Diabetes.

After picking up Dave in Spokane, I regaled him with the many tales of the drive west and the walk across Washington. Already the memories had piled up, and together with the inspirations caused sensory overload. Washington ended with a walk following the Pend

Oreille River, now in near flood stage, into the Kalispel Reservation. I presented my program twice over the next two days, and in between, the tribe gave us a map to a peak, their sacred mountain. Some of the members of the tribe were extras in the movie "The Postman," filming to the north of the reservation. We were given the choice of driving up to the location where we might get to meet Kevin Costner or doing the climb. We chose to climb 3,000 feet to the craggy summit of South Baldy. It gave us a 360-degree vista of where I had come from in Washington and where I was headed tomorrow, the lake country of northern Idaho. It really put things into perspective, and along with the wonderful people on the reservation, gave Dave a grand welcome.

I continued following the river into Idaho, the first state crossing of the walk, to where it turned into Lake Pend Oreille at the town of Sandpoint. We had been warned of white nationalist encampments spread throughout this part of Idaho. A billboard welcoming travelers into Sandpoint was encouraging as it read, "Sandpoint is a walking town!" Dave and I couldn't believe our good fortune and how we once more had our low expectations shattered.

Sandpoint was a hippie town full of coffee shops, Volkswagen buses painted with Day-Glo colors, and bookstores. I will always remember buying my first copy of "Women Who Run with the Wolves" by author/psychotherapist Clarissa Pinkola Estés in Sandpoint. It would become one of my favorite books. We took a break by the lake and watched a few sailboarders, then hit a few bars and walked to the north of town. The next morning, we continued due north into Bonners Ferry, where we were very near the Canadian border, and the next day we crossed into Montana.

Since we left the Kalispel Indian Reservation, we had not had one diabetes presentation. Over the next few days, we travelled in such a wild country that there were no towns of any size until Whitefish. It rained for three straight days, and Route 2 was under construction, making it a complete mud fest. It was the worst of the walking conditions so far.

Dave and I took turns calling home from a phone booth in the middle of nowhere south of Libby, crowded in tight to get out of the rain. Both of our wives could sense we were a bit weather-beaten and feeling down. The weather cleared as we entered Whitefish, but our program at the medical center was canceled. From here, it would get even more remote, as we soon would enter Glacier National Park. On

Dave's last day, we had a thrilling walk along the Flathead and Clark Fork rivers. It was time to drive south to the airport at Great Falls, where Dave would exit and the next crew would appear. I felt bad that Dave would miss Glacier, though he at least saw the southern part of the park as we drove east and south. I also knew he would be back one day in this western wonderland. Our last camp was in Choteau, where we attended a rodeo. Therefore, Dave's big sendoff came from rodeo clowns. It said a lot about this entire endeavor.

Chapter 12

Among the Cathedral Towers of the Alpine Deities

"See the carpet of the sun
The green grass soft and sweet
Sands upon the shores of time
Of oceans mountains deep."

— Renaissance, "Carpet of the Sun"

I was beyond excited. My oldest daughter, Adrienne, was flying into Great Falls in a few hours. Now 14 years old, she has inherited that part of me that gets restless remaining in one place too long. While she had travelled way more than I had at her age, she had never been to Montana. Now she would see it at 25 miles a day, a nice, easy, all-day pace. Accompanying her was one of my best friends, Linette, who was so glad I was going in the summer when she was on vacation from her job as an elementary school teacher. Linette had been on other adventures with me as my crew chief and lap counter during ultramarathon events and as a runner in a 24-hour relay.

During the wait, I followed a trail along the Missouri River where I could witness the great falls that gave the city its name. In the summer, Montana can get into 90-degree temperatures, but it immediately drops back to 40 degrees when the sun sets. Sunburn is a possibility because of the many days where skies are blue all day (the state's "big sky" motto is dead on). The airport is big for Montana but has only two terminals. As I walked toward the arrivals gate, the girls came bounding out glowing, having just traded the humid air of the East Coast for the low humidity of the big West. Adrienne had colored her blond hair reddish, leaving the bathroom a mess at home and getting in trouble with my wife, who was probably glad for the two-week vacation. Amberly was five years younger and not yet knocking heads with her mother.

We all jumped into the motorhome and headed north to the entrance to West Glacier, where I would start walking tomorrow. Upon arrival, we had time for a one-hour hike along the banks of the Middle Fork of the Flathead River before it got dark. It ran fast, pure, and cold as hell. Then the stars started popping on, replacing the blue with the glitter of the Milky Way. You could see the magnificence of the state seeping into the girl's new-to-Montana consciousness. Tomorrow that would not only continue but also ramp up a notch or two. We were now in the holy land, the throne room of the mountain gods.

My first 10 miles took me to the last grocery store we would see for many days. We had plenty of food, but half of it was the remaining 20 cans of vegetarian chili John ate most nights. He had started this adventure, now over a month ago, with 75 cans. It gave bad gas to everybody but John since he was used to it. At our morning re-supply, Linette insisted on buying me a big bottle of grizzly bear spray to carry on my belt. Also, she got us all bells to tie around our packs. Native Montanans liked to call the bells "grizz diner bells." There was no doubt they were out and about here. The real trouble begins if you get between a sow and her cubs. Every year, this happens a few times, and people get mauled and even killed. I had a lot of experience with black bears, but grizzly bears are a whole other level of danger. As grizz researcher Doug Peacock said, "It ain't real wilderness unless something can kill you." So we took every precaution available and then tried not to worry too much.

Lake McDonald is so long that it took me and the girls almost two days to walk along it. We kept cutting out on trails that led to long, wooden docks. The walking was effortless because we were in a constant state of enchantment. At our campsite at the foot of Going-to-the-Sun Road, we noticed newspaper clippings of recent bear attacks in this neck of the woods. The alert level rose again.

Going-to-the-Sun Road was a serpentine route of cliff-blasted passes, huge dropoffs, and continual climbing. It would be a good measure of my fitness. Going-to-the-Sun Road also would be a portal to some of the most stupendous alpine scenery in all of America. I felt a lot safer once I rose out of the lowland fog and mist. For a few miles at the start, I would not have been able to spot a sow crossing the road ahead of me or any lagging cubs behind me, putting me right in the middle as a threat. Now on the open passes with pull-over vistas, though, I felt as if I could see clear into next week. Soon the trusty little beast of a motorhome passed me and parked at one of the vista pullouts. Linette, raised on a farm, was used to handling trucks and tractors. Adrienne told me she had full confidence in Linette's driving even in the most hazardous of conditions. We all hugged and bounded around in a state of excitement. Glacier could wear out your capacity for wonder. It was sensory overload, again and again.

The girls couldn't wait to tell me about their wakeup call that morning. At the crack of dawn, something began shaking and bumping the side of the motorhome. When they slid back the curtains, it revealed a huge bull elk. No need for me to think they were being melodramatic — the proof was in the still-visible drool, fur, and dents.

As I continued ascending, the snowbanks were so high where they had been plowed through that they rose above my head. It was the Fourth of July, and we had eight-foot snowbanks! The climb continued, yet I felt like a million bucks. I moved swiftly and steadily, smelling the overheating radiators and brakes of the vehicles as they passed. Meanwhile, I gave off the sweaty odor of the heavily working human animal, the result of the right mixture of fuel (food) and self-administered hormone (insulin). My blood glucose was 123 mg/dl. Then, suddenly before my eyes, all the earth dropped off into infinity. It was the last of the pullout vistas and offered a view of serrated peaks and the ribbon-like gush of Bird Woman Falls to the northwest. My two trusty kindred spirits were parked and gazing in reverence. I walked up to them, we linked arms, and together we experienced one of those moments that's hard to duplicate in real life. I go to that moment every time I read copies of the girls' journals.

"It feels like we are standing at the edge of the world looking upon an awesome landscape of scenic mountains, lakes, and glaciers," Linette wrote. "It is more beautiful than I ever imagined."

And Adrienne added: "I have been awakened from my Dramamine-induced stupor by the majestic scene in front of me. Oh my, Toto, we're not in Pennsylvania anymore."

I reached the zenith at Logan Pass. Even though the ascent had gained 4,000 feet elevation in the last 14 miles, and despite the 40-degree temperatures and 25 mph wind, I felt no signs of fatigue. I was on another spiritual plane, one where weariness did not exist. At 6,680 feet, this would be the highest point of the Walk Across America for Diabetes. It was all downhill from here!

We did a hike, leading out of the visitor's center, of about five miles. That brought us to the edge of a glacier. We were caught off-guard by how casually a mountain goat would stroll past us. Then it was back to the road and the partial descent of eight miles, where other than the dramatic landscapes, the feature was sightings of Rocky Mountain sheep high up on the cliffs. I walked through a series of tunnels leading us to Sun Point Nature Trail, where the three of us felt like we were hiking in a walk-in freezer.

We camped within view of St. Mary Lake, which tried to compete with the big blue sky as to which was the bluest. That evening, we cooked over a campfire and watched the light fade, the sun having long ago disappeared behind the peaks to the west. The chill brought us closer to the fire, and we started to feel the tiredness of a day in which the constant bombardment of visual stimuli would not end. It soon got quiet, like the end of time. Then Linette broke the silence with, "I feel like I haven't a care in the world. I've completely lost track of time and home." I knew what she meant. We were in a marvelous time warp consisting of only movement through a land that looked and felt like a fairy tale. That night, we all slept a dreamless sleep, as deep as any I have ever remembered.

Most of the next day was spent walking the road and hiking the trails along the shores of iconic St. Mary Lake. Throughout that day, you could not escape the mix of big blue sky, shimmering blue lake, and continued vistas of the snow-encompassed pinnacles of Glacier. It was a deeply holy experience to just walk there. It was a peripatetic all-day prayer to a benevolent creator. That night, our last in Glacier, we watched a sunset from our campsite. Tomorrow I would walk east, dropping into the Great Plains, heading toward the reservation and surrounding lands of the Blackfeet Nation.

Glacier was not done with us yet, though, During the fading darkness of early morning, we saw a huge thunderstorm off to the west. It was safely distant but visceral to experience. As the light of morning broke, Linette went outside the motorhome to brush her teeth. Very soon she was yelling to us from a garbled mouth full of toothpaste. Directly over the mountains of Gunsight, Reynolds, and Heavy Runner, had appeared a double-helix rainbow. The lake sparkled from the rays of the rising sun as we stood transfixed. It was so quiet that I swear you could hear the mist slowly enveloping the edges of the rainbow. That scene will forever remain in our memories — something to remember on our deathbeds. At least, we hope our memories last, because we were so transfixed that none of us took a photo. Sometimes a photo would not have recreated the experience in a way that memory does, though. I was honored to be able to share it with my compadres.

***

It was sobering to look out onto the Great Plains of America. I had been in the mountains for almost a month and a half. Soon, for almost 400 miles this year, and another 300 miles the next year, I would walk in the northern Great Plains. Once there, I immediately found my walking groove, one that had been developed and expanded upon for most of my life. This is what I had prepared myself for. This flow conjures up memories and gazes into the future. But mostly it puts you wholeheartedly into the Zen-like present, the rhythmic footfalls of a metronome, gliding across the landscape, nothing escaping your apotheosis. I didn't need to engage in death-defying activities to make me feel alive. I had found that sweet spot, a consciousness that would last forever.

Two days later, as I approached the town of Browning, the headquarters for the Blackfeet Nation, I spotted Adrienne and Linette walking toward me so we could walk back to the motorhome as a group. Even though we still had a bunch of days left together, I started to put into perspective the effect my two kindred spirits had on me during this adventure. It was a great bonding experience to have Adrienne with me out here. She was growing up fast. She would leave for college in another four years. Our early backpacking adventures had prepared her well for the next few years of walking across America. It was not just physical prep but also mental and spiritual. She had inherited a lot of my good qualities, and since we are human beings, some of my foibles also. Her sense of humor was keyed right into mine, to the consternation of those around us. One thing that made Linette such a great fellow adventurer, for many years, was that she was also keyed into my, and now Adrienne's, offbeat sense of humor. She also had it in spades.

One of my reasons for choosing Linette to accompany Adrienne was that she would serve as a great role model, with an intelligence and maturity that would influence my daughter. Instead, Linette slipped down to Adrienne's level, listening to Adrienne's music, laughing at her gutter humor jokes, and reading out loud at bedtime from a book of "Politically Correct Bedtime Stories." Adrienne had a repertoire of movie lines memorized and would spit them out continually. Her current favorite was "Jerry Maguire." She knew damn near the entire movie dialogue. Linette wanted to memorize it, too, so Adrienne took heartily to that task. I would ask them important logistical questions concerning our ongoing quest, and they would answer me with "Jerry Maguire" dialogue. I would get testy, but they kept up the charade. It was confounding to say the least. To give even more ammo to their cause, they ran into Cuba Gooding Jr., one of the stars of the movie, in an ice cream shop in East Glacier Park Village. We couldn't believe the coincidence!

***

It seemed every white person I had talked to in the last two weeks had told me only of the destitute situation on the Blackfeet Indian Reservation. They called it wind-whipped and dusty, with horrible dirt roads. They told me it was dangerous and that there was a physical impairment of some of the tribal members. We entered and met our liaison, Ivan. He was a tall, well-muscled Blackfeet health leader and champion kickboxer who had served as a bodyguard for Arnold Schwarzenegger during the star's stint as head of the President's Council on Physical Fitness in Washington, D.C. Ivan also had been a trainer for the San Francisco 49ers football team. He was well-educated in both the ancient ways of tribal healing and in the modern ways of physiology, kinesiology, and psychology.

Ivan's first question tested me on my devotion to my cause of helping his people. He asked me if I was interested in doing some weight training with his recovering alcoholics group at the tribal gym. Even though I had walked 23 miles, I answered in the affirmative. Ivan led us down into a warehouse basement smelling of sweat and testosterone. The gym was full of proud but struggling Blackfeet warriors. Big muscles, tank tops, and tattoos were the uniform of most. Ivan informed them that I would work out with them. It didn't get much of a reaction. After a pause, Ivan told them that I had had Type 1 diabetes for 25 years. That got me some glances. Another pause, and then Ivan told them that I had walked 23 miles that day and was walking across America. That did the trick. Many came over to shake my hand and offer their advice and help with the lifting. I did a 45-minute workout of bench pressing, bicep curls, and back presses, while Ivan taught Adrienne and Linette some kickboxing moves on the heavy bag. Ivan used sweat lodges, vision quests, tribal dancing, hiking, and weights to build back the confidence, power, and spirit of the entire tribe. For the rest of the three days I spent there, I had some mighty warriors as buddies. All those preconceived notions about the Blackfeet were slowly shattered, and we were treated with the utmost in hospitality and respect.

We had the perfect timing to be on the reservation during North American Indian Days. In the days that followed, Ivan gave us a tour of the economic strengths of the tribe, the factories and their tribal savings and loan bank. We got to meet and have discussions with the elders and the tribal council about diabetes and health, after which we were invited to march in the next day's parade. All that was in addition to my usual presentations and group walkathons. Our accommodation for both nights was a teepee where Ivan instructed us to sleep with our heads together and our legs fanning out like the spokes of a medicine wheel. Ivan had given us a master class on the historical strengths of the medicine wheel and its applications to the modern way of living — mind, body, and spirit.

Back in 1995, Linette had served as Miss Pennsylvania in the Miss America pageant in Atlantic City, New Jersey. As one of her biggest supporters, I camped out at a buddy's house in Ventnor City Beach for the weeklong preliminaries leading up to the Saturday night pageant finale. Though Linette could not have any personal contact with friends or family, I wrote her notes of encouragement and stupid jokes to help her through the grueling process that these pageants entail. In solidarity, I kept her informed about my subsequent schedule during that week: wake before dawn, walk 10 to 20 miles, surf and boogie-board the Atlantic Ocean waves, attend each night's competitions, then party in the hotel bar where her supporters were staying. Linette appreciated my support and solidarity but did inform me that her schedule was even tougher than mine.

We recalled those days during our stay on the Blackfeet Indian Reservation, especially after Ivan took us to meet his wife, Shelly and four children, Nicole, Ivan Jr., Ivy, and Twyla. When he introduced Linette as having been in the Miss America pageant, his older kids remembered watching the event on the family TV, courtesy of a rooftop satellite dish. Meanwhile, Adrienne had a spirited discussion with Ivan's kids concerning suggestions on music, books, and movies, and some of it overlapped. It felt good not being the person everyone wanted to talk to. They made us feel like family, and it warmed our hearts and souls that here in such a remote part of America we could feel so welcome. I still occasionally call Ivan's office phone just to hear his answering machine message: "Sorry, I can't talk to you right now because I'm too busy making Browning the healthiest reservation in America." He was a great warrior, kind soul, tireless leader, and true renaissance man. Ivan and I vowed to keep in touch and meet again somewhere down the road.

Instead of walking east on our last day, Ivan drove us west, back into the Rocky Mountains. He wanted us to see Two Medicine Lake and Falls, a Blackfeet sacred site. It was an experience of great reverence. On the hike back to the vehicle, we saw a sow grizzly and her two cubs come out of the water on the far shore and effortlessly run up the lower flanks of the mountainside. It was poetry in motion, viewed from a safe distance — the best way to see grizzlies in the wild. Then, right as we reached the parking lot, a double rainbow materialized to the south, out of the dark skies of a far-flung storm. Ivan told me it was a gift to me from the Great Spirit, Great Mystery, for the work I was doing for the tribes. He said I would see more along my journey.

On our last night on the reservation, we walked to the powwow at dusk as the sun set over the Rockies. It was a supreme show of surrealistic colors, which glinted off the snowy summits. In the semi-dark of the foreground, you could still see the lodgepole pine tops of the teepees. I stopped, and Linette continued walking ahead. I got my camera ready and called her name. As she turned toward me, I took a shot, with the flash lighting up her celestially tanned face and highlighting her magnificent bone structure and mysterious, bright eyes. It turned out to be one of the best shots I have ever taken. We didn't know till I returned home and had the slides developed how that shot summed up our collective experience. The three of us would always have a record of our time together in Montana by looking at that slide.

After the girls headed home, I was alone for two days. I did still have a presentation for Lions Clubs in Shelby and Havre, but there was no denying that in the motorhome or while walking, it felt like someone had sucked the air out of the atmosphere. I was reminded of my loneliness by one of the Lions Club members who had met us at the pow wow in Browning. He was a tall, jeans-and-cowboy-boots-wearing guy who also had noticed Linette. He drew out a long "Hmmm," and with a western drawl, asked me, "Well now boy, where are you hiding that pretty little wife of yours?"

"She may be pretty, and she may be little, but she's not my wife, and she flew home two days ago," I replied.

He looked disappointed and strolled away.

Some of these lonely days I actually had to walk from where I camped to the 25-mile mark and get somebody from either of the Lions Clubs or one of the three reservations to give me a lift back to the motorhome so I could move it forward. The most important component of having a motorhome, beyond having a cheap place to sleep and cook out of, was to haul all my audiovisual equipment, including two projectors, two boomboxes, four trays of slides, power cords, and other miscellanea. Route 2 across northern Montana was a fairly quiet road, so, traffic was not a problem. Once or twice a day, Amtrak's Great Northern Emperor flew by, and soon they became familiar with my presence and alerted the passengers. I could see their faces pushed against the windows. I wondered how many of them, especially kids, thought to themselves that one day they too would walk across America.

I began to notice three features of walking on the scope of the Great Plains. First, since it was hot in the day but got cold at night, almost like a desert, the big rattlesnakes would crawl onto the blacktop to retain the heat of the road. I saw a lot of dead rattlesnakes and some live ones, which meant that if I started early in the dark of morning, I would have to be aware. More so if I went into the brush to go to the bathroom. There were a lot out there. Second was the sight of town water towers. You could see them ahead, figuring you soon would enter that town, and yet it could take you all day to get there. Third was the fact that it was so flat, especially as I made my way deeper into the plains, that I could see the curvature of the earth.

I was in a very lonely place. It was very monastic wherein I could work out many problems in my head. I also could count my many blessings and feel deeply the presence of the creator, Great Spirit, Great Mystery.

Josh joined me as I entered an oasis, a temperate band of hills then mountains that rose and drew me to them. It offered a respite from the flatness and dryness. This island in the plains included the home of a band of Chippewa and Cree tribes on a reservation called Rocky Boy's. I immediately noticed a banner hanging outside the health center, welcoming me. Josh was also impressed with the mountainous terrain, because he thought he had drawn the least interesting and flattest stretch of the Walk Across America. In fact, from here to North Dakota, we would both be impressed by the beauty of the Great Plains and its inhabitants.

I knew Josh only through my good friend Megan. They had joined me on multiple adventures a few years earlier. It now seemed slightly awkward because their relationship had ended. I was still good friends with Megan but had lost touch with Josh. He had contacted me when he somehow heard I needed drivers for my walk. But all was well. Megan had moved to Vermont, and Josh now lived in New Paltz, New York, where he was refurbishing old barns for actor Robert De Niro. His location afforded him access to the Shawangunks rock-climbing area, where he climbed to a fierce degree almost daily. In winter, he had plenty of snowy areas close by to indulge in his first love, snowboarding. I remembered how, when I visited Megan at an old farmhouse where she lived with Josh and his snowboarding buddies, in the summer they would try to keep an edge by jumping on and off the furniture with their snowboards. Now that awkwardness melted away as Josh's arid humor and laidback stoner demeanor fit the terrain we were crossing.

One of the features of my time spent at Rocky Boy's Indian Reservation was the three tribal walkathons we participated in. We took three routes through the hills, meadows, and creek drainages, even stopping at a few tribal members' houses or, in one case, a farm. These people all had Type 2 diabetes, and we discussed the difference and similarities between theirs and mine. One afternoon, I walked past the tribal gym when a familiar face stuck his head out the window, calling out, "Hey, Bob!" Huck Sunchild was director of tribal fitness, and we had talked together back in Browning during American Indian Days, where Huck danced. He performed at powwows every weekend all over the American West and Canada. Later that afternoon, he would set out on a marathon drive to Albuquerque, New Mexico, where he would dance in the biggest powwow in the world, called "A Gathering of Nations." I thought of Huck as having the same first name and wandering spirit of Huckleberry Finn, combined with the warming rays and gracefulness of his Cree-given last name, Sunchild.

I awoke each morning at 4:30 to the static of the clock radio alarm. There were no stations out there. I walked part of my mileage on my own and finished the afternoon with the tribe. We had a big ceremony before I finally headed east toward my next reservation where we exchanged gifts of T-shirts, jackets, food, and recipes. In a state of immense distance and stunning scenery, it was the First Nations people who were becoming the highlight of my walk across Montana.

***

The next reservation I walked to was Fort Belknap, home to the Assiniboine and Gros Ventre tribes. The heat on the unobstructed Great Plains meant that I got shake-and-baked most late mornings and early afternoons. Some days, we swam in the Milk River to cool off. It felt primal. The few small towns here and the one larger town, Glasgow, all claimed the title of "Mosquito Capital of the United States." As I entered the reservation and the town of Harlem, I had trails of both wet and dried blood on my arms and legs, looking as if my veins were atop my body. The natives soon came to my rescue with bottles of 90-percent Deet. The chemicals could not have been healthy, but it was the only thing that worked. Melvina, a tribal elder, was my contact here, and she told me her tribe had grown accustomed to the summer skeeter onslaught.

The next few days, we continued with group walks and diabetes presentations. I knew that there was no better way to get to know people, landscapes, tribal practices, and diabetes than walking and talking in unison. It was practical yet uplifting. One afternoon, in the heat of the sun, the tribe took me to the top of Rattlesnake Butte, its sacred mountain. The reason for going at that time of day was that the rattlesnakes stayed underground. It would be very dangerous as the sun set. The view was 360 degrees, with a look back to the Bears Paw range I had come from. Off in the distance, we saw a herd of antelope running across the plain to the southwest and the tribe's buffalo grazing to the east, while a golden eagle soared in the sky above us and the serpents of paradise lay in the rocks below us. This was a holy, terrestrial landscape. We all turned slowly in each of the four directions and prayed to the Great Mystery. It was then that I realized that I was not just on a walk — I was on a pilgrimage across the Holy Land.

Later that night, the tribe hosted a dance and ceremony where Josh and I each received a drum and a luxurious Pendleton wool blanket. We were instructed to wrap the blanket around us as our way of accepting it. As the campfires blazed and Josh and I glowed with a supreme sense of gratitude, I swear I felt like I was in the movie "Dancing with Wolves."

As we slowly approached the North Dakota line, I cut south a bit to walk along the mighty Missouri River, which was dammed up to form the Charles M. Russell National Wildlife Refuge. I had walked on the banks of the Missouri River Breaks, a wild, lonely slice of Montana, the day before. The mosquitos continued to dive bomb us. To try and use less Deet, we switched to Skin So Soft. As I applied it, I swear I could hear the mosquitos laughing. One day, the mosquitos did not bother us. Instead, we encountered three thunderstorms that moved across the flat prairies where, standing upright, we were the tallest objects. The rains came down in sheets, and then soon cleared as the next storm raged toward us. After three storms, we were once more witness to another necromantic, double-arcing rainbow.

The next and last reservation for that year's pilgrimage was at Fort Peck, home to the Northern Plains Sioux Tribe. One of the tribal elders, its medicine woman, told me and the audience at my slideshow that night that she sensed that I missed my family back home. Then, she asked me to return to two slides in which she had sensed big medicine. One was the Pinnacle Mountain on the Appalachian Trail of my youth, of which she was dead-on. I always considered it my sacred mountain. The second slide was of the swirling Loyalsock Creek in

Worlds End State Park, as seen from a high mountain peak, another of my holy places back home. I thought I would never see those places in the same way again, but in reality, we always sort of knew they were places of big medicine. She had just reinforced that.

The last day of the walk took me to the confluence of the Yellowstone and Missouri rivers just above Sidney. It was a magnanimous spot to complete year one. As I climbed into the passenger seat, the homesickness hit me like a ton of bricks. Eight and a half weeks was a long time to be on the road. The homesickness was followed by an emotional cocktail of weariness, elation, and fulfillment. I slammed the door, rolled down the window, cranked up some Neil Young tunes, and told Josh to gun us across the rest of the continent. I return to this very spot next year to start all over again. America would call me back.

We made a quick stop and hiked in the North Dakota Badlands, where we saw our fifth rainbow in three weeks. Ivan of the Blackfeet was right. Then we rolled south and east through Fargo, Minneapolis, Madison, Chicago, Indiana, Ohio, and most of my home state. I saw the sign welcoming me to Kutztown. One mile later, I fell into the six arms of Amberly, Adrienne, and Nancy. Odysseus had returned.

Chapter 13

The Divinity of the American Landscape

"The air is getting hotter
There's a rumbling in the skies
I've been wading through the high muddy water
With the heat rising in my eyes
Every day your memory grows dimmer
It doesn't haunt me like it did before
I've been walking through the middle of nowhere
Trying to get to heaven before they close the door."

— Bob Dylan, "Tryin' to Get to Heaven"

In a way, it was like leaving the year before. A soft summer evening, the fading light, a tearful family group hug goodbye. The differences also were stark. This year, I would fly home after three weeks for a three-day interlude to attend my nephew's wedding. Additionally, my daughter Adrienne would join me for the drive west and the first two weeks of walking. The drama of the goodbye for my family thus was lessened. Adrienne had turned 15 a few months earlier and soon would become a big asset when she could drive the motorhome, which she itched to drive now.

 As we headed toward the sunset on Interstate 80 through Pennsylvania, excitement and mirth ensued and continued for the next 14 days. Also joining me for the drive to the Montana-North Dakota line were two friends, Tina and Emma. Tina had helped me with lap counting and crewing during my ultra days. She was the cousin of Linette, who joined me in the walk across Montana the prior year. Keeping it in the family made the transition from year one to year two seamless. Tina shared some of Linette's qualities, including a fine-tuned sense of humor. In fact, Tina might have ramped up the humor quotient. Her laughter was cacophonous and backed by high-octane energy whether driving or walking. The big skies and wide-open prairies of western North Dakota swallowed up and muted sound except when Tina was in gear, which was almost always.

 Emma was the same age as Adrienne and a last-minute addition. The rest of us knew her only from the church we attended and its Sunday school. Somehow the walk across America brought out the best in everyone who participated. Emma fit in immediately and soon brought forth a series of witticisms describing the passing scene. She continued to broadcast what bounced around in her head, which we dubbed "Emmacisms." She kept us on our toes as we tried to figure out these pronouncements that came from Emma's truly unique mind. She named our little house on wheels "The Very Minnie Winnie" as we headed west and north along much of the same route as last year's return journey.

 We parked at the O'Hare International Airport in Chicago and rode the train downtown to stretch our legs with a walk along Lake Michigan. Our bliss was interrupted when a quick but mighty thunderstorm scared the bejesus out of us. We all got soaked to the skin as we ducked into a sleazy-looking restaurant straight out of the 1950s. The maître d' was not happy about us dripping on his plush suede carpet, so he shuffled the girls off to a downstairs bathroom to try to dry their clothes. A private party that might have been a bachelor party was going on. When the three girls, led by the maître d', came down the steps in wet T-shirts, they got a round of applause, as the group thought they were the entertainment.

After eating, we took the train back to the airport. We had had enough of the big city. Our focus was on the wilds of western North Dakota.

We blew through Minnesota with a rising heat gauge. A hard westerly headwind overworked the engine and caused our gas mileage to run up the expenses. I ran a tight ship expense-wise, so we would have to make cuts elsewhere. Fargo was a blip on the radar; maybe we expected more, or maybe we didn't have time to notice anything of interest. When we reached the capital of North Dakota, Bismarck, we headed south to present a diabetes program at the Fort Yates Hospital on Standing Rock Sioux Reservation. Afterward, the tribal members led us to our campsite for the night on the shores of Lake Oahe. Sioux leader Sitting Bull was buried there, and later we took a walk along the lake, actually the dammed-up Missouri River. The river still haunted my consciousness. The primal howling of a coyote sung us to sleep. We were back home in western America.

We arrived on the powwow grounds of the Fort Berthold Indian Reservation, home of the Mandan, Hidatsa, and Arikara tribes. We parked and started wandering the festival grounds where everything was in place. We had a lot of free time since my programs and tribal walkathons were scheduled for a week later, when I would walk onto the reservation. Because of the heat, some of the native kids were jumping 40 feet off a trestle bridge into the Missouri River. The girls thought they would jump too. In the end, only Tina dared it, leaping with perfect form, her arms out like a cross and toes pointing down.

During the dances, a few Sioux dancers exuding maleness and with big muscles approached me, asking how many horses I would take in exchange for my daughter. I told them they might get a better deal from my wife, since she and Adrienne were butting heads. I, however, considered her priceless and, at 15, too young for trading.

That night, the girls and I crawled onto the roof of the motorhome and had a ceremony as sage burned in a kettle on the kitchen table and rose through the ceiling vent. It was the perfect setting to watch the dancing from our lawn chairs, surrounded by the river, buttes, and festival lights, all taken in from our skybox. It was one of those celestial-like nights we would never forget.

The last stop on our drive west was in the North Dakota Badlands, where we took two hikes. It was important for me and my crew to view the pristine, ancient landscapes of the tribes whose lands would surround us for the next week. It would give us both reverence and a preview of what was to come.

***

It truly was an inauspicious beginning for year two of the Walk Across America for Diabetes. My first steps carried me into downtown Williston, North Dakota, from the city's northern fringes. In the semi-darkness of an August morning, with enthusiasm running high, the girls and I missed the turn for Highway 1804 and instead headed west, back the way I had come last year. When the sun finally peaked above the horizon behind us, I knew my earlier hunch was right. We were headed in the wrong direction. This was no big deal – just four miles in the wrong direction compared to the 1,150 miles I had walked to this point and the 2,250 miles I had yet to go to the Atlantic. I did have some Williston Lions Club members and some newspaper and TV media waiting to do interviews ahead, so I picked up the pace toward a fiery burst of reds and oranges, the full-on rising-of-the-sun star.

We moved at 15 minutes per mile on Highway 1804, named for the year the Lewis and Clark expedition returned via the same way we were walking. The Missouri River lay ahead of us, which we would follow along its northern shore back to Fort Berthold in a few days. The landscape gave a sense of the big medicine the tribes speak of — an inspiration to drive you onward, something primordial and aboriginal. The rising reddish-brown buttes were majestic in the same way as snowcapped mountains yet also different, with a parchedness and no surrounding vegetation. I had worried about the walk being anti-climactic compared to the epic landscapes I had walked through last year. Being there, though, I saw that would be unlikely.

My walk was almost migratory now that I had time to think about it. Nomadic writer Bruce Chatwin said, "I have a compulsion to wander and return — a homing instinct like a migratory bird" — a seasonal leaving then returning. Other things ate at me during these long solo passages. Why couldn't I be content during those ten months back home? I had a good life, a good family, a good business. Usually, though, a month or two after returning home, the creature comforts surrounding me wore off, and I started to miss the gritty "boots in the dust" life on the road. The voices would get louder, calling me back to that hardscrabble life. But out there, it was never something fun. Sure, it had its moments, but they came few and far between. There was that something — a certain monasticism, something decipherable in the clear night sky, the communitas among you, your comrades, and other kindred spirits you meet on the trail. I was, as Joseph Campbell wrote, following my bliss, east through the western panorama.

At four o'clock in the morning, the radio alarm played powwow music broadcast from the tribal station in Newtown 50 miles away. The only light to be seen came from the reflection of a partially starry sky in the waves of Lake Sakakawea. There was an unsettling sense of change in the air, in the sky, on the surface of the lake. I exited Lewis and Clark State Park on foot, watching the stars slowly disappearing, gobbled up by a blackness I could barely discern. It was spooky yet fascinating.

I now saw clearly that multiple storms were present. In the goosebump-inducing chill of the pitch-dark prairie morning, I was treated to the natural pyrotechnics of storm after storm, all non-threatening because of distance. Lightning and brightening clashing with each other to see who could give the earth the most fire. In my peripheral vision, I took in heat lightning to the north, like a lamp being turned on and off. In front of me came a solar hint of orange over the eastern flatlands, and to my right and south, a more vicious storm over the Badlands, with searing bolts and booming thunder. If I walked backwards, facing west but moving east, I witnessed a third storm with fewer bolts but still crackling. Rolling thunder moved like a freight train out of the distant buttes over Montana. I smelled the rain, though none reached me. With the last of the darkness fading, I caught a glimpse of a falling star, brilliant against the last wall of darkness. Quite a show for one walker in one morning.

The sun had now risen, and the road began heating up. I was 12 miles into my day with only the sun to the east and three faint images moving rhythmically toward me on the road. That could mean only one thing. Other than the sun star, there were only three stars left in my universe. Adrienne, goddess of blonde; Emma, goddess of witticism; and Tina, goddess of laughter. In less than one week, their jubilant love of the adventure of life had become an energizing force in the life of my quest.

Adrienne had changed little in the year since we walked together in Montana. She had grown maybe an inch or two in height, but she still masked her intelligence in a Valley Girl-style dumb blonde persona to keep people off-guard and wondering. Over the years, it was amazing how each adventure she took with her father added many inches to her mental and spiritual growth. These adventures had given her a new perspective on life, exposed her to a diverse cross-section of American people, and helped open her mind. By walking and driving toward the far horizons with her father, Adrienne had broadened her inner horizons.

***

Our two-day presentation at Fort Berthold had had an addition since the previous year. I had added about 15 slides from the walk across Washington, Idaho, and Montana. It was hard to remove some to make room for the new, and it was hard to limit the new ones to 15. Yet the idea was to keep it succinct, on point, focused. I reveled in the question-and-answer portion of the program. It caused me to dig down and answer with wisdom from not only experience but also heart. Sometimes I had to admit that I wasn't sure about an answer but that I would research further and follow up with the reservation's diabetes educator. Sometimes the Q&A continued after the program, spilling out onto the parking lot of the rec center or hospital. Many times, the questions reappeared during the next day's tribal walkathon. All this could be tiring, but I also found that simultaneously it exhilarated me.

On our last evening at Fort Berthold, we were invited to a concert at the outdoor arena next to the tribe's casino. The headliner was Billy Ray Cyrus, who that morning had hiked up to the holy butted ridge above the reservation, where he wrote a new song inspired by the landscapes and the members of the tribe. I wasn't a big fan of country music, but I figured it would be fun to be part of the scene. At this concert, I noticed a wild child running and wrestling with the Indian children, her loud voice almost rising above the concert. My tribal liaisons, Carla and Ivetta Spotted Bear, told me the energetic girl was Billy Ray Cyrus's daughter, Miley.

My surroundings changed more and more as I walked east and off the reservation over the next few days. I entered central North Dakota, where endlessly flat grasslands replaced the jagged buttes and the Missouri River. It was an existential hit on my psyche. I felt a fear of failure — a dread of not being able to mentally and spiritually continue. It only lasted a few hours but reemerged a few times in the next few days. This is where your teammates become positive forces for moving you forward. Their spirit was not always consciously presented. Instead, it was the everyday stuff that happened. With my three comrades, it was a constant swirl of activity that helped me tamp down my fear and concentrate on one major fact: I was on the adventure of a lifetime amidst a lifetime of adventures.

One day on the Great Plains, I was chugging along in one of my trademarked bouts of flow when I heard a familiar horn blowing, followed by manic laughter. My vehicle was passing, headed to our last rendezvous meetup for the day. But what was crazy was that the vehicle was being driven by my daughter. She was finally getting her wish to drive, albeit about nine months earlier than legally allowed. They had noticed young farm boys driving pickup trucks many times, even one where the pedals had blocks on them and a Sears catalog on the seat. Adrienne didn't need that, but she also could not make the claim that she needed to drive for a farm. She was enthralled driving the Very Minnie Winnie through the American flatlands. Yes indeed, my little girl was growing up fast. Hopefully her mother would not find out about this.

Emma was an enigma. We tried to figure her out, but she constantly changed her emotional colors. Emma also had nomadic tendencies, which always makes it hard to fit in with families during downtime. I was very empathetic with her there. With this crew, there was no problem fitting in. All my crew members were travelers, and most had plenty of quirks that made them interesting. But Emma took unique and idiosyncratic to another level. I marked her meditations on the passing scene in my journals with the symbol "$E=mc2$," short for Emmacisms. At times they had an Einstein quality to them, other times they seemed prophetic, and a few times she blurted out something we still haven't figured out.

She also had a vivid imagination and used it to illuminate any situation. When we camped at Theodore Roosevelt National Park, we all noticed that one of the rangers took a liking to Emma. It was obvious. But in Emma's mind, drawing from a large repertoire of slasher movies she loved, he was an axe murderer who would stealthily attack us during the night to steal Emma away. Later, she invented him in her mind as an alien. One night, Emma sat at the far end of a pier along Lake Oahe, totally at peace smoking one of her stash of cigars, the lighted end the only light in the darkness, blowing barely seen smoke rings into the air. She was only 15. One day, she revealed to us a horribly mangled, twisted, swollen second toe of her left foot. We laughed for 10 minutes, not at the foot per se but at the thought that Emma found it hilarious. Emma also made a prediction while riding the elevated train through the rows of cars in the O'Hare Airport parking lot that in the future we would shop and pick out cars this way.

On our last few moments in Roosevelt National Park, we prepared to leave after a long group hike. Emma was out on a promontory that featured a stunning view of buttes, mesas, and the Little Missouri River. She danced like nobody was watching, her headphones blasting Debbie Harry and Blondie. We signaled to her that we were ready to move on. And then we took notice. Somebody was watching. We noticed the creepy ranger observing Emma, hidden behind a pinion pine tree. The axe murderer watched with glee as Emma danced the dance of life, grooving to the metaphysical rhythms of the universe until we halted her reverie and rescued her safely back into the motorhome.

Tina was one of those rare breeds of humans who always seemed to be on a natural high, always ready for adventure, someone who never seemed to have an off switch, except on long flights where she charged her batteries by sleeping from takeoff to landing. She was our crew's drill sergeant who kept our ragtag group of bohemians moving forward. At the same time, she could get down into the world of the two teenagers, thereby gaining their confidence, thus able to be relatable. Tina loved challenges and dove into them feet first, just like she did when she jumped into the Missouri River from the bridge. Another example of Tina's take on life happened when we encountered a monster bull bison as we rounded a curve during a hike in the badlands. My heart was still thumping minutes after he charged off into the brush, but Tina, looking thrilled but unfazed, merely stated, "That was cool, way cool."

All of the crew who accompanied me on my quest would become lifelong friends. The experiences we shared, though short in time, seemed long because of their intensity. Those experiences coalesced into one wild adventure, even in the most mundane of landscapes. These were essential ingredients on a long walk across the breadth of a continent. My walk mates gave me an energy I could not always find in myself, one that stayed with me when I was alone. As Tina would say, "That's cool, way cool.

We entered Minot, North Dakota, at the end of a long day of walking through the flatlands. Tomorrow, the old guard girls would exit, and the new guard girls would arrive — trading one traveling circus for another. That morning, during Adrienne's segment of the walk, we discussed this ritual of coming and going. We were learning not to concentrate on our nearing separation but instead on her reunion with those she missed back home. It would always be hard to miss the energy of the Walk Across America for Diabetes. She had to learn as I did to find that energy in everything back home, to treat every part of life as if she was still out here. And then in no time, the next year we would return. Fathers can only hope to have some small positive influence on their offspring. Our shared journeys in the wildlands, since she was 8 years old, were set within our longer journeys through life. They were all part of life's rich pageant.

***

As my old road crew departed, I spent the day walking around Minot while awaiting the arrival of my new road crew. In the book "Road Trip USA," it says of the town, "Snug in the Souris River Valley, Minot evokes ambivalence from most travelers. Some loathe it for its apparent nothingness." I had one moment of loneliness as I spotted the plane ascending out of my sight, thinking of Emma and Adrienne joking around while Tina slept the sleep of the innocent. My curiosity kicked in and lifted me from my saudade longing. How many times would I, or anybody really, have a day to spend just hanging out and taking in the sights, on foot, of the largest city in North Dakota? There was a small zoo, an Air Force base, missile silos, and a small university. Then in the afternoon, I returned to the airport and recognized two figures sitting behind the motorhome. Road crew No. 2 had appeared, prepared for duty.

Kathie had accompanied John and I for the first three days at the start of the Walk Across America the previous year and had thus acquired legendary status as a member of the triumvirate of that crazy drive west. Kathy's face was a mix of excitement, tempered by a look that said, "I hope this portion of the trip will be less manic." John wasn't there, and that could help tone things down, but I couldn't guarantee anything. There were too many variables. Kathie was accompanied by her daughter, Kaitlin. The prairie winds blew through Kaitlin's long, curly hair, which she occasionally swiped from her eyes. She sat serenely, Buddha-like, on the tarmac ready for the walking and the adventure. But beside all that, Kaitlin was here to teach and to learn about her Type 1 diabetes, which she had for 11 years, since she was 5 years old. She knew of the struggle both of us were going to have to endure for the rest of our lives. But she also knew that she was here to rise above the struggle, crank out some prairie miles, and meet others to teach and learn from along the way.

The three of us walked to the edge of the city, and by mid-morning, Kathie and Kaitlin turned around and headed back to get the motorhome. After our first break, at the eight-mile mark, I prepared to begin the next leg. High humidity and encroaching darkness settled in, an ominous lack of light although it wasn't even noon yet. My blood glucose readings were extremely high. I had always reacted to high and low barometric conditions, especially a rapid change from high to low with frontal systems on the move. Immediately upon exiting the city, there was very little sign of habitation.

The night before, I had explained the "policy" to the new crew: "Let me come to you." When you reach our predetermined meeting spot, you wait there until I arrive. Under no conditions do you drive back to look for me. I could be off-road, going to the bathroom, or knocking on the door of a farmhouse to get water. The possibility was that you would drive right by where I was. We had no cell phones.

The coming storm soon was upon us. The rain came down as hard as I had ever seen or felt it, and I had walked through a lot of storms in my life. This rain came down so hard that it hurt. Another problem presents itself during a rain this heavy when there is no way to get out of it — I cannot check my blood glucose with my meter. Therefore, I have to guess what my blood sugar is and try to balance it. As the storm steamrolled toward me, a few lightning strikes got way too close. I looked for a place to get out of it, but there were none. I thought about crawling into a drainage pipe, but they were metal and overflowing with rain runoff. Then a bolt hit so close in front of me that I walked into the wisp of smoke it left behind. I could smell the sulfur so strongly that it conjured up Hell in my mind. Was I already dead and about to enter Hell? But two angels saved me. I saw the motorhome driving toward me. The women had not been here a full day and already had broken the rule. But I was eternally grateful that I would be spared from the searing bolts, the flash flood, and the gale-force winds so I could continue walking across America. Rules were made to be broken.

Over the next few days, we walked right past the obelisk outside Rugby, which represented the midpoint of the North American continent, which I thought would be hokey, but then I realized it also represented the halfway point of my walk. Then we headed due north to a line of hills rising from the flat patchwork fields near the Canadian border. Our destination was the Turtle Mountain Reservation, home of the Chippewa Tribe. After presenting my programs, the tribal members held a walkathon around one of the many lakes. The Indian Health Service checked the blood glucose of all 200 walkers, before and after. I held the line, testing at 120 before and 94 after. I continued exploring some lakes the next day, just happy to be back in the shade of the trees. The night before, several storms had passed through, leaving the atmosphere saturated with a stifling humidity. It was one of my least-favorite atmospheric conditions, but I had to expect and accept it as I progressed further east. I swam a few times in some of the cold lakes, which was a wakeup call each time.

For the next three days, we traveled backwards: west to Minot International Airport, then south by prop plane to Minneapolis, where I presented at the American Association of Diabetes Educators conference. For part of each day, I worked the floor at the MiniMed insulin pump space, where I took photos with a cadre of nurses and dieticians. Shop talk about diabetes ensued throughout the conference, even during the Minnesota Twins-New York Yankees baseball game we attended and the 10K race we ran in along the Mississippi River. Minneapolis turned out to be a welcome escape from the wildlands we had walked through. It was a real cosmopolitan city with giant skyscrapers, cool music and bookstores, and even nightclubs. I also got to reconnect with my MiniMed liaison DeNetta. I continued to try and talk her into driving and crewing for me next year, and she seemed to be enticed enough that a good possibility existed for her to sign on. For now, though, it was back to the prairies of North Dakota and miles to go before I'd sleep.

It was weird that the apparent "nothingness" of Minot did not keep us from returning for the fourth time in a week. It was a small airport, but it was the only one around. Minot had thus gained legendary status in the annals of the Walk Across America. It had become a home away from home, a place that I returned to after epic sojourns into the heart of the American dream.

One day of walking took me to the Spirit Lake Nation Reservation, where the Sioux welcomed me with open arms. The feature of the reservation was a huge, dying body of water called Devils Lake (the tribe preferred the ancient tribal name of Spirit Lake). It took a day of walking to encircle it amidst algae, gasses, construction, and mud. The humidity remained stifling into the last two days of solo walking to the Minnesota state line. I soon would fly home for the wedding of a close nephew. Kathie and Kaitlin, had flown home from Grand Forks two days prior. While awaiting the flight, Kaitlin and I had time for one more walk together. She was fast gaining an independent spirit, a bird preparing to fly from the nest. It would be hard on both of them but especially on Kathie. Katlin was her only child, and Kathie had done a wonderful job of preparing her for the exit into adulthood, especially in the years-long battle they both waged with diabetes. It would be extra hard to accede total control over to Kaitlin.

I knew both would do okay, though; I felt it in my heart. Both would flourish in different ways. My example of how I not only survived but thrived was what I was out here to show to the world. I would soon leave the great and wild American West. Its landscapes had inspired me, and it had given me many new friendships from both the people I met along the way and from the ragtag bunch of those wonderful souls who came to walk and crew for me. Many of those were old friends, and of course, one was my daughter. All those relationships had deepened. The West had worked its magic on all of us. We would never forget those epic adventures.

***

All adventures are an exercise in problem solving, sometimes in ways that are totally unexpected. The next two weeks would test me to the core. The first test was the fact that Northwest Airlines had gone on strike while I was attending the wedding back home. I had barely made it home before it happened. Northwest was the only airline covering the areas for my walk, and I would be in those spots for a few weeks. The second test was I would have two old-timers with me, my 73-year-old father, Bob Sr., and my 73-year-old father-in-law, Irvin. It would be a challenge to direct them to find me at the resupply points each day, and except for the mile or two that they would walk with me, I would walk alone.

But first, we had to get to the starting point on the North Dakota-Minnesota border. I appealed to higher management at Northwest Airlines. They were afraid that the media surrounding my walk would shed a bad light on them, so, they got Air Canada to honor our tickets, and right on time, we flew to Toronto and then on to Winnipeg in the Canadian province of Manitoba. From there, we were driven by limousine to Grand Forks International Airport, where the walk would begin anew the next morning. The Old Guys passed the first test with flying colors, getting a kick out of seeing places they would not have ever seen otherwise. We were ready for Minnesota to welcome us the next day.

It's magical thinking to expect everything to change at state lines, but the first 70 miles of Minnesota look no different than North Dakota. It was still flat, treeless, and hot. Three days of walking brought me to what I craved — forests of pine trees, cooler weather, and a moose-crossing sign. It was September now, so the cooler weather would be inevitable.

There was a series of Native American reservations spaced out every couple of days on my route through the state. I hoped to introduce the elders of my tribe to the elders of the Anishinaabe. This would get very interesting. Since I would walk alone most of the time, I started to get deep into my psyche, digging around into the far edges, trying to further my relationship with religion. I was raised a Lutheran, baptized, confirmed, and later became a deacon. My dad was very involved in every aspect of church life, and as a family, we attended every Sunday. My mom was not as devout, sometimes seeming to be going through the motions. Even though I taught Sunday school and Bible school, distributed communion bread and wine, and presented sermons when the pastor was on vacation, I oftentimes felt like my mom when it came to church life. I studied two years to be a deacon and knew the Bible inside and out, but I noticed that as devout as my dad was, even he doubted and questioned, trying to wrap his eighth-grade education around some of the deeper facets of theology. His favorite apostle was "Doubting" Thomas, and he was very confused with St. Paul. As my dad grew older, he questioned even more, so I soaked a lot of that into my understanding of religion.

Then along came the Beat writers and their introduction, for me, into Buddhism. I soaked up the Hinduism of Gandhi and dabbled in Islamic Sufism. Always existing around the edges were Jung's ideas on archetypes, the collective unconscious, and synchronicity. All that came flooding in. Then the music of John Coltrane introduced me to quantum physics. More Buddhism followed through the writings of the Dalai Lama, who I would later meet. Then there was the mystic Catholicism of Jesuit priest Pierre Teilhard de Chardin, who also was a paleontologist. And in the last few years, I had started meeting medicine men and women, hallowed souls from many tribes, which would continue for the next few years. All this swirled around in my brain, especially during long solo walks across holy landscapes. All this was also influenced by the fact that because of my many life-threatening diseases and injuries, I always felt that I was living on borrowed time, even more so than average human beings who, let's face it, are all living on borrowed time.

Another factor that came into play was the atrocities committed by the church throughout history in the name of religion, right up to the present, and the holier-than-thou-attitude on display by politicians and leaders. That caused me to constantly question and doubt. Part of this long walk would be to further organize all these influences into something I liked to think of as a rich tapestry of paths of life. I didn't know if I would ever find these answers, but I do believe that what's important is the searching and not necessarily the finding. I always would be a seeker. The beauty and solitude of Minnesota were, at least, helping in this process.

***

The first Native American reservation we came to was White Earth, known for having a seeping spring that would become the mighty Mississippi River. Also, White Earth was the home of Winona LaDuke, who ran as the vice-presidential candidate with Ralph Nader in the late 1990s. Our contact here was a familiar face – Miriam, the tribal nutritionist on the Rocky Boy's Indian Reservation in Montana from the year before. She had since transferred to White Earth. Upon meeting us, she introduced us to tribal historian Andy, who in turn introduced us to radio DJ Joe. They regaled us with stories then invited us to appear on Joe's radio show the next day. The old guys were already showing their age, getting tired of living in the 19-foot confines of the motorhome and the snoring of my father-in-law. As we parked beside the auditorium where I would present my program that night, I started to carry my equipment in to set up. Upon returning to the vehicle, the Old Guys confronted me with, "What are you going to cook for us for dinner?" I told them that I had walked 25 miles and now had to prepare and present my program, so I would eat dinner later that evening. It was a consequence of living on the road and being on a quest. They gave me sour looks of disappointment. I showed them where the food, pots, pans, stove, and sink were and then left to go back to the auditorium to prepare. They eventually figured it out and did not starve. It was an enriching experience having them with me but also a challenge.

The next day was the Old Guys' day to shine. I let them do a big portion of the talking on the radio program. Joe taught them Anishinaabe words and had them pronounce them. In return, the Old Guys taught Joe and his listening audience Pennsylvania Dutch words, which are derived from the Black Forests of southern Germany, where my ancestors come from. I don't really know much of this language, so hilarity ensued as there was now a mismatch of three languages being spoken live on the air. For the next two days, whenever tribal members saw us, they wanted to shake the hands of the two Old Guy comics. As we exited White Earth on foot, I was taken to the sacred site where the mighty Mississippi sprung forth. The ebb was low because of the end-of-summer drought. Winona LaDuke was away on a book tour, so unfortunately, I didn't get to meet one of my heroes.

The heat returned with a fury, causing me to wake early and walk in the coolness of pre-sunset. At least here there were trees. We had an evening program at a university in the pleasant small city of Bemidji, where there is an iconic statue of Paul Bunyan and Babe on the outskirts. One night we camped by a lake, and in the afternoon, my dad and I rowed a borrowed boat across it. It was my fifth lake since entering Minnesota. I had only 9,995 to go.

My father-in-law seemed a little homesick, maybe missing his wife. My mom and dad, though, were glad for a week's separation. Another day of walking took me to the Leech Lake Reservation just in time for the Ojibwas' annual powwow, where the Old Guys would get to see some amazing dancing and eat both traditional and American junk food. They both seemed hungry and tired of the motorhome food. I gave a speech between dances, though I wasn't asked to dance. The

Old Guys seemed nervous when I told them they might have to dance in the arena in front of huge crowds.

My dad and I slept in a teepee that night in a beautiful grove of white pines, and before leaving in the morning, we had a tribal two-mile walkathon. The anticipation ramped up as we got closer to Lake Superior, and so did the preponderance of large grain trucks hauling their wares to the docks on the harbor. We stayed overnight and then had a program on the Fond Du Lac Indian Reservation. As I walked east, I recalled the lines of the Longfellow poem about Lake Superior: "By the shores of Gitche Gumee, By the shining Big-Sea-Water." The next day, the forest on top of a ridge opened up suddenly, revealing one of the wonders of the world. The sunlight glinting off Lake Superior burned my eyes. I switchbacked down a series of dirt roads, always seeing glimpses of that shining lake. This was one of the hallmarks of the Walk Across America for Diabetes. It was the first Great Lake on the route, and yet it was the biggest of the five. It made me feel bigger than my six-foot height.

The Old Guys were supposed to fly home from Duluth, but the Northwest Airlines strike was still on. The Old Guys would have to stay here for maybe another week and for as far as Green Bay, Wisconsin. My next driver, Barb, also couldn't get here. I broke the news to the Old Guys, and they both seemed just a little bit troubled. To placate them, and to please myself, we headed north, off-route, along the shores of the mighty lake. I walked on lakeside trails as Superior grew larger and larger. I was in a state of enthrallment, and the Old Guys' spirits rose again. We made lemonade from the bitter lemons of the airline strike.

Duluth was a mix of metropolitan and frontier town, always within the stunning backdrop of the lake's beauty. Then we concocted another plan: I would drive the guys south to St. Paul, where they would get on an Amtrak train that would arrive just south of where we lived the next day. Barb found an airport in central Wisconsin that had one airline other than Northwest. I would drive due east after dropping off the Old Guys in St. Paul. Then, Barb and I would drive back north to Duluth, where the walk would begin again. It was exhausting yet gave me no walking mileage. But adventures are a series of problems that need to be solved. I solved this one so the walk could continue. And after a tiring day-and-a-half of driving, I, with Barb in tow, was back on the path again.

***

It was cool for me to get to show Barb Lake Superior and the hip city of Duluth. She exited the small prop plane a little shaken. It had been rainy with high winds all day. Barb's plane had flown through all that storm and turbulence. She took a few deep breaths, picked up her one duffle bag, took a few steps, and said, "I'm ready for whatever the Walk Across America for Diabetes needs me to do." That was exactly the attitude I needed right there, right then.

"You have to ride three hours on bumpy roads in an old motorhome to a frontier town located on the wild shores of one the biggest freshwater lakes in the world," I told her.

Barb, without missing a beat replied, "Reporting for duty, captain." She was all in.

The day after Barb's arrival, I crossed into Wisconsin, still following the shores of Lake Superior, this time east. It wasn't until partway through the next week that I began, in a comical sort of way, calling Barb, "Barbarrific." It was a sort of a tribute to Jane Fonda's character, a female superhero, in the 1968 film "Barbarella" (without all the weird, futuristic, sexual themes, of course). Barb's script had her battling and beating cancer and then becoming an advocate and counselor for others going through the same thing. Barb was a real-life superhero. The "terrific" part came as a change from last week's problems with the continued airline strike, the Old Guys having to stay beyond their limits, and a heat wave that hit central Minnesota. All that was in the past as Barbarrific walked tall and mighty through the streets of old Duluth.

Wisconsin felt cooler within the first hour of me striding through it. Soon the boreal forests appeared and stretched on into the Upper Peninsula of Michigan. There were occasional dirt roads heading north. All of them took a walker a few miles to a beach on the immense shore of Lake Superior. These forays gave me extra mileage but also inspiration. One morning, we took a ferry out to Madeline Island just beyond the gorgeous Apostle archipelagos. The islands' deserted beaches were strewn with driftwood, and inland there were cemeteries full of the remains of Ojibwa tribal ancestors. It took me most of the day to circle the island on boardwalks, roads, and rickety piers.

That night, while sitting on a pier after returning to the mainline, came the first in a line of evening sunsets. They started out pink and ended with bright fire. We had gorgeous weather for most of the week, which made us thankful, for the stories were many of the maelstrom storms that caused shipwrecks.

One day, we walked into Bad River Reservation, where the descendants of those buried on that island live. Spread aloft was an effervescent blue sky, resplendent here at the end of summer. I thought I was daydreaming as a band of ancient Ojibwa warriors walked toward us. But they were real, modern, and walking to meet us. The first to reach me was Louis, who actually was an Apache warrior. He had long, black hair and a dark complexion, and he was married to an Ojibwa woman. Louis was the youth health leader. We walked onto the tribal grounds, and Louis observed that, even from afar, my legs moved like the turning of a prayer wheel, like the flapping of prayer flags. He told me that if I prayed while I walked, my prayers would be carried directly to the creator. This made the very act of walking holy. That was a unique concept. Louis had moved my consciousness of walking into another level. Here on the shoulders of an American highway, among the tribes of the Ojibwa nation, from the mind of an Apache medicine man, came a metaphor of Himalayan Buddhist spirituality that was passed on to a pilgrim of Swiss-German descent, who would carry that message the rest of the way across America and eventually to the rest of the world. It would be a message of transformation and healing.

We spent two days with the tribe, which included a 13-mile tribal walk, two presentations, a game of basketball with the kids, and plenty of feasting. The tribal elders thought I needed some fattening up. My weight definitely had diminished thanks to the 25 miles I did each day.

More dirt roads leading to remote, primal beaches were a continuing feature as we moved east. I barely noticed that we had crossed into the Upper Peninsula of Michigan. On Saturday morning, I felt something strange pulling me along. It wasn't atmospheric; the skies were an unending clear blue. No, it was some kind of anticipation amidst mile after mile of forest. We came onto the shores of Lake Gogebic, at the end of the day, and I asked Barb to drive us north into a little town where we could hopefully rent a motel room or cabin. They had one unit left, and the television had been hooked up one day before. That night, on that TV, we watched the Miss America pageant. My friend Linette, who had walked with me in Montana, had been in the pageant three years earlier. My interest tonight was the fact that two contestants, Miss New York Deana Herrera and Miss Virginia Nicole Johnson, were Type 1 insulin-dependent diabetics, whose platforms were education programs to stem the rising tide of life-damaging diabetes across America. In other words, I shared that same message and goal. If one of them could win, it would be monumental. Both wore the same MiniMed insulin pump that I did. A strange phenomenon had led us here and made everything fall into place so we could watch. Stranger yet was how connected I had become to this pageant since Linette was in it.

The drama rose in degrees. Nicole Johnson made it to the top 10, then the top five. Her talent was singing. It was now between Nicole and one other contestant, and then Nicole was crowned Miss America 1999. It was a miracle that we were able to witness this historic moment, in the middle of nowhere, in that space and time. The next day, I would have to find a payphone and call MiniMed to remind them that I would finish my walk across America in Atlantic City, New Jersey, where Nicole had just won the pageant, and that it would happen on Memorial Day next year. I needed Nicole to walk the last two miles with me!

As the walking portion of Barbarrific's time in Wisconsin and Michigan ended, we prepared to head south to the airport in Green Bay. We finished our last walking day in Iron River. Then it was a two-hour ride south to the airport. Barb's time here was exactly what I needed to keep the spirit moving through a uniformity and remoteness that could be crushing. Especially if you throw in the homesickness that was uncharacteristically starting to haunt me. Barb became another kindred spirit during this time together. In the three and a half months that I had been walking across America, the number of kindred spirits was beginning to pile up. Barb boarded the plane, and I waited for the next spirit to make its appearance.

***

John walked into where Barb had just boarded. He had wanted to get a hug and say hi and goodbye to her, so he sweet-talked the ticket handlers and the flight attendants into letting him onto her plane. He had a certain persuasiveness with the ladies. Of course Barb was totally discombobulated when she saw him, knowing he was arriving, almost thinking that she had gotten on the wrong plane. They hugged, and John deplaned back into the real world. John, in typical dramatic fashion, had returned to the Walk Across America for Diabetes.

During the drive back north, John regaled me with tales of his wild and wooly, just-completed 26-hour bus ride, laced with vivid stories told with animated hand movements. He told of dramas he had observed starring a cross-section of Americans, with some of the lead parts played by a female bus driver, an 18-year-old exotic dancer named Gina, and a world-famous chef with a handlebar mustache that seemed to twirl when Gina displayed her obvious attributes. John was drawn to these situations as someone who, with wide-eyed wonder and fascination, watched and heard the human condition swirling around him. In turn, saints and sinners also were attracted to John, so the show never ended. More situations, and thus stories, would now appear in real time as we made our way across the Upper Peninsula.

Before leaving Green Bay, we decided to take a walk. I had never been there and more than likely would never return. The Lake Michigan waterfront was underwhelming to the point that I wouldn't count it as the Walk Across America's dramatic first sighting. Downtown Green Bay was a mess of torn-up streets in the middle of a dramatic rebuilding that supposedly was long overdue.

In the midst of this chaos sat a lowly Irish restaurant. It was now being run by a Mexican family, and with the chaos outside, lack of parking, and the language barrier, it would be a tough row. One of the energetic daughters took our order of blueberry pancakes. She giggled as she wrote it down. We both ordered soda, and she asked if we wanted Mexican or American soda. We asked what the difference was, and that got a bigger laugh out of her. It took her a minute, but we finally understood that Mexican soda is served in bottles, and American soda comes in cans. Otherwise, there is no difference.

When our pancakes were served, mine had cashews in them, and John's had apple slices. Neither of us had blueberries. The owner came to apologize, and he was a funny and likeable character. Though the menu had many egg dishes, we overheard him promising an elderly couple to have eggs next time. It seemed like most people were not getting what they ordered. We'll always wonder if that Mexican restaurant with the Irish signage would overcome its disadvantages to make a go at success. We hoped it would. Green Bay, at least on the surface to us passersby, desperately needed the spirit of the American Dream.

***

Over the next few days, I walked through the Scandinavian-settled towns of Iron Mountain, Quinnesec, Norway, and Vulcan. It rained hard most days, leaving my feet soaked. I always was lucky with blisters, and even now that luck held. I soon started looking for an ark being loaded by animals in groups of two as the flooding began to reach biblical proportions.

John and I saw advertising for pasties every few miles. Thinking of Gina the exotic dancer, we thought it was the name of an almost-topless strip club. Turns out that pasties were meat pies, a well-known regional delicacy. John was a vegan and returned to cans of vegetarian chili he cooked on our stove. I was not a big meat-eater, but I reckoned I would try a pastie somewhere in the next week. We joked that maybe we could find tofu pasties but didn't hold our breath.

The official sighting of the mighty Lake Michigan happened in the sleepy town of Escanaba. Once again it was a little underwhelming, though that soon would change.

We were scheduled to do a TV news interview while walking out of town. The young, red-headed news anchor was not having a good day, what with the continued bad weather and her being stuck, career-wise, in Escanaba. Now she had to deal with two smartass long-distance walkers who were trying to cheer her up. Other than downpours, we had not showered for a few days since the shower never worked in the motorhome. Even our usual overabundance of charm could not brighten her day. She carried on for the one-mile interview then jumped in the news vehicle and shot back to Escanaba. It was hard to imagine anyone being immune to the brimming-with-fun personalities our on-the-road selves displayed.

Eventually the rain and storms got to us, too. There were long stretches of silence, something totally out of character for us. It got so bad that I started hoping to find a pastie at a roadside restaurant. I finally found one, and even that was underwhelming. Our moods were rather grim.

We detoured out to a long spit of land at a state park. That night, I called my wife from a payphone at the ranger station. The trees continued to drip around me, but it looked like it might be starting to clear. The call did not lift my mood. Nancy was on a bad-mood bender. She did not appreciate these long absences. I tried to talk her out of her mood by reminding her that I would be home in a week. The phone started cutting in and out, not helping the situation. She then complained that I would be so busy working to make up for lost time that the family still would barely see me. She never asked me how I was feeling until finally she sensed that maybe I was not exactly living the high life out here in the continual wetness. She always could sense my moods, even through a badly functioning phone. Then she accused me of only calling because I was down ("You don't call when you are having fun"). Eventually we called a truce and vowed to take this up when I got home. I left her with one positive note, that I could see the stars coming out over the Lake Michigan beach. Then she admitted that she wished she was there with me. She always was a sucker for a good beach.

After the call, I walked out to the shoreline and thought of the lyrics of the Joni Mitchell song "Blue Motel": "I've got road maps from two dozen states. I've got coast to coast just to contemplate. Will you still love me, when I get back to town?"

The sun did come out the next day. We found this part of the lake to be wild with state parks, lighthouses, and rugged coastlines. I walked past Manistique, where the lighthouse was a stunning bright red. We presented for a Lions Club in Gulliver and at a Native American casino in Naubinway. We walked on a steel suspension bridge that spanned a waterfall at Mallorquins' Point and encountered sweeping dunes at Pointe Aux Chenes. The trees started changing into a bright array of colors. We glided through a fairy tale land of enchantment.

I slept on the dunes one night at a park with a full moon as my companion. Its brightness swallowed some of the closer stars, but there were plenty of them on the far fringes of the night sky.

Our third Great Lake was in sight, on the other side of the five-miles-long Mackinac Bridge. Crossing it would not be an option, as there is no walkway. To make up for it, we instead would take a boat out to Mackinac Island, which sits out in Lake Huron. John and I walked around the shore of the island, taking in the caves and history along the way. No motorized vehicles are allowed on the island, which was idyllic.

***

We jumped into the old Minnie Winnie and headed north to Canada, where we got a glimpse of Lake Superior at Sault Ste. Marie. We headed home once more. The homesickness bug rarely infects me while walking, but just like last year, as soon as we hit the homebound road, a homesickness pervaded. We rolled through the night past Sudbury, Toronto, and Hamilton, crossing back into the United States at Niagara Falls. Tired and ragged, we drove past the Finger Lakes and soon into our home state of Pennsylvania.

We had plenty of stories that we shouted above the din of the perpetual music. Stories of past adventures. Stories of just-completed adventures. And anticipated stories of next year's finale, year three of the Walk Across America for Diabetes. We would head north again on this very route in the motorhome the next April.

With four hours to go, we stopped in Wellsboro to say a quick hello to friends. We apologized for being dirtbag travelers; once again, our last shower had been days earlier. Then we traversed familiar landscapes, ones John and I had walked on during my multiple sclerosis walk to Allentown a few years prior. My kids laughed at how ragged and rugged we looked as we crawled out of the vehicle. My wife just shook her pretty little head. The itinerant wandering fools and saints had found their way home again.

Chapter 14

Walking My Way Back Home and on to the Ocean

"'Michigan seems like a dream to me now'
It took me four days to hitchhike from Saginaw
I've gone to look for America."

— Simon and Garfunkel, "America"

Year three of the Walk Across America began with the drive north, back to the straits of Mackinac and three Great Lakes, though the bulk of the walk would happen along Lake Huron. The drive basically reversed the route of last year's homecoming. My good buddy John was back again, as was Kathie, as she and John both made their third appearances. In my journal entry from April 3, 1999, I wrote:

"The musty smell of the motorhome after a winter in storage, the sight of Pa. highway 61 unfolding ahead of us in the pre-dusk darkening, the sounds of Kathie and John, once again, debating the merits of the physical life vs. the intellectual life, then compromising on the importance of the spiritual life — all of these realms of the senses

— sight, sound, and smell — brought back to me, in a rush, that exhilarating sense of adventure."

John did the lion's share of the driving, tiring around Buffalo. Then I took the wheel in Canada with the heavy early evening traffic in Toronto putting me on high alert. The music, as always, calmed me a tick or two — Willie Nelson, Gillian Welch, or, when I needed ultimate road stimulation, Jim Morrison and the Doors ("Take the highway to the end of the night. Take a journey to the bright midnight").

It was midnight when I pulled over at a rest stop to sleep. The combination of the thrill of being on the road again mixed with the stress of large metro driving caused my blood glucose to spike to 320. I took a correction bolus of insulin from my pump, set my alarm for two hours, and at 2:15 a.m., my blood glucose was slowly easing back to safe levels. In the morning, John rolled us onto the Bay Mills Ojibwe reservation on the shores of Lake Superior, where I did a program guided by the tribe's medicine man. Later, we walked to Point Iroquois Lighthouse in a bitter, driving rain, with both wind and water blowing through our storm gear. The big lake seemed malevolent though it was just Superior in early spring. Next came a drive south and the crossing of the five-mile Mackinac Bridge in very scary wind bursts. In Cheboygan, the Lions Club, who would walk with us the next day, hosted us. The drive had ended. The mileage would now proceed at 25 miles a day.

It was cold and windy on our first walking day. Everyone, including the native northern Michiganders, were dressed as if winter had never left. Sunglasses were a must to cut the glare of a now fully risen sun reflecting off the ice of Lake Huron. We journeyed toward that fire of Father Sun until our paths diverged hours later, the pilgrims to the southeast and the sun arching to the west.

Just like the last year, I decided to sleep on the beach, though this year it was much colder. I shivered with anticipation as I approached our possible campsite at 40 Mile Point Lighthouse. Later, as darkness fell after exploring the beach, I gathered up my warm sleeping bag, ground pad, and other supplies. I could gaze at all the splendors and visions of the night sky, maybe even the mystical colors of the Aurora Borealis. I slept at the base of the lighthouse, the blinking light cutting down on the stars' visibility every 10 seconds. Off and on, the stars filled the sky, and I drifted off to sleep — the sleep of a man who has returned to the tiredness that 25 miles of walking in the frosty air of the north can produce. Though, I also felt I could have watched the sky all night.

I started tossing and turning around dawn. Even in my sleeping bag there was a noticeable chill, with a hard wind coming in off the waves of Huron. When I peeked my head out of the bag, those waves were almost upon me, all the result of a storm blowing in from the north. I grabbed my bag, threw it behind the lighthouse to block the wind, and crawled back in for one more hour of sleep.

Upon waking inside the motorhome and venturing out to the beach, Kathie and John were aghast that the spot where I had been laying was covered in the ebb and flow of the tide. I eventually awakened to their frantic calls and let them know that I had not been carried to a watery grave in the middle of Lake Huron.

***

The shores of Lake Huron were sparsely populated; even the few campgrounds would be closed until Memorial Day weekend. By then, I would be in New Jersey with only a few days left in my walk across America. The beaches were long and a delight to walk upon, especially on the hard sand of a receding tide. P.H. Hoeft State Park was open and gave us some woodland trails as a diversion from the shore. Another long stretch of deserted beach brought us to Rogers City, a resort-type place and the most civilized area we would encounter until Bay City and Saginaw, more than 150 miles away. We passed some huge eagle nests before entering Rogers City.

Two days later, we were in another resort city, Alpena. This city was hopping because of a statewide Lions Club convention, where I would be the keynote speaker. In my speech, I made a few jokes about the Michiganders from the Upper Peninsula, and to balance it, I added a few about the lower Michiganders. I felt the convention needed some lightening up, and everything was done tastefully and all in good fun. But the "oh-no-he-didn't-say-that" look on John and Kathie's faces was worth the risk.

The next day, Kathie hitched a ride with a husband and wife from the convention to the Flint airport, where she flew home. Things were a bit slow in this part of Michigan, and they weren't going to pick up soon, at least until we got further south. But the big lake put on another show for us at Sturgeon Point Lighthouse, where John and I got caught in a sudden snow squall way out on a thin spit of land. It was elemental. Another highlight came when we reached a marker that claimed it was halfway between the equator and the North Pole.

One night in a deserted campground, John and I were so lonely that we took on the voices of Bill Clinton (John) and Ronald Reagan (Me) as we reviewed all the highlights of the Walk Across America since the start back in Washington. I think loneliness was starting to crack us.

At a Lions Club presentation, we met a tall, fiery, redheaded exchange student from Germany. Our slideshow of the beauty of the western parts of America from years one and two must have awakened her nomadic spirit. She told us all she did was chores for the house mother, go to school, and study. She had seen nothing of America. We felt bad for her and agreed that she definitely should see more of the country. I guess we encouraged her too much, to the point that in a miscommunication she thought we had asked her to ride along on our way to New Jersey. We were lucky that we didn't get run out of town. We did feel bad for her, but there was no way that she could have joined our quest. To console her, I suggested that she return one day with friends, rent a motorhome, and see the real America.

On another night, after a program hosted by a retired general, he and his wife asked us back to their house, where he proceeded to tell war stories until 1 a.m. We were so tired and fighting off sleep. John succumbed and lightly snored. Even the general's wife soon nodded off. The poor woman must have heard those darn stories a million times.

After Tawas City, I raced John to the Flint airport, and then it was time for the changing of the guard once more. I would miss John. He was a central character in my quest and in my stories. But I knew he would be back. Maybe sooner than later.

***

Husband-and-wife driving team Julie and Joe joined the walk starting with a Lions Club meeting in Bay City. It was the last we would see of Lake Huron. Then it was on to our last Native American reservation at Isabella. This was our 16th reservation. We did our usual round of programs and took one tribal walk south to the reservation's edges, led by the tribe's medicine man, who carried a holy staff. We were no longer in the wilderness, nor would we be at least to beyond Pittsburgh. The medicine man told a lot of stories, many having to do with the corruption of religion. He took the conversation to another level with a bunch of esoteric ideas, and I could have talked to him all day. The big problem with Christian groups doing good service projects to aid the infrastructure of the reservations was that it came with so much evangelizing. I knew what he meant. I had witnessed this also, first-hand, and had read a lot about it in history. I myself needed no proselytizing or evangelizing.

Joe and Julie brought their own special mix of energy to the Walk Across America. Laughter was a feature, even rambunctious laughter from Julie. We walked through downtown Saginaw, which literally was falling apart, as it seemed half of the houses were boarded up with plywood. Even those wooden sheets were starting to rot and fall off.

"You the man I saw on TV last night," called a man from a decaying front porch, and I nodded. "You the man walking across America." I nodded again. "God bless ya, man, God bless ya."

It was the kind of thing that could carry you for many miles. It started raining just north of Ann Arbor, where we did three programs. Between the cold rains all day and the amount of talking I had been doing, I came down with a bad case of laryngitis. I made it through the second program, but then Joe and Julie took over. They had seen me do five programs in the last five days, knew the drill, and handled the job flawlessly. Michigan flattens out south of Ann Arbor, looking almost like the Great Plains, and our trip there even included a "Wizard of Oz"-like nasty thunderstorm. We scanned the landscape for houses being dropped on witches.

Then we crossed into Ohio, our third-to-last state, and our fourth and last Great Lake, Lake Erie. I had never seen a Great Lake before my walk, and now in less than a year, I had seen four. We walked around the fairly big city of Toledo, including the small bay so I could dip my walking pole into Lake Erie. That was all I was going to dip, as it was still raw and rainy out. Then we went south to be hosted at the Toledo Diabetes Camp for Kids. We had a great time there; the counselors and kids were so welcoming and willing to learn how to control their diabetes so they could one day walk across America or take on their equivalent challenge/adventure/discipline. I got out my list of "50 things I want to do in my life," which I had started when I was 14, four years before I had diabetes. I had accomplished and checked off many things but also added more, so the list never got any smaller. I told the campers that I hoped to die at a ripe old age having accomplished many things, but the list would always be around 50. I encouraged them to start making their own lists. They, too, could live the "life of the list." In another five weeks, on the shores of the Atlantic Ocean, I would check off another major line on my list, but today I also added another: "Go on a tour around the United States just visiting kids' diabetes camps."

Another changing of the guards took place at the Toledo airport. I felt a little bad for Julie and Joe, for it was not one of the most scenic routes on the walk, and the weather was challenging most days. But like all my crew, no matter what section they were on, they brought the fire and grit, the humor and spirit, that kept us moving forward giving me memories that I would never forget.

***

A unique test awaited me at the airport. My dad and younger brother Craig arrived as Joe and Julie flew home. I noticed that my dad seemed troubled, and my brother seemed like he had been dealing with a troubled father. It turned out my dad had tried to bail at the last minute. In the words of my mom, whom I heard from later, she practically had to push him onto the plane. For most of his life, he had dealt with a mild sort of depression. Most days it was barely noticeable. Exacerbating the depression, however, was his other battle with epilepsy, which caused grand mal seizures. He had been diagnosed as an 8 year old after being hit in the head by a baseball. I hadn't noticed this deep of a depression on last year's walk with him in Minnesota. The last few months had started to affect my mom, usually a gregarious and upbeat soul. She had really looked forward to the week-and-a-half vacation from my dad's worsening malaise. Now Craig and I would have to help him deal with it through Ohio.

I have never had much of even a touch of depression. I normally was a high-energy achiever, greeting the day to explore whatever it might bring. Dealing with long-term diabetes could cause a form of depression in most diabetics. Once more, I had empathy for anyone suffering from that. My dad's condition was systemic, however, and passed on through the generations. Even my brothers had had mild bouts with depression.

We had planned to camp out along Lake Erie each night, even on a few of the offshore islands reached by ferries. I now especially felt that a nice lakeside campfire would be good for his soul, but he felt an ongoing chill and was always shivering. I gave him some of my northern Michigan gear to wear, having to retrieve it after packing it away just days before. We talked and reminisced and told bad jokes all around the campfire on a star-filled Lake Erie evening — a father and his two sons on an adventure of a lifetime. But our dad was struggling, searching for something that we knew not what. The Walk Across America had become an experiment in the search for the light, an existential clawing and scraping of the psyche to find the meaning of life itself.

We took a ferry to South Bass Island from Catawba Point. There, my brother and dad rented a golf cart to tour the edges of the island while I walked the shoreline. Unlike Mackinac Island, from last year in Michigan, South Bass Island permits vehicles, but at this time of year they were far and few between. As I walked, I caught sight of the two guys zipping around, following the grid work of roads across the center of the island. Being out in the open air, however, my dad's chill continued, even though, once again, he layered up in my northern Michigan storm gear. At one point, our routes converged on top of a small mound on which a lighthouse spiraled into the sky. Back on the mainland he immediately sought the protection of the motorhome, almost as if the roof and walls could keep him from the demon of his depression.

We had another calming fire that evening on the edge of Catawba Point, the silver-tipped waves shining from the light of the near-full moon. It was quite a peaceful setting, but dad still wallowed in the mud of his cynicism. Tomorrow would start a series of Lions Club meetings and walkalongs, plus some TV and print media engagement. I hoped that might pull him from his funk. Though I was optimistic, I knew that difficult days lay ahead.

For many years, the byproducts of my dad's depression and epilepsy were seasonal light disorder and wicked pessimism. He talked at times of wanting to escape his mind, usually by engaging in some sort of labor-intensive activity. That was one of the reasons why, after 44 years of hard labor in an iron foundry, he came to work for me the day after he retired. He enjoyed reading and studying the Bible and going to church, but during these bouts of depression, he radiated no sense of spirituality; his cynicism crowded out any life force. He never lashed out or exploded into violence, instead moping along to get through the day. Of course there were times of brightening when we could discuss professional sports or the Bible, his two religions, but even there he started concentrating on the negatives. Hopefully a period of brightening was on the horizon.

A group of men and women with the valor of warriors and the hearts of lions and lionesses appeared on the bleak horizon. The first wave came in the town of Port Clinton, where members of the Lions Club met us on the sun-drenched shores of Lake Erie. My father crawled from the cold chambers of the motorhome into the sunlight. He was intrigued by the laughter and conversation found when Lions meet. They talked of life in Sandusky County, Ohio, which then was interwoven with talk of my father's life in Berks County, Pennsylvania.

The thing about Lions Club International is that it had some of the same goals surrounding diabetes that I did. For them, it was ending blindness around the world, and the leading cause of blindness is diabetes. We continued into Sandusky, where we rode a roller-coaster at Cedar Point as they tested it for the grand reopening that weekend. Then came more Lions Club meetings in Vermilion as we walked closer to Cleveland. My dad was rallying, maybe seeing a little light at the end of the tunnel. Sometimes when that happened, he would pass that sliver of light off as mere illusion. But he did admit that he noticed the sliver. I thought of a quote by Carl Hammerschlag: "The light at the end of the tunnel is not an illusion, the tunnel is."

Just before the big city, I walked out on a dock where a fishing crew was coming in for the day. The crusty old skipper yelled to me, asking if I was the man walking across America. He had seen me on the news the night before. He exclaimed to his crew, "It takes balls the size of grapefruit to walk across a continent." I returned with, "Thank you, but it actually has more to do with feet, legs, heart, and spirit." He roared out a laugh and said, "Yea, those also," as his crew laughed with him.

Cleveland was a bit of a letdown. On a Friday afternoon, downtown was empty, and later we had trouble finding a place to eat dinner. Cleveland was still climbing out of its post-industrialized past and into its renaissance. My brother and I walked out to the Lake Erie shoreline where the Rock and Roll Hall of Fame was. We did not enter because our adventure budget was tight.

The next morning, I walked out of Cleveland past what was then known as Jacobs Field, home of the Cleveland Indians, heading south toward the airport where another changing of the guard was to take place. My dad was still on a slow upward trajectory, but at least I was sending him home in a better state than when he came out. He even admitted that it would be interesting to continue with me into the western Pennsylvania of a few years ago, when he and my mom crewed for me on my wild walk across the state. Hopefully, my mom had enjoyed her time during this last week and my dad's upward climb would continue a bit longer when he returned home. I was lucky to have my brother Craig's warrior nature to help me ease my dad's early suffering. I would miss them both, but they would see me again somewhere on the path, somewhere along this holy road I was walking upon, seeking redemption and clarity as I set my compass toward the Atlantic Ocean.

***

The next gang of rowdy friends arrived by car. John had only been gone for less than three weeks, and now he drove seven hours with Anna Mae, a mutual friend, along Interstate 80, arriving at Youngstown-Warren Regional Airport, where the next gang of drivers were arriving by air. John and Anna Mae would only be on the walk for two days before heading home. John couldn't stay away from the walk for long, and Anna Mae was always up for anything. Both of them had energy to spare, so a long drive to nowhereville Ohio was not a leap of imagination.

While we waited for the next crew on the airport parking lot, I rolled down the windows and cranked up the music, bluegrass from the Del McCoury Band. We started an impromptu hoedown with Anna Mae calling the "swing your partner" and "do-si-do" and "four hands all around." That is the scene my daughter Adrienne, Barb, and Barb's daughter Jackie landed in. After grabbing their bags, they entered the parking lot and immediately joined in on the hoedown, setting the tone for a crazy but typical few days on the Walk Across America.

After camping at a weird but hilarious Jellystone Park campground near Akron, the walk took me toward Warren, Ohio. We had a scheduled television station interview in a city park near the end of the day. While walking toward the park, I realized a coincidence was taking place. Anna Mae was in the process of recovering from the sudden death of her husband only four months earlier. Their shared vision of a life of travel as they approached retirement was now shattered. Anna Mae's husband's name was Warren. Here in a city in eastern Ohio that shared the name of her beloved husband, Anna Mae was taking one more step in her recovery from deep mourning. The night before, around the campfire, she told us humorous, entertaining stories about Warren's life. Many sages and pilgrims believe that a mythic quest, like the one that I was in the middle of, could easily be used as a metaphor for life itself. If that was true, then one was blessed for the guidance through all journeys, real and mythical, by the ghosts of those who have passed on and by the friendship of those who still walk this earth.

I walked into a thick, stifling air surrounded by the postindustrial ugliness of a city in ruins. Or at least that is what I felt like. I thought of the lyrics of a Bruce Springsteen song: "My sweet Jenny, I'm sinking down. Here, darling, in Youngstown." But once again I was rescued from the doldrums of living in my head by the exuberant nature of my crew. Adrienne was her usual bright light, undercut with a deep sense of satirical repartee. Her high school friend Jackie brought her own brand of some of those same qualities. I would have to elevate my game or accept that I would be constantly dunked on. You would expect that at least I would have Barb as an ally, but sometimes she joined the girls in the piling on.

This was Barb's second appearance on the walk; the first time she saved me in the wilds of Wisconsin. Barb knew the shakedown. We visited her parents in Youngstown, where she had grown up, and they helped put me in touch with the Lions Clubs in that area. Then we crossed the state line into Pennsylvania, at Sharon, continuing through New Castle and Butler, home of Miss Pennsylvania 1996, GiGi Gordon. We had no time to visit, and she was old news anyway. The new Miss Pennsylvania, Mayra Acosta, would join us in a presentation in Lewistown.

We eventually walked our way into Pittsburgh International Airport, where the four of us flew from to a Diabetes Athletes Conference on the shores of the Pacific Ocean in Santa Cruz. There I gave a keynote address and led a walk on the cliffs, which I was familiar with from my coastal walk five years previously. I met amazing, focused athletes with Type 1 diabetes, including Olympic marathoner Missy Elvin Foy. My crew and I had dinner with my buddy and mentor Bob Blackburn, who walked with me during those coastal storms back in 1995.

Though I was in one of my favorite places in the world, I was eager to return to the route of my quest. The conference was stimulating, but the deep power of the Walk Across America for Diabetes beckoned. My pilgrimage called to me from the humid, industrial, polluted hills of western Pennsylvania, drawing me away from the Garden of Eden-like coolness and spectacular, mystical Pacific coast. In a spiritual calling, comfort and scenery are only sugar-free icing on a fat-free piece of cake.

***

I would soon walk toward Indiana, Pennsylvania, through a vast tunnel of springtime greenery. As we left the parking lot of the Pittsburgh airport, driving to the point north of the city where I had stopped before the California idyll, my new driver, DeNetta, was amazed at this show of endless greenery. DeNetta came from the inner and outer deserts of Los Angeles, where she worked with my biggest sponsor, MiniMed, inventors and producers of my Insulin Pump. DeNetta, who also had Type 1 diabetes, served as my liaison to the company. She had never been east and was in culture shock. DeNetta was a blithe spirit, a searching soul, always on top of her game. But she would have to get used to the east, eventually to my buddy John, and to motorhome life on the road.

DeNetta would spit out questions, barely waiting for the last one to be answered before moving on to the next one. "Why are there so few black people in this part of America?" she asked after being stared at in a crowded truck-stop diner. "Why do the mountains bunch up like someone kicked a carpet into a corner?" "Why is there so much roadkill on the highway?" I jokingly told her to stop and throw one of those dead animals into the motorhome, and I would gut it and cook it up for dinner. DeNetta was not amused. She was a deep study into the psychology of the human condition. I got the distinct notion that, with DeNetta, there would never be a dull moment.

I walked on back roads paralleling Pennsylvania Route 422. We would soon follow in my own footsteps from when I walked across the state in 1993. This was not my favorite place to walk through. I had seen so much splendor in the six preceding years that I had to bear down and repeat my mantra, "The goal is the path," to glide through the center of my own state and state of mind. Things picked up in Altoona, where, just like during the Ultra Walk for Diabetes, I presented two diabetes programs in two nights. Dick McCaulife was, once again, the Lions Club extraordinaire who planned and hosted my presentations. He has used a wheelchair since suffering a diving accident almost 40 years ago and was a highly motivating figure for many miles, including the following day when a long trek took me into State College.

While waiting for my extended family, DeNetta took me down the rabbit hole that was the "Life of DeNetta Elmo." She had been an intensely talented track and field runner and hurdler in high school and college. She still displayed that tall, lithe build and attitude of a national-class athlete. Not too long before, she met Muhammad Ali in an elevator at a diabetes fundraiser in Los Angeles. She held her own against the witty repartee Ali was known for and even physically, as they playfully punched and ducked as the elevator doors opened to a now-amazed group of people waiting to enter. DeNetta also met another of her heroes, guitarist Carlos Santana, at one of the many concerts of his she attended. After knowing her better, I began to think of her every time I heard the Santana song "Black Magic Woman." He could have written it about her, for surely she had to have dabbled in the black arts, and probably still does.

***

It was a historic weekend for the Walk Across America as my youngest daughter, Amberly, now 11, along with my 12-year-old niece, Allison, were making their first of many appearances. Both were wired, high-energy personalities with vocabularies way beyond their years, and both had volumes of stories to tell. The sound of silence no longer existed. I did worry a bit that the smooth organization of the inside of the motorhome, and the walk itself, was about to be thrown out the window to be fed upon by the Nittany lions who roamed the surrounding mountains.

The day after that, my lovely trouper of a wife made her first appearance along with my mom and dad. My dad was in a good mood, probably remembering his comical standup routine that he had performed here during my infamous walk across Pennsylvania back in 1993. Nancy said he actually tried out new material to use in the Lions Club brunch presentation that day. My wife and mom talked him out of some of the more risqué material he wanted to use, advising him that it was too early in the day for the blue portions of the act.

Next came Julie for her second appearance. My brother Craig and his wife, Tracy, had brought the young kids up after school the day before. Julie arrived right as the Lions Club brunch ended. It was beginning to feel like a television show: "Bob Scheidt, This Is Your Life!" Who would show up next, John? That was unlikely, as he had only been home for a few days after his stint in Ohio.

As DeNetta and I descended into Lewistown near the end of my walking day, I saw a distant human gliding up the switchbacks toward us. Long before I could make out any recognizable features, DeNetta commented that the figure was, lo and behold, John. I wondered for one second then exclaimed, "Now wait a minute. You never met John." DeNetta said, "I heard enough stories about him that I feel like I know him and can recognize him from afar. Maybe it's some kind of cosmic connection. But I'm telling you, that is John." And indeed it was! My guess is that anyone who hears any of my crazy stories is going to eventually feel like they know John. Because in my life, crazy constantly swirls around me, and it's very likely that John will show up somewhere.

That night in Lewistown, I was serenaded by three Miss Pennsylvania contestants. Miss Juniata County, Miss Centre County and the winner and actual Miss Pennsylvania, Mayra Acosta. Mayra announced that she would dedicate the song she was about to sing to me. It was called "Stormy Weather," popularized by Billie Holiday, and Mayra prefaced it by saying, "I'm sure Bob has had plenty of stormy weather during his walk so far." She was right about that. I had a feeling that we would see and hear from Mayra somewhere down the road.

Meanwhile, we left Amberly and Allison back at the motel. They had seen my slideshow plenty of times. When we returned, the management told us that the kids had been running up and down the hallways in my mom's spare wigs and nightgowns, singing and laughing. They both had loud Scheidt voices. After herding them back to our room, we discovered that they had pretty much trashed the room like rock stars.

***

I followed Route 522 east, stopping to pet kittens at an Amish farm. We now had five vehicles in our contingent and one full-time walker — me. Then we moved on to McClure and Middleburg as more and more cars left to head home. DeNetta had flown home to Los Angeles from the Harrisburg airport earlier in the morning. John had driven her to an airport hotel the night before. I think John was infatuated by DeNetta after only meeting her for half of a day. There was some heavy charisma going on between them.

The following day, I walked into Selinsgrove, where we had another changing of the guard. Everyone had now gone home, but I would not be lonely, for Barb's oldest daughter, Heather, showed up. She brought with her a head full of arcane philosophical knowledge and a ton of theories and postulates. I would not be lonely in the least.

The familiarity of home came rushing back to me as in a dream. I walked through the anthracite coal slag heaps, a light mist touching down. It was much warmer now than when I walked through here many times before. I only had to walk through one more county before I would be back in my home county, Berks.

The night before, Heather and I presented a program at the hospital in Lewisburg. After that, we found a Dairy Queen just moments before it closed, Blizzards of ice cream cooling us in the warm night air. For the next few nights, there were no programs scheduled, as the entire regional Lions Clubs had consolidated to hold one big program in Pottsville. That gave us free time to stretch out to see one of the most unique sites in all of America: the town of Centralia. It was the subject of numerous books, newspaper articles, documentary films, and even a play, all because of a massive evacuation that had happened because of a coal mine fire burning underground. Wisps of smoke smelling of sulfur leaked from cracks in the roads, which were closed to cars but not to cross-country walkers.

Heather was beyond fascinated. This had all the elements to send her searching mind on flights of fantasy, to the possibility that we were as close to Hell on earth as possible. In the humid, sweat-inducing air with that foul smell, it sure could have been Hell. We carefully scanned the cracks for red horns and the sounds of a scraping pitchfork. Long after exiting the ghost town, we were now enmeshed in discussions of good and evil. Heather had just completed her sophomore year at the University of Pittsburgh, where she majored in philosophy. She also participated in the debate team, which was one of the best in the country. Though I often dabbled in philosophy, I was a mere dilettante. To up the ante, we met a teenager as we walked into the Schuylkill County coal town of Ashland. He suddenly emerged from the mist and told us he was heading to the monastery high up on the mountain. He had walked all over Europe, in all kinds of weather and terrain, studying at monasteries and was considered a prodigy among the Catholic priests both locally and overseas. We walked three miles together, and the philosophical and theological discussions amplified and continued unabated. I could have written a book on those three miles alone. Heather considered it one of the best days in her life.

In the city of Pottsville, we received a huge check for our charities at the banquet they held for me. The Coal Region had come through once again. There was so much goodwill coming from Schuylkill County, one of the poorest and hardest-hit areas in the new economy. Its people always supported my charities and endeavors.

Before and after the banquet, Heather and I watched reruns of the TV show "The X-Files" in a motel room the Lions had given us. For the next few days, I was given a tutorial on every component and intricacies of that show. As we walked up to the summit of Hawk Mountain Sanctuary, I not only entered Berks County but also was at the site of the birth of the Walk Across America for Diabetes. It was a humbling moment to think that I was now only nine or 10 days from the finish.

Heather and I had spent the night at the log cabin home of my friends Todd Gladfelter and Cindy Ross. They were world travelers and had hiked all the triple crown trails: the Appalachian Trail, the Pacific Crest Trail, and the Continental Divide Trail. They were always very encouraging to me when I dreamed of big, multi-week adventures. I felt bad that we were too tired to be engaging or humorous around their campfire. It doesn't happen often, but that night, we were burned out.

Heather and I then crossed the Appalachian Trail and climbed the 10 miles, up and back, to my holy mountain, the Pinnacle. The "X-Files" discussions continued. At the vista on top, I could see that lower ridge to the south where I had grown up and longingly looked up at this very mountain. All my origin stories were piling up, memories stacked as high as the slate and granite rocks that were the very reason the ridge still towered after glaciers cleared the valleys during the last ice age. I surged my way toward home, like an ice age myself, sweeping into a campground five miles from Kutztown. The next day, a huge crowd of hometown Lions and Lionesses, friends and family walked with me on roads I had traveled most of my life. Even my mother-in-law and father-in-law were on the route. Downtown, we had a picnic organized by my wonderful friend and trainer, Ina, at the site of her gym, Fitness by Ina. Most of the walkers who had done sections of the Walk Across America were there that day. Five miles of walking was time enough for only a small fraction of the stories waiting to be told. I was back home again.

***

I still had seven days of walking to reach the Atlantic Ocean. Once again, I travelled on familiar roads and trails to Topton, through the Lehigh Parkway of Allentown, where my old walking buddy Louie joined us. Then we moved along the trails of the Lehigh River in Bethlehem and Easton. There, I switched rivers to follow towpath trails along the Delaware River and then crossed a bridge at the site of George Washington's famous crossing into New Jersey. Maybe mine was now the second-most famous crossing.

My crew consisted of John; his two kids, Justin and Ryan; and another of my friends, the professorial Len. It was getting very warm as we closed in on Memorial Day. We swam in the river most days. Then we crossed through the Pine Barrens of southern New Jersey, and soon we could smell, taste and feel the salt water of the Atlantic Ocean. My emotions welled up and spilled out in tears and manic laughter. It was really hot now, and my clothing was soaked through, but I barely noticed it. The end was in sight.

During most of the last few miles, I seemed to be in a haze, almost like watching a man who moved through the hot Jersey air at four miles an hour or seeing it all on a snowy old television screen. That man moved like a metronome, like he had all the way across a continent and across his life. This man was just a simple man. Walking was his thing. Years ago, he was asked by a newspaper reporter about the claim that walking was his artform. And this is how this simple man had framed it: "I want to walk like Miles Davis played the trumpet. I want to walk like John Coltrane played the saxophone." This man was not such a simple man.

Mayra, Miss Pennsylvania, surprised us at the five-mile mark, ready to walk with me to the ocean. Then groups of the usual suspects, having arrived in a bus from my hometown, joined in the walking festivities. It was almost synchronized in the way groups came in waves. The smiling faces of Nancy, Adrienne, and Amberly arrived on foot in different groups, causing me to break down in tears all three times. Linette, my driver back in Montana, showed up, as the number of former Miss America contestants now numbered two.

A bunch of yellow-vested southern New Jersey Lions Club members who, along with Ray and DeNetta from MiniMed, planned the festivities for my finish. First was a set of speeches with two miles to go. Then I noticed a face I had not met personally. I would never forget that look of pure joy I witnessed on the TV, in middle-of-nowhere Michigan, when Nicole Johnson, wearing the same MiniMed insulin pump and touting a platform of education for people with Type 1 diabetes, won the Miss America pageant. Now Nicole was only two miles from where her life-changing event had happened. Now she was here to walk two miles with me to that very spot, to crown me with a crown made of insulin pump composites. I almost felt as if I had won the Miss America pageant.

During the speech segment of the festivities, I was the last to talk. When I got up, I realized the chair had a pool of sweat on it, the byproduct of the heat I had walked through. I winced as Nicole sat down on that chair, so I apologized, but she deflected it and exclaimed, "Of course it's sweat-soaked. You just walked across America." I thanked everyone involved in my quest for the three years it took me to walk. The list was very long, culminating in my biggest thanks to my wife and daughters. Then it was time to head back out for the last miles, led by a marching drum and dance ensemble. I walked with Nicole and talked about the intricacies of diabetes control. She told me that it always gives her hope for the future to see someone of her own tribe, who also fought daily battles with Type 1 diabetes, accomplishing a challenge like my walk.

We reached the sand and waves of the Atlantic as I strode without pause into the ocean water and stuck my walking stick into the salty sea. Three years before, I had done the same in the salt water of the Pacific Ocean. My quest was officially over as cameras flashed and the holiday tourists looked on quizzically. Ray and DeNetta held a MiniMed banner that read, "This Bob was made for walking. Powered and Pumped by MiniMed." Then 20 or so of my craziest comrades and I spread out on the sand, held hands, and sprinted into the cold spring waters, washing off the metaphorical dust and weariness of walking 3,000 miles across the very bulge and bulk of the American continent. Each of those faces told a shared story. We had gained in immeasurable ways the knowledge of how America nurtures the soul of a pilgrim on a quest. Tomorrow it would really feel like we were home, but during those six months of walking, we were always home.

***

Over the next three days after completing my quest, I did a press junket in New York City with John, DeNetta, and Ray. Now joining us was Miss New York, Deanna Herrera. We had to race around the city doing 12 TV, print, and radio interviews. The first one was "Today" at 5 a.m. Ann Curry handled my interview, and I also got to meet the gracious, imaginative, bundle of energy that was Katie Couric. That set the tone for the next three days in which I honestly found myself more fatigued than I had while walking 25 miles a day. And just like those days across America, I was buoyed by my compatriots, especially Miss New York. She also had had Type 1 diabetes since she was young, so that meant that the Miss America Pageant that past year actually had two Type 1 contestants, each with diabetes platforms.

Deanna was a wonderful soul, soothing out the rough edges of this frenzied press junket. There were times during our shared interviews where she picked me up in the middle of a concept I was trying but failing to get across to the media. After three days, we began to finish each other's sentences. The strangest moment came during one of our many taxi drives through the traffic-clogged city as we raced to the next appearance. I was so tired that I fell asleep next to Deana, and my head slowly slid onto the shoulder pad of her couture dress. Then I started to snore. The rest of the crew cringed and tried to wake me up, but Deana shushed them as she whispered, "It's okay that he's tired. He just walked across America."

John and I took the bus home from the big city to my little hobbit hamlet of Kutztown. We walked the mile over the cemetery from the bus depot to reach my house, because what's another mile when you just walked 3,400? What do two old friends of the road, experienced seekers extraordinaire, talk about after all that had transpired during that friendship?

"Well John, we better start planning the next big adventure," I said.

"That's a big 10-four good buddy!"

Chapter 15

Circumambulation

*"I have spoke with the tongue of angels
I have held the hand of the devil, it was warm in the night
I was cold as a stone
But I still haven't found what I'm looking for."*

— U2, "I Still Haven't Found What I'm Looking For"

Were we really going to return to the Pacific Ocean and continue down the West Coast? I had workshopped the idea, researched it, compiled a cost analysis, and proposed it to my corporate sponsorship. The toughest sell of all would be to my wife, she being the angel who sits on my shoulder, with very coherent reasons, and tells me I should say no to walking around the perimeter of the United States. On the other shoulder sat the devils, souls from the past, those intrepid explorers who were my inspirations. They counseled emphatically: "Go forth and prosper." I could totally be sympathetic to the rational view of my wife, but in the end, I sided with those dastardly devils.

The idea made way too much sense to be ignored. Since I had walked a very northern route during the Walk Across America for Diabetes, sometimes very close to the Canadian border, we had only three more sides — 5,600 miles — to complete the journey around the rim or, as the Buddhists call it, a circumambulation. The total would be 9,000 miles for an eight-year adventure. We would have to cover a little over 1,100 miles in each of the five years.

I planned to start in August 2000 and finish in December 2004. Since we would be in the deserts and the deep south, we would do those sections in the late fall to avoid the extreme heat. In a twist, we would switch to bicycles and ride from the western Texas border all the way to St. Augustine on Florida's Atlantic coast. The second twist would involve kayaking the inland waterway from Florida to Atlantic City, New Jersey. So instead of just a walk, we would call it "Adventure on the Rim of America." Early on, I grew less fond of the kayaking idea; I will always be a land animal, a walker. The bicycling was still cogent, because I did bicycle a lot and did not love the southern parts of the United States. I could finish that section more quickly on bicycle. That was the loose plan, and almost everyone who had been involved before, plus a few new crazy people, signed up again, and we were off and running.

We left home at the beginning of August. The two nicest months of weather in Washington and Oregon were August and September. It boded well for being an epic journey down the coasts of those two states. Adrienne was back for her fourth appearance, Jackie for her second, and Chuck, the newbie, for his first. The drive west would be our furthest yet, all the way out to the San Juan Islands. Then we would move on to Washington's mainland to the furthest western point of the lower 48 states at the Makah Indian Reservation, situated at the mouth of the straights of the Strait of Juan de Fuca.

Some of the drive out through the North Cascades would follow the route I walked in 1997, only in the opposite direction. I wanted Adrienne to see the beauty of the Cascades. More and more, during each year's drive out and the return home, I became disenchanted with the Midwest. We sped through everything up to the Dakotas. I know it's bad to call it flyover country; the residents do not like the term. I'm someone who can find enchantment almost anywhere — for God's sake, I found a deep spirituality on a quarter-mile track in southern New Jersey I walked around for six days and nights – but Ohio, Indiana, Illinois, Iowa and Nebraska's landscapes just did not interest me. The people might have, but they didn't seem that interested in us. Bring on the deserts, the mountains, the plains, the oceans, the Great Lakes, and the Native American reservations. That's what I wanted to see!

We rented bicycles to ride on a dirt trail through the Black Hills to beyond the Crazy Horse Memorial and then tour the battlefields of Big Hole in southwest Montana, where the U.S. cavalry slaughtered Nez Perce soldiers, women and children (Chief Joseph survived but could not quite escape, as he was captured just before the Canadian border). From there, we followed the Nez Perce route backward, stopping in Missoula, Montana. During all these stops we walk some miles, still training for the actual big walk, now only days away.

Then, with respect and reverence, we followed the trail onto Nez Perce lands in Idaho, where we spent a day doing programs at the big reservation near Lewiston. Once again, we found that Type 2 diabetes was rampant among the tribes there. We had driven through some wild country along the banks of the Salmon, Lochsa, and Clearwater rivers. After my presentation, we sat with my tribal liaison, Casey, at a picnic table next to the teepee we were going to sleep in. Casey was from the Yakama tribe of Washington, and his wife was from the Nez Perce tribe. As we spoke of spirituality, chronic disease, and sacred landscapes, a sickle moon rose above us amidst a sky filled with stars from horizon to horizon.

Heading north the next day, we drove through Shoshone and Coeur d'Alene Indian lands. The flatlands of Washington gave way to foothills and eventually the mighty North Cascades, where we hiked for an afternoon at Rainy Pass. This was a historic crossing of the Pacific Crest Trail, where Chuck began daydreaming of a future end-to-end hike of the 2,600 miles. Down and off the pass, we encountered the eye-popping, cerulean blue lakes of North Cascades National Park. Then it was a hop, skip, and jump to Anacortes, the gateway to the San Juan Islands, where the walk would begin in the morning.

My crew was spirited and up to the challenge of movement. Adrienne sometimes complained a tad, but she knew that all of the traveling, which she loved, would involve some work and foot mileage. She accepted the tradeoff with goodwill, and I absolutely adored having her with me. I already dreaded the loss of her essence when she would have to fly home to go back to school. I never got used to it.

It seemed that Jackie always was a great friend of Adrienne's and, like her mother Barb and sister Heather, seemed created to do a chunk of each year's mileage with me. Jackie was sharp and had a weird sense of humor that always livened things up.

Chuck worked for me for a few summers while he pursued a fine arts degree in photography at Kutztown University. Then one winter, he told me he was thinking of hiking the 2,100-mile Appalachian Trail. So off Chuck went, starting in Georgia and ending five months later in Maine. He had plenty of tales to tell while working long hours with my crew. In fact, it became a standard for me to choose workers. If you pursue outdoor adventures and journeys, it generally makes you a hard worker, someone used to adversity, and you would bring back stories that made the rest of my workers feel as if they had been with you. Chuck fit the bill. Now we were on a shared adventure in the far northwest corner of America.

***

After driving across a continent, you need to ease into the not-so-subtle shift to covering only 20 to 25 miles a day on foot. If you throw into that mix the need to keep on schedule to honor the commitments to the hosts of my presentations, it can get very regimented. We always had to remind ourselves that this was not a vacation. Sometimes it felt like it would be nice to stay, even for a day or two, in some of the most gorgeous settings on earth. But that was not our life. We were on a quest, and it was almost ecumenical. If you knew that the Holy Grail was hidden in the sands of the 50 or so beaches we would walk on, why would you want to do anything but hunt for it? In effect the grail was, metaphorically, out there waiting to be found. But on the other hand, we did not rush or speed our way to break any records or win a race. The Walk Across America for Diabetes had several goals, but in the end, it was to control my diabetes and inspire and teach others to do the same. I would accomplish that by putting one foot in front of the other for two months for the next few years.

We would walk the San Juans island by island, but in between a ferry would bridge the gaps between them. We planned to walk on Orcas, San Juan, and Lopez islands before heading to the mainland at Port Townsend. The first day, Chuck and I headed south from where another ferry took people to Victoria, Canada. It was mostly flat and easy walking. Chuck was younger than me and used to carrying a pack, but even he could feel the weariness of back-to-back-to-back big mileage days. The ferry rides gave us rest breaks. Chuck's humor was drier than John's, but he exhibited some of the same ability to mimic local accents and folksy dialogue. On the drive across the continent, he did a redneck rant as we drove through Butte, Montana, basing it on stories he had heard from CDT hikers who stayed there for a day or two. Chuck was a self-proclaimed semi-redneck originally from Georgia and now living in Kempton, Pennsylvania, which has the reputation of being outlaw country, so he wasn't exactly making light of anybody. Here, the local accent was hard to detect, but we did hear a lot of Canadian sounds, and since this was somewhat of a touristy area, there was a mix of unusual sounds and language.

Little things enliven your day when committing to just walking. Chuck found a cache of discarded CDs in a ditch just off the road. It was a mix of cheap classical shit and motivational spoken-word stuff, in addition to one Chuck called, with a Freudian slip, "Dolly Parton's Greatest Tits." The only one we kept other than Dolly was Sarah McLachlan's "Surfacing." Then, just beyond was a stack of rubber-banded letters and then a few pornographic Polaroids. During the rest of the walk, we theorized what transpired to cause the dump, and when the girls walked back to meet us, they jumped right in. Maybe someone started a new life and wanted to get rid of old memories? Or was it just a simple case of accidentally leaving them on the roof and driving away? What CDs did this distraught person choose to keep? If you could only keep 10, what would they be? During all this, the miles flew by.

***

We got two bad messages from home in Oak Harbor. First, my friend Linda Pottigeir had passed on after a prolonged battle with breast cancer. I had co-taught Sunday school with her for a few years, and she was the wife of our church pastor. She was a lovely person and a deft teacher. We each brought different skills that blended well during the difficult job of teaching eighth-graders. My wife and parents would represent me at her funeral. Within the next hour, Chuck got a call from home letting him know that his grandfather had suddenly passed on to the next world. Chuck told us stories of how close their relationship was, and so we made plans for him to find his way to the Sea-Tac airport so he could attend the funeral. Eventually, we walked and ferried him to Bainbridge Island, where he took another ferry to downtown Seattle and then a taxi to the airport.

The girls and I headed to the mainland at Port Townsend, and during the next two days traveled through Port Angeles and past the stately, snow-dusted spire of Mount Olympus. We were in the rainforest microclimate, the only one in the lower 48 states, and with it came buckets of rain from the skies and gale-force winds. I forced myself to adjust to it just as the locals had to, especially as the tribal fisherman in boats were jostled about in the wild and stormy seas of Cape Flattery. We were now on Makah tribal lands, where I did a diabetes program and where we stayed in ramshackle but dry barracks. Amazingly enough, they had a shared lounge area where you could watch television, including MTV music videos, so Adrienne and Jackie, when they weren't walking, were happy.

I walked along the cliffs each day and marveled at the salmon boats, the skies continuing to throw down torrents of wetness accompanied by the omnipresent wind. One evening, the elements let up enough for us to have a shared meal outside in a park, where we ate delicious baked salmon that the tribe had caught that very day, the charred black skin of the fish flaking off. We prayed for the journey of the souls of my friend Linda and Chuck's grandfather and their entry into the spirit world during a ceremony, and then Adrienne and Jackie were presented with tribal-made earrings as gifts. We headed further down that wildest of coasts until it was time for the girls to head back home from Seattle, another changing of the guard.

***

Next up as driver/walker was professor Len from last year's segment in Pennsylvania and New Jersey. He was here for some more amazing coastline, lasting through the crossing into Oregon. I was lucky to have a day of walking with Adrienne and Jackie up into north Seattle before they flew home. Then I went down along the docks and piers, remembering four years ago, the day before the Walk Across America began. That already seemed like such a long time ago. I was sad because I missed the girls, but already things were getting better. The Prof was in the house, or at least the motorhome, which in effect is the house.

Our first order of duty was an overnight at the southern edges of the Quinault Indian Reservation followed by a walk through the towns of Moclips and Pacific Beach, which is also a state beach. This is a primal Pacific Ocean landscape with wave-lashed rocks jutting just offshore, littered with driftwood. I eventually cut inland at Ocean Shores toward Grays Harbor and Aberdeen.

Len did all the driving and some of the walking, claiming he would cook some monumental meals. I reminded him that I was happily married in case he was auditioning for the role of my husband. The enchantment faded a bit when, in a moment of irritation, he called me a barbarian because I didn't have a spice rack, save for one small bottle of cinnamon powder. Len relaxed a bit in Aberdeen where he procured a satisfactory spice assortment, complete with a rack, which he installed above the stove. It was his contribution to the Adventure on the Rim of America.

We headed back to the beach, past South Bend and along the inner shores of Willapa Bay. While walking together, we found an old shack on an overlook selling fresh seafood. Since Len had to walk back to collect the motorhome, he could procure seafood of every type imaginable and begin to cook the feast for dinner that night. During the meal, I praised his expertise and admitted that there were tastes I had never experienced before.

"Welcome to the modern world, Conan the Barbarian," Len said.

We didn't have any presentations during this stretch. The few shore towns and villages were lightly inhabited, especially as we neared the end of summer. Back along the mighty Pacific shoreline in Long Beach, Len took a break from cooking, and we ate at Little Richard's House of Pancakes. How could one not eat there? I was entering that phase, a few weeks into walking, my first state almost completed, where my appetite leapt and I started to shed weight.

We started to see a lot of tsunami warning signs since we were on a fault line and at risk in the event of an earthquake. We camped at a trailer park in Seaview, and I could walk off course, heading north on a thin stretch of land to a town called Ocean Park, where I ate lunch, turned around, and walked back. It was some of the best walking I have done anywhere. Flat, on the beach, on hard sand when the tide was out, with sand dollars scattered everywhere. It was luxurious except for the continued tsunami warnings every few miles. I comforted myself, rationalizing it with, "What a great place to breathe your last breaths." In fact, the next day, I walked the same route up and back. It was one of the highlights of the walk so far.

Back at camp, Len told me about his conversation with an experienced long-distance cyclist who was starting a cross-country tour. He saw the man dip his back wheel in the Pacific. Len had entertained the idea of getting into bicycling and asked the rider for some tips, specifically about whether it was necessary to wear padded Spandex bike shorts. The biker laughed and asked Len if he had done any mileage.

"I did a 10-mile ride a couple weeks ago in the heat of a Pennsylvania August," Len said.

The biker asked what he wore, and Len said jeans. The biker asked how that worked out for him.

"I got so chafed that I could barely walk for three days!" Len said.

The biker almost fell off his bike laughing as he composed himself and said, "Get the shorts good, buddy." Len heard faint laughter as the biker rode east into the adventure of a lifetime, across the heart and soul of America. After retelling the story to me, Len said he would get the shorts and then continue to dream of a continental crossing. I told Len that he would find it hard to carry a spice rack on his bike.

Before crossing into Oregon, we hiked the trails of Cape Disappointment and then inland to Chinook. We had to cross a huge bridge over the Columbia River, one of the biggest rivers in America which by now was a raging torrent. Where it empties into the Pacific was also the place where the Lewis and Clark expedition reached the turnaround point and wintered, so this indeed was a historical point both in the past and today, for I would enter my second state on this walk and my 11th on the rim.

The first of many Lions Clubs in Oregon was here to get me safely across the bridge on foot. Traffic was heavy, and I could not have done it without them. Also waiting on the other side was the Volkman family of long-distance biking fame, who I had met in the North Cascades in 1997, travelled with for many days into Spokane, and kept in touch with all these years. They, along with their parents, organized my presentations and fundraising all along the Oregon coast, biked my route and camped with me and my crew each night. The difference this time was that their 2-year-old daughter, Tam, would ride in the trailer with Penny the dog. I was glad Len could meet them, as they bonded over their shared interest in ham radio.

After a Lions Club presentation that afternoon, we stayed in a motel, and the next day I walked through Seaside and Cannon beaches before driving inland to the Portland airport. I dropped off Len, picked up John, and headed back to Cannon Beach. It was a monumental and very tiring day, but it also was the start of one of the most epic and far-reaching stretches of adventure and landscapes I would ever walk on God's good earth.

***

The striking pyramid of Mount Hood faded into the rearview mirror, a most impressive hulk of alpine landscape. John's alter ego, Neal Cassady, appeared as he took the wheel and deftly handled the curves paralleling the Columbia River. It had been a long day of walking and driving for me, and a long day of flying and driving for John. He came alive when, after four years, he renewed his friendship with the Volkman clan, including newbie Tam, at a campground on the beach at Seaside. The next morning, I would begin a two-week walk down that most pristine of coasts, but for that night, we had a lot of catching up to do. We had so many stories to tell that we could have stayed up all night and not gotten through half of them.

Cannon Beach, with its famous rocks rising from the waves, fell under my feet. This scene had been captured in many postcards, coffee table books and calendars. Next came Oswald West State Park, where we camped for the night. It was a small park with unique, almost rainforest-like foliage.

Kelly told us of her fascination with motorhome inhabitants. The vehicles could be large, some 40 feet in length (ours was 19 feet), and were almost always driven by men. They usually towed a car and an electric golf cart, which they used to get around campgrounds. They were scary to bicyclists, more so when the roads were narrow. Kelly has observed that most of the vehicles' inhabitants were overweight because they didn't walk or make too much effort, and she took to calling them "pasty butts" because of their wide girths.

I had two points to be aware of on tomorrow's beach walk, Humbug and Hug. I realized that I need a reliable tide chart so I would not get caught between the two points. Some of the bigger points had trails switchbacking up the sides and descending to the next beach. We later heard that some were ancient Native American trails.

John and I climbed up and over Arch Cape, but it was so foggy that we would only see a few feet in front of us. Supposedly it was one of the more stunning vistas on the coast, so much so that they used a picture of it on the cover of the trail guide. We held the picture in front of us and settled for that, but even the guidebook faded into the fog if we held it at arm's length.

John headed back to move the motorhome forward, and the fog lifted as I continued south into Nehalem Bay. I stopped at a small store and ended up talking to the owner for 20 minutes, leaving me to wonder whether I was becoming John. But I decided no, because John would have talked for an hour. Further on, at Rockaway Beach, the state of Oregon used orange-suited inmates from a nearby prison to pick up litter. I figured that if I ever committed a crime, it would be here where the landscapes were pure splendor.

I saw John walking back toward me at Tillamook Bay and the village of Garibaldi. I felt bad that John had to repeat some sections, but his childlike sense of wonder informed him with the idea that things look different when you witness them going in a different direction.

The Lions Clubs in Oregon planned many presentations over the next week. First came after a drive inland into the Coast Range, where I hung out for a day at Gales Creek Camp, a diabetes camp for kids with Type 1 diabetes, most of whom wore MiniMed insulin pumps. Some of the counselors also had Type 1 since they were kids.

We now had a new feature in the program, a sock puppet show for the younger ages. After setting up for our show, we helped with meal prep for 40 kids and 10 counselors. John had fun flirting with the older women cooks, telling a million stories, totally in his element. Before heading back to the Pacific coast the next morning, we took a two-mile hike with the kids and counselors through towering pine trees, a hint at the redwoods to come.

Another day arrived, and jocks from a radio station picked us up and drove us inland 26 miles. The premise was that a bunch of rock-jock radio DJs and I would walk the 26 miles back toward the tribal casino right on the ocean. If we made it in six hours, we got a $500 check from the casino plus various other checks from organizations, including the Lions Club of Lincoln City, which helped organize the event. I knew I can walk a five-hour marathon, having done it 12 times before. However, I hoped the DJs and their entourage, who would jump in and out at various junctures, could keep the pace. We would stop occasionally for live radio and newspaper interviews, so I would have to keep the pace lively. I really wanted those checks to go to my five charities.

Throughout the walk, John kept up his usual shenanigans, flirting with the women, telling stories, and listening to stories. He surely was the spark plug during any day on Adventure on the Rim of America. And I am eternally grateful for John being John. At one point, he was changing out of his long pants into shorts when one of the women DJs opened the back door. All the other DJs said it was the first time she was ever speechless.

All went well as we approached the finish. We neared the six-hour cutoff point, but I could see the casino and smell the ocean behind it. In fact, one of the women suggested we slow the pace a bit so that we would make a dramatic entrance with a minute left on the clock. We entered the casino doors with half a minute to go. After ceremonies and a meeting of the Grand Ronde tribal members, I was presented with checks totaling $2,000. I was so honored that it left me speechless, and I could barely give my live radio and TV speech. John then met with the tribe and the casino to announce his bike ride across America, which would begin right here at the casino, and they pledged to send him off in the same way they welcomed me.

The following day, I walked to and took part in festivities at the Siletz Reservation powwow. We did programs, and I gave a speech in between dances, though thankfully no one asked me to dance. The next morning, 50 tribal members joined me for a four-mile out-and-back course, which gave me ample time to talk to a bunch of the walkers. After another speech, I was off and walking down the coast, preceded by a 10-mile walk along the wonderful Siletz River, for which the tribe is named. Next came a steep climb up to Cape Meares. We started to notice heavily laden bikes and riders heading south on the Pacific Coast Bike Route. I added that to my list.

Another new feature of our walk popped up in Lincoln City. The Oregon Lions had loaned us the use of their medical testing lab bus, staffed with a driver and volunteer nurses who did diabetes screenings and tested cholesterol, hearing, and eyesight. They drove ahead of us and set up shop in a parking lot in the next town or city, moving ahead once again after we arrived. They also advertised our evening presentations down the coast. This caused crowds of 50 to 150 people to show up at those evening programs. It was a brilliant concept, and I began to dream that we could have something like this for the next four years. The bus blazed a trail through Newport, Waldport, and Yachats. The section after that was a pristine wilderness of huge waves, waterfalls, big trees, and vistas from headland lookouts. It took our breath away. Four state parks and beaches were linked together. The town of Yachats, leading into this area, gave me an eerie feeling of familiarity. I felt like I could definitely settle down in this coastal town one day.

John and I got a sense of something big happening up ahead in the city of Florence. The Volkmans felt it, too. In fact, even Penny the nomadic dog couldn't stop barking, while baby toddler Tam just smiled. We saw our medical bus in the parking lot of a grocery store, which was good since we needed to stock up on food. There was another DJ set up in the parking lot waiting to interview me. As John and I approached, we could hear the radio station playing Tony Bennett.

After the interview, as the number of people waiting for the medical testing bus dwindled, we asked to meet some of the volunteer nurses. And then Skip, Kelley, John, and I were introduced to Janie, a Florence nurse and diabetes educator. Within 15 minutes, she started to enrapture us with stories of her travels, including a rafting trip down the length of the Amazon River, a long walk across Poland, and trekking in the Himalayas among the highest peaks on earth. Her intensity and demeanor reminded me of British blues singer and guitarist P.J. Harvey. She agreed to attend my presentation that night to further delve into the theme of diabetes and adventure. I asked her to give a short talk as part of my program.

That night, Janie showed up with her energy intact, but I also noticed a laidback, soft-spokenness. She knew how to listen to your story even though she had a lot of story to tell herself. Her quietude eclipsed her deep spirit, though eventually her light appeared. More adventures poured forth, and all four of us kept up a barrage of questions, eventually learning that her nomadic tendencies caused rifts with her family at times. All of us shared in that. The janitor of the community hall had to finally "lights out and lock up" the building. The conversation spilled out onto the parking lot for another half hour until finally our energy sagged, and we returned to our campground at Jessie M. Honeyman Memorial State Park.

At least once a year I meet one or two kindred spirits out there in the wide world. Three years ago, it was the Volkmans in North Cascades National Park at the beginning of my walk across America. Now they were present as I met another one. This is one of the monumental aspects of a pilgrimage/journey. The energy of those meetings can carry you many a mile down the road of your current endeavor and beyond, and even down the road of life.

John had to leave to pick up his sister Lisa in Eugene, which she traveled to by bus after flying into Portland. I walked right out of Honeyman State Park carrying enough supplies for 24 miles of beach walking. At the four-mile mark, I came to a river inlet draining into the Pacific. The weather was sublime, with temperatures in the 70s and low humidity as I prepared to cross the river. I walked back inland a few steps since the river had less depth and rush the further inland we went. I took off my shoes and walking shorts and crossed, the water rising to my waist. Upon reaching the far bank, I got out my map and saw that I had three more rivers to cross, almost one every four or five miles. I decided to walk naked the rest of the day. It was a complete wilderness except at either end, so I figured this would be one of the few times I could have this unique experience. I applied suntan lotion to strategic locations, places suntan lotion had never been applied before. The rest of the day went swimmingly. Just as I got a bit warm, it was back in the next river. Up to that point in my life, it may have been my most transcendent walk yet, where no covering impeded the cosmic elements from soaking into all of my skin.

Late in the afternoon, John returned with Lisa in tow. We found all four Volkmans at the campground at Tugman State Park. Little Tam had already become a seasoned traveler, which was good since Skip and Kelly were thinking of doing another transcontinental crossing, which would be Skip's 11th, Kelly and Penny's second, and Tam's first. Everyone got to know Lisa that night around the campfire. She was John's youngest sister and had all the attributes of her brother, lots of go power, and the curiosity to be up for the next experience. She collected experiences and took them back to her classroom, where she passed on the world to her students. She was 6-feet, 2-inches tall and played intense basketball at the high school and collegiate levels. After a tiring day of flying, bussing, motorhoming, and walking, she was asked by the locals if she wanted to take the infamous dune buggy ride across the dunes. Lisa answered in the affirmative without a pause. She truly was up for anything. Three years earlier at the Blackfeet reservation I was given the moniker of "He Who Walks Across Continents." Here on the Oregon coast, I bestowed names to the rest of my crew: John was "He Who Never Sweats." Kelly was "She Who Dances Like the Wind." Skip was "He Who Is Huge in Body and Voice." Tam was "She Who Asks Why." And Lisa I named "Woman Who Slam Dunks."

I approached the end of this coast of dreams, and Oregon had become a major challenger for the title of my favorite state so far. We continued having a full slate of presentations at schools, Lions Clubs, Native American reservations, hospitals, and even senior centers, which took place at noon and included a full meal with leftovers being sent back to our motorhome's refrigerator. One day, we did three programs and I still walked 20 miles. It was both exhausting and exhilarating, leaving us buzzed to the max.

One night, we drove back north to a 24-hour Relay for Life to raise money and awareness for cancer. It seemed counterproductive time- and energy-wise to go off-route like this. In an interview in my local county newspaper, my MiniMed rep and my driver the prior year, DeNetta, told the reporter I had a lack of corporate mindset. Instead, she said, "Bob prefers to look into people's hearts." Janie invited us to attend and asked me to speak about surviving with chronic disease. Once again, we were worn out but euphoric. The fact that we were back with Janie kept us moving forward. Then it was time to say goodbye to her, feeling like she was an old friend already.

As we headed back down to another state park to camp, we stopped for fuel at an all-night yogurt shop. We had been discussing how Oregon state parks rent out octagonal Tibetan tent platforms called yurts. It must have stuck in John's head. When it came time to order our much-needed treat, John was falling asleep while ordering. Lisa and I let him go on just for the pure entertainment value. When the girl working the counter asked John what yogurt he would like to order, he said, "Yurts." She asked him again, and again he mumbled, "Yurts." She told him they did not carry that flavor, and finally Lisa cut in and ordered for him.

We spent a few more days heading down the coast on foot, witnessing resplendent sunsets past North Bend, Coos Bay, and the mystical towers offshore in Bandon to just beyond Port Orford, where we would pick up the trail again the next year just north of Gold Beach.

On the last day of walking, Lisa and I went down a rabbit hole, with the conversation turning to theology and spirituality. She had attended and graduated from a Catholic university, though back home she was very involved with the Lutheran church, similar to my situation though in different locations. When the conversation turned to Eastern religions, Lisa had many questions. Her intellectualism and bright, shining mind helped her to create unique queries. This continued for a big chunk of the day, all enhanced by the sheer, unending beauty of the Oregon coast. The conversation affected Lisa's original idea of what this trip with her brother would entail.

The following day, when we dropped her off at the bus station, she admitted she was impressed. She had thought that John and I were only on the road for kicks and high adventure, and some of that was true. But she had observed how, during the last four years on the roads of America, this had evolved into a spiritual pilgrimage, like the faithful on hajj to Mecca, like the pilgrims on the Camino de Santiago in Spain, like the circumambulation of a sacred mountain by Buddhist monks in the Himalayas. We hadn't yet found what we were looking for, but we were still out there searching.

***

On the long, 3,000-mile drive back home to Pennsylvania, we stopped in to say goodbye to the Volkmans in their hometown in the coast mountains of Corvallis, Oregon. We had created lifelong memories and cemented deep bonds with them, and we would always remember these magical days on the big Oregon coast. Then we made another stop at the base of the mighty Cascades, where John and I climbed to the top of South Sister, Oregon's third-highest peak. From the volcanic top, it felt like you could reach out and touch Middle Sister and North Sister. John's wandering mind caused him to utter, "Once you've been on one sister, would you always wonder what the other sisters were like?" The blue sky was so clear that, looking north, you could see the snows of Mount Jefferson, the Fuji-looking cone of Mount Hood, and even the rubble of Mount St. Helens. That night, our campsite was draped in a firmament of twinkling stars as Oregon gave us her last goodbye.

On into Idaho we went with two quick stops in mind. First was a hike around Redfish Lake in the Sawtooth Mountains. Later in the day, we visited Ernest Hemingway's last home in Sun Valley, where he ended his lifeforce in an act of suicide. The wheels of our old beast of a motorhome rolled on through Utah and Wyoming. The beast experienced some bucking problems, so we cleaned the carburetor and air filter. It worked for a while, but the long, slow passes of Wyoming's Great Basin Divide strained the engine. Things smoothed out a bit along the Platte River of Nebraska and then on through Iowa. We only moved toward home then, no longer looking to hike, sightsee, or anticipate anything but our destination. I had now been away for eight weeks, but even during the hustle and rush of "just going home," we maintained a sense of adventure and pious wonder. Under the archway in ole St. Louis my cell phone rang. It was Janie, who felt she must tell us something.

She told me, "I am a deeply devout Seventh-Day Adventist who fasts, prays, and worships from sundown on every Friday till sundown on Saturday." I replied, "That's fascinating, John and I love to read and discuss theology, even, or maybe more so, from religions we are not familiar with."

It turns out Janie wanted to join us next year for a part of Adventure On the Rim of America along the California Coast. She would bring valuable skills and energy, and we in turn would accommodate her spiritual needs. However, we would not deviate from the diabetes journey we were on. Raising awareness and demonstrating what a person with diabetes could accomplish was not our religion, but it was the quest we were in the midst of.

We rolled straight through Illinois, Indiana, Ohio, and the long breadth of Pennsylvania, back into the loving arms of our families, barely even thinking of our just-completed adventures or those of the years to come. But after a few days home, it all began to bubble to the surface once more.

Chapter 16

The Enchantments of the Empire by the Sea

*"No I'd rather go and journey
Where the diamond crescent's glowing
And run across the valley
Beneath the sacred mountain
And wander through the forest
Where the trees have leaves of prisms
And break the light in colors
That no one know the names of."*

— The Byrds, "Wasn't Born to Follow"

We have begun a new ritual, a sacramental ceremony before leaving on the next stage of our eight-year journey. It included invocations from standard Lutheranism, Catholic mysticism, Buddhist compassion, and Native American wisdom. This year, year five, would involve two days on the Oregon coast and then six weeks along the California coast to Santa Monica. The long drive west would loosely duplicate the route John and I drove to get home the year before. John was back, again but that's where the norm ended.

There would be many new fellow adventurers, a slightly newer and larger motorhome, and 850 miles of an entirely new state. We looked forward to the new while still maintaining and celebrating the best of the old.

Husband Larry and wife Dianne came along for the ride west. They were old in years, middle-aged in body, and young in mind and spirit. Dianne had a dry wit about her, and Larry's was even dryer. The first half of any drive west was so drab that we needed all the humor and wit we could get. W.E.B. Du Bois said, "The history of the world is the history, not of individuals, but of groups." And to parallel that, a quote from Paul Rosenfield: "Complex works of art speak not through individuals, but ensembles." I liked to think of my Adventure on the Rim of America as both history and art, and I gathered a vital group in my motorhome. It was time to let the creation begin.

In South Bend, Indiana, we pulled into a truck stop for gas. I ran inside to peruse the musical choices of cheap CDs and found plenty of Ted Nugent, patriarchal country music, Molly Hatchet, and Lynyrd Skynyrd, to name a few too many. Music to torture foreigners with, and us, too. Somewhere in Iowa, we camped well off the road, and at dusk I walked down a lonely dirt road onto an overpass above Interstate 80, where I looked back east under a starry sky, thinking of my family. I missed them already. Then I turned and faced west, and the possibilities of the adventures to come elevated my heartrate.

Just before crossing the Platte River in Nebraska, Larry braked hard as a car pulled out in front of him, and the entire roll of paper towels unrolls like a parchment scroll from the back of the kitchen all the way to the front of the motorhome. Finally, right before crossing into Wyoming, we saw our first butte. That meant we officially were in the west. Next up for our viewing pleasure were the distant, jagged towers of the Wind River range. My buddy Todd, who had seen mountains all over the world, said he believes the Wind Rivers are the most beautiful. We went for a short hike along the Green River, Edward Abbey's eternal river of no return, right before it flowed into orphic Utah. We moved into Mormon country and stopped in Salt Lake City, where John, Dianne, and Larry went on a tour of the Mormon complex and cathedral. I chose to see an upcoming bluegrass folk band called Nickel Creek in a bar. To each his own spirituality.

In Nevada, we presented a short diabetes program on the Pyramid Lake Paiute Tribe Reservation and then rolled into California to give a diabetes presentation near Sacramento for a Lions Club. They invited us to give the keynote presentation at a northern California conference a few weeks down the road. Heading north toward Oregon, we sailed by Mount Shasta, the furthest south of the indomitable, cylindrical, volcanic spire towers. Snow wisps spun off her summit. After crossing into Oregon, we voted about how to drive over a mountain. I voted for staying on the interstate, which would take us two and a half hours to get to the coast at Gold Beach. The other three voted to cut time in half and follow logging road shortcuts. It turned out to be so rugged with steep descents that we burned out the brakes, which would have to be fixed the next day. At the Lions Club presentation that night in Gold Beach, the members shook their heads and exclaimed that us eastern flatlanders should learn to never take the logging roads lightly, especially in a motorhome. That's why I voted no!

 I officially began the walk south at Gold Beach with Larry and Diane in tow. Meanwhile, John got the breaks repaired, feeling a little guilty for voting yes to taking the shortcuts the previous day. If the procedure took longer than a day, he would have to rent a vehicle to move our gear and presentation equipment to get ahead of me. Other than that problem, I was in a fantastically upbeat mood, back in my element, riveted to be back on the Oregon coast. I would miss the Pacific Northwest, but I simultaneously looked to California with an anticipation that sent my heart racing.

 Just south of Golds Beach, we witnessed another of those seminal scenes of the Oregon coast where seven sentinel rocks rose from the Pacific, all within a half-mile of walking. It was so stunning that I forgot to photograph it, which was great since I then had to walk back and shoot it. I could have done that stretch all day long.

 For our last night in Oregon, we stayed at Whaleshead Beach Campground, where Diane and Larry were treated to their first Oregon beach driftwood campfire. Oregon sent us into California with a gorgeous, pine tree-lined path that looked spooky in the morning mist and fog. We quickly passed through Brookings, and a few miles later, we entered the state in which we would walk for the rest of that year and for part of the next year, a total of 1,000 miles — a landscape where dreams are conjured and walked through, a coast where surely the Holy Grail would be found.

***

Our introduction to the California coast was a big ol' wooden, landlocked schooner. Then came Crescent City, where the California we all know and love shows her beautiful face, with beaches, lighthouses, big waves, cliffs, year-round flowers, and, of course, surfer girls. Even the fresh scent differed from Oregon, not better or worse, just different. Toward the end of our walking day, we skimmed the edges of Five Mile Beach. Later, the sun set like a fireball, leaving the sky full of embers that contrasted with the bluish-purple of the inevitable night. A lone surfer carrying his board for his last ride of the day entered the waves with the cinematic panorama of colors all around him and a huge rock monolith rising in front of him. I shot a photo that turned out to be the masterpiece of my wanderings so far. I slept outdoors on the ground with the sweeping beam of the lighthouse for my only companion. Sometime a few hours before dawn, the skies rained down, sending me into the motorhome. The wetness lingered into my walking day and then cleared as I traveled inland toward giant redwoods. In the afternoon, we walked through Del Norte Coast Redwoods State Park and Trees of Mystery. If this continued down the entire coast, our capacity for wonder could become overused and burn out. Or, more likely, we would stack the revelations one upon the other until we attained nirvana.

We got a phone message with directions and an invitation to a private campground. Upon meeting a Chile native named Marcella, we also received a great meal of fresh-baked salmon, a bottle of Chilean wine, and an invitation to do our puppet show at her daughter's school. The girl, Tiffany, was a fast learner and helped John work the puppets as I did the narration the next day. The show told the story of our walk from the last four years with a simple diabetes message backed by my old "50 things I want to do before I die" list. The puppets of the characters we met along the way were rather crude, having been made by hand in a New Jersey campground near the end of year three.

We also had amassed a collection of all the animal wildlife we met along the way. They were miles ahead of the sock puppets, but who's counting the miles? We stayed a few nights with Marcella, her husband Bill, Tiffany and Bill Jr. The elder Bill was a commercial fisherman on the Klamath River, which we hiked along for many miles to where it emptied, just beyond the redwood forests, into the Pacific. We engaged in evening campfire discussions with these new friends, who by the time we left had become old friends. This truly was a place of big medicine.

More big medicine presented itself inland on the Hoopa reservation, in what looked like Bigfoot country. I wore a size 13 running shoe, so I hoped no one tracked me. The reservation school where we presented sat on a bluff overlooking the Trinity River. We hiked through towering hillsides of pine, first with tribal members and then on our own. It reminded me of the Black Forest Trail back in Pennsylvania. We passed an ancient earth shelter village where the spirit world was sensed. Then we headed back to the coast, where we hiked through Patrick's Point State Park, now known as Sue-meg State Park, and saw a huge bull elk off in a meadow. The next day, we bought an elk puppet and added it to our show.

The coast there had pullout parking areas for surfers to get to the big waves, and those pullouts gave us splendid, awe-inspiring vistas. While waiting in the motor home for the rest of us to hike in, Diane witnessed other sights, that of surfers changing out of their wetsuits. She claimed that after those rear views she barely remembered the glorious vistas of the Pacific. Next up was the town of Trinity. I was led there by the sound of elephant seals barking.

In Arcata/Eureka, Larry and Diane's two-week tour of duty came to an end. Like all my crew members, they contributed to my quest and journey with their unique brand of humor, knowledge, and inspiration.

***

John and I now had a novel adventure to challenge us: driving 125 miles south to Oakland, where I would give the keynote speech at the big Lions Club conference we were invited to during the drive out. We then would have to return north to resume walking. The Lions claimed they will make it worth our while in donations to our charities. Thank God my good buddy John was here to take the wheel. When John was there, everything became an adventure

The conference went well, and the checks would be mailed (my wife handled the finances for the walk). My friend Julie, who drove for me in Michigan, showed up in Oakland. Then we were three, and after a walk around downtown Oakland, we headed back north. Julie expounded on why she would fly all the way west from the East Coast and then travel north by motorhome for a few more hours. She knew where we were heading: Avenue of the Giants, one of the most concentrated bands of giant trees in the world. It took us two days to walk them, end to end. Just sleeping among them that night was magic. You could feel the majesty and wisdom both in dreams and in waking, and of course during the next two days spent walking.

The mists of time permeated the forest. Occasional showers drenched us. But there among the living, breathing trees we did not complain. All this moisture that drifted in from the Pacific was why those trees grew so stately. After walking among them all day, we, too, felt that we were growing. On any adventure you expect some, if not many, days of rain. There it added mightily to the atmosphere and to the mood. The sky-high treetops hid and revealed as they shivered a bit in the breeze. Sometimes we shivered as well, not from the dampness but from something unseen, possibly something from the spirit world or the animal world, bears or mountain lions. And, yes, we were still in Bigfoot country. What we reasoned those shivers were, after two days of walking among the redwoods, was pure and simple: a sense of awe.

***

The Forest Service campground showers were under a foot of water. Julie was a tough egg and decided to brave them anyway until I remind her that Bigfoot might be using them. The rain continued into Garberville, Humboldt County, the logging, hippie, marijuana capital of the United States. All three of those personality types lived there in harmony because most inhabitants were usually all three rolled into one. Railing against one part of the holy trinity was a bar that had crude homemade signs stating, "No patchouli allowed." There in Garberville, they did not judge you for your appearance, politics, or religion — only for your fragrance. Julie, either in an act of defiance or solidarity, tore down one of the signs as we exited and then pasted it in the motorhome. She claimed it was just a souvenir and memory of these high times.

The three of us jelled well together. The laughing rarely abated, and no one ever complained. We looked for Julia Butterfly Hill, the "save the giant trees" activist who climbed up and lived in redwoods and sequoias so the timber companies couldn't cut them down. John and I had met her at a presentation at a college back home and both fell in love with her spirit. When she was not high up in a tree, though, she was on the road.

Continuing the walk south, Julie and John took turns driving and walking with me. Pacific Coast Trail cyclists on gear-laden touring bikes passed us, battling the hills and wetness. We came out of the forest and hit a long stretch of road right on the shores of narrow beaches. This eventually led us up switchbacks and canyon-spanning bridges. By the time we reached Fort Bragg, we are dripping in exhilaration.

Two more pilgrims then joined the party: Julie's husband, Joe, also from the Michigan portion of my walk from two years earlier, and Janie from Florence, Oregon, and the prior year's walk. The conversations began in a bar on a bluff overlooking the Pacific and lasted into the evening. I knew it would be lively because both Joe and Janie wore their spiritual convictions on their sleeves. In contrast, for the last four days, Julie, John, and I barely broached the topic of religion. But evidenced by the revelatory call Janie made to me on the drive home from the previous year's adventure, she would have some catching up to do. And Joe was not a slouch when it came to proselytizing. He was the cantor back home at his reformed church and a trained gospel singer. Julie, John, and I buckled up and watched from the cheap seats. Since we were all tired and imbibing in a wee bit of demon alcohol, not all of the discussions were processed. But we all heard in plain English when Janie trumpeted her claim that the Pope was the anti-Christ. I shut it down right there, and we all took a nighttime walk along the Pacific, the crashing waves asserting their godhead as Julie and Joe peeled off behind us to amorously make up for the last week they had spent apart.

We had entered Mendocino County. Sleeping would be tight in the little traveling home of ours, so I slept outside in my sleeping bag, never minding occasionally awakening to the sounds of the peeling breakers. The next day our four walkers and one driver rolled south along the never-ending oceanside show. Russian Gulch State Park, Van Damme State Park, Manchester State Park — each beautiful in its own way — passed by at our slow but steady pace. At Point Arena Lighthouse, Janie and Joe walked on a precarious spit of land out onto the ocean. Then the ground started breaking away and tried to drag the two daredevils with it as the heavy waves crashed. All five of us breathed a huge sigh of relief as they made it back to solid land. These two may have had different forms of religion, but my guess was that both prayed to the same god as the bedrock earth tore away beneath them. We crossed into Sonoma County at Gualala Point and continued past Moonrock, Fort Ross, and Wrights Beach. At Bodega Dunes Beach, Joe and Julie headed home. Joe's time was short but spectacular, and Julie's longer time was beyond spectacular. Both were already talking of next year or maybe the year after that. In my mind, this adventure would continue till the day I died. And since I didn't plan on dying soon, we all had plenty of time for many more adventures.

***

We were soon approaching the San Francisco portion of the walk, the halfway point of the year. My family would arrive the next day, the Thanksgiving holiday. The night before, John, Janie and I camped on a far-reaching point of land, Point Reyes Lighthouse. There wasn't a soul in sight as the fog came down heavily, causing a kind of whiteout. You could hear the Pacific but not see it. Every step was calculated because I knew, from talking to rangers, that these waters were rife with monster sharks. At dusk it became eerily dark. We thought it would be cool to go to the beach, but you could barely see your hand in front of your face. Even going to the park bathrooms was a spooky excursion. Janie made John walk with her to the bathroom, almost causing an awkward moment when she heard footsteps and doors slamming yet saw no one. John, a true gentleman, asserted his comforting presence, carrying a can of grizzly bear spray from Glacier National Park in Montana without entering Janie's stall. Were those sounds made by the spirits of drowned fishermen or the spirits of shark attacks? There was no way to tell if anybody alive or dead was on that point. Would bear spray work on ghosts? Personally, I think that incident served to further bond John and Janie.

The next morning on Thanksgiving day, the atmosphere had cleared, and thank God, because it was an extraordinary vista looking beyond the lighthouse where the Pacific crashed onto rock islands. We dropped into Stinson Beach, an old hangout for the beat writers and the Grateful Dead. Then it was up and over the Marin Headlands to the Golden Gate Bridge, where I met my family, who walked from the south as I came from the north. That sounds so romantic, like something out of the pages of a mythical novel. In actuality, my family — wife, daughters, niece, and a friend — had reunited with me the night before, tired, cranky, suffering from motion sickness and yet still manic (at least the kids were). But for epic storytelling purposes, let's say we met on the bridge.

We were a gang of eight now. My wife had been on three short stints so far, two in Pennsylvania and one in New Jersey, the same as my youngest daughter. My oldest, Adrienne, was here for her sixth appearance. It was old hat for her. She was on break from her first semester at Susquehanna University and thrilled to be on the West Coast again. Our friend Jackie was in her first semester at the University of Pittsburgh. She was here for her fifth appearance. It was a tossup for who was more thrilled to be in California, although future California girl Jackie might have won that distinction. And my niece Allison was here for her third tour of duty. When her and Amberly teamed up, trouble usually brewed, just like two years earlier during the walk in Lewistown.

For my good buddy and mentor Bob to open his house on a holiday to a ragtag gang of eight was beyond generous. His wife, Barbara, and their children and grandchildren also were present. He lived in the Oakland hills and had walked with me seven years prior when I trekked from San Francisco to L.A. amid strong coastal storms. I had rarely met anyone as eclectic, and inspiring, as Bob. He was one of a kind. After the big family dinner, we swam in the pool, and many were the stories that were told that night around a fire with the lights of the Bay Area spread out below us. It seemed like a mini homecoming for me.

During the next couple days, the gang walked around San Fran then down the coast, first on Ocean Beach and then up the cliffs and down the beaches of Montara and Half Moon Bay. My family's short time there had come to an end. We said our goodbyes, emotions running the full gamut, though I would be home in three weeks. John drove them back to the airport while also picking up our next pilgrim, then met me down the coast as I walked toward Santa Cruz. Monterey, Carmel, and Big Sur were waiting to dazzle us. The challenge here on the Pacific coast was how to take in all that beauty without being completely overwhelmed.

***

Dave was back for his second tour of duty. He had walked with me in Idaho and western Montana during my first year. I had felt bad for him back then since he had just missed Glacier National Park. But with these Pacific Ocean landscapes looming, he was going to level up for sure. The wonders began in Pescadero State Beach, Pigeon Point, and Año Nuevo State Park and continued as we walked inland to the giant redwood trees of Henry Cowell Redwoods State Park. One great feature of walking among the giant trees was the soft, pine-laden trails. Although it had the occasional root, it might have been the best walking surface in the world.

Dave entered the fellowship seamlessly, always up for a challenge. He also was stoic about the less-than-ideal living conditions that John and I were, after almost five years, fully indoctrinated to. Dave had only one request, and that was to drive inland to a hallowed climbing area called Pinnacles National Park. Dave and his son, Kyle, had climbed Devils Tower National Monument in Wyoming and City of Rocks in Idaho, and they had their sights set on the big walls of Yosemite.

Another seven miles of coastal heaven brought us to one of my favorite places in the world, Santa Cruz. It wasn't just about the scenery, which was spectacular, but also the vibe — the surfer shacks, the old motorhomes in parks on the periphery, the beachside amusement park that looks like 1950s Americana. I hoped that it would never change. John accompanied Dave inland to the Pinnacles, so I was left to wander over every inch of Santa Cruz. What I found was the beginnings of the change. Big money was trickling in from San Jose and Palo Alto. The tech industry would need a respite from grueling workdays, and Santa Cruz as it then existed may not have been good enough. So I spent the day soaking it all in with the wonder of a child who also knows that he is growing up and will have to uproot to other wonders or stay and fight for what he wants to preserve. Maybe a bit of both.

The climber boys returned with their bodies undamaged and spirits invigorated. The walk proceeded south slightly inland through the vegetable fields of Castroville. Then it was back to the beach on a bike trail paralleling 17-Mile Drive in Monterey. Luckily, the famous golf course was empty and so we could walk upon the greens, for no other reason than to be incendiary. That night, we slept in a shopping center parking lot in Carmel and waited for a visit from Mayor Clint Eastwood to talk cinema and jazz but never politics. Dirty Harry never showed. During the night, a storm front blew through with a wind-driven rain sounding like the hoofbeats of 1,000 horses ridden by the

Spanish conquistadors on the roof of "Ragged Glory," newly named by Dave. It reminded me of six years previously when a series of storms washed away the bridge into Big Sur. This storm was short, so I was able to cross the bridge to walk along the northern end of Highway 1 in Big Sur. I prepared myself for the enchantment, finding the reality far exceeding even my imagination.

Dave rented a bicycle in Carmel with instructions to meet me in Point Lobos State Reserve, the first of the parks heading south. So, our triumvirate traveled on foot, on bike and by motorhome. Dave had a bit of trouble finding us, and when he asked for help, he mistakenly asked for "Los Lobos," which was a Tex-Mex rock band. Everyone told him that the band was not scheduled to perform anywhere that they knew of. Finally, we all connected, and at our break, we blasted a Los Lobos CD out the windows. Everything came full circle.

Big Sur is one of the phenomena of the world. It consists of 90 miles of twisting, winding roads on cliffs above the wild Pacific. It has occasional pullouts where you can park to take in the extraordinary scene. The mountains rise behind the road and lead to inner wilderness. The distance is divided up by parks and state beaches. Then, to top things off, when you get to the end, you see a castle high up in the hills. The Native American holy men called it a place of big medicine.

When we got to Big Sur, we crossed the infamous Bixby Creek Bridge, an engineering feat, a work of art, the star of many movies. It may be the most stunning 15 minutes of walking I have ever taken, challenged only by the North Cascades, the top of Going-to-the-Sun Road, or my walk down the aisle when I got married. Only three respites appeared from this sensual bombardment: the beer and the barmaid in the only bar within 90 miles, and the Marc Chagall paintings in a Big Sur art gallery.

A bit further on, a luscious waterfall poured lime-green water into the cerulean blue of the Pacific. More points to measure progress appeared as we walked south: Lucia, Ragged Point, and finally the exit at San Simeon and Hearst Castle. Finally, after four days of walking, I could finally catch my breath. Walking the length of Big Sur will be one of the last things, after family and friends, that I will remember on my deathbed.

Dave headed to his home back east, taking a bus from San Luis Obispo to Los Angeles International Airport. I bought some more music in San Luis Obispo, including an album that would immediately become the cinematic soundtrack to our journey down the Pacific, Wayne Shorter's "Native Dancer." I had always been a huge fan of Wayne's many musical periods and incantations. The gala rhythms and Brazilian voices performed on "Native Dancer" still take me back to these weeks on the Cal coast. John and I hung out with the surfers at Morro Bay and camped at the nude beach in Pismo Beach. I can honestly say we didn't see any nudes, but I can't honestly say that we didn't look.

We walked into Santa Barbara County, veering inland a bit between Guadalupe and Gaviota. Then we found the bike path that ran on top of the cliffs, with drops to the Pacific, from Refugio State Beach to beyond El Capitán State Beach. We thought that after leaving Big Sur our sense of fascination would be ruined. Yet here more magic was present. Next, we moved on to one of the most beautiful cities in the world, Santa Barbara. The inland mountains rose above the piers, and red-tiled roofs made us feel as if we were on a movie set where we were the stars. Then, two movie stars showed up: the glamorous Barbarrific and her traveling sidekick, the Angel Gabriel. Barbara was there for her fifth appearance, and when people back home asked her where she was traveling to, she said "Santa Me!" Gabriel was one of my best friends and lived in New York City. He occasionally would take the bus south to Kutztown, where he would work for me, sometimes for weeks at a time. My wife and kids also loved Gabe for his humorous take on anything and his high spirits. Back in Kutztown High School, Gabriel played the male lead in every musical production, singing, dancing, and especially joking his way to stealing the show. In New York, he was still finding his way by doing stand-up, auditioning, and attending acting classes. He immediately started interacting within our close circle and beyond with people we met along the way. Barbarrific and Angel Gabriel would be with John and I for the rest of the walk to Santa Monica and the entire drive back home. This would truly be a time of high adventure.

Barb commanded the motor home as the three guys walked south along more beaches, including Summerland and Carpinteria, where we soon crossed into Ventura County. On the beaches we walked three abreast, a spiritual and creative triumvirate equal to any in the history of people walking the perimeter of America. Toward evening, we did chores at a grocery store, a laundromat, and beach-side showers, where we camped for the night at Emma Woods State Beach. "Surfin'

USA" became our siren call as Ventura Beach lasted for miles and miles. This spot had some of the best waves on the coast. Then we drove inland and on U.S. Route 101, the Ventura Highway, blasting, what else, but songs by "America," including "Ventura Highway." An inevitable southern California traffic logjam brought us to a standstill, but soon we were in front of the towers of MiniMed Corp., makers of my insulin pump. We parked and participated in a marketing meeting where we added our two cents. Next up, we piled into two cars and were hauled to Children's Hospital of Los Angeles. With the city in perfect view, I felt like singing out the window to a girl walking by, echoing Jim Morrison's alliterative lyrics: "Are you a lucky little lady in the City of Light? Or just another lost angel?" At the hospital, we presented our puppet show and hung out and played with the kids, who had a wide range of medical troubles. One little girl told us it was the best puppet show she ever saw. One day, that little girl may be a famous, oft-quoted movie critic, never to be satisfied because our phantasmagorical puppet show spoiled anything to follow in her life.

Even though I had been in the state a multitude of times, it still amazed me how everywhere I went in southern California, the songs of musicians popped into my head. The next day's walk took us past Zuma Beach (Neil Young), Point Dume (Bob Dylan), Laurel Canyon (Joni Mitchell, the Mamas & the Papas), and, later, Sunset Boulevard (the Eagles, Beck, Tom Petty), the Whisky a Go Go (the Doors), and any of the beaches (the Beach Boys). We walked past McGrath State Beach, Oxnard Beach Park, and Leo Carillo State Beach, where we crossed into Los Angeles County.

On our last evening in California, we slept at the most expensive campsite of our five years on the road. Set on the side of a hill overlooking the ocean on the northern fringes of Malibu, it was worth every penny, even including the weird assortment of characters inhabiting the hot tub, some of whom were buck naked, others sporting nipple rings. Gabe jumped in, sans suit, while John and I wore our shorts. Barb stayed away, claiming we all were going to get E. coli and die before reaching home. We were in Malibu but still not among the beautiful people.

Gabe and I had climbed down a steep bank with our sleeping bags to camp on a small bluff with a view and the sounds of the mighty Pacific and Highway One. We sat up talking most of the night, subjects of deep mystery and global reckoning. The arts, philosophy, metaphysics, Carl Jung and Joseph Campbell, Henry Miller and Pierre Teilhard de Chardin. It was cinematic and novelistic, one for the ages, and it set the stage for us to exit and begin the epic journey back to our homes.

On our last day of walking for year five, we met Robert Downey Jr., and talked a bit with him. Later, in front of Pacific Palisades, in a flowing hooded cape, we encountered an ethereal Nicole Kidman.

We visited the pier at Santa Monica, acting a bit like tourists on the beach, and then we drove east toward the late afternoon, up and over the San Bernardino Mountains as night fell. We may have been going home, but the adventure continued.

As Hunter S. Thompson wrote, "We were somewhere around Barstow, on the edge of the desert when the drugs kicked in." For us, just beyond Barstow, in the Mojave Desert, we stopped to urinate. John, Gabe, and I stood outside the motorhome in a night so dark that you could lose all connection with the past and future. In the present, three streams of urine caught a flickering light from the shine of myriad stars. The simple act of relieving oneself of liquid became transcendental. Back in the motorhome, Gabe threw Neil Young's "Tonight's the Night" into the CD player and cranked it as we rolled into and out of Las Vegas, with no time for play. We had an appointment on the Navajo reservation in the morning, so John drove through snow and cold through Kingman, Williams, and Flagstaff on the Mother Road, old Route 66. We arrived on time, as usual, exhausted but euphoric.

At the Navajo Evangelical Lutheran Mission, we presented two programs and had a group walkathon. Later, Medicine Man Philip walked us to a sacred butte with some climbing involved. It was so cold we could see our breath, a notable difference from the California coast. Our contact, Floyd, told us a bunch of stories in the two days we spent there. I received an invitation to stop back the next year on my way to the start of the walk in Santa Monica.

One last major happening awaited us before we bolted for home. I had never been to the Grand Canyon. A few years earlier, my dad joined a church group to travel to the Lutheran Mission to do some repairs and fixups. In the afternoons, they toured some of the sights of the Four Corners region. My dad chose to stay back on the rez to talk to the residents and help with more chores. His line, now immortalized, was, "What's the big deal about the Grand Canyon? It's just a big hole in the ground." It was now my time to see for myself.

One can never prepare spiritually for the first time you walk up to that rim. All the praying and meditation will not help. The shock electrifies your body. That day, there was snow on the rim, maybe making the gash more pronounced. As we descended into the canyon, the snow soon expired as the temperatures rose sharply. We had no time that year to hike down since Christmas was days away. The next year, I planned to descend and ascend in a day, hoping to soak in the mysticism and big medicine. For the current year, though, I felt content to watch and photograph my crew. Barb, John, and the Angel Gabriel, wearing woolen berets that we kept in the motorhome for rare bouts of cold weather, frolicked in the whiteness underfoot with the Colorado River far below, still carving the rock of the canyon walls. My three traveling compatriots and I stood on the escarpment of the Grand Canyon, all raging across and around America, all standing on the escarpment of life and death.

The West faded behind our wheels as we uneventfully travelled home through Oklahoma, the Amarillo panhandle of Texas, and the swamps of Arkansas, crossing the mighty Mississippi River into Memphis, Tennessee. Memphis was a place I'd like to spend some time in, but not then. Onward we went toward Knoxville; Tennessee has the finest highways in America. Then north and east we headed through Virginia, West Virginia, Maryland and Pennsylvania, traveling from the arms of America into the arms of my loving family.

Chapter 17

The Deserts Stark and Holy

*"I'll show you a place
High on a desert plain, yeah
Where the streets have no name."*

— U2, "Where the Streets Have No Name"

The following year's drive west would be a re-creation of my first drive west back in 1977 with my wife and my cousin Mike. To make it official, Mike would join me all the way to Santa Monica, over 3,000 miles away. John was back for his sixth year of Adventure on the Rim of America, my stalwart compadre of the road. He was here to continue his role of Neal Cassady to my Jack Kerouac. Inspirations, kicks, and epiphanies were sure to turn up around every corner.

Since I was going to walk in the deserts of California, Arizona, and New Mexico, we started later in the year to avoid the heat. That meant we could encounter some wintry weather in our drive over the Rockies. We traveled on Interstate 70, a road we had not driven on during the five prior years of the rim walk. It turned out to be a real connection for Mike and I, dredging up so many memories of the past. Mike was my best man when I got married. Then, a year later, he,

Nancy, and I headed to Colorado to climb and backpack in the San Juans and Rocky Mount National Park. Since that time, Mike and I had rarely seen each other. There had not been a falling out in our relationship; we both were just extremely busy in a lot of other endeavors. Mike got into banking, got married, had two sons, and eventually became the president of a mid-sized bank. On this drive, we immediately fell back into the buddy vibes of two cousins back on the road together. John continued being John: amazing driving skills, puns spilling out as part of the dialogue, and a keen sense for the divine female form and essence. I probably said the phrase "There would never be a dull moment" too many times, but no truer words were spoken.

We hustled our way across the east and Midwest, and soon the Rockies towered before us. I looked forward to our first diversion, heading north from Denver to Boulder to visit another old friend of mine. Laura Hutchings had acted and danced in our local high school musicals. Both of my daughters were also involved, though they were a few years younger than Laura. I built and painted sets after rehearsals, and Laura sometimes stayed and helped me. We played some of our favorite music and discussed both serious and commonplace matters. Working with Laura and other members of the cast gave me a positive feeling about the state of the students in the school that my own kids progressed through. Now Laura was in law school at the University of Colorado. She invited us to her apartment, where we camped in her living room and together had dinner that night and breakfast the next day. For a minute, Laura entertained the idea of skipping the next few days of classes to travel with us to the Navajo reservation and then onto Santa Monica, where she could fly back to Denver from LAX as the weekend ended. In the end, she decided not to. She would have fit right in, though. I got a feeling there would be future adventures with Laura. Time would tell.

The three musketeers headed down Interstate 15 and turned west below Colorado Springs, trying to beat the snow over Wolf Creek Pass. We pulled over for a few breaks at awe-inspiring vistas. Winter had come to Colorado, but we were headed to the desert, the Four Corners, the Navajo reservation. We had only the snows of the lower hills of the San Juans to get through. Our newer, heavier motorhome was now in its second year and had dual rear wheels in the back, so it was steady in bad weather. I had gotten a great deal on it, and even though it had 35,000 miles, it still looked and smelled new. Both my motorhomes represented home and home away from home.

We presented our programs with the Navajos, including a puppet show for the kids, and another stark dirt road walkathon around the buttes. Shaman Philip told us of the Navajo word "nizhónígo" which translates to "walk in beauty." The Dine, "the old ones," wanted us to take that with us on the rest of our walk through life.

From the Four Corners we headed to the rim of the Grand Canyon. This time, we were going all the way down. Soon after descending, you notice the change to hotter temperatures, especially down at the bottom. Halfway down into the canyon, John had a conversation with a few huge condors sitting on the railings of the lookout; he had a deep connection to all living things. On the climb back up, John ran the last stretch. He had not carried enough food and was getting mighty hungry. When Mike and I reached the top, John was sitting at the rim, devouring half a loaf of bread with peanut butter and jelly. Watching him was a large group of Japanese tourists, all laughing and taking photos. Only John could divert attention away from one of the most amazing views in the world. John was just being John, again and again.

We zoomed through Arizona, now on the same route as the prior year. Again, Las Vegas came and went. There was no time for gambling and debauchery. I wasn't averse to those things, but we had the rim of America to walk around. The next day, we had a brief panel discussion/lunch meeting with Alexis and the crew of marketers at MiniMed in Northridge. Alexis gave us a valuable contact — her brother — who worked for Giant Bicycles, which gave us a possible way to procure sponsorship and bikes for the next year when we hit the Texas border. After MiniMed, we took a glance at the Hollywood sign; made a quick stop for more CDs at Amoeba Music on Sunset Boulevard; took a 10-minute look at Grauman's Chinese Theatre, where the handprints of famous people are in the sidewalk cement; and landed back at the pier in Santa Monica. It felt like we had never left.

***

Year six of Adventure on the Rim of America began with a walk to the end of the pier and then south past Muscle Beach in Venice. We all flexed our biceps, but no one noticed, except maybe a few who laughed at the absurdity of it all. Later, the beach weather evaporated. The rain poured, with more forecast for over the next two days. Heading out toward the Pacific on the bicycle trail and nearing LAX, I spotted a raggedly dressed but well-equipped bicyclist. We talked a bit, and I learned that he had cycled over the last five months from the Arctic Circle in Alaska down the Canadian and American Pacific coasts. He was Swiss, and after I asked how far he was going, he said, "Ten minutes to the airport, where I will fly home to Zurich. I'm arriving right on schedule." We both felt that we were kindred spirits, especially after I told him that my ancestors were from northern Switzerland and southern Germany. We could have shared many stories, but the rain continued, so much so that we even forgot to exchange contact information. I would have to imagine the wonders he saw, but that was easy for me since I had one hell of an imagination.

My mission now was to follow the serpentine coast to the Mexican border. The rain continued for the third straight day then cleared around Marina Del Rey. My friend Tina, who had driven for me four years ago in North Dakota, lived in an apartment there. We joined her and her friends for meals and walking and camped out on her floor. My cousin Mike flew back home the next day; his quiet presence and solid companionship would be missed. John drove inland for a day and night to join Oregon Janie for a Seventh-day Adventist conference. He told us he was interested in the church and was thinking about joining. He didn't fool us. He knew that we knew that he was interested in the lovely Miss Oregon Janie. That left me and Tina to walk down the coast past Hermosa Beach, Redondo Beach, and Seal Beach, where we crossed into Orange County. From there, a bike trail ran along the cliffs for a heavenly walk from Huntington Beach. During the walk, enigmatic Tina told me she was thinking of living in her friend's boat in a slip in the marina for half a year. She was born and raised in Pennsylvania, where I lived, but I sort of knew she'd never leave southern California, so it surprised me when she mentioned possibly taking physical therapy jobs in Key West, Florida, or Lake Tahoe in central California. Tina was nomadic by nature, feeling comfortably at home in whatever space she inhabited.

John returned, and Tina headed back to work. John and I would be the sole participants well into southern Arizona. On our first day back together, we walked along the continuing coastal bike trail into Newport Beach. We camped two nights on the cliffs at a state park near

Huntington Beach. Just like in the real estate business, it was all location, location, location. In Newport, we were picked up by Jackie, president of the PADRE (Pediatric Adolescent Diabetes Research and Education) Foundation. Working together with MiniMed, Jackie had me fly out to southern California a few times in the past. Sometimes I opened for the Pump Girls, four teenage singers and dancers who had Type 1 diabetes and wore the same insulin pump as me. I always took the Southwest Airlines redeye via Las Vegas, where I would sleep on the plane and at the layover in Vegas to maximize my time in the Golden State. That day, Jackie had us do a few programs and the puppet show at Children's Hospital of Orange County. My programs were a nice diversion from the walk's occasional grind, and they always made the return to the walk feel fresh. The goal was still the path.

Our trek continued through Laguna Beach (one of my favorites), Dana Point, and Doheny State Beach. In San Clemente, John and I searched for the ghost of Richard Nixon. He always walked those beaches from his home nearby, right up until his death years earlier. Both of us tried doing our best Nixon impressions, hoping to conjure his spirit. Can you imagine having a conversation on a two-mile walk with Tricky Dick? Next came Carlsbad and the renowned Trestles Surfing Area, where the waves thundered. The following day, we passed La Jolla and then moved on into San Diego. It was hard to find parking for the motorhome, so we procured a campsite out on a spit of land to the west of the city for two days. That allowed us to walk along Silver Strand Beach through Coronado and then back into San Diego for dinner. We returned to the camp in the twilight and watched the city light up in green neon, reminding us of the Emerald City of Oz. Toward the ocean, untold clusters of glimmering stars drew our attention from the urban dreamscape we walked away from. Day two on the strand consisted of walking south with the bay on one side and the light surf on the other. It was another sensational day.

My last day on the Pacific took me along Imperial Beach right to the Mexican border. I composed a meditation in my head as a memorial to the California coast: "Walking early this morning is to be witness to the opening of the universe. The dark of night fades, the new day glows red over the Mexican hills to the southeast. And I, on foot, take it all in. I breathe the world."

***

We stocked up on supplies in San Ysidro, and then the path took us along the border wall. A crushing heaviness invaded my psyche. In the past five years, I walked along many rivers, lakes, and creeks, with the last two and a half of those years spent right along the Pacific Ocean. Now I would be in the desert for the rest of the year and half of the next year. I had never walked in a desert before, and I missed the ocean immediately. An existential dread materialized. John, usually upbeat and positive, felt it too. Would this be like a death march through Hades? We probably reacted way too negatively, but that's the problem when you have an overactive imagination. Normally it inspires you, but it can turn dark, too. In reality, we had the shelter and water capacity of the motorhome. We had each other to spot any early heat-related problems, and it was the middle of November. We minimized the threat by rationalizing while still worrying ourselves silly.

The Pacific Crest Trail starts on the Mexican border in the village of Campo and travels north for 2,600 miles to the Canadian border in Washington. We decided to walk 60 miles of the trail, first north from Campo and then from Pine Valley Campground to Anza-Borrego Desert State Park. Though it was the desert, it was not flat. In fact, I found it fascinating. You could see passes further ahead no matter which way you looked. We prepared by carrying plenty of water.

On our first night in the campground, we saw a stunning display of stars and a meteor shower. I had taken a shower earlier in the evening in the camp bathrooms. If watching the celestial meteor showers counted, then I didn't need another shower for days. Toward morning, we were awakened by the border patrol looking for five illegal immigrants. The next day, we walked north and returned, then drove north to an elementary school in Julian to present the puppet show. Only a few days in and we were thoroughly enjoying this part of California. It was great to have pre-existing notions shattered once again. That is the beauty of travel.

Eastward through El Centro and Calexico. We started to know the border patrol from seeing them all the time and engaged in a few discussions with them. They seemed like good guys. Days later, we entered Yuma on the Colorado River right where it empties into Mexico, eventually finding its way to the Sea of Cortez. We, however, turned left and headed north, first on foot, then in the motorhome, following the Colorado River. That is the state line, and so we now were in Arizona.

We had programs to present at Parker, on the Colorado River Native American reservation, which hosted four tribes: the Mojave, Hopi, Navajo, and Chemehuevi. We had a monumental reunion awaiting us on the reservation. Ivan and his family, whom I met five years earlier on the Blackfeet reservation in Montana, had been transferred to the reservation we were traveling to. Since Ivan worked for the Indian Health Service and is such a valuable commodity, it wanted to share his knowledge and spirit with other tribes. My first question to him was, "How does someone living at the foot of the Rockies, on the edges of Glacier, Montana, adjust to living in the desert?" The professional Ivan responded with, "Modification and adaptation." Then that coyote trickster turned it around and asked me, "How does someone who walks across and along the mountains, plains, and oceans of America adjust to walking in the desert?" In unison, we replied, "Modification and adaptation." And with that, the learning and inspiration that I always get from Ivan began anew.

We presented our programs, hosted two walkathons along the river, broke bread together at meals, and played basketball in Ivan's driveway court. Ivan's quiet yet effective way of teaching, and his dry, subtle reservation humor, impressed John. Together, they made plans for John to bring his church group out to Montana when Ivan returned to his real home, not to evangelize and proselytize but rather to do some fixup projects and to share in each other's wisdom. Before Ivan and his family came to this reservation, they did a spell at the White Earth Reservation in Minnesota; I had missed them there by one year. I also made plans to meet back there in Arizona on my way to next year's starting point in El Paso. It would be another wonderful chance to connect with Ivan, his wife and kids. We all had become one, a family of the road.

***

The true Arizona portion of the adventure started as we made our way from Quartzsite through Salome, Aguila, and Wickenburg before dropping down into Phoenix. Just north lay the mystical buttes and towers of Sedona. They called to us, but we had appointments in the big spaces of the Sun City. I hoped to visit Sedona the next year.

For now, though, John and I prepared ourselves to enter the tempestuous world of a one-time Kutztownian shaman who became the prophet of a desert metropolis.

We arrived and were greeted by husband Larry, daughter Laura, granddaughter Karina, and, in all her raging glory, wife, mother, and grandmother Janet. The merriment and reconnecting of the early evening proceeded into late evening. I apologized to Janet for shaking up the family routine, telling her, "You didn't have to stay up late partying just for us," and Janet replied, "I do this most nights." She was fast asleep when John and I slipped out early for the first of two days of walking the bike paths paralleling the Phoenix irrigation system. To the northeast, I could see Camelback Mountain, permanently etched in my head from seeing it during the 450 laps I made around a quarter-mile track at the 48-hour race back in 1988.

We presented a program for a Lions Club and again later for Janet and her family. Of the many hundreds of shows I've presented, this was the most festive. There was no need to present the puppet show, as Karina was too young and Laura too old. The family took us out to a Mexican restaurant and then back home to the continuing party-like atmosphere. It was hard to keep pace, but Janet never wavered. She must have been well trained, as her hoarse whiskey and cigarette voice rose above the din. We tried to get her to join us for a few miles the next day, but Janet slept in to recharge her batteries for the next party. It would have been nice to talk to Janet over a few quiet miles, to be the vessel of the enlightenment I knew existed in her, but alas that was not the way of Janet. She walked her own path, searching for transcendence in her own novel way. Who was I to say that my way was better? I did know that my way left my voice a lot less hoarse-sounding than Janet's.

Adventure on the Rim of America headed back to the actual rim, south to the Mexican border in Organ Pipe Cactus National Monument. We passed through Ajo on Thanksgiving, and I was feeling low, the combination of some abnormal blood glucose swings from high to low and back again plus a deep homesickness. As I went by a small shack in the middle of the vast desert, some young kids were playing soccer in the front yard. One of the young boys called out to me in a Spanish-inflected voice: "Mister, mister, I want to wish you a very happy Thanksgiving." He had no idea how those few words lifted me out of my funk. These people were the salt of the earth.

We spent two days camping and walking Organ Pipe's surprisingly mountainous terrain. We met Janice, a lovely park ranger from the village of Sonoyta, Mexico, who was a font of information. She told us to stay away from the western part of the park because of sightings of human traffickers called "coyotes" and drug cartels. Among all this danger, Janice remained stalwart and invited me to present a program to her hometown when I returned the next year, as diabetes was rampant there. One night, I took a full-moon hike to a small peak, where I saw the lights of Sonoyta in the distance and thought of Janice.

To get to and from Organ Pipe, we had to go through the small village of Why. Both times we debated stopping. "Should we stop in Why?" Both times we answered ourselves with "Why not?" And both times we did. As we headed east, John began a three-day bout with some kind of intestinal bug. He slept in as I walked onto the Tohono O'odham Indian Reservation. It was so remote that even traffic on the nicely shouldered state Route 86 was minimal. Being alone for three days was valuable in that I finally was able to muse a bit about the desert. Physically, it was perfect for walking: 70 degrees, low humidity, the sight of showers off to the south toward Mexico, the chance of a rainbow sighting, abundant bird life, four-legged coyotes at dusk, and at night, as the musical group the Eagles sang, "with a billion stars all around." Mentally, one could problem solve and sing lyrics, both hemispheres of the brain working simultaneously. And spiritually, we already knew that most of the great religions had their origins and ascendance in the deserts of the world. The desert was a holy place.

We camped for two nights at Indian casinos and had no TV. There was no need to have a TV. We had all the entertainment we needed watching the white trash entering with pockets full of money and leaving, if they were lucky, with empty pockets and just the clothes on their backs. It was a psychological study of the faces of losers. We weren't losing, only because we weren't playing.

If you walked 30 steps in any direction with your back to the neon, you would be swallowed by the dark of night, the sounds of coyotes serenading you to sleep. On the last day of John's maladies, I had to hitch a ride with one of the tribal members to drive the motorhome back. Then the sickness disappeared, and sick John became vibrant John once again.

We spent two days in Sells to do programs with the tribe. One day, a group of wonderful tribal members walked with me as we split the difference between Kitts Peak National Observatory slightly to the northeast and the tribe's sacred mountain, Baboquivari, rising solemnly from the desert floor slightly to the southeast. We had grown very close to Marlene, Monica, Phyllis, and Orville the last few days. We exchanged gifts, and they invited me back the next year with the possibility of a climb up Baboquivari. I would need another week next year just to revisit all these places. Then we had a tear-stained goodbye, and John and I were off to the next drivers' exchange. Even though I loved all my volunteer drivers, who all brought their own palpable energy, I had to admit that when John left, things got quieter and maybe just an iota or two less energetic. He had been with me for way more than half the miles during those six years. Cassady now returned to his home back east, and Kerouac remained, pointing his feet toward southern New Mexico.

***

My friend Marian flew into Tucson and prepared herself for life on the road, this being her first appearance during Adventure on the Rim of America. She was a diabetes educator, working at one time in hospitals and recently for the County of Berks health department. Her most valuable skill was her deeply caring attitude to her coworkers, patients, neighbors, and people at her church. Even though this was Marian's first time on the rim, she always swirled around other aspects of it with contributions, having me present at conferences and for various church groups, and checking in to hear how things were with the adventure and personally with my diabetes. She was like the Godfather in how she had influence and connections, only she had a high degree of empathy and compassion. Marian also had a wicked sense of humor backed by a pervasive laugh. She would feel right at home on the road in southern Arizona and New Mexico.

Our first stop was at the San Xavier del Bac Mission, a school nuns ran for children of the Tohono O'odham Nation. We spent two days there, and the funniest incident for me was watching Marian try to maneuver the puppets by herself — generally a two-person job — only hours after arriving in Arizona. Most of the kids just laughed, thinking that Marian's jetlagged attempt to control the puppets to be part of the act. She agreed that even if you would know in advance you would be asked to work puppets, how could you even prepare? To get some walking mileage in, I woke early and did a two-mile loop to the apex of a butte where there was a cross. My first mile was in the faint light of dawn, but as the desert sun rose, I spotted two tribal members hugging the 15-foot metal cross. I asked them if it was okay to take their photo, and just as the cross diffused the rays of the sun, I shot a few slides, looking south to a mountain on the Mexican border. The seven times I climbed to that cross left me feeling exuberant beyond measure with a bunch of piety mixed in. It prepared me for the tasks of the day with the nuns and the children of the tribe.

On the next two nights, we stayed in a campground on the edges of Tucson, awaiting a program I was to give downtown at the University of Arizona. On day one, I walked around and through that downtown, the city smaller and more charming than Phoenix. The next day, I walked all day around Saguaro National Park while Marian took a less-mileage group tour. Even though you could see the city in the distance, this was a raw, cactus-filled desert, the kind one thinks of from movies and cartoons. A few road runners crossed my dusty path several times. I feared that they would take me for Wile E. Coyote and drop an anvil on me from one of the buttes. Though it was hot in the midday, this was a December desert heat and totally survivable.

Next, we headed due south again to Sonoita, Huachuca City, and the six-shooter gunfights in the streets of Tombstone, where a walk around the cemetery revealed stones of famous outlaws and sheriffs. I wasn't fearful because outlaw Marian, packing heat and gunslinger reflexes, was by my side. I now knew why I chose her for this section.

Continuing east, we encountered wild Apache landscapes while walking toward the copper mines of Bisbee and the Pedregosa Mountains, very close to the Mexican border once more. Bisbee is known for having over 1,000 steps spread around on the hilly periphery of the immense mines. I spent an entire afternoon climbing and descending every single step. Six weeks into this year's adventure, I was achieving peak fitness, with my blood glucose readings in excellent range other than the usual expected high or low deviation, which is quickly corrected. Marian understood all this way more than any other member of my team. Next up was a walk through Coronado National Forest which, along with Chiricahua National Monument, was a totally different environment with stunted pine trees, pine needle trails, and moonscape rock formations rising up 40 feet. I was not prepared for this after all that desert. Both Marian and I were jazzed up from viewing it at a walker's pace.

We had to drive north to present the program at a hospital in Silver City, Arizona, right on the continental divide. This gorgeous small city sits at 7,000 feet with mountains and a robin's egg-blue sky that was so brilliant it hurt your eyes. This was another one of those places I collected on my route as future landscapes to settle down in. The hospital was state-of-the-art, and the downtown was hip with bike shops, bakeries, and coffee houses. It was a supply stop for the Continental Divide Trail. The programs went well, and I was invited back to be part of a conference right around when I would return the next year. We hiked on the CDT north toward the frontier of the rugged Gila Wilderness. Then it was on to Las Cruces, New Mexico, and down into El Paso, Texas. I wasn't done with New Mexico yet, though I needed to do the last driver exchange of the year at the airport. Marian's stint had reached an end. After brightening up my walk for the last week, she would now do the same back home. Brightening up the lives of everyone she came into contact with was Marian's modus operandi.

***

My daughter Adrienne had returned. She was here for her eighth tour of duty, and accompanying her was her sidekick, Jackie, here for her sixth phase as driver and walker extraordinaire. They would be here with me to finish up New Mexico and then the long drive back home, chasing Christmas. This was the longest stretch I had gone without seeing Adrienne, and I broke down a bit as the girls exited the aeropuerto. They had bigtime smiles because they had escaped the east once more, but there was also a hint of a smirk upon seeing the happy tears rolling down my cheeks. It would be a memorable time indeed.

The first rule of travel was to return near to where I had stopped yesterday. We camped at Oliver Lee Memorial State Park on the edges of Lincoln National Forest. It was a spirited walk up and onto the escarpment, a mix of cactus and pinion pines. At the top, it was flat for miles with a 360-degree panorama unfolding into wilderness. There was even a lonely creek making its serpentine way across the landscape. To the north, you could see Alamogordo, where we had a scheduled Lions Club presentation two days hence. This was a great introduction for the girls to this part of the West.

On the way to Alamogordo, we stopped for a hike up and down the dunes of White Sands National Park, where a light rain shower surprised us and created lingering little lakes that reflected the dunes. Then we walked and drove further north to the Mescalero Apache Reservation in the foothills of mighty Sierra Blanca, whose snowy summit reached over 12,000 feet. We had a wonderful two days of presentations, celebrations, and conversations with the tribal members. Our campsite was near the casino and gave us access to many trails. We were no longer in the desert.

It was time to head home. Christmas was approaching, and we had some road mileage to cover. We had only two destinations to stop at on the drive east. The first was back in El Paso. I thought it would be interesting to walk over the Paso del Norte International Bridge into Ciudad Juárez. There was talk of an outdoor market only two blocks after crossing the bridge. But once over the border, the scene was harrowing. A sea of young men, many of them crippled, lined the sidewalks, begging for money. I hustled the girls back across the bridge, and we jumped onto Interstate 10, flooring it all the way, without stopping, into downtown New Orleans.

The 1,000-mile drive across Texas took us 18 hours, followed by a couple more in Louisiana. We only had a few days till Christmas, and my wife would have killed us if we missed that deadline. None of us had ever been to New Orleans, though, and we felt we could not miss the magic we were sure to find there, so we decided to drive all day and night. The plan was to rotate every couple of hours, to have one person driving, one person keeping the driver alert, and one person sleeping on the sofa in the back. Jackie took the first shift, and I was next. I drove while Adrienne rode shotgun, and it turned out to be some of the best father/daughter hours we have ever spent together. The music shook the walls of the motorhome as I disc jockeyed the beginnings and endings of every song. It was a primer for my daughter to hear what music made me tick at different stages of my life: Steve Earle's "Texas Eagle" through Van Horn, Tift Merritt's "Bramble Rose" north of Marfa (her hometown), Black Sabbath's "Paranoid" through Fort Stockton, Glen Campbell's greatest hits through Ozona, Gram Parsons and Emmylou Harris through San Antonio, Son Volt through Gonzales/East Texas, Tori Amos' "Scarlet's Walk" (a shared selection) through Houston, Liz Phair (another shared selection) south of Beaumont, and finally Rage Against the Machine into and through the rest of Louisiana. I had driven almost the entire way with no stopping except for pee breaks. This meant we would have almost one extra day in the French Quarter. When you falter, always blast Rage Against the Machine!

It was all worth it. New Orleans was magic indeed. Of course there would be plenty more music, though now live. We had our own driver assigned to us by our hosts at Best Western. It was a slow time just days before the holiday. He was an older local, born and raised, and we had so much fun together that we tried to talk him into driving us home. We took walks along the Mississippi River. Adrienne played a five-gallon bucket with a local drummer. We toured the outdoor markets. We sampled all the local delicacies. It was warm, and it didn't feel like winter was just days away for us. All was a whirlwind and then it was time to ramble north, keeping our senses honed for chances of snowstorms. Mississippi, Alabama, a small slice of Georgia into Tennessee, then, just like the year before, a big chunk of Virginia into Maryland, and we were back in Pennsylvania. It had been eight weeks since I was home, and it felt like I had seen the entire United States. Indeed, I had seen most of it in the last six years. But I wasn't done yet. Two more years to go.

Chapter 18

Texas Radio and the Big Beat

"I'll tell you this...
No eternal reward will forgive us now
For wasting the dawn."

— The Doors, "The WASP (Texas Radio and the Big Beat)"

My Father passed away in March 2003 at age 77. It was sudden and unexpected. He had a massive heart attack and never rallied; too much of his heart had been damaged. He had lived a hard life, wearing a big back brace almost every day of the 44 years he worked in an iron foundry in Reading, Pennsylvania. He needed the brace because he had been born with a missing vertebra. They found evidence of black lung during the three days where he barely clung to life in the hospital. Since age eight, he had suffered from grand mal seizures and later occasionally fell into deep depressions he had to pull himself out of. But not all was misery. He experienced periods of adventure in the forests of eastern Pennsylvania, and of course he had joined the Walk Across America at five junctures. He excelled at the hard-work parts of his life and would not have lamented about any of it. He always managed to drag his tired body out to play baseball with my two brothers and I after his energy-draining job. He did that because he loved baseball, and he loved his three sons. When you put both loves together, you get a love supreme.

My brother Craig decided that we should dedicate the beginning of this year's Adventure on the Rim to our dad. Craig would join me for the long ride back to the deserts of the West and my starting point in El Paso, Texas. We would search for traces of our dad in the landscapes of the West and in the wilderness of our collective memories.

We set out in the late afternoon on a Sunday in early November with winter knocking at the door. Two hours in, we stopped for dinner in Carlisle, just before getting on the Pennsylvania Turnpike. My daughter Adrienne drove from nearby Shippensburg to say goodbye. She was in her junior year at the university there, and during our meal, I could see the longing in her eyes, her wishing she was heading west with us instead of south and back to school. She liked college and had joined the school newspaper to write and edit, but Adrienne, from years of adventures with me, knew there would be an untold number of exploits that led to learning experiences on the road west. But in six weeks' time, at the beginning of her winter break, she would join me in the panhandle of Florida to finish year seven of Adventure on the Rim. That journey would take us to the Atlantic Ocean and then north on the long drive back home. As busy as she was now, I was touched that she took a few hours to see me off. A few tears rolled down my cheeks as she said, "Bon voyage!"

After a long bicycle ride on the Katy Trail in Missouri, I let Craig play DJ for the next portion of the motorized journey. We had a lot of crossover tastes in music, so I knew it would be energizing. He spun some Tears for Fears, Elvis Costello, the band Kansas when we crossed from Missouri into Kansas, and some Ambrosia. I mixed in some Radiohead, Stevie Wonder, and Tori Amos, whose "Scarlet's Walk," had become an Adventure on the Rim staple. And, of course, the omnipresent Joni Mitchell, our patron saint of the road, who reminded us that "the drone of flying engines is a song so wild and blue. It scrambles time and seasons if it gets thru to you" as we flew through the great plains of a raw western Kansas night.

The high passes of the Rocky Mountains in November are always going to be tricky. I drove as night came down and a full-on blizzard enveloped us. The stalwart motorhome held strong and true, so when we finally descended into the deserts of western Colorado, we were safe but beyond tired. After a few hours of sleep at a rest stop outside Grand Junction, where we chowed down on omelets, we felt sustained and ready for hiking and biking in Utah.

First on the list was a hike around Fischer Towers, where we observed and later talked with the climbing bums. It was a quick but fascinating window into their life of extreme exposure. Then we drove past Arches National Park; bicycled all around Moab; hiked around Wilson Arch; and bicycled into and out of the mysterious Canyonlands National Park, where we also hiked out to the ledge overlooking the Colorado River, just south of its confluence with the Green River. Throughout Canyonlands we saw petroglyphs on the faces of rock walls. Heading south, we stopped to watch the sunset over the towers of Monument Valley, where we recreated a photo of my dad sitting on a wooden fence taken 10 years before. We took turns sitting on that same fence trying to match the photo of our dad. Then we moved on to Arizona and the Navajo reservation where we would present programs and lead walkathons for the third year in a row. Our dad's spirit hovered all around these landscapes. His presence was so strong that we felt he was our third wheel.

We had one day left before Craig would fly home from Phoenix. He had completed his duty of acting as my road buddy, to safely guide me to the beginning of my quest. And it wasn't over yet. We had a few more mini adventures to complete. The first was a hike to the top of a ledge looking out on Spider Rock in the south of the Navajo reservation. We followed that with a hike into Canyon de Chelly National Monument, the canyon out of which the towers rise. I kept a promise to myself from the previous year that I would hike and climb in Sedona. Craig and I completed that endeavor just before he flew home.

I would be alone for five days, all of them spent fulfilling promises from the year before. First on the list was a stopover with Ivan and his family on the Colorado River Indian reservation, where I presented programs at the tribal casino. I rode my bicycle to Havasu City for a televised presentation and then back south to Parker; the entire scenic route followed along the Colorado River. Next up was a return to do programs on the Tohono O'odham reservation. The much-anticipated climb up to the sacred summit of Baboquivari had to be canceled because of flooding from a few fast-moving, gully-washing thunderstorms. I was lucky to have gotten off the reservation, as many roads and bridges were washed out. Third on the list was the San Carlos Apache reservation to the east of Phoenix, where I did two walkathons, a puppet show at a school, and a shared keynote speech at a men's health conference. My co-speaker was Billy Mills, the Oglala Lakota (Sioux) athlete who won a gold medal in the 10,000 meters at the 1964 Olympics in Tokyo, Japan. His shared speech with me was fantastic; I learned a lot from him, and our conversation inspired me for weeks.

Between presentations, I took long bicycle rides around the reservation, careful of the excessive amounts of broken glass beer bottles on the shoulders of the highway. Last on the list was a return to Silver City and a diabetes conference where I was the keynote speaker. Before the start of the conference, I dropped off both bicycles at a bicycle dealer just down the street from the hospital, where they did a tune-up and donated the cost to my charities. The last 10 days had been a whirlwind of activity. I was dog-tired yet rapturous, and my bike ride across Texas and the deep south was just beginning. It was time to rise to the occasion and continue to follow in the footsteps and bike tire ruts of the brave souls who went before me.

***

I was standing in front of the motorhome, which was standing in front of the highest point in Texas, Guadalupe Peak. John and I arrived there in the dark after I picked him up at the airport in El Paso, driving out of the city past myriad strip clubs and adult bookstores. Our anthropological studies would have been enhanced by visiting a few of those fine establishments, but we had some vast and empty spaces to bike across here in West Texas. The scene was visually intoxicating but also intimidating. I wanted so badly to climb to the top of Guadalupe, though I'm not sure if a 360-degree view would reveal anything further. There was no sign of any civilization — no cars, and even no wildlife — though I was certain there were some creatures out there. Gazing south I saw a dirt road leading into the loneliest landscape I had ever seen. That was the way I was heading.

Other than size, John's bike and my bike were identical. Both were Giant brand touring bicycles, which meant they were more rugged than road-racing bicycles but had thinner tires and more comfortable, stretched-out frames than mountain bikes. They both had racks on the front and back for attaching panniers. We didn't need those because of the motorhome, but in the future, as I had in the past, I would take week-long rides, staying in campgrounds and carrying a tent, sleeping bag and pad, lightweight stove and food. It was so freeing that I could see myself biking across any of the seven continents in such fashion. In fact, I would read such tales all the time, and those accounts would electrify me. But that was not now. I was on an entirely different mission, a quest of a different sort. Walking was still my thing, but we thought of shaking things up to be more interesting, more challenging, to make it Adventure on the Rim, instead of the Walk Across America (hence the bicycle and kayak portions). That brought us to where we now stood under a lonely mountain, mournful, because we didn't have time to climb her.

    The road turned into blacktop as I started climbing switchbacks, up, up, and away. Once again, rarely are the desert or plains just flat. I changed a blown-out tire 15 miles into the ride using a patch instead of my only spare tube. I waited for it to fail, but it held the rest of the ride, including during the riveting descent, head down on the drops, safely handling the curves like a great bicycle should. Alexis from MiniMed had made good on her promise to talk her brother into getting me a great touring bike, but only one, so I split the difference, and John and I each paid for half of our bikes. John deserved at least that much. His friendship, dedication to my quest, and role as the energizing force in all road matters made him worthy of many bicycles. For now, the one he got for half price could be spotted off in the distance coming toward me, just as planned. When John reached me, he turned around, and we headed 25 miles into Van Horn, located on the same Route 10 Adrienne and Jackie had driven on with me on the long ride home a year earlier. The only other vehicles I had seen in the first 25 miles were two tractors. Big blue skies, low humidity, and sunburned faces made it one of my favorite days of On the Rim so far. That's saying something. There were many contenders.

    Since I was always more of a walker than an actual bicyclist, some days I would walk a few miles, usually on single railroad tracks in the middle of nowhere, but still staying near the two-lane dirt or blacktop roads. I walked with a purpose: to meet Willie Nelson. He was rumored to run his daily five miles on railroad tracks. Indeed, he had done so in a town north of where I lived while he gave a concert at the fair in Kempton, Pennsylvania. The first few times on the tracks, I did not run into Willie. The search for him now took on another dimension:

rickety old-time bars in the middle of nowhere. We heard the same old story from every bartender: "You guys just missed him. He was here last night." So, we broadened our search and included fancier bars in bigger towns. All this searching for Willie led us to spending too much time in bars drinking. But even in the bigger town bars we got the same old story: we had just missed him ("He was here last night!"). John and I aren't the sharpest tools in the shed, but finally we realized this was the standard line used on all the tourists looking for Willie in West Texas. We weren't tourists, but we were still being played. We never did meet Willie. He is usually somewhere else in the world, on the road again. Though, we did feel solidarity with Willie. We were on the road again, too.

As we started angling south and east, I came to the unmitigated realization that I loved West Texas. We camped in Fort Davis at the base of the observatory, which sits on top of McDonald Peak set in the gorgeous Davis Mountains. The next day, I walked the mostly uphill switchbacks for 17 miles, and that night we got to see the stars, planets, galaxies, black holes, and nebulae through the giant telescope. I had met a bicyclist late in the day, a kid from Ireland who was biking across America in the opposite direction of us. That night at our campsite, a million stories were told under a sky full of the most stars any of us had ever seen. Days later and further south, we watched the eerie, mystical Marfa lights off in the distance. Earlier, we had looked for the recording studio of one of my favorite singer-songwriters, Tift Merritt. Supposedly, we had just missed her also. Maybe Tift and Willie were together, somewhere on the road, laughing at two fools searching for two musical artists who are rarely ever home.

The Rio Grande was dry most of the autumn, all the way from El Paso toward Big Bend National Park. We crossed over the emptiness and prepared to ride our bikes into the Chihuahuan mountains for a day, from Presidio, Texas, to Ojinaga, Mexico.

Though the landscape looked the same across the border, something felt different. John and I were in a euphoric mood while cycling toward the hills and mountains wrapped in a haze of heat and clouds. Just the thought of escaping the rigid structures of Adventure on the Rim accentuated that mood. We were still on an adventure, but we were no longer on the rim of America. We had broken through to the other side. It felt like we could have kept going for days, up and down those mountains, maybe angle toward the Sea of Cortez, take the ferry to Cabo San Lucas, or keep pedaling to the Pacific coast of Mazatlán. Reality brought us back to what our true quest entailed. John and I were no longer young. We both had families back home. And though we had not done any presentations in Texas because of the remoteness, in a week we would enter a more populated East Texas and keep some scheduled appointments. Maybe those few hours in which we felt the freedom of a buddy bike trip into Mexico was enough for now.

On the way back to our real lives, we came across barricaded streets in Ojinaga. It was Mexican Independence Day, and there would be parades and festivities all afternoon and into the evening. After pushing our bikes a few blocks, we saw the parades were just starting. The sidewalks were crowded with people cooking on portable fires, roasting cobs of corn, vegetables, and different meats. We ate everything we were offered, hoping for the best stomach-wise. Then we watched all the school children dressed as Mexican revolutionaries — Zapata, Obregón, Huerta, and more — marching and on horseback carrying toy guns and wearing fake mustaches and gun belts. The afternoon overflowed with festivity.

We had another reality check coming back over the border. John had forgotten his passport, and even his driver's license, in the motorhome in the morning. Our ease in entering Mexico did not sound any warning bells in his head. Coming back into the United States was a different matter. We were held at customs for an hour, and I almost had to bike the five miles to retrieve his proof. But eventually, two amigos were released back into the arms of America.

A couple of days took us into Big Bend National Park, down a frightening series of descending curves, rollercoasting a few bumps near the bottom, and back to a broad, Altiplano-like flatness, the wild desert in all its raging glory. It was 90 degrees on the afternoon of Thanksgiving, which called for a dip in the waist-high Rio Grande. To cross the river would put us back in Mexico once more. We hiked through the narrow stone-walled canyons, thrilled to be in this holy cathedral of the natural world. Next, for a few days we encountered a mix of dirt roads, two-lane blacktop, and sometimes no road at all. We followed the arc of the river, becoming ever more intimate as we cooled in its waters, again going east and south to Del Rio. Some days the wind was a murderous westerly, pushing me onward but tough on John as he came back to meet me.

It was time to do programs again. We actually started to miss meeting locals and engaging in the people's world. Part of the reason was that there were Native American reservations in remote areas of the further western states. I had been on 32 reservations in the last six years, and the last one for Adventure on the Rim was back in New Mexico. For the rest of the trip there would not be any, making it harder to find audiences in remote areas. To make things more interesting, after presenting a few programs for a school, Lions Club, and hospital, including three walkathons, John and I crossed the border once more. Acuña had a bright array of pastel-painted houses on very narrow streets. It was like another world, and we were delighted to see it all from the seat of a bicycle. In the afternoon, we did a puppet show in an elementary school with an interpreter. The puppets were having a great time, some of them even committing to learning Spanish for the next time.

The big cities were just north of us. First up was San Antonio, a surprisingly major metropolis. We were still used to the nothingness of West Texas. Through the traffic, I started having a series of stomach bugs. I cycled through them to Austin but then had to take two days off to recover. The outdoor music scene in the state capital sure helped bring me back from the edges of nausea. From here on began a major problem that would continue throughout the Deep South. It was an empty feeling in the middle of Texas that had me re-thinking the advocacy of my quest. No one was interested in any of my programs or walkathons. All the usual contacts were notified six months in advance. No one got back to me. And the eventual irony was that we were deep in diabetes country. It started in Texas but became even more prevalent in the Deep South. I constantly tried to find answers. It would take me years to understand this negativity and denial of a killer disease.

***

John prepared to fly home as my next crew entered the story. Julie was back, now for her sixth tour of duty. Julie's cousin, Amy, was out here for the first time. She had no idea what to expect, but she knew how wild her cousin was, so she figured it out, and all expectations were sure to be met. John would leave the next day, so his time overlapped by one day with Julie and Amy. What followed were two days and one night of revelry: many foot miles around San Antonio's riverwalk, a climb of the Tower of the Americas at dusk, and a tour of the city's bars. If you only have one drink per bar, it doesn't sound like a lot, but there are a lot of bars in downtown San Antonio, and it's never too many miles to walk for my crew. In any group of revelers, it always helps to have a Type 1 diabetic along, or at least me. I haven't been drunk since high school, so I am available to shepherd groups of party animals in any setting, though it can be like herding chickens. One particular bar was staffed by comedians whose job it was to insult the patrons. They loved my crew because we playfully do that to each other all the time. My crew knew how to give it back.

The next few days took us on roads paralleling Route 10, heading east past La Grange, San Felipe, and a couple of Texas barbecue joints. We didn't use our stove once during that time. I bought a big ol' red cowboy hat, and at one joint, the girls flirted with a tall Texas Ranger out on patrol. That was good in case we got pulled over. Hopefully we would have been forgiven for sporting a Pennsylvania license plate.

Houston was a sea of traffic and an impressive array of skyscrapers. From Houston, I angled south and in 50 miles came upon a shining sea of big water in Galveston. It was the first big water I had seen since San Diego more than a year earlier.

One good thing about not having scheduled programs was that it gave me room to be innovative with routes. I was so taken by the Gulf of Mexico that one morning Amy and I started pedaling south toward Corpus Christi and South Padre Island. She and Julie flip-flopped, with each driving for half the day while the other biked. Traffic was sparse here in the off-season. We crossed many small bridges over inlets, and the sun peeked in and out of the clouds, reflecting off the stunning gulf waters. Partway through that idyl, I received a phone call from a medical center in the delta city of Houma, Louisiana, which would be days ahead, located southwest of New Orleans. The center was going to try to set up an impromptu diabetes conference and wanted me to speak at it. We were glad for the offer, but we also would have liked to keep heading south to Corpus Christi. We were not sightseers or tourists, though. As I had done many times before, I reminded myself that we were on a quest. It was time to head back to Galveston and cross the state line into Louisiana.

On our first night in Louisiana, we camped on the gulf at Holly Beach. The girls went out for some partying at two shack bars, two of the only buildings in the very small town. I chose to stay at the campsite and work on a keynote address I would give at a Diabetes Exercise and Sports Association conference in Chicago in a few days. I would have to break from the bike ride and fly to Chicago for three days. I wanted my speech to be an over-the-top inspirational message written from the road while in the middle of an adventure. Meanwhile, Julie and Amy had so much fun drinking and storytelling all night with the locals that they returned to the park as the sun came up and I was ready to head out on my bicycle. They were both red-eyed and sleepy, their voices hoarse from yelling "One more for the road." I hadn't been worried. They were both tough characters who knew how to handle themselves. They told me that they would sleep a few hours then meet me down the road.

Over the next few days, we biked along the gulf, heading around bays and estuaries and through swamps on wooden bridges. It was quite exhilarating. As we approached the turnoff to Houma, we got word that no one had signed up for the conference there. This was the continuation of what had happened in East Texas. It was a harbinger of the quest's future through the Deep South. The one good thing was that we would have more time in New Orleans.

Bicycling along the Mississippi River levees into New Orleans was some of the most exciting pedaling I have ever done. The path was situated a few feet above the river, and occasionally small, wooden piers were built from the levee banks out onto the flow for fisherman. The Mississippi was very wide there as it headed toward the delta.

If you want to learn new things, all you have to do is stop and talk to the old fishermen, who appeared at least once each mile. We talked about jazz, blues, traveling, types of fish, the idiosyncrasies and changing moods of the river, and, of course, the weather. It was such a supercharged affair that we camped near the zoo on the western edges of the city and rode back out and in again the next day.

Our first night in the French Quarter was a rather tame affair. I thought Julie and Amy would own New Orleans, attracting many beads and green leis, turning the one-drink minimum into multi-drink and jumping onto the stage to sing with the bands. It seemed that between the long days spent biking and the parties down on the Gulf Coast a few days earlier, they were just recharging their batteries. They had one more night in New Orleans before flying home, and my guess was that their last night would be over-the-top madness. I couldn't wait to hear the stories.

I flew into Chicago the next day. It was amazing to leave one cultural giant of a city and enter another, all within the scope of a bicycling adventure. All my fellow diabetes warriors and kindred spirits were present at the conference: director Paula, Bill, Judith, Noah, Missy, Dave, Guy, Doug, and many others. Not only were these some of the best diabetes athletes and adventurers in the world, but they also were the best period. Type 1 diabetes was just something they lived with and adjusted to in their everyday lives. I felt honored to be among them.

My new speech was titled "Seven Mythical Archetypes for Diabetics to Live By," and a revised slideshow accompanied it. I had worked hard on it for the last week, but it had circulated in my brain for many lonely miles before that. I had used these archetypes for many years to help inspire myself through metaphorical rough and steep patches of trail. During breaks in the conference, I traipsed around the scenic Lake Michigan waterfront for mile upon mile. To top things off, during the banquet on the last night, I was named DESA athlete of the year along with two others and was presented with a $5,000 check. I felt humbled and grateful. The money would further fuel my adventures, as it was intended to.

After flying back to New Orleans and arriving by taxi at my motorhome, I saw my next driver, Dave, sitting outside waiting for me. The first thing he asked me was, "What the hell happened here with Julie and Amy?" I had hoped to hear from them soon as they were now back home. Dave couldn't wait to show me. He led me into the motorhome, and hanging from the ceilings, from the cabinets, and from the curtain rods were at least 50 beads, necklaces, and Hawaiian leis. I now knew what kind of night the girls had had in the debauchery of the French Quarter on their last night in town. Julie and Amy, as they always did, left their mark on the French Quarter, on the state of Louisiana, and on Adventure on the Rim of America.

***

Dave was back for his third tour of duty, having joined me in Idaho/Montana and along the central coast of California. After one last night in New Orleans, we would bike along the gulf coasts of

Mississippi, Alabama and Florida. The next morning, it didn't take long to bike across the rest of Louisiana and into Gulfport, Mississippi. Seven people showed up for our presentation there, and I was happy about that. In the Deep South, this constituted a monster crowd. Three even stayed for the walk around the city afterward. I took the "Seven Mythical Archetypes for Diabetics to Live By" and merged it with the original slideshow. "Archetypes" was great for medical conferences like in Chicago, but it was too esoteric for the general public. Yet, there were some parts of it I wanted to retain, hence the merger of the two.

On day two in Mississippi, Dave and I did all our mileage walking on the dirty beach, past high-rise hotels and casinos. The roads near the gulf were traffic-heavy and not too good for cycling. At our presentation in Biloxi, five people turned up at the community building, and two walked out halfway through. At least that was better than the next and last town in Mississippi where no one showed up, and the woman organizing it felt so bad. She also was not surprised. I felt like an aging rock star who could no longer carry a tune and command a decent audience.

Thanksgiving Day looked awfully somber. We had a presentation scheduled at noon at a hospital in Mobile, Alabama, but Dave and I didn't expect anyone to show. The morning bike ride was terrifying with holiday traffic. The somber mood was lightened just by the very act of survival. But then a series of fortunate events happened. Because my event was held in the hospital, many patients showed up, and some brought family members. My organizer was a young nurse, a real go-getter, and her enthusiasm was infectious for her patients and for us. Along with all that, she displayed a true Southern accent. We ended up with 72 people in the audience. After the program, the nurse/organizer invited us to eat Thanksgiving dinner in the hospital cafe with her and her patients. It was one of the best Thanksgiving meals I ever ate.

Part of the program I presented showed me changing my insulin pump infusion site on my abdomen. As we packed up our AV equipment, the nurse asked me in her accent, "Since I saw your infusion site, do you want to see mine?" I looked over and saw Dave's face turn red as he took a sudden interest in infusion sites. He had shown no interest in mine. I told the nurse that I had not known she was diabetic, but in the interest of medical science, I would love to see her infusion site. She proceeded to hike up her dress, just enough to show us her site attachment with her plastic tubing dripping insulin into the subcutaneous fatty tissue of a beautiful thigh. Never was I so glad that someone else was controlling her diabetes with an insulin pump.

The next morning, we held a walkathon through a park next to the hospital. Twenty walkers showed up, many with Type 2 diabetes. Dave and I got to see some beautiful parts of Mobile, a city I had really taken a liking to during the last two days. Then it was back to the gulf along scenic Mobile Bay encompassing Fairhope, Alabama. On one of those days, a storm left a heavy wind in its wake, so heavy that we switched back to walking through Foley and Orange Beach.

In no time, we crossed into Florida, our 19th state. Pensacola was a traffic-ridden hellscape with crappy-looking resort beaches. I'm sure there were some nice spots, but we didn't see any. We stuck to the shore, hoping to drum up some programs, but to no avail.

Hiking and biking to some more remote spots proved fun and interesting. We saw some amazing sunsets along Alligator Point and St. Joseph Peninsula State Park. During downtime, Dave and I discussed the pros and cons of owning businesses that were hard, tiring, dangerous, and not that lucrative. We both owned painting and decorating businesses specializing in high church steeples, towers, and the interior of gothic cathedrals. We often helped each other out, working together for weeks at a time. What we did get was a sense of creating visible beauty and being our own bosses, which left us in control of going on long adventures. Another key element was the ability to hire fellow adventurers who we encouraged to go forth and bring back stories to tell while working long days. We could talk about past, current, and future adventures. Active adventurers are some of the hardest-working souls and are used to adverse conditions. The funny thing is, since we were in the middle of an adventure, Dave and I talked a lot about our work and the many scallywag characters who inhabit the painting business.

No programs continued to come up on the radar through Fort Walton Beach, Destin, or Santa Rosa Beach. The roads were crap for cycling until Panama City Beach, where you could use roads only used by tourists all the way to Panama City. They were lovely because it was December and the off-season. In Panama City, we presented at a lightly attended event at a community college and then continued east to the state capital, Tallahassee. Dave had one more day left, so we biked 20 miles both ways on a bicycle trail, taking us south through swamps to a shack on the gulf serving great fresh seafood. It was one of the better rides of that year's adventures. Then it was time for another changing of the guard as Dave flew back home. We had had a challenging time in unlikely conditions and landscapes. But when Dave was along for the ride, hike, or climb, it would always be interesting and stimulating.

***

My daughter Adrienne and her sidekick, Jackie, flew into Tallahassee and reported for duty. Adrienne had been along every year for Adventure on the Rim, and Jackie had been there almost as much. We decided to use the bike trail one more day. I biked in the morning, and we all walked in the afternoon and then drove to the roadhouse, where a raucous dance party ensued that night with a live, motley band. I was nervous that the entire deck was going to crash into the Gulf of Mexico from all the shit-kicking. The next morning, we reversed direction and headed back to Panama City Beach so the girls could see that part of Florida and I could do some more bicycling on those roads. That night, to get in the spirit of the coming Christmas, we went to see the movie "Bad Santa." It was a bit shocking but also hilarious and starred one of our favorite actresses, Lauren Graham.

It was so much fun when Adrienne joined me somewhere along my route. It made me ponder the gift of children, not only when they become part of your everyday life or you become part of theirs, but more when they become part of your grand endeavors — when you are at the peak of your joy and they witness you converting that joy into creating a better world, or at least the world you are traveling through. Adrienne had witnessed that for seven straight years now as she joined me on Adventure on the Rim of America.

We angled east and south to Gainesville, where we presented at another lightly attended program on the edge of the University of Florida. Afterward, we were given a tour of the massive football stadium. I enjoyed some nice bicycle trails through swamps and estuaries heading toward our end for this year in St. Augustine. It was our last chance for a program, but none happened. We spent a day hiking all around the old city and then on the dunes and waves of Anastasia State Park. Even though it was cold, we felt we had to wade in. It was a defining moment of the entire seven-year adventure. We had once more made it to the Atlantic Ocean.

We hung out in St. Augustine at a taco food truck parked next to the entrance to the beach and close to a surf shop. It became one of our favorite food memories. We ate dinner there twice then packed it in and headed north, once again hoping to beat any winter storms as we moved up the East Coast. Christmas was coming, and missing it with the rest of the family would have been grounds for divorce. Interstate 95 through Jacksonville, Georgia, the Carolinas, Virginia, Washington, and Baltimore was for me some of the most boring road found anywhere in America. But I was okay. I had great company and damn good music. Even a bad road can still make for a grand road trip.

Chapter 19

Chasing Autumn Along the Atlantic Ocean

*"And in the quick of a knife, they reach for their moment
And try to make an honest stand
But they wind up wounded, not even dead
Tonight in Jungleland."*

— Bruce Springsteen, "Jungleland"

The eighth and final year of Adventure on the Rim of America was upon us. Only the Atlantic Coast remained: 1,200 miles to go to reach the grand total of 9,000. We had been out for two months every year since 1997. Three of those years had encompassed the Walk Across America along the far northern borders of the United States, followed by four years along the Pacific and the southern border. It seemed like we were on the precipice of the grand finale, but we still had a lot of adventure to go.

We slowly realized that kayaking up the Intracoastal Waterway was not going to happen. None of us were great kayakers and hadn't put in the time to get proficient. The idea seemed grand, especially looking at the calm bays in South Jersey where my family vacationed a couple times each year. But eventually, those calm waters would give way to where the Delaware River entered the Atlantic Ocean, and then to where the Chesapeake Bay did the same in Virginia. There would be the danger of encountering bigger ships, and the rendezvous with the motorhome each night would have been a reconnaissance boondoggle. We still needed to haul the two projectors, four slide trays, two boomboxes, the duffel of puppets, and many electrical cords. Logistically, it seemed like a headache.

Over the last many years, I had come to the realization that I was a land animal. Surfing, swimming, and boating were things I did but nowhere near with the passion I had for walking. We decided to split most days into half biking and half walking — still human-powered, and still an adventure.

Dave and I shoved off on a gray day at the beginning of November in Atlantic City, New Jersey. It seemed strange to drive only two and a half hours to get to the start for the year, a place we knew well from the ending of the Walk Across America for Diabetes more than five years previously. Dave was back again, and it seemed like he had hardly left. Only 10 months had passed since he flew home from Tallahassee.

The start was a nine-mile walk down the beaches from Atlantic City to Ocean City, New Jersey. We would battle some cold temperatures and winds until we got further into the warmth of the South. The next morning, a rain shower caused the Ocean City boardwalk to turn dangerously slippery. We biked past Avalon, Stone Harbor, and the three Wildwoods before camping in Cape May. In the morning, a ferry took us across the Delaware Bay to the state of Delaware, Adventure on the Rim's 20th state. Traffic was light, and a cold northern wind pushed my bike south, though it chilled me at the same time. We would only be in Delaware for a half day, passing through Rehoboth, Delaware Seashore State Park and Bethany Beach. I couldn't believe I was already in Ocean City, Maryland, calculating my speed as excessive. But what I had not known, not having been in that part of the world for 20 years, was that the city had been built up far into the north. Even though I had crossed the resort city's line, I still had 10 miles to go, and then south onto a peninsula to camp with the wild horses of Assateague Island National Seashore.

That night, around a lonely campfire, it was Dave's night for storytelling and regaling me with his wisdom. Normally he was a man of few words. He was used to the quiet of the alpine world, high up on a western rock wall where the closest human could be over 100 feet above or below, leading or belaying. But I had heard rumors that at the base of those big walls, around campfires, Dave was quite talkative. Rumor also had it that it may have had something to do with a few drinks, as climbers can sometimes indulge to calm their nerves from exposure. Or, it might just be how a campfire brings forth stories from even the quietest of adventurers.

That night in Assateague, we had no alcohol, so my guess is that it was the campfire. Two of the many platitudes Dave brought forth that night still stick in our heads, years later. First, he commented on the dangers of hanging out too much with women friends. To this he warned, "Laughing with another woman in public is the worst form of infidelity." His second pronouncement had to do with how much I was really into maps all my life, worshipping them like the Dead Sea Scrolls. At home, if I couldn't sleep at night, I would slip down the stairs where I would get out my stash of maps, lay them out on the kitchen table and start to plan a future adventure. My wife would sneak down the steps and try to catch me in the act of tracing my finger on the carnal body of the landscapes, imagining the wetness of the rivers or the contours of the mountains. But I was prepared. I had an old Playboy magazine my father-in-law had given me, so if I heard a step creak, I would quickly stash the map into the Playboy. My wife would say "Ah ha, I caught you," but then see that I was just looking at a Playboy magazine. To this scenario, Dave exclaimed, "Maps are the new pornography."

It was possible to walk 20 miles along the beach to Chincoteague, Virginia, where it met with Assateague. You could not drive a vehicle or ride a bicycle. I considered walking all the way down, but toward morning the rains came down in buckets. We had been chased into the motorhome as we slept on the beach. Instead, we walked down 10 and back, then headed inland and crossed into Virginia.

The next day, with the cold rain still pouring down, we walked up 10 miles from Chincoteague and back. Dave and I were in foul moods as George W. Bush had just won a second term over war hero John Kerry, even after Bush's Iraq debacle in his first term. The rain finally started to let up, so we biked for two days through lightly populated areas to the start of the 32-mile Chesapeake Bay Bridge-

Tunnel. Crossing would be impossible as part of the crossing was under the water in the tunnels. Next, one more day of biking carried us into beautiful Virginia Beach with its four-mile cement walking and biking way. That night, we camped on the shores of the bay amid the dunes with a view inland to the lights of the bridge we had crossed earlier. All night, big tankers came down the mighty Chesapeake Bay and headed into an even mightier Atlantic Ocean. It was almost a sin to waste the night sleeping with such a window into another world.

Dave flew home from the Norfolk airport the next morning. I would be alone all the way down through North Carolina. It was hard to find drivers at this time of year. None of my usual suspects were tempted because of the cold climate. South Carolina would bring forth some fellow drivers, walkers, and riders. Until then, I would have to backtrack or hitchhike back to move the motorhome forward.

There were very few towns along the 100 miles of the thin strip of beach called the Outer Banks. I biked north a bit to Duck, then turned around and it was all south through Nags Head, and Rodanthe, where I camped for the evening. It was a small park of about eight campsites right on Pamlico Sound. Across the street lay the wind-swept beaches of the Atlantic Ocean. The camp was run by surf dudes from Southern California, who were packing up their rentable kayaks, canoes, surfboards, and windsurfing equipment. The season had ended, and the cold air was driving them back to the warmth of the Beach Boys' sun. This was a place and vibe I hoped to one day return to.

I noticed a pannier-laden touring bike beside a small, one-man tent. The owner strode out from the shower/bathroom and introduced himself as Gil, a Canadian who had just graduated from university and decided to circle the United States on his bicycle. He was well-equipped and self-sufficient, following my route with some stretches in the opposite direction. It turned out that he was just as eager to find out who owned the funky, logo-plastered motorhome. We had both found our tribe. Together we walked down to the Atlantic, a light but chilling air coming off its waters, then ate in the one small restaurant left there at season's end. We told stories over dinner and committed to bike together for a few days. I had to drive ahead then bike back to Gil just so I could turn around and bike with him. That method took us past Cape Hatteras Light Station and to a ferry to Ocracoke Island, where we camped. I was so happy that I was not as lonely as I thought I was going to be.

Moving south, there were more ferries to Cedar Island and an entrance to the low country surrounding Morehead City and Jacksonville. It rained hard most days, a miserable rain we both peddled through with mutual encouragement pushing us forward. At Atlantic Beach, I parked the motorhome right on a ledge, the windows revealing a stormy coastline. Gil was glad to be able to cook and sleep in the motorhome instead of his drenched tent.

We wound our way past Wrightsville Beach toward the city of Wilmington. John Knabb flew in to drive and bike the rest of the way with me. That night, the three of us went to a concert in an auditorium on the edge of the Cape Fear River featuring singer/guitarist Holly Golightly. The place was packed with good ol' boys and good ol' girls, everyone drinking Pabst Blue Ribbon beer. We ordered the same because that's all they sold, as John and Gil bonded instantly. I had two programs to present at the Wilmington hospital, so Gil decided to take a rest day and attend my slideshow, talk, and discussion. Two days later, we said goodbye as he headed south to cross into South Carolina and continue along the perimeter of America. We would follow in his tire tracks a day later. We would exchange stories by phone and letters, wild sagas of the adventurous life at junctures of our now separate roads.

John and I took a long walk around the environs of Wilmington in the morning then led a group from the hospital on an afternoon walk on Wilmington Beach. That night, I repeated my program for a new audience, which now included the local newspaper and television station. John and I started to plan our further adventures south. We soon would cross into South Carolina, Georgia, and Florida. Adventure on the Rim of America would reach its official end in St. Augustine. Adrienne and Jackie would soon fly into Georgia to accompany us to the historic point, tying together the route from where it came from the west last year at this time. It would be a slow, dramatic build toward the goal I never could have imagined years earlier. We would continue down the Florida coastline toward Miami, so we still had a lot of adventure to come in these next weeks. The place names rolled off our tongues: the southern charm of Charleston; the broad beaches of Hilton Head Island, where we had a program scheduled; and the city of Savannah. The temperatures would get comfortably warm as we traveled the small coast of Georgia with its many Islands and the bike paths that circled them, and then we would reach the big redneck city of Jacksonville, Florida. We talked late into the night, excited for what lay ahead.

We decided to bike to the eastern edge of North Carolina, past Kure Beach and Carolina Beach. It was a pleasant ride that still had me on high alert because of the amount of work vehicles that carried contractors to a large-scale building of vacation homes. On the way back to the motorhome, I tested out my new long-distance trained body against an always fit John. I was about five minutes ahead of him when a pickup truck came roaring up behind me, and in my rearview mirror, I saw him on the phone and dangerously close to my path. He came so close to me that I felt the wind of his mirror on my left ear. As I concentrated on the danger, I did not notice the railroad tracks I was about to cross. As I hit them at a good speed, I went down hard and fractured my right tibia near the same spot I had broken it in the car accident 24 years earlier. The truck never slowed down and never looked back. Luckily, a guard inside a fence of an industrial park saw it all happen, though he was still too far away to get the license plate number of the truck. He called the hospital, which was only two miles away, with his walkie-talkie. John came up on his bike right as the ambulance arrived.

The hospital turned out to be one of the best in the country for orthopedics. The staff set the bone and then drilled a hole in my knee, slid a titanium rod down to my ankle, and gave me a bunch of painkillers. Our adventure over, John drove me home. All of our sightseeing plans fractured along with my bone. I wondered how much damage I had done. I was in my 50s now and couldn't heal as easily as when I was young. The trauma, pain, and nastiness of those painkillers all mixed into a cocktail of drowned dreams. Would I be able to come out of this and continue, not only this adventure, but future adventures too? I would have to dig down deep within my store of inspiration to get through the healing, the rehab, and the new training to get back out there again. I always knew I had it in me. I had gone through this many times in my life before. But at this moment, my drug-hazy view looked quite bleak from the sofa of the motorhome as we headed north to Pennsylvania too soon.

Chapter 20

Islands, Keys, and the Ghost of Ernest Hemingway

"You know it never has been easy
Whether you do or you do not resign
Whether you travel the breadth of extremities
Or stick to some straighter line."

— Joni Mitchell, "Hejira"

I immediately began my difficult journey back to a semblance of health, and not just fitness — more along the lines of wellbeing, equally balanced between the mental, physical, and spiritual. My body literally had broken in the bike crash of 2004. It would take a while to heal my way back to working, walking, and bicycling strength. But the layoff would give me time to work on the mental aspect — reading, learning, and having long conversations with people smarter than me, which included a large group. I could tweak, refine, and make my presentation more illuminating and vital, not that I had a lot of bookings on the road down south where I would complete my Adventure on the Rim of America for Diabetes during the next year. The South continued to be the South, disinterested and non-compliant.

I would take whatever bits and pieces I could get, though. The spiritual aspects of my healing were similar to the mental portion: reading, learning, and having conversations, along with some meditation thrown in. The difficulty with the meditation was that I usually practiced it while walking. Once again, that was going to take a while.

My first hurdle was getting off those nasty painkillers. Luckily, I always had a high pain tolerance. Maybe the gods had me penciled in for a load of pain on those lists they keep, the challenges they put you through. If they were benevolent gods, I was lucky that they also gave me a high pain threshold. Anyway, all the pain I seemed to fight my way through in life could have just been a bad roll of the dice. But the Oxycontin made my recovery difficult. Initially, I needed it for the pain, but very soon I weaned myself off it. It gave me too much fuzziness in my head, making it tough to concentrate on reading or even watch bad television, which is most television. It was even difficult to watch my favorite movies, so I threw away the pills.

Then I did what I had done during my first broken leg: spend miles walking with crutches, building up to two miles a day. Unlike my recovery 29 years earlier, it was winter, not summer. Ice and snowy sidewalks could cause problems. Eventually, I started to heal with a lot of help from my wife, daughters and friends. And that help was mind, body, spirit!

Another key element in my recovery came from a new source. Adrienne started dating a Kutztown University student named Brian. After she started her freshman year at Susquehanna University, Brian and Adrienne transferred to Shippensburg University. Brian was interested in hiking and backpacking, and a few months into my recovery, we started backpacking on the Appalachian Trail with the goal of eventually heading north to the sensational trails in the north and central parts of the state. I could now introduce these trails to Brian just like the old-timers had done for me. I used to joke with my daughters that when they really became interested in a possible partner, I would do some three-day backpacking treks with said partner, putting this new person under duress of mileage, bad weather, and discomfort so I could really get to know them. Throw in conversations while walking and campfire discussions at night, and I would really know them better. When my daughters were still young, they would just laugh at me when I told them of this plan. They often laughed at me during the conveyance of life lessons. But now the time had come to put the first of the mates to the test. As it played out, this was ne going to be a macho endurance feat or a deep probing of their menta acuity or their monastic sense of piety — not even close — and my girls knew this. Good old dad was going to be good old dad. They knew I just wanted new backpacking partners.

***

Year eight of Adventure on the Rim had unfortunately turned into year nine. The important thing was that I was back. For a while during the recovery, I had some mental letdowns. Nothing major, probably some of it the byproduct of trauma, but it was palpable. Sometimes it was that creeping malaise that always swirled around me since I had been diagnosed with Type 1 diabetes, that sense of a diminished life. I started to notice the beginnings of some complications and difficulties in the people I knew that also had Type 1 nearly as long as me. It both terrified me and drove me even harder forward. That was the frame of mind with which I returned to my quest.

I started out alone but only for the drive south and a few days of bicycling and walking. Then John Knabb would join me in Charleston, South Carolina. I left in the late afternoon/early evening and had a long, lonely drive ahead of me. It was 1 in the morning when I reached my destination in Virginia Beach, and I slept in before parking by the fishing inlet at the southern end of the four-mile boardwalk. Most of the afternoon was consumed with biking both south and north on boardwalks, bike trails, and park roads.

Though it was cold, I found the physical effort to be warming, the scenery pleasantly stimulating. That prepared me to give a rousing presentation at a Norfolk hospital that evening, after which I drove south through the night to Wilmington, North Carolina, the scene of the accident the year before. The following day, I gingerly got on my rough-and-tumble bike, amazingly undamaged from the accident, and faced the fire to re-bike the same route. I "got back on the horse," so to speak, after getting bucked off. Next came a presentation at the same hospital where, the last year, an amazing group of orthopedic doctors pieced me back together. After all that rush of blood to the head of the first three days of my trip, the rebeginning of the Adventure on the Rim would commence.

bout those solo days to illustrate a point. They seem so why even include them here in the adventurous story nce again, I have an objective to convey: to show the pacing. Whether it be walking, bicycling, driving, public speaking, life itself, I have damn good pacing. I know how to parcel out my energy, to not just to get through the day or night but to make it celebratory, a ceremony, maybe even holy. It is one of my greatest talents.

This time I made it into South Carolina. Bicycling through Myrtle Beach, I learned that the traffic is so bad that a few years after they built a bypass around the resort city, they had to build a bypass around the bypass. Luckily it was now December and traffic was lighter. More beach towns dotted the map heading south along with a pleasant sidetrack into Francis Marion National Forest. In Charleston, I walked all around the city during the day since John's plane was due to land in the late afternoon. As John appeared, just like every year for the past eight years, any semblance of loneliness or boredom evaporated. Once again, he brought that big John energy. The spirits of Jack Kerouac and Neal Cassady were back on the road again.

We bicycled into and around another famous resort city, Hilton Head Island. The beaches formed a flat circle and were so wide that it took a good walk to reach the Atlantic. The December warmth of the southern states felt welcoming. That night, I presented my program to a small but vocal crowd at the city's medical center. Most of the audience consisted of retirees, since Hilton Head was full of elderly snowbirds who come from the north for the winter. A lot of them had Type 2 diabetes, and they came prepared with questions and ideas. The following morning involved a long beach walk, a few miles of which were taken with some of my audience from the night before.

Georgia only has about 100 miles of coastline but does have a few beautiful islands with light traffic and bike trails. We were going to bicycle around a few of them, which would be such a novel adventure. First up was Tybee Island with a short bridge from the mainland. We immediately noticed how the tropical foliage abounded and how the afternoon heat became quite tangible, even though it was December. Tybee had a modicum of traffic and a few trails. These islands probably are busy year-round, especially on weekends, but luckily we were traveling in the middle of the workweek.

Next came St. Simons Island and Little St. Simons Island. The big island had more traffic, and though there was a bicycle presence with a bike lane through the towns, my caution beacon was on alert. The little island was more like a park, with light traffic and a few dirt trails.

Jekyll Island was our favorite with a long bridge approach over the Intracoastal Waterway. This was what we would have paddled through if we had stuck to the original plan. It may have been dangerous, but at least I would not have broken my leg. Bicycling around Jekyll was sublime, with hardly any traffic and bike trails on the edge of the Atlantic beaches. The campground was so inviting that we stayed two nights. Among our neighbor campsites was a cross section of American peoples and even a few tourists from other countries. Jekyll Island turned out to be one of John and my favorite places of the last nine years. Our time there was laidback but unfortunately so since we had no programs scheduled for the rest of the trip.

***

Conversations with my kindred spirits who had travelled with me during Adventure on the Rim, plus my family and even my hometown friends and neighbors, brought forth one unifying concept for the completion of this grand endeavor. Since it had always been, and then evolved even further, into a spiritual pilgrimage instead of just an adventure, the grand finale should have a man of the cloth — a pastor, a priest, a holy man, someone with that official background. I agreed, and so I booked a buddy of mine, Lutheran and Reformed Pastor Jimmie Lee, to fly into Jacksonville, Florida, and to preside over and bless the last few days and the completion in St. Augustine. I made the announcement to everyone initially on the importance of such matters. But with that announcement came a question: would John be along for the grand finale? Almost everyone knew John and of his supposed roguish reputation, so another collective suggestion was put forth: since John would be there, it might be a good idea to have two pastors present. I booked another friend, Lutheran Pastor Dave, to join us. We probably needed an entire busload of popes and holy men, but enough was enough was enough.

Upon entering Florida, John and I made our way directly to the home of a mutual friend who lived just south of Jacksonville. Colleen had already saved us time and traffic headaches by picking up the two holy men at the airport. After dinner, she led us on a hike from her backyard around and along some ponds and streams. There was not a hint of the big city to the north. We all kept our eyes on the surrounding bush, on high alert for alligators and water moccasins.

The next day, John and I headed east toward the ocean and then south along the beaches and swamps. The pastors met us on a broad beach where we had a small invocation. Then it was on to St. Augustine and the official ending of Adventure on the Rim of America. We decided to hold the finale ceremony on the beach at Anastasia State Park instead of the old town of St. Augustine. As I approached the culmination of the blood, sweat and tears of nine years, of a project that had been at times an obsession that had almost consumed me, had almost killed me, I let my emotions flow and baptized the sand and salt water with a mix of happy and sad tears.

After the ceremony I called my mom, and of course she was on the move, out and about, so I left a message on the answering machine. I always knew where I had gotten my wandering ways. Next came a call to my wife, who was at work, so it was short and sweet, though not short enough to keep her from reminding me that someone had to work to bring home some money. I called Adrienne at college, and we both felt sad that this was the only year, out of nine, that she would not be appearing. I could sense that she would go out on her own soon and on adventures with her future family. But, oh, what a mighty run it had been. We were able to bond amid amazing landscapes and meet the wonderful souls of the American people who lived along the route, including the souls of the Native American stewards of those lands. It was a time of adventure that we shared, something that would be hard to duplicate in everyday life. Then, finally, I called my sweet but not-so-little anymore daughter Amberly. She had grown up during this adventure. It was a short call; Amberly always had an agenda to attend to, but I did promise her that sometime, somewhere, in the future, the two of us would have the same bonding time I had had with her big sister. I got goosebumps just imagining those future adventures.

During the last few miles, John and I did what we always did at the emotional end of a grand adventure. John said, "Where are we gonna go next?" And I replied with, "We sure did cover a lot of territory on this one, but there's a lot more out there!" Then, simultaneously, we blurted out, "Tonight we will get out that list and follow up with the maps." The end of every adventure is the beginning of another.

***

The official ending had come, but I tacked on another week away. My two main interests were Key West and the gulf coast of western Florida. After a hike on Daytona Beach and a drive to the Orlando airport, I officially said goodbye to John and the pastors. A five the next morning, I headed back to the Atlantic below Cape Canaveral and started biking south. I flip-flopped the motorhome ahead through Stuart Beach, Jonathan Dickinson State Park, Jupiter, and Delray Beach. Eventually I arrived in Hollywood Beach outside Fort Lauderdale, where I slept for one of the very few times in a hotel. I swam that afternoon in the warm, greenish-blue ocean, and when I came in from the water and onto the beach, I saw my brother Craig walking toward me. We hugged, me getting him all wet, and he said, paraphrasing what Stanley said to Livingstone in the deep, dark, central Africa of the 1870s: "Dr. Scheidt, I presume?"

Craig made his sixth appearance on Adventure on the Rim. Officially it was no longer really that, but then again it sort of was. He would be with me for the next week, including the drive home. We continued south on an early Sunday morning, the perfect time to bicycle through Miami. It was quite exhilarating, some of the most exciting biking around. Craig parked the motorhome just south of the city, and together we biked out onto Key Biscayne, a thin strip of land going due east packed with runners, walkers, bicyclists, and tons of rollerbladers. Everyone wore the least amount of clothing legally permitted. Returning to views of beaches and city high-rises was quite stunning. From there I started to bicycle south toward Key Largo into the swamps that had been drained to become row upon row of strip mall shopping centers. It was an eye-opening contrast with Miami. The traffic was thick and ugly, full of shoppers two weeks before Christmas. I flagged down Craig, threw the bike on the rack, and announced, "I'm done with this shit."

Past Key Largo, it got gorgeous again: 90 miles of riding like you were floating on the ocean. Once again, the contrast between the keys and that swamp not sufficiently drained of humanity was wide. We overnighted in Marathon. My friends Kate and Don had given me the keys to a condo located right on the inlet, and that night there was a boat parade. The last 50 miles were ridden into Key West to the southernmost point in the continental United States. From there, it was just a 90-mile swim to Havana, Cuba.

Craig and I did a one-hour lunch interview for the highest-circulation gay magazine in Florida. The writers asked the toughest but most meaningful questions I had ever been asked. They shot pictures of us in our sweaty bike clothes, calling us "brothers in arms," and put it in the centerfold.

On our last day before heading home, I took the Hemingway house tour, peeling away from the small crowd, climbing over the chain divider, and sitting in Hemingway's chair, at his desk, with the descendants of his cats crawling all over me. His ghost could have been present, but then again it could have been south in Havana, or north in Idaho, or over the Atlantic in Spain or France. It would have been a real adventure following his ghost to those places. Later that day, I added those spots to my list right under the two I recently marked as completed: walk across America and bicycle and walk around the perimeter of America.

It was a quick drive home. We were done with the sightseeing. We cut across the Everglades and saw one monster alligator, then headed north along the gulf coast, stopping only to ride the 32-mile bike trail from St. Pete Beach to Tarpon Springs that included a wild offshoot to Honeymoon Island State Park on a narrow strip of bike path. I thought wistfully that this was the same Gulf of Mexico I marveled at on first seeing it in Galveston, Texas, more than two years earlier. So much had happened since then. I was now 50. In another five years, I would pass the threshold the doctors told me would be difficult to attain at the time of my diabetes diagnosis. But how vital can I remain, how long can I set difficult challenges in front of me that push me to thrive, not just survive? I thought about that a lot during the long drive home. Without a grand plan in front of me, would the next years see me falter, maybe survive but not thrive? I thought about that long after I arrived home. I thought about it through the next few years. I felt the heavy weight of the extreme perils and danger that lay upon the path ahead.

Chapter 21

The Poisons and the Panaceas

*"In the clearing stands a boxer
And a fighter by his trade
And he carries the reminders
Of every glove that laid him down
And cut him 'til he cried out
In his anger and his shame
"I am leaving, I am leaving"
But the fighter still remains."*

— Simon and Garfunkel, "The Boxer"

The wonderful feeling of accomplishment and the vivid memories of each and every day of Adventure on the Rim of America carried me forward most days. I was surrounded by the love of family, indispensable and interesting friends, a thriving business, and more adventures on the horizon, even if they were smaller in scope. But just like on the long drive home from Florida, that nagging sense of cataclysm, a failure of systems, the possibility of a downward spiral, all returned. In reality, there existed no cogent justification for that way of thinking. It was just a feeling, a gut feeling, thinking from the lizard brain. That feeling brought on an annoying inertia, Newton's First Law of Motion: "a body at rest stays at rest." I sat around waiting for the inevitable to manifest itself.

Obviously, I didn't conjure up anything real. But that didn't mean that bad shit didn't start happening. Maybe it was just negative foreshadowing. The first plague that struck was an enveloping tiredness. I especially felt it at work; the apex of this tiredness happened 70 feet up, inside a bell tower. I pushed myself to stay awake, not to let down my guard while hanging out to paint the exterior of a church steeple while being belayed by a coworker. More dangerous yet was when I was the belayer.

Finally, I went to see my family doctor, who ordered a comprehensive set of blood tests. All was good except for one: my TSH thyroid numbers were way off. My autoimmune disease — my overactive immune system — had attacked another endocrine gland, the thyroid. It would take the medication Synthroid a while to kick in, and finding the right dosage would be a continuing experiment. But in only one week, my usual high energy slowly returned. I had to take one Synthroid pill first thing every morning with lots of water and let it settle before eating breakfast. Other than waking up with low blood glucose and having to eat some carbohydrates immediately, this was not that big a deal. Adjusting it and having to do this for the rest of my life was a bit more of a big deal.

The next curse was the sudden death of my wife's mother. She was 84 and died of a failure of her cardiovascular system — a long, slow, wearing down of her heart and lungs — though she showed no effects until the end. Catherine was a quiet soul, a sweet woman of the soil and earth, content to be home on the farm they sharecropped from. It always amazed me that she could sit quietly on a rocking chair for hours with no tv, music, or book after the chores were done. She and my father-in-law eventually moved to a retirement housing community on the edge of Kutztown. She was known to have some psychic qualities, the ability to tell fortunes and predict future events. It was uncanny how often she was on target, although of course she was also way off at times. I gave the eulogy at her funeral and compared her subdued lifestyle with that of poet Emily Dickinson, merged with the famous prognosticator Nostradamus.

Throughout this period of a few years, I battled the plague of a series of dangerous low blood glucose reactions. I had lost the ability to feel a low coming on. I never had any reactions during adventures or training, although at those times I probably had my guard up more intensely, especially when I was out on solo adventures. I had a bunch of severe lows that brought on seizures, and the falls from the seizures sometimes broke bones. I would live my life and then wake up in the hospital eight to 12 hours later.

One seizure happened at home during the middle of the night, and I unknowingly fell down the steps and broke several ribs. I broke more during a seizure at work when I fell against a cement curb next to my van. I had a low blood glucose seizure while taking care of Adrienne's house while they were on vacation, and another when my daughters and I were camping at the Rattlesnake Roundup in Morris, Pennsylvania. That happened during a severe thunderstorm as lightning flashed all around. Nasty drops in barometric pressure, right before storms touch down, can cause the blood glucose to spike or drop off exponentially (you could never guess which way it would go). I had an extremely dangerous seizure while visiting my daughter at Penn State University right after she had finished a 46-hour dance marathon to raise money for children with cancer. I almost walked across a busy street full of fast traffic but luckily fell on my face onto the bolts of a light pole, breaking several bones and making me look even more gruesome than usual. It also added more scars to an already scarred face.

After 48 years of arresting lows, my go-to methods included a piece of fruit, usually a banana, or some fruit juice if the low was mild. In the field, I used glucose tablets or Clif Bloks. If it was urgent, I turned to a glucose gel in an aluminum squeeze tube, which I could easily carry in a pack or pocket. The gels have a bit of caffeine in them, which gets the glucose into the bloodstream more quickly. Generally, it takes five minutes until you feel the wonderfulness of the gel arresting the low. In extreme situations, with only a few minutes pre-seizure, I used a glucagon, which is a syringe either pre-filled or fillable from a vial of pure glucose. The filled syringe is then jammed into the fatty tissue of a thigh or arm. This arrest of the low blood glucose takes one to two minutes.

The seizures left me wrung out and nauseated for days and raised some new concerns. Since my dad had grand mal seizures from epilepsy, some neurologists worried I had inherited epilepsy. I had to endure several brain scans and electroencephalograms done while I was in an agitated state of heavy breathing so as to best determine the reason for the seizures. I was never diagnosed with epilepsy.

I had a sneaky low at a cafe in Kutztown while working on my writing one Sunday morning. The significance of this seizure takes me to the last plague/poison. While recovering in the hospital, doctors found some inconsistencies with my bloodwork and decided to hold me for the night and do a catheterization in the morning. The results were indisputable. My arteries were blocked, three of them at 80 percent. It was a shock to me. I thought I was in decent shape; however, the intervening years since Adventure on the Rim of America had seen me gain 10 pounds around the middle, and without the goal of a big expedition, I had let down my guard a bit. Yet, only one week before the diagnosis, I had done my weekly repeat sprints up the steep cemetery hill behind my house with my neighbor Alison and felt no pain in my chest or abnormalities in my breathing.

The day after the diagnosis, I underwent open-heart triple-bypass surgery. All went well. I could do steps slowly only days later and was rehabbing within the week. The problem was that my chest cavity breastbone had to be ripped open and my left lung deflated. I would henceforth lose about 20 percent of my breathing capacity in my left lung. Another problem was that I couldn't lift anything for a few months because of the gluing back together of the breastbone. No work meant no pay, and we faced hard times again. I started searching for some of that good ol' Scheidt gospel inspiration. Getting older, drifting toward my middle 50s, the grasping for anything positive was getting harder and harder.

In the intervening weeks, I learned why my heart had clogged. The three major ones were my dad's heart attack death at 76; my mother's crippling stroke, which left her wheelchair-bound for life at 77; and my continued battles with long-term Type 1 diabetes, at this point going on 40 years. All three put me in an at-risk group — three more bricks in a wall being built around me. I had to step things up and crash through that wall.

There were many facets to my clawing back to positivity, mind, body, and spirit. First were a series of three-day backpacking trips with my son-in-law, Adrienne's husband Brian. We did the Susquehannock Trail on two trips, completing two-thirds of the 86 miles. We hiked the Black Forest Trail in two three-day trips covering the 46 miles. I don't know if Brian realizes how much he contributed to my comeback, beyond us just having fun and adventures.

Next came a return to bicycling, with shorter rides with my wife and longer-distance rides with my younger daughter, Amberly. We started training for and competing in a few races each year, completing the Donut Derby, the Brake the Cycle of Poverty Ride, and Shoo-Fly Classic Charity Bicycle Ride. The toughest one we built toward was the Fall Classic, which went 50 miles and had three steep climbs. The climbs had tracking cables at the bottom and top, and the rider with the fastest cumulative time would win the King of the Mountain award. I really felt the strain on my lungs more than ever, but slowly, I started clawing back to a semblance of fitness.

Around this time, I was honored to be asked to give the commencement address at Kutztown High School. My wife, our daughters, a bunch of my friends, and even my father-in-law had graduated from there, but I was an alumnus of hardcore rival Brandywine High School in neighboring Topton. For some reason, my own alma matter had not yet asked me to speak there. I was being thrown into the lion's — actually the Kutztown Cougars' — den. To counter, I stacked the audience with some Brandywine allies, including my trusty brothers.

At the beginning, I figured most of the audience thought I graduated from Kutztown since I had lived there since 1979 and often helped build and paint sets for the school musicals and volunteered with other projects, along with some chaperoning. I started my speech by admitting the truth: "I graduated from Brandywine." It precipitated a shouting match between the heavier in numbers home team and my much louder allies. When it finally quieted down, I added, "At least I didn't graduate from Fleetwood." That school was an even bigger rival to our two schools, and that brought the crowd together as they cheered against Fleetwood.

Next, I incorporated the comic rule of three. I mentioned how we were living in extraordinary times and listed a bunch of events that had either happened already or could possibly happen later that year. One of these was that writer Diablo Cody had won an Oscar earlier in the year for her screenplay, "Juno." I announced that other than being an excellent writer, at one point early in her career, Diablo was a dancer and stripper at an exotic nightclub. I got a few chuckles for that. Then

I mentioned that I aspired to be like all the people I had mentioned earlier, then added, "Well, maybe not the stripper!"

My speech was based on "Five Cliches Most Commencement Speeches Use." Cliche number three, the Art of the Compromise," happened at the halfway mark, about nine minutes in. I told the graduates that in life most of them were going to have to compromise somewhere during their journeys. To demonstrate, I explained, "Most people know me as wearing cargo shorts all year, even in winter. My wife told me I had to wear long pants to give this address. But the art of the compromise had me countering with, "Okay, but only for half the night, which happens to be now." I then sat down on a chair, on the stage, and quickly unzipped and removed the lower half of my pantlegs, leaving me in cargo shorts, and I threw the legs into the crowd. Back at the podium I reminded the audience, "Remember that stripper I talked about earlier? I may have more in common with her than I first thought." Everyone agreed and laughed. That brings up another cliché: the fact that most high school graduates, years later, don't remember much from their commencement address. This class would remember that the man giving the speech took off his pants at the halfway point, even if it was only the legs.

***

The Diabetes Exercise and Sports Association was having its yearly conference at Harvard Medical School. Just like for the Chicago conference six years earlier, I was asked to be one of the keynote speakers. Amberly was preparing to start an internship in the Philadelphia hospital system, which would, upon her passing numerous exams, make her a certified licensed dietician. She would follow that with further study and become a certified diabetes educator. Together, we drove north to Boston, hauling our bicycles to ride the trails in and around Burlington, Vermont, after the conference. That side trip also would include a visit to my friend Megan, who had backpacked with me in the 1990s.

I revised my "Seven Mythical Archetypes for Diabetics to Live By" and presented it with new slides from new journeys, and new slides of me using new diabetes products while on those journeys. Meeting my tribe and hearing the stories and tales of their latest challenges and undertakings made me now more than ever want to get back out there, to plan and engage in a monumental adventure. I needed to break on through to the other side again. With the latest problems I had encountered, though, that was easier said than done.

In September 2009, Adrienne married Brian in an outdoor wedding. Brian had passed the test to be my son-in-law during our many backpacking hikes through rough terrain. When my daughters were young and I spent time with them on snow days, I always told them that I would sing to them at their weddings. The time had come for me to keep that promise. During the reception, the rest of the family performed, in jest, an interpretive dance to Michael Jackson's "Off the Wall." The rest of my family were good dancers; me, not so much. Even my father-in-law joined in playing a toy guitar like Prince, though he did not wear assless chaps. The dance served the purpose of getting everyone on the dance floor. I also am not a singer, so I practiced a lot to sing one song to my now happily married daughter: Frank Sinatra's version of "The Way You Look Tonight." I often practiced at work while rolling paint on ceilings, figuring that if I could hold a decent tune while doing that, it would be presentable at the wedding. I did pretty well at the reception, singing a capella and remembering the words, and I actually stayed in tune. But most of all, I kept my promise and, as a bonus, made my daughter cry.

***

I felt the early aches and pains of advancing age throughout my body. The training and recovery took longer, dogged by years of accumulated injuries and the resultant trauma that can start to permeate the consciousness. I started to see the tragic complications in my local diabetes community. Some friends and acquaintances who had been diagnosed with Type 1 back in the 1970s, around the same time I had, had lost toes, feet and legs. Others were slowly losing their eyesight, some had started on kidney dialysis, some had undergone open-heart surgery, some had organ transplants, and some awaited transplants. Some had even passed on to the next world. All these complications are quite common among long-term diabetics.

After 40 years with this malady, life was a shitshow of battlefield wounds, a loss of positive attitude, and the grinding down of my lifeforce from too many hours spent adjusting, maintaining, and correcting the blood glucose. Every night, there was the thought that when I closed my eyes to sleep, my blood glucose could drop off and I may never wake up again. I had lost fellow diabetics this way. For the survivors, this was a slow descent into the pit of despair, a loss of the spirit, the beginnings of a form of post-traumatic stress disorder.

In 2011, I started to feel the weight of all that bearing down on me. I felt maybe I should feel glad to have accomplished what I had up to this point. Maybe I had been the lucky one and now there was nothing left to prove. I started mentioning those thoughts to my family. They thought about it for a week or two and knew it was uncharacteristic of me. Then they sprang into action, sitting me down for an intervention. They did the equivalent of a slap to the face or dumping a bucket of ice-cold water on me. They ranted and raved, telling me that this life I had lived was not all that I got. It was not deep down to the core of who I really was. The rising up was my modus operandi. I would have to do what I always did: find a new adventure and research it, map it, make lists for it, pack for it, proclaim it to friends and family, and then collect those friends and family members and create an esprit de corps to accompany me. Amberly added one more thing: "I think you've had enough with the North American continent. There are six more continents left. Start with one and see what flows from there, and I'm coming with you!" They may have saved my life.

Chapter 22

An Awakening on the Way to Santiago

*"Travel the days of freedom
Roads leading everywhere
Come with me now, and show how you care."*

— Renaissance, "Ashes Are Burning"

I was in the Philadelphia Airport waiting to board an Iberian Airlines flight to Madrid, Spain. My heart beat so hard and so fast that I hoped my bypassed arteries, now four years old, could handle the acceleration. During my 58 years, I had been on so many adventures, big and small, fantastical and provincial, that I feared I did not have enough life left to tell all the stories in an adequate fashion. But I did have the time, I hoped, to tell this one.

Poet Evan S. Connell wrote: "Each life is a myth, a song given out of darkness, a tale for children, the legend we create. Are we not heroes, each of us in one fashion or another, wandering through mysterious labyrinths?" I chose three heroes to accompany me on my first adventure on a new continent. First was my youngest daughter, Amberly, who admonished me to leave the adventures of North America behind and begin anew on the other side of the Atlantic. She would bring her Tigger-like exuberance for the beginning two weeks.

Her Penn State University sidekick, Lauren, would bring her extreme athleticism and a drive she displayed in college, one that woke her in the darkness of mornings to row crew for hours in an icy-cold lake before her classes. Brigham was a tower of power and deep thinker with a drive like that of his mate, Lauren, causing him to think the Camino de Santiago trail was a race he was trained for. Only one day in, all four of us but especially I, learned that it was not a race — it was not just an adventure — and we were no longer in America. My awakening had begun.

A taxi took us into downtown Madrid, where we found the apartment of a friend from back home who had married a Spanish woman and lived here for many years. It was a third-floor apartment with a deck looking south. Amberly immediately noticed Alan's cat while I strolled onto the deck to view the highest mountain range in Spain, Sierra Blanca. Snow crowned the summits as they rose in far-off Andalusia.

We slept that first night on the floor then began a system of travels north by metro, train, and bus to the monastery of Roncesvalles, just over from the border from France. There was snow all around, with a light flurry in progress. This was why we had avoided the climb over the Pyrenees from Saint-Jean-Pied-de-Port, on the Route Napoléon. I planned to walk across France the following year and come up and over that part of the Camino de Santiago trail in May. We attended Mass in the monastery, ate a great meal in Hotel Posada, and met our first pilgrims, Sheila, Stella, and Diego from Brazil. They had not brought enough warm clothing with them, but luckily there was a huge box of jackets left behind by other pilgrims who brought too much clothing in the warmer months. Little did I know that I would happily run into these three pilgrims all the way into Santiago and would always be able to recognize them from afar because of those fleece jackets.

***

The sun rose late in Roncesvalles because it was hidden behind the summits of the Pyrenees Mountains to the east. We walked to the west in melting snow and mud. A sign showed that I had only 790 kilometers to reach the holy city of Santiago de Compostela. We had to wait to take a photo in front of the sign. The Brazilians had beat us to it and were flashing their wide smiles. None of us could know anything at this point of all the wonderful moments that would follow, mixed with pain, heartbreak, nasty weather, and all kinds of pure sublimity. Thirty-five days from now, we would know all of that and more.

We walked in Basque, Spain, AKA Hemingway country. He had come there to fish in the creeks outside of Burguete, the town he passed through, in the 1920s. Hemingway had needed a break from the partying during the bullfights in Pamplona, which we would walk into two days hence. This was a continuation, for me, of following Hemingway around the world.

Our first night in an albergue, a hostel/dormitory with bunk beds for pilgrims, was in the town of Zubiri, which we entered by crossing a charming bridge. In ancient times, that bridge supposedly offered cures for several maladies to the pilgrims crossing it. If that was true, then that bridge would work overtime as I crossed it. We had our first pilgrims' meal with people from all over the world, and we met several pilgrims who would become further characters in our stories. One was Bernd, a German fighter pilot with a heart of gold and a big smile. Then a huge Canadian named Yve appeared from the shower room, wearing only a too-large sweatshirt and too-small tighty-whitey underwear as he introduced himself to Lauren and Amberly. The next day, they would suddenly break out in chuckles while we walked toward Pamplona. He would repeat this routine for the next few nights, and the next day the girls would chuckle again and again. As holy as pilgrimage is, there is something that brings out the mirth of the everyday living on the trail. Laughter abounds.

We entered the medieval walled city of Pamplona through a portal. Passing by the huge bull-fighting ring, we noticed a statue of Hemingway at the entrance. I was still following in his footsteps. Pamplona is a large city in which the modern coexists with the ancient, the tourist with the pilgrim. At night, it comes alive. You can barely move through the streets. At this point in my life, Pamplona was already on my list of favorite places I had walked through.

Our albergue was staffed by Germans who spoke good English with German inflections. This caused Amberly to entertain us while walking by also speaking English with a Germanic flair. When she goes tired of it, she switched to her go-to accent, Russian. No reason why, but she had been doing it for years. Walking the streets of Pamplona, we again bumped into our Brazilian friends.

We climbed a mountain in a sea of mud. The weather was gorgeous, but the byproducts of the latest rains still poured forth from the hillsides. At the summit, we saw the windmills we had walked toward all day. The name of this place translates to "Where the path of the wind crosses with that of the stars." I would have loved to have been up there at night. The usual Don Quixote tilting-at-windmills literary annotations are entered into many a journal on this sacred mountain.

After a steep descent, we stopped for an outdoor lunch in Uterga, where we learned of a Navarren custom. When the waiter came to take our order, he brought four glasses and a bottle of wine, no label, with the cork already popped and sticking out. He told us it came from the vineyards behind us and then asked if we also would like a bottle of water. This was the beginning of my love affair with European wines.

We partied into the early evening with the Brazilians in the town Puente la Reina. Stella was a bit tipsy, having trouble speaking in either Portuguese or English. That night, Amberly was awakened by the rustling of food wrappers. She thought I was having a low blood glucose reaction, but instead it was Lauren eating a Clif Bar. Our appetites had spiked, and we had only been walking for four days.

The town of Cirauqui stood on a mound, rising from the flatlands and acting as a beacon pulling the pilgrim up to a place consisting of just a few old buildings, and then it was right back down again. Moving on, one could not help from turning and staring back at the prominence of Cirauqui. Such are the wonders of pilgrimage.

The route took us through Estella, though we did not see the Brazilians in the town Stella could have been named after. Right outside the town was the infamous wine fountain where you could fill your bottle from an outdoor tap. We were here in the morning, as were most walkers, thus limiting the amount of wine being drunk.

Descending from the ruins of a castle in Villamayor de Monjardin, we soon walked through a desolate landscape, made more imposing by an advancing black sky. The rain pelted down but for no more than 15 minutes. Later, we were accompanied by an unobstructed sun into dusty Los Arcos. After checking into our albergue, Brigham once more completed his routine of pushups and doorframe pull-ups, the 15 miles of walking with a backpack being a mere warmup. After dinner, during a Facetime call home, we noticed the Brazilians approaching, so I introduced them to my wife, thus making Sheila, Stella, and Diego an official part of our family.

Two more days brought us into the city of Logroño. During the last seven miles, we battled a windblown mix of sleet and rain that stung our faces. My merry band of fellow pilgrims had reached the end of their time in Spain. They would take the train back to Madrid and then fly home the following day, returning to jobs in the real world. The three of them had been so vibrant and wonderful, and I would miss them so much. I now faced one of the more daunting trials of my life: being all alone for the rest of the walk in a foreign country with very little Spanish in my vocabulary while battling a bunch of nasty health problems. I would enter a monastery consisting of over 700 kilometers, some of those quite remote with a deafening silence as a soundtrack. I would have to turn to prayer, meditation, and atonement to survive. Then again, the chance existed that I would find the Holy Grail in the catacombs and dungeons of the Knights Templar castles enroute. Out there, the chance existed that I would meet God. To balance all that, I would also share stories with new pilgrim friends from around the world, drink lots of wine, meet roguish characters, and delight in the physicality of the daily walking. This mix of the sacred and the profane, though always hovering around the peripheries of my life, would now precipitate exponentially.

***

I walked fast and long through the vineyards of Rioja. It became my favorite wine, and I was told that it equaled or even exceeded the wines of Bordeaux, France. Next, Navarrete, Nájera, and Azofra fell under my metronomic pace. Before entering Santo Domingo de la Calzada, I heard the polyrhythmic sound of walking poles striking the solid dirt road. I slowed my pace and met Sheryl and Glenn from North Carolina. We instantly fell into a rapport that lasted for the next few days. I occasionally lost them for a spell but then heard their laughter in a café or felt piety wash over me and notice them in a cathedral at Mass. I was amazed at the conversations Glenn could strike up with anyone, no matter the language barrier. Sheryl and I got into deep theological discussions that would continue in the years to come. At this time, those discussions were still in an exploratory phase. Humor was another part of both Sheryl and Glen's modus vivendi, with laughter often ensuing each day. They also knew of the three amigo Brazilians, and thus Sheryl and Glen became part of my Camino family.

There existed a cave, I was told, on a hill above the monastery in Belorado. The story said a monk who lived in the cave sent blessings and benedictions into the town and its surroundings. After checking in to the albergue, I climbed the switchbacks and found the cave. I then came up with an idea: later that night, I would wear my headlight, take my sleeping bag, climb up and sleep in the cave.

A Polish mother and her teenage daughter were climbing up as I descended. I met them a day earlier and happily told them of my plan. I never went back up. It started to rain around nine o'clock, plus I didn't want to stir up any problems. I'm sure it would have been epic, as much for the view of the lights of the town of Belorado and of the stars as for the spirituality of pretending to be a holy monk.

I walked with Sheryl and Glenn again. In the morning, we climbed a mountain and were on a remote trail heading toward the monastery in San Juan de Ortega. We went slower than usual and had to stop for lunch on a bank along the trail. It was slim pickings. I had three rolls, and they had a bag of figs, so we made fig sandwiches. I would have felt embarrassed if any pilgrims walking past would have heard us enjoying those fig sandwiches. We all agreed it was one of the best lunches we ever ate. On Camino, it is as much about the companionship as it is about the food.

Torrential rains followed me into the city of Burgos. I was nervous to pick up my first medical mailing at the correos. I peeled away from the other walkers and crossed a bridge over the River Arlanzón. My package was waiting for me, and several postal workers helped me to efficiently add the insulin pump attachments, food for raising blood glucose, blood-testing strips, medications in pill bottles, and a bunch of other miscellanea into my pack. That light pack would now be heavy once more. I found the people of Spain courteous and very helpful. They have taken care of pilgrims for hundreds of years. In this kind of weather, with my anxiety level cranked high, they made the transfer just another part of the pilgrimage experience.

I entered the Burgos albergue dripping rainwater onto the floor. It was scenically located right behind one of the most stunning gothic cathedrals in the world. That night, we all decided to cook in the kitchen and have a boisterous, communal pilgrim dinner. Two pilgrims volunteered to brave the storm to pick up the ingredients at the supermarket. There were some new faces from Australia, South Africa, and France plus old faces I had not seen since the beginning, including Bernd, Yve, and others. Yve was having leg problems, including lots of swelling, and one leg was turning a ugly shade of purple. I advised him to see a doctor first thing in the morning. Later, after the meal, I learned Eve was a literature professor in Toronto. He noticed my copy of Thoreau's essay "Walking" and then gave us a rousing tutorial on the value the essay held for all of us. We had found comfort from the storm in the warm embrace of a Camino community.

***

We were 20 kilometers outside Burgos, gazing west into the beginnings of the vast, windswept Spanish Meseta. It was quite sobering. From the top of the hill, we saw the village of Hornillos del Camino and the dirt road curling to it through a hardscrabble landscape. It would take half an hour of walking to reach that town. I had trekked across the plains and deserts of North America, but this seemed different. I couldn't imagine crossing the Meseta in the summer. For us, the weather was cold with constant gusts that slowed our pace. Rumor had it that pilgrims sometimes go mad partway through the Meseta from the stark psychological intensity of the desolation. Others skip the entire eight days, taking the train from Burgos to León. I was walking with Sheryl and Glen plus new pilgrims Jenny and Jill from Australia and Jane and Evan from New Mexico. For us, there was a certain comfort in numbers.

That evening, at a community diner in ramshackle Hontanas, I learned that Jane had graduated from medical school and was preparing to choose her specialization. She figured walking the Camino de Santiago would help her to decide. For the next week, I would lobby her to consider endocrinology, which covered the pancreas and thyroid, adrenal, and pituitary glands. I had problems with three of the four. There was a severe shortage of endocrinologists in America yet increasing numbers of patients who had the same problems I did. This was the beginning of a quest for me to encourage medical students toward endocrinology. I would go on to meet many such students from around the world and would present my case, let them observe the day-to-day struggles I went through, and let the Camino work its magic. It seemed that a special contemplative element a pilgrimage conjures up, whether you want it or not, can be a guide into the future.

Over the next few days, we all ended up walking many days alone. It was not a conscious decision but more like introductions into solitary experimentations, seeking and searching. We would occasionally run into each other for brief spells. I shared Sheila's headphones for a few minutes as she listened to Brazilian heavy metal music, but the unwritten rule was to let the Meseta wash over us as imperfect souls struggling through life, to see what we could become at the other end, eight days later.

During my long, lonely solo walking, I found some strange things happening to me. I broke out in tears not from the loneliness but sometimes from thinking of the earthly lives of friends and family who had passed on into the next life. Other times, a feeling of mild homesickness arose, and sometimes there was no reason for the tears at all.

However, I liked walking alone. I started to think of those Camino tropes, undeveloped in my mind but talked and written about by long-term pilgrims, psychologists, anthropologists, and even quantum physicists. I went deeper and deeper down that rabbit hole during the ensuing years of walking pilgrimages. Thoughts in the early stages of my consciousness focused on how the ancient pilgrims walked at night using the Milky Way, the Via Lactea, to guide them. The stars in northern Spain, especially on mountaintops, were bright to the point of feeling like they could drip on you. Powerful magnetic ley lines ran under the earth, a form of "places of big medicine" like the Native American shamans had talked about, thin places where the fabric between different worlds let one to travel betwixt and between. The concept of liminality was like a threshold that, upon entering, takes you to the edge of things, through the doors of perception. I understood this entire walk was way bigger than me. Something was happening out there. It was palpable. I looked forward to investigating and feeling these concepts further.

***

I met three more Brazilians, and my old buddy Sheila started hanging out with them. One night during a communal diner in Terradillos de los Templarios, Sheila, Antonio, Ireneide, and Luiz Edwardo held a ceremony where they pinned a Brazilian flag on my pack and pronounced me a "friend of the people of Brazil." Sheila had to interpret, but I was so choked up I could barely speak. One of the things we had bonded over was the Brazilian music of bossa nova and samba, especially that of composer Antônio Carlos Jobim. I listened to that music all the time. Sheila wasn't as into samba and bossa nova, as she liked the heavy metal of Sepultura, but I actually liked that, too. The next day, in Sahagún, all of them except for Antonio took the train to three days ahead of us on the Camino. They were behind schedule, and unfortunately, I would never see them again.

Walking the old Roman dirt road to the middle-of-nowhere town of Calzadilla de los Hermanillos, I started to feel a loss of energy. Two miles before I reached the town, I came across a desolate playground and my new Brazilian buddy, Antonio, swinging to his heart's content. He guided me into town, where we all enjoyed a Camino communal dinner. I had no appetite, and a strange woman from Wyoming was annoyingly acting as mistress of ceremony. Everyone had to stand up and talk about how much they missed their pets back home. I was already agitated from not feeling well, and maybe Miss Wyoming read me, but I told everyone that I missed my cat Peaches en Regalia, who was named after a Frank Zappa song. Miss Wyoming commented that cats barely counted; it seemed everyone else had dogs. I got defensive, telling her that Peaches was a diva and thought she was Barbra Streisand or sometimes Lady Gaga. Peaches had one hell of a voice. A woman named Judith sitting beside me defended me. I immediately liked her, and I later ran into her off and on all the way into Santiago. She became one of my favorite people on the Camino. That night I tossed and turned, which was uncharacteristic for me. Plus, I did miss my cat. Oh, and my wife, too.

I hit the dusty old Roman road right at sunrise, lacking sleep and with my stomach gurgling. The first few miles flew by, but then my blood glucose started spiking, and over the next stretch of road, it was soon in the high 300s. I slowly became nauseated. Evan and almost-doctor Jane sensed my discomfort, and in an act of solidarity, they told me they would guide me into the next town, which at this point was 15 kilometers away. It was good timing to be walking with Jane, as I felt as sick as I ever had. Those last miles were some of the hardest I had ever walked. It was flat, but the sun beat down mercilessly. Twice I had to stop and take a 15-minute nap. I saw the town of Mansilla de las Mulas in a drunk-like haze, and it just would not get any closer. At the albergue, Evan and Jane signed over my care to Carey, a young woman from the Philippines I had met a few days before. I crawled into a lower bunk with my sweaty, dusty walking clothes on as Carey pulled off my shoes, and that's where I spent the next 17 hours. Nurse Carey checked in every hour and made me drink some water and check my blood glucose, which had risen to 400. A virus or infection was almost certainly present.

The next morning, I felt better and was able to eat a Clif Bar and drink a glass of orange juice cut with water. The city of León was a flat 19 kilometers away. I was able to rally myself into slowly walking it in. I even stopped on the edge of the city and ate a ham and cheese bocadillo at a bar. But something was not yet right, so I booked myself into a nice room with a personal bathroom in the beautiful Hotel Spa Paris. I sat outside my pension with 10 of my old friends who were all moving on, including a new guy, Carlo from Belgium. I only met him for a minute, but Carlo would, in the next few years, become a stout pilgrim companion on many Caminos. I was very sad to be losing my Camino family. Even if I could recover quickly, I would always be at least a day behind.

That afternoon the shit hit the fan, almost literally. During the next two days, I spent half my time on the toilet. I talked to my family back home on the phone, and we figured it must be food poisoning. I almost checked into the hospital, but the symptoms finally slowed. I had played it well, having room service deliver me yogurt, bananas, and fresh-squeezed orange juice that I again cut with water. At one point early on, I dashed up the street to a bookstore that had one shelf of English-language books. I grabbed two, Hemingway's "For Whom the Bell Tolls" and Zafón's "The Shadow of the Wind," both about the Spanish Civil War and together encompassing over 1,000 pages. I read both in the next two days and then left them in an albergue in Astorga for future readers.

My third-floor room fronted the main promenade in León, a festive, lively city. I left my windows open, and all through the night, the sounds of northern Spain entertained me. I was never down and out. I took everything in stride or, in this case, no striding but still enjoying the space I inhabited. My Camino family had moved on, but my new Camino family was right around the corner, in front of another breathtaking cathedral waiting for me to introduce myself.

***

    Camino families are a big part of pilgrimage. You can find and lose these families several times over 500 miles. It teaches you to accept loss while almost simultaneously making your heart sing as you find a new tribe. New relationships deepen again. I came to realize that it was a plus to lose a family if you or they move ahead. You now get to meet more people from around the world. This is what happened to me in front of Santa María de Regla de León Cathedral. I met Judith from Nebraska (for the second time), father and son Nick and Sigurd from Copenhagen, Michael from Germany, Chloe from France, Matt from Australia, Agnes from Hungary, and Nadine from Switzerland. They looked to be a rowdy, fun-loving bunch, and eventually their energy carried me into the holy city of Santiago de Compostela.

    My pace was slower the next few days, allowing me to gradually recover. I entered the walled city of Astorga through a drawbridge-like portal at the beginning of Semana Santa (Holy Week). A Gaudi-designed cathedral/castle rose from within the walls. Outside of a church on Sunday morning, trumpets and drums played in the distance, taking me to a distant time in history. I carried my walking poles on my shoulders, like spears or lances, and felt like a Templar returning from the Crusades. Or, as I wrote to those back home, "I think I just had my 'Game of Thrones' moment."

    Chloe carried a ginger root in a plastic bag in her pack. She would boil it in a pot in the evenings and mornings and drink the tea. When the root was depleted, she would buy another one at outdoor markets in the bigger towns. She told me the tea was good for many ailments, including my nasty trees and grass allergies. I had several cups over a couple of days, and it truly helped me.

    Chloe had been walking since January, almost four months, having started in the foothills of the French Alps until the snow got too deep. She then switched to a Camino path further south toward the Mediterranean Sea in Arles, France. That way eventually took her up and over the Pyrenees and into Spain at snowy Col du Somport, and she then joined the Camino we were on now at Puente la Reina. She looked totally comfortable, taking her time, at home in her environment, in it for the long haul. She became an inspiration to me.

    It was good that I had walked myself back into shape. The mountains were looming as we climbed toward Rabanal del Camino,

Foncebadón, and Cruz de Ferro. In a little town partway up, I came upon Judith repairing the blistered feet of Matt, who was in agony. His feet looked like slabs of raw meat. Judith was all goodness and light, not at all daunted by the task at hand. I thought she must surely be a nurse, but I came to find out later on a different mountain that she was an artist. Witnessing her healing properties, I called her not nurse Judith but rather St. Judith for the rest of the way. Matt, meanwhile, healed and became one of the most entertaining of our family of misfit regal pilgrims.

***

 We climbed up and over the summit of the rocky hill where a large cross stood, puncturing the sky, surrounded by stunted pine trees. It reminded me of the North Cascades or the High Sierra back home. People get very emotional here; at the base, you could leave a stone you carried from the land of your ancestors or where you lived. That stone represents a burden that now can be left behind — petty fears, anger, psychological hang-ups. It's not that I don't have any of those, but I forgot to bring a stone. I was a bit underwhelmed, somehow not feeling the rush of spiritual significance. What I did see and feel, though, were the distant, snowy peaks of the Cantabrian Mountains, which drew me across seven kilometers of trail and made my heart race and my spirit soar. Those four miles were my Cruz de Ferro.

 The descent, however, sobered me up fast. The loose sandstone boulders make the footing, as my buddy Bradley says, like that of walking on moving, slippery soccer balls. I got a bit nauseated coming down, and upon checking my blood glucose, I found it was 400. It could have been a mix of the altitude, excitement, pine tree allergies, or a return of my stomach infection. Of course, later it crashed and had to arrest it with a glucose gel. Just another day in the life of a Type 1 adventurer.

 The Knights Templar castle in Ponferrada was another Cruz de Ferro substitute as a high point for me. I spent half a day wandering around its ramparts, towers, and dungeons, waving from within to all the pilgrims admiring but slowly walking past the castle. I searched for the Holy Grail in the dirt of the catacombs, not finding it but almost feeling like I had as I continued walking with exuberance through the vineyards of the Bierzo region and right up to the top of the mountain at O Cebreiro.

Warnings of an approaching winter storm arose as I climbed up and into Galicia, the last region of Spain I would walk through. With a slow but steady pace, not counting breaks in the three small villages you pass through, you can finish the climb in three and a half to four hours. I made it to the top as the first snowy flakes touched down. I could feel the barometric pressure of a major storm deep in the marrow of my bones.

The albergue had a huge capacity of 104 beds. Most of my new family was there, along with 96 other pilgrims. Father Nick and son Sigurd were not present, so Judith and I worried. As darkness fell, I was about to go looking for them when they entered the albergue. There were no more beds, so I offered mine since I had a bivy bag and a small camp mat. They chose to sleep on the floor and make the best of it. I was already bundled up, so I took a walk around the small village as the roaring wind rose and the skies started dumping snow. I walked out to the lookout and saw the few lights in the valley get swallowed in thick cloud cover. It was one of the most primal moments of my life.

All night, the wind and snow pounded against the windows, but it was warm and cozy inside, a classic case of the "many cows in the barn body heat theory" that all farmers know. Judith jokingly said, "Are you calling us cows, Bob?" In the morning, O Cebreiro was covered with a three-inch blanket of white snow, with the wind still howling. Everyone put on every stitch of clothing in their packs. We agreed to stay within sight of each other so as not to miss any arrows, though once the first tracks were planted, we knew which way to descend. The laughter flowed as freely as the wine and cafe con leche in the bars of the mountain towns that appeared every few miles. That descent took most of the day because it was so gradual and there were two small climbs mixed in. Further down, the flurries turned to rain, and the wind abated. This revealed a stunning, ongoing vista of the flora and fauna of the lush valleys of Galicia. It was like descending into another world. We all made it down. Surviving the storm created a bond between pilgrims that would last for our final week of walking into the holy city.

***

I detoured to the Monastery of San Xulián de Samos on forested paths where I passed what looked like uninhabited old cottages. It was like walking through the Shire of the hobbits. Then I reached a cliff, the huge, squared monastery lay below me, though it still took two kilometers of walking to circle down to it. Set in the charming village of Samos, the monastery is still staffed by monks who make their own chocolate and whisky. I vowed to stay in Samos the next time I passed through. For now, it was onto the city of Sarria and then through the farms, hills, and habitations of Galicia. We had only 100 kilometers to go.

    I walked across a long, lake-spanning bridge into Portomarín. After checking into an albergue, I went to claim my bed. There were only a few left. A middle-aged Brit claimed the lower bunk, so I threw my stuff on the upper. Douglas introduced himself, saying he was originally from Brighton, a resort city on the English coast. He suggested we find a place to have dinner, noting, "I like to get to know the people I'm sleeping in the same bunk with." I must have looked a little taken aback. Doug gave me a big smile and said, "Just joshing with ya, Captain America. You stay in your bunk, and I'll stay in mine, and things will be just fine." It was the start of an amazing friendship.

    We walked the streets of Portomarín, past the ancient cathedral that stood in a plaza where we sat at an outdoor restaurant. Doug told me he had started his Camino a few days before I did and had actually climbed the snow-covered pass over the Pyrenees and the Collado de Bentartea. He had started in Saint-Jean-Pied-de-Port, where the people had warned pilgrims to use the lower-elevation Valcarlos route or take a bus to Roncesvalles like I had because of the forecasted early spring snowstorms. But Doug was what the Brits called a "tough egg," complete with a stiff upper lip akin to a British explorer like Sir Richard Francis Burton in the 1800s. Just like Burton, Doug had been in the British Foreign Services and also in the Special Forces as a paratrooper. We didn't talk much about military history or experience except for our mutual love of the movie "Apocalypse Now." Doug did mention that he had survived the blizzard over the Pyrenees but had gotten lost in the blizzard on O Cebreiro a few days earlier. As the skies darkened, he had seen the lights of the village two mountains away, so he dug a trench in the snow under a towering pine tree, set up his bivy bag, cut up some dead branches for a fire with his big knife, and was totally happy. He missed the beer and whisky and Spanish women he was sure to have met in O Cebreiro, but otherwise he was snug and content. He got a real kick out of the fact that I, too, carried a bivy sack, but I lost a point or two on Doug's tough-man gauge when I told him I slept in my bivy during the storm but inside the albergue. I followed with, "Hey, Doug, it was because I didn't get lost!"

The Doug and Bob banter sideshow continued as we climbed steeply into Gonzar. There, we caught up with the rest of my Camino family at an outdoor cafe. We sat inside as a chill descended and steady rain fell. Matt, Sigurd, Nick, Michael, and Judith were, as usual, in full discussion mode. I introduced Doug, and he described our unlikely friendship with some valid points.

"Bob hardly drinks, and I drink too much," he began. "Bob doesn't smoke, and I smoke too much. Bob is a highly evolved spiritual being. I don't have a spiritual bone in my body. Bob is an American man married to the same wife for 40 years. I have been married three times and divorced three times. I am, however, working on my fourth, a German pilgrim who finishes in Santiago tomorrow. She owns and operates a bar in Florence, Italy. We already had our honeymoon two weeks ago in the Spanish seaside town of Finisterre."

I interrupted with, "So are you still working on your fourth marriage..." and Doug cut me off.

"Yes, fourth marriage and probably fourth divorce. It likely won't last. She's a tough woman and won't take my usual shit, but over time she'll get tired of that, and I won't change. So let's all have another drink with me and my wonderful life."

He proceeded to fill in everybody on his survival of the blizzard and other Camino hijinks. I had known Doug for 18 hours, and yet it felt like I had known him all my life. Now the rest of my Camino family felt the same.

There was still a surprising bit of up and down through the Galician forests. The flatlands had long since ended. It also tended to rain a lot in this province, and with the vast Atlantic Ocean cliffs, the mist and fog of morning, and the legendary mysticism, it was no wonder why the Irish Celts had settled there many centuries earlier and why Irish pilgrims feel at home in Galicia.

One evening, Doug, Judith, and I slept in a new albergue set back in the woods where we were the only pilgrims. It was strange, as all the albergues were usually filled. We all felt a little creepiness swirling around. For dinner, we walked in a thick fog to a restaurant where we met another pilgrim, a woman from Canada. She was staying in a pension above the restaurant. She, too had felt the creepiness of the albergue we were staying in. Doug and the Canadian woman hit it off, but after drinking too much they started arguing. Later, Doug said I shouldn't worry because that was just how he wooed women. Plus, he admitted it usually doesn't work. Maybe it was a defense mechanism.

That night, Judith was awakened by the sense that someone was looking in the windows. There were human shadows about but hard to decipher because of the mist. She was afraid to go to the bathroom. I wasn't scared because Dougie had his big knife under his pillow, but something weird happened outside that night. As the morning sun rose, our survival now bonded us as Camino brothers and sisters.

Many kilometers down the Camino paths, Doug and I decided to have a picnic lunch outside Arzua. I had picked up my last medical package at the correos and was flying high. All three of my packages had been mailed and picked up, in three locations enroute, with no problems. We bought some picnic food at the supermarket and walked one mile on a forested trail, where we sat on a thin log. Just as we got out our scrumptious spread of food and drink, the log broke, sending everything spilling and crushing under our weight. We couldn't get up because we were laughing too hard. And it had to happen right as two young Spanish pilgrims walked by, shaking their heads at two holy fools who they probably thought were drunk. We had not even had one drink (well, at least I hadn't).

On our last night before entering Santiago, my Camino family had a big pre-completion celebration. Nick and Segurd were absent because Segurd had some sort of stomach bug. He was going to rest all night and try his best to drag himself into the holy city the next day. At dinner, we met some Irish women, one of whom said it was her 24th birthday the next day. She invited us to join in the celebration, which would involve hitting all of the bars spread over the last 20 kilometers (virtually one every two kilometers). It was going to be a Camino pub crawl extraordinaire.

That next day, the last of our journey, was interesting to say the least. At the first bar, of all things an Irish pub, Doug explained to the girls that I was the perfect walking partner since I don't get drunk because of medical problems. I could be everyone else's sober guide toward Santiago, "the designated walker." Another two kilometers along at the next bar, Dougie passed on some of his holy wisdom in a toast: "As an expert, the general rule was that Americans don't drink until after 12 o'clock noon, Canadians never drink before 11, Brits start to drink after 10, Scots drink after nine in the morning, and the Irish drink at any time, day or night. So today, we are all Irish." Ambassador Doug had brought the nations together as one.

We all wondered if the finish – which would take us through the portal of Santiago, past the fountain, through the tunnel where Galician bagpipes play, and finally turn onto the Praza do Obradoiro — would be somewhat of a letdown. But it was fantastic and more, full of that feeling of accomplishment and a sense of exhilaration at all we had seen. After hugging everyone in our family, then hugging other pilgrims we had met along the way, and even hugging people we didn't know, Doug and I stood gazing at the 300-foot-high Gothic Romanesque towers built in the late 1100s, and I noticed Doug starting to cry. He took one look at me and said, "Promise me that you will never tell anyone about me crying in Santiago." A tear or two rolled down my cheeks as I told Doug, "I'm not gonna lie to you today in front of the tomb of one of the apostles of Jesus, St. James, in front of the third-holiest cathedral in Christianity, here amidst the presence of God. I'm going to tell everyone about what I have witnessed here today." And now I have.

Not to get too maudlin, Doug searched through his pack and pulled out a one-pound plastic blowup donkey. He had trouble blowing it up because we were laughing too much. Those sacred tears of minutes earlier now mixed with tears of joy. It was getting too hard to distinguish which were which anymore. Doug explained that his coworkers had given him the donkey as a going-away present, and he had carried it 500 miles.

"The name of this beast is Hotie. Donkey Hotie," Doug said. "Just like the ancient novel 'Don Quixote.' Because sometimes I can be a real ass!!"

Then the partying began. After we all cleaned up, we started hitting some of the many cafes, restaurants, and bars that line three tight cobblestone streets through old Santiago de Compostela. Outside one of the bars, Doug put a cigar in my mouth, made me hold two half-empty bottles of whiskey, one in each hand, then made me put my arms around Agnes and Nadine. Then he took a picture of me, telling me he was going to send it to my wife if I told anyone about his crying in front of the cathedral. I headed him off at the pass and showed it to my wife soon after I returned home. She didn't believe it; she sensed it was staged.

Once again, I acted as designated walker, taking drunk pilgrims to their hotels. Nadine helped me because she was only 17 and not drunk either. Not that that stopped her from drinking. I saw her drink two big steins of beer, really fast, after which she said, "Hey, don't worry. I'm Swiss."

As we walked to the first bar, I asked Doug what made him want to walk the 500 miles on the Camino de Santiago.

"My mother told me a year ago that I had to get my life together," he replied. "I was drinking, smoking, and womanizing too much. I was gonna die young. She was a hardcore Catholic, so she told me of this Catholic pilgrimage in Spain. Now that I completed it, it's amazing how much it has worked."

"I don't want to rain on your parade here, Doug, but I still saw a lot of smoking, drinking, and chasing women during this last week," I said.

With a twinkle in his eye, he said, "But you didn't know me at the beginning of my pilgrimage. I have improved. I'm a work in progress!" Doug, like the Camino, was a supremo mix of the sacred and the profane.

***

To cross the entire continent, a trail leads you three days to the western Atlantic coast at Cape Finisterre. About 10 percent of pilgrims walk it; most take a bus. It translates into "the finish of the land." The following day, while most pilgrims sleep off their hangovers, I started walking, figuring on taking seven days. I would walk further north to the seaside village of Muxia, then follow along the shoreline south for 30 kilometers to the cape. It was raw and lonely. I barely saw anyone except a few villagers in very few villages. One exception was when I ran into Michael, though he was walking the opposite way. Michael was an amazing pilgrim, having walked to Santiago many times. He knew every bit of landscape, all the side trails, the history, the architecture, the esoteric, the psychological, and, of course, the deeply spiritual aspects of the way. We talked for a few minutes and then we continued our separate ways.

It rained most days, the skies a mix of overcast gray and tempestuous, darker gray. The terrain outside the towns remained devoid of living things, except for farm dogs and a handful of pilgrims. The views of the rock-strewn ocean from the cliffs were truly primordial. I really got into being alone. The spirituality had a few good days to soak into my consciousness, to drench my entire body. It provided me a deep clarity, and the empty spaces of my mind started filling up. There was a deep joy balanced by a low level of euphoria.

The sun came out as I entered the "ends of the earth" in Finisterre. I witnessed the sunset over the lighthouse, and the next morning I turned and started to walk back to Santiago. I followed along bays and estuaries, which brought me to the seaside towns of Corcubión and Cee. And then, on a whim, after suddenly tiring of the walking, I hopped the bus back to the holy city. My pilgrimage had come to its end. This gave me an extra two days in Santiago, where I ran into Evan, Jane, Stella, and Diego. They had rented a car and driven to Finisterre, though Jane told me they had feared for their lives because Diego had driven like a madman.

On my last day, I went back to a bookstore that had a few English books. Before walking to the ocean, I had inquired if they had a copy of book five of the "Game of Thrones" series. They said it had not come in yet. Now, five days later and without much hope, I checked back. It had arrived the day before, in English! I gave the elderly Spanish woman a kiss on both cheeks, paid in euros, tipped in euros, and took the copy, all 800 pages, out on the Praza do Obradoiro. Then I sat in the sun against an ancient column and read for four hours. At the end of each chapter, I gazed at the resplendent cathedral. I read 250 pages. It was some of the best four hours of my life.

I took one last walk around the city on my final evening. There was live music on makeshift stages in most plazas. They brimmed with merriment. I saw Michael sitting at an outdoor cafe with three pilgrims and a pitcher of sangria. They invited me to sit down, and I realized that one of them was St. Judith from Nebraska. She said she had a feeling I'd turn up one more time. The next morning, I took a train six hours to Madrid and flew home the next day with a buzz I could not tamp down. I had not found the Holy Grail. I had felt the presence of a God but had not met him face to face. Yet, there was no question about what I had found: my way back to health, vibrancy, and a new way of living that would get me up in the morning during tough times. The feeling was palpable. I had been reawakened on the way to Santiago. I wanted to return again and again.

Chapter 23

Across France in Search of Jeanne d'Arc

"The wanderer has far to go
Humble must he constant be
Where the paths of wisdom lead
Distant is the shadow of the setting sun.

Bless the daytime
Bless the night
Bless the sun which gives us light
Bless the thunder
Bless the rain
Bless all those who cause us pain."

— The Strawbs, "Benedictus"

A walk across France would not be easy. There would be lingering winter snow at the top of some of the climbs a pilgrim has to navigate in the Massif Central. In between those summits would be steep descents into and over river systems carving their way through the hillsides. I also would be dragging some baggage along from home — a nasty case of plantar fasciitis in my left foot, possibly caused by too much twisting while shoveling a record amount of snow over the months preceding the walk.

My youngest daughter, Amberly, and two friends, Tina and Rebecca, joined me as we flew to Lyon in eastern France. Next came a train ride to Saint-Étienne. We were supposed to take another train from there to the start of the Via Podiensis in the village of Le Puy-en-Velay, but we learned that a landslide had obscured the tracks. This is quite common in that steep terrain. A bus ride would be our only way in. I hate bus rides, and I soon remembered why. The driver had a heavy foot on the gas pedal, even around switchback curves or in the towns with speed bumps that did not slow him down. Most people in the half-full bus looked awfully sick, and so did I. Tina slept peacefully through the entire ride so I tried to copy her, but I kept waking up, which brought on a deep and head-spinning nausea. I did manage to peek out the window, and all I saw were steep ravines on top of which sat archaic castle towers, buttresses against long-ago invaders. I tried doing breathing exercises, but that barely helped.

Finally, we arrived. Relieved, everyone rose out of their seats, but many could not keep their footing, falling into seats in front or behind them, most of their faces covered in a sheen of sweat and a sickly pale color. It still felt like we were moving. As I exited the bus, I promptly threw up on the sidewalks of the city. I noticed other passengers running behind the station to do the same. I took five wobbly steps and vomited again. There was no way I could run behind the building. I checked my blood glucose, and it was 350. Then I remembered my aching left foot as we headed down the sidewalk to our room. I looked up and saw seven steep mounds of earth — puys, or domes – one of which had a cathedral on top, reachable by an exterior spiral staircase. The top of others had giant statues. It was like something out of a fairy tale or Disney movie and unlike anything I had ever seen. So, with the taste of vomit in my mouth, dizzying motion sickness, a nauseatingly high blood glucose, and a foot I could barely walk on, I was still entranced by the kingdom of my surroundings. All my miseries became mere irritants, pushed to the back of my psyche to make room for awe and adoration. Such are the wonders of pilgrimage.

This part of France was once known for the Black Virgin statues that stand in the cathedrals. The evening before and on the morning of our departure on foot, we worshipped in a Mass in the Cathédrale Notre-Dame du Puy, set high on a hill on the edges of the city with a long set of steps that took us steeply down to the cobblestone streets. Those steps were the beginning of the Via Podiensis, the modern-day GR 65, the pilgrimage trail that takes you from the Auvergne region of southcentral France west to the Pyrenees Mountains on the border with Spain. The Black Madonna here was burned a long time ago, but pictures and talk of it formed the start of my fascination with the Cult of the Black Virgin. Later, it would build toward near obsession.

The weather was overcast and warm as my gang of merry prankster pilgrims descended into the city and then immediately began to navigate a series of ascending paths through farms and woodlands. It was both ordinary and quixotic. There were eight of us now. Cheryl and Glenn from North Carolina, whom I had met a year ago in Spain, had returned to the pilgrimage. The walk we were now on was the result of a longing discussed on one pilgrimage to someday be on another. It might be weeks, months, or years, or in this case one year later, that the vision would become reality. I learned how this longing was a pilgrimage trope. Through the bodily pain, the miseries of foul weather, and the lingering homesickness, a real pilgrim sometimes brings up future pilgrimages. This phenomenon has something to do with viewing your entire life, and maybe beyond, as a pilgrimage. Cheryl and Glenn were bona fide pilgrims.

Tina and Rebecca were both friends of mine, and both were from California. Tina grew up in my Pennsylvania neck of the woods, and most of her family still lived there. She had been on many past adventures with me, including the canyons and buttes of western North Dakota, where her bellowing laughter resounded off the landscapes. Rebecca lived in Los Angeles, but some of her family still lived in the place of her ancestors, the deserts of Mexico. She complimented Tina in both spirit and laughter. And what became important during the early miles of the adventure was that Tina was a physical therapist, and Rebecca was a physical therapist assistant. Before the walk even started, they had laid out a plan to alleviate and rehabilitate my pace-slowing injured left foot.

Carlo was from Belgium, and we had met for just a few minutes the previous year in León, Spain, right before I got sick. He was a nurse and artist who showed his amazing paintings around Europe. Carlo integrated easily into any group of pilgrims with his combination of humor and caregiving.

Jenny from Australia also was a holdover from the past year's Camino when I walked with her in the vast, open Meseta. She was short but mighty, with a fast stride that could last all day.

Our gang of intrepid pilgrims progressed steadily up and down the flanks of the Massif Central, through the villages of Montbonnet, Saint-Privat-d'Allier, and Rochegude. Occasionally, we passed those same castle towers I had groggily noticed out of the windows of the speeding bus. Most days continued to be overcast and foggy. Many times, I contemplated the amazing humanity this wonderful mix of personalities displayed and how we began to gel as pilgrims walking toward the holy lands. Especially rich were the deeper bonds being created between my daughter and I as we progressed across France. We descended steeply into Monistrol-d'Allier one day and had lunch. There, we added a new pilgrim to our ranks, someone who would play a role in this adventure for weeks to come. Sylvie was from France and lived and helped at a gîte d'étape (pilgrim sleeping quarters) hundreds of kilometers ahead of us. Sylvie was a blithe spirit, a woman of earth and sky. She became part of us from our first meeting.

A few kilometers before our destination for the night, the pilgrim resort of Domaine du Sauvage, we took a wrong turn. The red and white markers of the GR65 were spaced further apart compared to the yellow arrows used in Spain. We only added one kilometer out and one back, but that it happened at the end of a long day had us grumbling. This is how it goes on pilgrimages some days, though. We stopped for a break in a beautiful meadow, surrounded by pine trees, and everyone took a long nap. Our wakeup call came from Carlo as he exclaimed in broken English, "We will lay here till they search us."

The next day, we added another pilgrim to our group, an older Frenchman named Louie. When he smiled or laughed, he displayed a set of sharp, pointed incisors, which, along with his black clothing, made him look like Dracula. Otherwise, there was nothing vampirish about him, and we all soon fell into a kinship with him. Louie spent a big part of his life on Camino because he was retired. Sylvie knew him because he occasionally stayed at her gîte d'étape. For a few days, Cheryl, Glenn, and Jenny got ahead of us as the terrain changed to a wide-open plain where the cold winds of spring blew. We overnighted at a series of farms, complete with home cooking that included our introduction to aligot, cheesy whipped mashed potatoes. It was an incredible taste sensation and so filling to a body just starting to crave more calories. The landscapes and weather produced an intense hunger out where the towns were few and far between. Aligot did take a lot of insulin, though, as I was on a learning curve to count the carbs of French cuisine.

One day was typical, a balance of humor and amazement. We were hiking on an open plateau through patches of snow where, in the middle of nowhere, there appeared a huge, shining, white statue of the Virgin Mary holding the baby Jesus. A fast-walking German man passed us, another common occurrence on a pilgrimage; as he barely slowed, he told us his name was Hansel. Without missing a beat, Tina answered him with, "Cool, my name's Gretel," as Hansel continued on, looking for the next gingerbread house.

Just beyond, we descended into Sarbonnel, a small resort town. It was getting late in the day. We all hurt physically, especially my left foot, and the guidebook warned us that the further descent into Saint-Chély-d'Aubrac was poorly marked, making it easy to get lost. We asked the woman at the front desk of the resort if she could call a taxi. A half hour later, a small taxi pulled up, driven by a funny, animated French woman. There were five of us — how would we possibly fit? The driver laughed as she pushed us and our backpacks into the full-to-capacity little taxi. Then she drove like hell down the switchbacks and pulled in front of the Gîte.

The town was full of pilgrims, including the rest of our gang, many hanging out on the front deck of an Irish bar. As we started spilling out of the car, the laughing driver threw our packs onto the sidewalk. Tina, Amberly, Rebecca, and Sylvie started circling back and re-entering the taxi, making it look like there were 20 people stuffed in. Even the driver joined in. Everyone on the deck of the bar witnessed this clown car ridiculousness. It seemed everyone in town was now laughing. It was just another day in the life of a pilgrim.

Tina and Rebecca started offering physical therapy workshops at our evening gîtes. I asked if it bothered them to work on vacation. They claimed it was a great way to engage with pilgrims from around the world. God knows there was a need for such a service with the many pains and injuries a pilgrimage could incur. I was one of the injured, limping along with my plantar fasciitis. One night, I laid out on a table as Rebecca pulled me by my neck and Tina pulled at my feet to stretch me out, and they told me to try and walk through the pain each day as normally as possible. If I could stand tall and heel and toe it, my injury would vanish about three-quarters of the way across France. It would not be easy, but I should trust them. I looked forward to this like I was searching for the Holy Grail.

My daughter and my friends from Los Angeles would head home the next day. On our last afternoon, all nine of my fellow pilgrims baptized ourselves in the cold water of the Garonne River outside the appealing village of Saint-Côme-d'Olt. Then it was a seven-kilometer walk into a splash of pastel-colored buildings and bridges in the town of Espalion. That night in the plaza square, we all sat outside at a long table, now joined by new friends from France and England. The conversation flowed in several languages, as did the phenomenal French wine. It was a fitting goodbye to three of our gang. That night I said my goodbyes to Amberly. We both started crying during the long hug, her because she would have loved to stay and keep walking, and me because of the lonely challenges ahead with the demanding terrain, my diabetes, and my painful left foot.

***

Three elements of pilgrimage lifted my mood as I left Espalion around noon. That morning, I climbed off-route up a mountain on the edge of town to the crumbling remains of a castle. Withered battlements were strewn all around as I gazed upon a view, in all directions, of the French Massif Central mountains. Then I descended back into town to be greeted by a huge outdoor market, where I stocked up on fresh foods for the coming days. I rested a while and observed the engaging humanity, the greetings and traditional kisses on both cheeks common among Europeans. The friendliness displayed to me and others filled my heart and sent me on my way west to the continuing sparkle and radiance of the French countryside.

A usual hedge against loneliness was my fellow pilgrims. However, Cheryl, Glen, Jenny, and Carlo were a half-day ahead of me. There was no way I would catch them with my slow left foot. I missed their merriment, but I also looked forward to the monastic sense of solo walking and praying. Here in France, it was easy to accomplish this as I walked toward a series of holy monasteries, abbeys, and cathedrals. Thus began a period of my life in which I would become devout and monk-like, unlike anything I had ever experienced.

Sylvie became my French guide to both the terrain and the spirituality. I caught up to her in the town of Estaing, and she led me to an Abbey up an old cobblestone alleyway. She had walked this route before. I had noticed a huge, ancient-looking cathedral with gothic towers shooting skyward, toward God, as I entered town along the river. Some of these stately cathedrals had remnants, or at least representations, of the Black Madonna. I would have gone there looking for lodging and Mass were it not for Sylvie intercepting me. We knocked on the weathered doors of the abbey, and a nun led us in. As we were introduced to other nuns, I realized that they all knew Sylvie as a devout pilgrim. She translated to me the rules of the night's stay as the Mother Superior laid them out in French. To receive a space to sleep among the bunk beds of a side room, a simple dinner meal, and breakfast the following morning, one had to wash and dry dishes, set the table before meals, and attend the Mass at seven. Then your entire stay is donativo, a donation. If you extended your stay, you would be given tasks, usually maintenance of the building, sewing, setting up for Mass, acting as greeter, etc. It was tempting to stay here for a spell. However, my spirituality was the path each day. This was a continuation, for me, of a period of fervid and pietistic worship, both on the path and at night in the future abbeys and monasteries Sylvie led me to.

I walked solo most days, checking in with Sylvie in some of the towns. I passed through Fonteilles, Golinhac, and Espeyrac, all set upon the tops of hills, which took a lot of energy to complete the day. We were coming to the end of the Massif Central, though there would still be climbs almost every day. My left foot felt fine during the ascents, but the downhills made me silently scream in agony. I persevered and was absolutely delighted in the combination of charming villages and rural French landscapes. I was rarely lonely, and the few times it eked its way into my psyche, I'd spot Sylvie sitting at a cafe or at the far end of a pastoral field cut by a singular path. She was in pain, too, as her pack was ill-fitted for her lithe figure. We each preferred the solitude of walking alone.

I descended into the holy pilgrim village of Conques and immediately checked into the abbey. The commitment was the same as at other abbeys in France. This one, however, came with a new request. It was Palm Sunday, the beginning of Holy Week, and for the evening Mass I was asked to read one of the lessons in English. This was a sign to me that I was on a devout spiritual path and the nuns and priests recognized that. Or, maybe Sylvie had phoned ahead. It didn't matter; I was extremely honored that they asked me to partake in the Mass. Sylvie checked in soon after me and also was excited that I would read that night.

Conques sits on the side of a mountain in a remote part of France yet still receives pilgrims daily as they enter on foot, bus, or by taxi. This being Holy Week, the town was overflowing.

The cathedral of Conques was one of the wonders of the Catholic world. The impressive architecture was amazing with an array of scary faces bunched together above the massive wooden doors. Inside, 12 stone columns rose 100 feet into an intricately carved and sculpted ceiling. I sat with Sylvie in the front of the cathedral, and when my time came to read the Palm Sunday story from the Gospel of Luke, she consecrated my reading with a pat on my shoulder to send me forward. When I started to read, I immediately slowed my pace. There was a huge echo off the hundred-foot-high ceilings. After the service, a few pilgrims were asked to join the nuns and priests in the balcony for an organ and chanting recital, presented with the lights dimmed low. I participated in many sacred services back home, but this one I would probably remember till the day I died.

Between the spike in blood glucose and my poor sleep resulting from the elation of the last evening, I started out slow up the major ascent out of Conques. It was maybe the hardest climb of the route, and the weather also grew warmer as I progressed west. I eventually caught up to Cheryl, Glenn, and Carlo, who had taken a rest day. We walked together into Figeac, where we had another rousing pilgrim meal as Carlo prepared to exit back home to Belgium. He walked for two or three weeks a year and would complete this trail to the Spanish border next year. During our conversations, we expressed mutual interest in walking the Camino del Norte in spring 2016.

I walked out of Figeac with a gang of three Frenchmen: Francis, Philip, and Gaston. I saw them again and again, sometimes with days in between sightings. During one crushing, 32-kilometer day, I walked the last 15 kilometers with them, descending into Cajarc on an extremely rocky trail. My foot once again screamed in agony.

Upon arriving at the crowded albergue, Gaston announced in loud, broken English, "I Gaston, proud Frenchman, age 69, with Type 2 diabetes walked 32k today. My new American friend, Bob" — which he pronounced "Bub" like most Europeans – "age 59, Type 1 diabetes and limping with a bad left foot, also walked 32k today." The crowd stood up and cheered for us. Gaston was my biggest motivator.

Later that evening, I was sitting on a bench in a park when Francis walked by. He wore a sporty shirt, plaid shorts, and sandals with socks. He didn't see me as I took a photo and sent it back home to Amberly. She immediately cracked up, remembering meeting Francis on the approach to Espalion, her last day on the walk. She said that's exactly how she would have expected handsome Francis to dress for his evening stroll.

Phil was even more handsome, with thick, dark, wavy hair. He reminded me of a director from the French cinéma vérité. Amberly was glad that between Sylvie and the three Frenchmen, I had found some interesting compatriots to walk with.

It was around this time that I noticed two things simultaneously. In most of the churches, of any size, even in some of the small villages, there would be a prominent statue of Jeanne d'Arc displayed near the front. She would be clad in armor, sometimes wounded, blood dripping, her sword or spear also dripping blood. I became quite infatuated, remembering the many books and movies I had consumed over the years concerning Jeanne d'Arc, even one written by Mark Twain. She now edged ahead of the Black Madonna as my new obsession.

Around the same time, I started noticing a young French girl walking at my pace but always half a kilometer or so behind me. I would stop to catch my breath after a climb, turn around and there behind me, on a distant hill, she would be gliding effortlessly, the optical illusion of mist surrounding her. This happened off and on for days. I began to think I was inventing her or that maybe she was the ghost of Jeanne d'Arc. She wore a floppy hat that could have been a helmet of armor. Finally, in a cathedral in Lascabanes, as I was telling Jenny from Australia about this strange, continual sighting, the girl showed up at the Mass. It was only the three of us and one priest. I gazed at the statue at the front of the church and then to the back of the church where the French girl was sitting and was amazed by the resemblance. I even got down-to-earth Australian Outback Jenny to admit that something weird was definitely happening. As part of this service, the priest recreated the act of Jesus washing the disciples' feet by washing our feet, including the feet of the "maybe ghost" of Jeanne d'Arc. As we left the church, Jenny rushed ahead to try and engage in conversation with the French girl. I was anxious that Jenny would break the spell, but the girl's two-word reply was "no English," said with a shrug of her shoulders. But even that was done with an air of timely importance — history about to be made, battles to be marched to, the providence of God surrounding her. Then she put on her floppy hat/helmet and proceeded to vanish into the meadows of Lascabanes. I saw her again the next day at the distant hilltop village of Lauzerte, her hand to her forehead to shield her eyes from the setting sun as she gazed ahead, looking for the battlements of the Hundred Years' War. A day later, she appeared in the gothic Cathedral of Moissac, and the next day across the river Lot, high on the escarpment of the storybook city of Auvillar. Then she vanished again, this time never to be seen again. I did, however, continue to see the magnifique statues in all the churches I entered across the rest of France. I was still following the ghost of Jeanne d'Arc.

***

Every epic adventure in which I have immersed myself comes with one equally epic city that stays in my memory long after I return home. Florence, Oregon; Missoula, Montana; Moab, Utah; Astorga, Spain; Negril, Jamaica; Santa Cruz, California: Manchester Center, Vermont; and Acuna, Mexico, to name just a few. As I descended a winding trail, before me appeared a French city surrounded by hills and encased by a horseshoe-like river. Cahors became that signature city for my walk across France.

A stop at information directed me to a sweet, elderly French woman's apartment, where I procured a two-bed room for the night. Soon, a young Australian pilgrim joined me. Uriel had grown up in France, was fluent in the language, and had moved with his family to Perth while still in high school. He had started on this pilgrimage in Switzerland months earlier and was walking all the way to Santiago de Compostela and beyond to the Spain's Atlantic coast. I was immediately intrigued.

Our landlady knocked on the door and advised us to close it if we did not want her new kitten to jump up on our beds and sleep with us. I looked at Uriel as we both told her that was okay with us. I knew then that Uriel and I would get along just fine across the rest of France, and, yes, the cat divided her attention equally between her owner, Uriel, and me.

We strolled around the city and took in its amazing plazas and abundant outdoor restaurants, with every turn taking us to another bridge across the omnipresent river. One amazing bridge had castle-like towers as balustrades, which, after crossing, would lead you up switchbacks to continual vistas of the city. This was the route of the Via Podiensis-GR65, which we would be walking the next day. I was so excited that I had trouble sleeping, plus the kitten kept snuggling me. Uriel and I made a pact to get to that climb as the sun rose behind us, giving us sensational settings for photography. The next morning at dawn, we climbed out of Cahors, capturing the cosmos as a record of a fantastic and unforgettable adventure.

I walked out of the city of Moissac in a light rain. The night before, I stayed in a wonderful gîte run by a wonderful Irish couple who hosted a bunch of us pilgrims for a big meal at a table in their backyard. My friend Jenny was back along with a new friend of hers, Anna from Barcelona. Uriel showed up, too. I had not seen him for a few days. Later, we gathered in the kitchen to help with chores, and I introduced everyone to my family via Skype.

I had three things on my mind this Sunday while walking on the bike path out of Moissac. One, I knew there were numerous abbeys and monasteries in the last two weeks of the walk. Two, Sylvie's gîte was only 15 kilometers away, making for an easy day for me. Three, my left foot was indeed beginning to hurt less, just like Tina and Rebecca had predicted. I hoped to soon walk at my normal long-distance pace and mileage.

The rain came down harder, so I ducked under a bridge overpass to eat lunch. I was soon joined by a French family consisting of mother Virgine, older son Theo, younger son Hugo, and grandma Vivian. Mom and the boys were walking for two weeks to Air-sur-l'Adour, while Vivian would walk all the way to Santiago. We shared snacks and made plans to stay with Sylvie a few more kilometers along in the town of Espalais. This was the beginning of a wonderful relationship, as they eventually adopted me into their family.

A few kilometers from Espalais, I spotted Sylvie walking back to meet me. I remembered that when we first met, I told her she reminded me of French movie actress Juliette Binoche. I had lost touch with her for the last week. Her boyfriend, Vincente, was running the gîte along with a cook from Italy. Espalais was a one-street town, though that street was gorgeous, lined with huge, leafy trees with the gîte at one end and an ancient church at the other. It all sat on the banks of the river Lot, which at this point was very wide.

Sylvie told me Vincente was into an expansive variety of music. During our communal dinner with the French family, he tested me, playing the first minute or two of a song to see if I could guess the musicians and the song. I got nine out of 10, surprising Vincente that I would know Pakistani singer Nusrat Fateh Ali Khan and one of Santana's lesser-known songs, "Singing Winds, Crying Beasts." I, too, had an expansive knowledge of music.

The following morning, Sylvie and I said a teary goodbye. I had so enjoyed her companionship, her translations, and her introductions to the spiritual elements of France. Most of all I would miss Sylvie's spirit and smile. We both hoped to one day walk together again. As I walked across the bridge over the river Lot, I put on my headphones, something I rarely do while walking, and listened to Santana's album "Abraxas," which begins with "Singing Winds, Crying Beasts." Ah, this was going to be a great day after all.

***

I had two weeks of walking to reach the Spanish border. The first week was thoroughly enjoyable. My plantar fasciitis was fading, aided by the gentle pace of my French family. French pilgrims tend to walk long and steady but also take numerous picnic breaks at cafe's, grocery stores, meadows, lake shores, and churchyards. Together we hit them all, with everyone contributing to the moveable feast. My specialty was buying freshly picked strawberries from the trailside farmers. My French family unveiled every cheese known to man.

While walking, Theo, Hugo, and I sang along to Michael Jackson and Stevie Wonder songs and Pharrell Williams' "Happy." We glided through the villages of Miradoux, Marsolan, La Romieu, and Castelnau-sur-l'Auvignon. In Lectoure, I ran into the merry French trio of Francis, Philip, and Gaston once more. We all stayed at the monastery, an extension of the soaring towers of the cathedral. A young, handsome priest gathered us for dinner, sitting across from me and my French buddies.

Since the beginning of my journey, I occasionally noticed a young Swiss woman with short hair who was a really fast walker, as most Swiss are, and then a week later, she would pop up again somewhere else on the route. Her name was Beatta and she was a banker based in Geneva. I had not seen her for a while, figuring she was way ahead of me, but I found her in Lectoure that night, where she squeezed in next to the young priest at the dinner table and started chatting him up. The French trio noticed right away as Francis proclaimed, "Just look at Beatta, hogging time with the priest." She looked across the table at us and gave us a wink and a nod.

The next morning, as I walked the streets of Lectoure, Beatta popped out of a pastry shop and walked with me out of town. This was the last day of her adventure. She had to fly into New York City on the morrow to meet with some international investors. She picked up the pace and disappeared over the next hill, walking right out of my life.

My French family was overjoyed to see me again when I found them sitting on the porch of a church. Theo and Hugo asked if I had any strawberries, and indeed I did. They once again had laid out a spread of food on a blanket. There was no way I was going to lose 10 pounds of body weight like I did the previous year in Spain. My French family invited me to a restaurant that night in Montreal-du-Gers to celebrate Theo's 14th birthday. Once again, I brought strawberries, and we added them to the birthday cake. We said our goodbyes two days later in Aire-sur-l'Adour, as they were taking a train back to Paris. Grandma Vivian continued toward the snowy Pyrenees summits to the west, where I also was headed. We all had a somber goodbye lunch in a bar, and when I wasn't looking, 12-year-old Hugo stole a big swig of my beer.

Cheryl and Glenn appeared again in Aire-sur-l'Adour, which took the edge off my loneliness. We slept that night in an old monastery, right in the main part of the church, where Mass usually took place. I was still searching for the Black Madonna and Jeanne d'Arc.

I walked the next day with my old Camino friends, even sharing my umbrella during some rain squalls. Then Cheryl and Glenn moved ahead, but not before we made plans to walk again in the years to come. I felt like I had known them all my life.

Most of the last week was a miserable slog through drenching, all-day rains and deep, shoe-clinging mud. There were times when I felt like I was walking on platform heels. I traveled alone most days, going deep inside myself, meditating, taking pieces of many religions and spiritual practices, welding and fusing them together to make sense of my pilgrimage, but still the dampness invaded, inside and out. It was so remote in this Basque province of rural France that I could not check in at home for four days. Then a phone booth magically appeared, and it was amazingly in working condition, so I made a credit card call to my oldest daughter's voicemail and left an eight-second message saying, "I'm okay, it's remote, goodbye." When I got the bill weeks later, I found out the call cost me $54. It was worth every cent.

    The mud and rain continued, day after dreary day. One time, around lunch, I saw three German pilgrims sitting on a log in their ponchos during a downpour. It was the saddest lunch scene I had ever seen. Yet as I passed by, they all gave me a smile as I chuckled to myself. I ended up eating my lunch in a leaky old shed near a farm. I walked past a church from the 1600s in Pimbo and stayed overnight on farms near Arzacq-Arraziguet and Larreule. Small epiphanies gave me joy. At dinner one night, a German pilgrim saw me doing my diabetes maintenance and told me his wife also had Type 1, which she used as an excuse to stay home. He took a picture of me and was going to show it to her, declaring that it was possible for her to walk with him. Another night in a gîte in Arthez-de-Béarn, where a Swiss father and daughter were staying, the daughter interviewed me about my diabetes as part of her pilgrimage documentation for her school back home. I walked into and out of the walled city of Navarrenx as my left foot returned to normal. On another night, while staying at a gîte on a farm, Uriel and I watched the latest "Game of Thrones" episode on his laptop. So, it wasn't all so gloomy after all. Fellow pilgrims make the worst of days all worthwhile.

    Two days before I reached the Spanish border, the sun made an appearance. To celebrate, I listened to Santana again on my headphones, playing make-believe guitar on my walking sticks, singing along to "Oye Como Va" at a vista of the now-prominent Pyrenees. An older Frenchman appeared behind me and said, "Ah, Santana." I must have sounded pretty good!

    I approached an important landmark at Ostabat-Asme where two other routes joined the Via Podiensis. Both came from the north, one via Paris and Orleans and one from Vézelay. At this point, we also were close to the holy city of Lourdes to the south.

I made a triumphant entrance through a portal into the revered and hallowed city of Saint-Jean-Pied-de-Port. Here, most pilgrims' journeys begin, up and over the Pyrenees mountains to Roncesvalles, Spain, and after a month of walking, they reach Santiago de Compostela. My journey should have been ending, but I had chosen to extend it with three more days of walking to Pamplona. From there, there would be a train to Barcelona and then a flight back home. It sort of felt like I was done, but a lot of adventure was still to come.

***

In early May, the Alpha- and Omega-point village of Saint-Jean was jam-packed with humanity. Pilgrims were everywhere. I waited in line for my gîte assignment for a long time, looking much dirtier and wearier than most of the other beginning walkers. I had been away from home for more than five weeks. When I checked into the dorm, my bunk was next to a guy named Marvin from New Mexico who wore a Tour de France jersey. In the bunks across the aisle were two young women, one with a head full of dreadlocks from New Zealand named Sasha and one with a noticeable "joie de vivre" from Georgia named Katie. They started asking questions about my Camino the year before and my just-completed route across France. We made plans to start early the next morning to avoid the afternoon heat. I had noticed the rising heat over the last few days.

It was cool and damp at 5:30 the next morning, lending an air of mysticism to our first footsteps on the cobblestone streets. After crossing a stream, the climbing began. We trended upward for the first half of the day. The Pyrenees are rugged and craggy, though not high in elevation. We were going to top out just under 6,000 feet. But because the mountains are not giants, unprepared hikers take them for granted, and a couple trekkers and pilgrims die on top in bad weather each year. For my group of first-dayers, though, the weather was forecasted to be superb. We took our time. This was the ending of my pilgrimage and a spectacular start to the pilgrimage of my three comrades. As an elder of the tribe, I was there to guide them on the route of "The Way of a Pilgrim," something I had been doing all my life.

Halfway up, we stopped at a food truck. If you wanted to impress your friends back home with photos of the ruggedness and loneliness of the Pyrenees, you had to make sure your photo did not swing wide to include the queue of pilgrims waiting for hot drinks at the food truck. My initial worry about the heat and dehydration during this climb was quashed by the constant cold breeze as we neared the summit. There was a mile of narrow trail with a dangerous drop-off that could have been nasty in a thick fog. But soon, we were back on a dirt road with wide paths as we crossed into Spain. Then came a very sharp descent and a view of the monastery of Roncesvalles.

I had reached my starting point from the previous year, though in March 2013, it was covered in snow. After checking in at the albergue, Katie and I went to the bar and sat outside at a long table that filled up quickly with both new and known pilgrims. I had met Allie and Michael of Florida at the trekkers' shop the day before in Saint-Jean-Pied-de-Port. Allie had walked the Camino the year before to decide whether to get married to Michael. After the pilgrimage, she said yes to the dress and brought him back now to walk the Camino as a married couple. Allie was a bundle of energy who played the character of Ariel, the Little Mermaid, in Disney World.

Also joining us were a Polish mother and daughter I met a week before in a grocery store in Lavalette, France. Then another mother-daughter team from Berlin lifted glasses with us and our ongoing toasts. I had met them a few days earlier on the French trail. Celia from South Africa said "let's go" when we invited her to join us. Martin from Montreal, Canada, filled the last chair. This is what the anthropologists called "communitas."

My second-to-last day on the trail took me through familiar places. Katie and I had discussed Hemingway off and on for the last two days. As I sat eating a breakfast bocadillo in the town of Burguete-Auritz, Katie walked by and later told me I looked like Ernest sitting there. Maybe I was the embodiment of Hemingway's ghost. This was the town he escaped to from the madness of the festival of San Fermin in Pamplona in the 1920s.

Later that day, I caught up to Katie. She would start grad school at Montana State University in Bozeman that fall to study to become a wildlife biologist. She had backpacked parts of the Appalachian Trail, including the Presidential Range of New Hampshire. At the end of her pilgrimage in Santiago, she planned to hike and train her way around other parts of Spain and Portugal. When she returned to Georgia, she was going to road trip her way to Montana. I saw a lot of myself, at that age, in Katie.

That night outside an Albergue in Larrasoaña, the wine flowed. Two Irish cousins and two Irish sisters joined us. They had met on the long train ride from Paris and were what we Americans would call "party animals." A lot of pilgrims go to bed early, but I like to stay up late, sitting outside at a picnic table reading, talking, or listening to music. Even the Irish called it a night before me. Of course, I wasn't drunk and hadn't been since high school. Katie hung out a bit longer, interested in what I was reading and/or listening to. I told her I had discovered a new singer/songwriter/guitarist named St. Vincent, aka Annie Clark, whose music, look, and being totally infatuated me. Katie smiled widely. She, too, was obsessed with everything St, Vincent.

My last day on Camino started out normally and then evolved into helping Katie walk the 10 miles into Pamplona. I hadn't realized that her blisters were as bad as they now looked. She had tried to make the best of it, obviously used to minor discomforts from past adventures. With eight miles to go, though, we had to stop. Her pain was intense, evident in her tears. She showed me the blisters again, and they looked even nastier, on the verge of infection, after the day's first two miles. Her solid boots had served her well in the mountains of New Hampshire, but here on Camino, they were too much, leaving her body oozing in parts.

She thought of staying at an albergue in Zuriain, but I encouraged her onward. We both laughed when she thought that eating a large chocolate pastry would lessen her pain. I kiddingly suggested she should have rubbed the pastry on the wounds. With seven miles to go, she felt she couldn't go on. The pain made her feel nauseated and dizzy. We were close to the outskirts of Pamplona, and I had another idea. She took off her boots, and I tied them around my neck. Next, she pulled out her flip flops, normally used for showering, and I got out my duct tape and taped the flip flops to her feet. Since her blisters were on the back of her foot, they would not get any more friction. This seemed to work. With a few bar breaks to keep hydrated, we crawled our way forward. Upon arrival in Pamplona, I suggested she see a doctor, get some prescribed antibiotics, shop for some soft running shoes, mail her boots ahead to Santiago, rest, and take the next day off.

Katie's new New Balance running shoes felt so good that she joined me for a walk to the train station, where I purchased my ticket to Barcelona for the next morning. Back in the albergue, it was time to change my insulin pump sub-q site, reservoir, and tubing. I always alert pilgrims to what I am doing and offer them an invitation to observe. Rarely does anyone want to watch. In a show of her curiosity and humanity, Katie watched and asked pertinent questions.

At night, we went for dinner in the Plaza del Castillo near Café Iruña, the bar Hemingway drank at in the 1920s. Pamplona is a fiesta city, even when there is no actual fiesta. Tonight was "Two Euros Tapas and Cerveza Thursday." The streets were so jammed that it was hard to navigate. We ran into the Irish Cousins and the Irish Sisters. I knew this was going to be a wild soiree. Once again, my gang was lucky to have me as a sober guide. They all wanted to celebrate the ending of my successful pilgrimage and the beginnings of theirs. We had to be back at our sleeping quarters by 10, which was going to be too close for comfort. It was like herding drunk chickens through the crowded streets of a Spanish city. Too many times I heard the Irish yell out, "We still have time for one more drink." They even suggested that we could sleep outside on the steps. I was not drunk enough for that. We made it back with two minutes to spare.

I noticed there were a lot of pilgrims with bad hangovers the next morning. Maybe this was part of the suffering that must take place for atonement, guiding one to a deeper spirituality. I had diabetes, Katie had blisters, others drank too much. Everyone works through some kind of suffering. Compassion for the suffering of others and then the helping of others through that suffering should be the basis for every religion.

It was time to say goodbye to my fabulous three-day pilgrim comrade. We walked down the now-deserted streets of Pamplona, her to a cafe to write, me to the train and a plane home to America. I asked Katie if anyone had ever called her Amelia Earhart, to whom she bore a striking resemblance.

"It happens all the time, especially in Georgia bars frequented by college students and professors," she said with a laugh. "In fact, I bought a bomber flight jacket and wore it everywhere just to further the myth."

We stood silently in the middle of the cobblestone streets, no one making the first move to walk away. Finally, we hugged and I whispered in her ear, "I adore your spirit! Thanks for sharing it with me," then turned and walked away, never looking back. A few blocks later, it hit me like a ton of bricks. We had just played out the final scene of the movie "Lost in Translation," where, after hanging out in Tokyo, Bill Murray whispers something into the ear of his platonic buddy, played by Scarlett Johansen. We never get to hear what it is. Many moviegoers have speculated as to what was said. Maybe he whispered what I whispered to Katie. Probably not. But he could have. I was thrilled as I boarded the train that my walk across France and the crossing of the Pyrenees ended with such cinematic flair.

***

Barcelona is one of the most beautiful cities in the world. Two days for a tired and homesick pilgrim would not do it justice. Of course, I walked and walked, seeing the amazing architectural works of Gaudi including the unfinished Basílica i Temple Expiatori de la Sagrada Família. The line to get inside was blocks long, and I didn't feel like waiting, so I sat outside at a café, eating an ice cream cone. That was my prayer. Then I walked through the zoo and down miles of sun-drenched Mediterranean beaches. After dinner that night, I walked down to the outdoor cabana bars and watched the couples dancing on the beach. That just made me miss my wife even more.

My journey had ended. One day I would do Barcelona slowly and see everything. In the here and now, though, it was time to return to the loving arms of my family.

Chapter 24

Camino Portuguese and the Most Fascinating City in the World

*"Only love is real
Everything else illusion."*

— Carole King, "Only Love Is Real"

August 2014 brought forth the birth of an ethereal child from, of all places, the banks of the Missouri River in the northwestern corner of Iowa. My first grandchild, Miles Robert, was born in the flat cornfields of middle America because of extenuating circumstances. My oldest daughter had several miscarriages over a period of a few years. After extensive testing, she and her husband were told that the most likely way to bring forth a child would involve expensive drugs, and even that would not be guaranteed. They thought about it for a while, then one day, they decided to adopt a child. They were present at the birth, and two weeks later, they drove 1,300 miles back home, thereby naming the bright-faced little boy Miles. When they called home hours after the birth, at four in the morning and told us that his middle name would be Robert, my wife and I broke down in tears. I now had even more incentive to keep myself in fine walking shape so I could one day walk pilgrimage trails for miles and miles with Miles.

***

I flew into Lisbon, the biggest city in Portugal, and arrived to a welcoming warmth. It was early March, and I had escaped the brutal winter of home. I immediately set off from Cathedral of St. Mary Major, aka the Sé, the beginning of the Camino Portuguese. Following the yellow arrows north, I would at least see the northern part of Lisbon as it receded behind my still-shaky jet-lagged feet. That welcoming heat now became a negative force. My winter body had to adjust by sweating heavily, and my face, arms, and legs needed sunscreen.

Ten kilometers along the narrow, cobbled streets, I ate breakfast in a wonderful little bar/restaurant. This was my first chance to practice my limited Portuguese language skills. During the last two years of pilgrimage in Spain and France, I had slowly acquired some competence in Spanish and French. Now I was starting all over again with my fourth language.

I wound my way out of the city, past modern high-rise office buildings, beyond any semblance of the old, festive Lisbon. I walked along a waterway crossed by bridges that were architectural works of wonder. I spotted jet planes taking off and landing at the airport I had arrived at hours earlier. Then, slowly over the next two days, the city faded to fields and marshes. I thought I would have seen more pilgrims by now, but it was still very early in the season. In fact, I would not see another pilgrim until 10 days hence.

I climbed a hill into the quaintness of what I considered my first pilgrimage city. Santarém sat upon that promontory, surrounded by castle walls and with a river winding like a snake below. There were vistas in almost every direction. I could see the plains from whence I came and to the vineyards where I would head tomorrow. I sat at an outdoor cafe at the edge of the wall and drank my first Portuguese beer. The icy coldness permeated my sweaty being.

Then came time to find my lodging. There weren't a lot of choices, and the few that were listed in the guidebook were not open till a month later. So, I let providence and the idea that the Camino provides play out. I walked through the village until an elderly woman opened her door and put her hands to her head like a pillow and closed her eyes. I nodded yes, after which she led me to a small bed in a third-floor attic. Then she made eating motions, and again I affirmed her suggestion. She refused payment. I thought of hiding some Euros but was glad I didn't. Some people said she may have been offended. I realized that I was really going to love walking in Portugal.

Walking through the vineyards and olive groves was pleasant, though they offered no shade to my white winter skin. In Vale de Figueira, a small van pulled up, and the driver opened the back doors to display fresh fruits, homegrown veggies, bread, and cheese. Perfect timing. I waited in line with the local women, unable to decipher the town gossip being thrown around as they laughed and shook their heads. I was falling in love with Portugal, but this was tempered by the difficulty I had finding markers after leaving the village. My instincts were good, though, and I stayed the course, even at two instances when there was a choice of three dirt roads. This eventually brought me into Azinhaga, the town where Portuguese writer José Saramago lived. I had read his books "Blindness," "Seeing," and "Death with Interruptions." In an albergue that evening, I downloaded and started reading Saramago's, "The Gospel According to Jesus Christ."

The next couple of days took me through the villages of Golegã, Vila Nova da Barquinha, and Atalaia. Then the city I had been anticipating revealed itself. The entry to Tomar was nothing special, even a bit industrial. But when a mighty hill appeared to the west, all my doubts disappeared. The Knights Templar castle was as epic as any I had ever seen. It was late in the day, so I decided to spend a few hours seeing every rampart, tower, and dungeon the next morning. When I got up on the high walkways, it seemed like each portal revealed a different piece of Tomar. Cathedrals, cottages, an ancient irrigation system, tree-lined parks — this was a place I would return to.

The next four days were mountainous, with few towns, bad trail markings, and, still, no other pilgrims or rumors of them. The weather was gray and drizzly, and I got lonely and disheartened. As I descended into the city of Coimbra, the first thing I noticed was the bridge over the river that led you downtown. Next, I saw a monastery that also served as an albergue for pilgrims. Then I saw a woman with a backpack reading a sign listing the open hours of the monastery. I was so excited to finally see another pilgrim after 10 days that I jubilantly yelled to her, so much so that I thought I might scare her off. Instead, I noticed she reacted the same way to seeing me. She also had seen very few pilgrims, and we had not run into each other before because she had taken the outlier trail west to Fatima. Since there was still an hour before the monastery would open, we decided to walk over the river and into downtown Coimbra. We had each found what initially seemed to be each other's kindred spirits.

Maartje hailed from the Netherlands and had travelled widely. For the next several days, we walked and talked through Mealhada, Sernadelo, and Anadia. The discussions continued during our late evening meals. We were making up for 10 days in which each of us had talked to only a few other people. It all came spilling out, a mixture of travels past, present, and future. Heartfelt stories on how certain books, movies, and music had influenced our lives. Politics and theology wound their way in and around the discussions. Always in the background were the joys and thrill of being pilgrims on the holy trails of the world and being pilgrims of life. Eventually Maatje had to speed things up because she was meeting her mom in Porto so the two could walk into Santiago together. I, on the other hand, had to slow down since my daughter was coming into Porto two days later. Maartje and my shared experience energized and motivated us northward, and it couldn't have come at a better time.

I was a bit lonely through Arcos de Valdevez and a few more towns. Then, in the bigger town of Águeda, I stayed with a wonderful hospitalero family. They did my wash and even hung it out to dry. Their Albergue de Peregrinos Santo António de Águeda was homey, and they made me feel like they were waiting for me to arrive. And, in fact, they were. Since Maartje was ahead of me, she sent me messages on where she stayed. Then she would alert the hospitaleros of the possible Americano showing up in a day or two. I could never forget Maartje. She kept leaving a bit of her spirit behind.

I met a gang of five Irish pilgrims in Águeda who invited me to join them for dinner. Bright and filled with enthusiasm, they got together every year to spend two weeks walking on Caminos in Europe, usually around Easter. They invited me to walk with them the next day. Just before Lamas do Vouga, we crossed a stunning stone bridge called the Ponte Medieval do Rio Marnel, after which there was a steep climb to a churchyard from which you could watch pilgrims cross it. From afar, the bridge looked like a pastoral watercolor painting.

In Albergaria-a-Nova, we stayed in a bar with upstairs sleeping quarters. Once again, they knew I was coming. I took notice of the friendly ribbing and pranking going on among my Irish buddies. It was a fascinating dynamic. When they eventually started pranking and ribbing me, I knew that I had been accepted into their Camino family.

Of course, I then had to pick up my game so as t͟ back to them. Further along in São João da M͟ into Porto. It was time for them to head home.

I would only be alone for three days. be on her way to Porto. In Grijó, I stopp͟ monastery to inquire with the monks about sleeping ͟ albergue. They told me that it was too early in the season and the͟ my name. When I told them, they smiled and fetched me the key, asking me to drop it off in the morning. I asked them to say a prayer for the safety of a pilgrim woman from the Netherlands. Again, they smiled, knowing exactly who I meant. Maartje was not God, but she was still looking out for me.

I ate breakfast the next morning at the same cafe I had eaten dinner at the night before. I was up early, buzzing with anticipation at what was on the horizon only 18 kilometers away: a rugged trail that crossed a little mountain with a huge cross at its apex that led me into the suburbs of Porto.

I felt hot, tired and a bit let down as I walked through the industrial suburbs. I had forgotten how that happens in the big cities of the world. I walked up a slight rise that was just high enough to hide what was ahead. I reached the peak of land, and laid out before me was one of the most astonishing sights I had ever seen. Travelers walked onto a foot bridge with the river Douro 1,000 feet below. Along the banks of that river sat lively outdoor restaurants and cafes. On the other side was an outdoor marketplace, where vendors and farmers sold wares just in front of port wine cellars dug out of the riverbanks. On both sides were ship docks because the Atlantic Ocean was six miles to the west, too far to see, though the saltwater permeated my olfactory senses. Trails on both sides led to the ocean.

Rising above the river was the city scape, a dazzling mix of modern office and university buildings amid ancient cathedral towers and the ramparts of a castle. That view that stopped me in my tracks would become one of the defining moments in my life, and yet it ranked second among the most joyous happenings of those two days. Tomorrow my sweet Amberly would arrive, my second-born daughter, one of the three lights of my life. And then I could show Amberly what I just saw. I could relive everything I saw today through her eyes tomorrow.

***

I crossed that heavenly bridge into the thick of downtown Porto. Another vista sent my senses reeling, this time of Liberdade Square, Praça da Liberdade, surrounded by cafes and statues of the many famous Portuguese sea explorers of the 1400s and 1500s. In the middle of the plaza was a reflecting pool in which I could see the stately cathedral at the far end. After walking up and down the plaza, I headed to another one, past haute-couture fashion shops, the Harry Potter bookstore, and the Porto Cathedral, one of the oldest buildings in the city.

On my first night in Porto, I stayed at the Wine Hostel. Hip and trending younger, it sat on the outskirts of a tree-lined park. It had a cafe downstairs and a fruit, vegetable, and nut shop run by a very old woman at the end of the street. She became one of my favorite people in Porto.

The next day, I switched over to the much quieter Duas Nacoes Guest House a block and a half away. As the noonday arrival of Amberly approached, I sat outside at the pension's cafe and enjoyed a salad and glass of red wine. I was living the high life, the first day on this pilgrimage in which I didn't have to rise early and shuffle along six to eight hours' worth of Portuguese trail.

A taxi tooted its horn, and out jumped that bundle of energy and joy that I had spent two weeks waiting for: Amberly Joelle, with a smile as big as Porto. She had left the cold and snow of Pennsylvania and stood gazing around her in the warmth of a Portuguese spring. That smile could not have been brighter; it would not leave her face. She plopped down at my table and took in more sensory overload. She still had not said a word. When she finally spoke, it was to the waiter: "I'll have a glass of semi-sweet red wine." That's all she needed to say.

After checking her into our spartan sleeping quarters, we headed to the infamous bridge that shook my world the day before. Since we were traversing it in the opposite way from which I had approached, I made her promise not to turn around and look. Then at the far end, I made her climb the steps of a chapel that took us higher up onto a rampart viewing wall. We got to the top, looked out, and the smile lit up again. Amberly now officially had been welcomed to the most fascinating city in the world.

That night, we roamed the cobblestone alleys, finding churches everywhere, and eventually descended to the neon-bright riverside, home to a mixture of dance clubs, cafes, and restaurants, where we ate dinner. We now looked up at the bridge and beyond to the ramparts we had stood upon earlier. Then as we ordered dessert, a full moon popped out of the deep black sky, cresting the height of that heavenly bridge. Porto was putting on an eternal show of beauty.

***

On day one of our pilgrimage, Amberly and I took a 10-minute train to the coast, where we then started walking north toward Santiago de Compostela, Spain, from the village of Matosinhos. This was the second time I walked along the ocean in the two and a half years on Camino, having been in Muxía and Finisterre at the end of my first year. There is a certain exhilaration to walking on remote trails along an ocean with the waves crashing. We both felt it. There were a few seasonal beach towns every five kilometers or so, but most of the cafes were not yet open for the summer. However, it was a treat when we found an open one where we could sit outside on a deck with a beer, wine, or coffee. We felt especially giddy if it wasn't even noon yet. We were free as birds. We had no schedule or timetable other than to walk. It was liberating and opened all kinds of frequencies for meditation and ideas.

Boa Nova Lighthouse, Labruge, and Vila Chã passed under our feet. Sometime toward the middle of the afternoon, we were sitting on a big rock, watching the waves get wilder while we got even more contemplative, when Amberly's phone broke the spell. As she listened, her face lit up even brighter than usual. A few days before leaving home, she had interviewed for a job in in-patient nutritional care at a hospital in Allentown. She had studied for four years at Penn State and completed a year of internships at a bunch of Philadelphia hospitals to prepare her for this job, and she figured that she would find out about it sometime after returning home. Amberly had only been in Portugal for a little over a day when she found out that she had been accepted. She told the caller that she was backpacking up the Atlantic Coast of Portugal with her dad. The caller already knew and told her to check in as soon as she returned. This was a moment we would never forget. I was so proud to be in that space, at that time, on a fabulous coastal adventure, sharing that moment with my daughter.

It was a long mileage day, but the weather was perfect, and we had no climbs. We were still a little tired when we reached our albergue in the resort town of Vila do Conde. The following day, we said goodbye to the ocean and headed inland. Now that we had a taste of the Coastal Route, we knew we would one day return.

Our first night on the Central Route, we stayed at the famous Restaurante Pedra Furada with hospitalero Antonio, who never stopped smiling. We ate dinner and hung out with a young German couple, Andy and Coralinda. Then, further on, we walked to the scenic pilgrimage town of Barcelos, where we witnessed the Easter parades in every little village to which our afternoon route took us. We could see the mountains appearing ahead and looked forward to the challenge and fruits they had to offer us.

Our first climb took us up to a modern albergue and a communal dinner with three new pilgrims, Philip and Lila from Germany and Renee from Holland. Lila bubbled over with spirit, whereas the other two were rather quiet. In fact, older Renee seemed downright grumpy. Later we learned he was a longtime pilgrim and was not as enamored with Portugal. He couldn't wait to get to Spain in a few days.

We walked most days in comfortable weather through picaresque woodlands and fields, with a village every five to 10 kilometers. We stopped to talk to local inhabitants, both human and animal. We were still in the learning phase of Portuguese, but we were both fluent in most animal languages since those come from the heart.

Our next sleeping stop was in the town of Ponte de Lima, a captivating city along the Lima River, with the bridge of its name coming to life in an array of sparkling lights. Then it was up and over a steep mountain. We took a break before the climb at a little country market. There we met two pilgrims, Mari and Charlie from England. After just two minutes of comical banter, Amberly and I knew that we hoped to run into them again somewhere along the way. At the top of the mountain, we took an hour-long break and napped on a slab of granite warm from the sun. The vista looked down to the village of Rubiães, our destination for the evening. On the way down, Amberly slipped on rock, spraining her ankle and skinning her knees. We would have to walk more slowly over the next few days.

That evening, we ate dinner at a bar with outdoor tables. Charlie and Mari took the hilarity to another level and introduced us to Megan from Toronto and Heidi from Belgium. They were both willing participants and sometimes just observers of the sharp hijinks swirling around Mari and Charlie. The Londoners mentioned that when they passed Amberly and I while we napped in the sun on the mountain, they thought it was so idyllic that it caused them to get sleepy.

It was slow going for Amberly with her poor ankle, so we downgraded our schedule, knowing she would not make it to Santiago de Compostela. Our new goal was Pontevedra, where she could catch a bus to Porto to fly home. We ran into Renee again and walked together into Valença. At our sunny outdoor lunch, his grumpiness faded because we could see Spain across the river. It was a dramatic setting as we walked through the labyrinths of a fort and then crossed a long bridge over the river into Tui, Spain. An iconic sign welcomes pilgrims with, simply, "España." Tui was a mini city on a hill with a massive cathedral and stately castle. I loved Portugal, where I had spent nearly three weeks. But like my buddy Renee, I felt wonderful being back in Spain.

The evening before Amberly departed the pilgrimage, we ate our last dinner together at a kebab restaurant. We laughed at how, on her last night in Europe, we chose simple Turkish food instead of fine Spanish cuisine. We laughed a lot, recalling the usual hilarious instances that always happen when Amberly and I are on adventures. Then, slowly, as the evening wore on, feelings described by the Portuguese word "saudade," a longing to just keep walking together, filtered in. I knew I would miss my Amberly, and I knew she would miss the brightness of the Camino, our fellow pilgrims, and maybe even her dear old dad. Amberly doesn't worry about me when I'm out alone, but she, more than anyone around us, knows of my daily battles with heart disease and Type 1 diabetes. It is part of her chosen profession. But she also knows deep in her heart that, out here, in the rigors of the day-to-day life of a medically compromised adventurer, is where I thrive. She understands that this is truly who I am.

***

I completed the last two and a half days into Santiago, walking through Caldas de Reis and Padrón. I was back with my family of Megan, Heidi, Mari, and Charlie. Then my longtime adventurer friend Tina from California showed up with her new husband, Mike, in tow. We were now seven. Tina and Mike's part would be a short stint, the last two days into the holy city. They had spent time in Madrid visiting a relative, a nun in training at an abbey, and would go back there in a few days. They fit right into my Camino family. We all bathed our feet in the healing cold springs that the town of Caldas de Rei is known for, and then we ate and drank our way into the evening. Everyone, including me, were amazed and amused that Tina and Mike would spend so much time on their vacation at an abbey in Madrid. Of course, who were we to judge? We spent our vacations walking all day in sometimes nasty weather with all kinds of aches and pains.

We entered the holy city of Santiago de Compostela, this being my third time, in high spirits with feelings of reverence. We went to Mass, cleaned up, and then the partying began. We sat for hours at an outdoor table, and other pilgrims we knew checked in. I had met a mother-and-daughter team of pilgrims from Siberia named Tatiana and Lava a few days earlier, and now they joined us at our table. All was well until Tatiana announced, "Now we drink vodka." Toughies Charlie and Mari, both veterans from the British military, said they were in. Mike, a big dude, said, "Salute." And then the mayhem ensued. Charlie and Mari dropped out early. Mike held his own for a while but eventually found his limits. Tatiana, who weighed about 100 pounds, showed no signs of inebriation. She claimed that most everyone from Vladivostok can handle vodka with ease.

Since I had two weeks left till my flight home, I decided to take the train east to Léon and walk back over the Galician mountains to the holy city. I said goodbye to the hilarious, rowdy dynamic duo of Mari and Charlie, the enjoyable wisdom of Megan, the elegant mysticism of Heidi, and the always-up-for-adventure souls of Mike and Tina. I knew this would not be the last time I would see them all. There was a good chance we would walk together on Camino again, someday, somewhere.

***

I figured walking from Léon would be a nice, quiet coda to my just-completed walk up from Lisbon. I knew the terrain and landscapes would be epic, but I had no idea how wild and crazy a time it would turn into.

I love riding trains in Europe. It was part of the attraction of returning to the pilgrimage city of Léon. I loved the time I spent there two years previously, even as I entered with a bad case of food poisoning. The people of Léon nursed me back to health, for which I will always be grateful. This time, I stayed in the albergue connected to the chapel where they have a Mass and evening vespers, which I attended. I had missed that element in Portugal.

I walked out of the city the next morning, through the industrial suburbs, one of the least-scenic sections of any Camino. It all changes when you get to the amazing stone bridge in Hospital De Órbigo. From there, the windswept expanses of the meseta still reigned supreme. On that remote dirt road, I met my first pilgrim. Jen was born in Cuba but had lived most of her life in New York City. Her Camino was a tool for planning the rest of her life as a possible world traveler. The aura about Jen made her instantly interesting to me. Then she took it up a notch.

After a few miles of walking, we came to a solo lookout tower, like something out of a medieval movie, rising 30 feet above the bleak terrain. Two young French boys were on top and yelled down to us with an offer of free cookies if we climbed up. A rusty iron ladder was bolted to the tower. I climb ladders for a living, so it was no big deal for me. Jen looked at me and said, "Let's climb it." So up we went. Since the pitch was so straight, it was strenuous. When we reached the top, the French boys were happy. No one had taken their offer till we did. I told Jen that she must have been hungry for cookies. She replied, "Yes, but also hungry for experience and challenges." She definitely would be a great walking companion as we entered the mountains ahead.

Jen and I walked into Astorga, which for me is one of the most intriguing places on the Camino. The city had a wall surrounding it, and people can walk on the ramparts. After checking into the municipal albergue, we walked into the plaza, where we sat in the sun of a cafe and worked on our journals. Later, we had dinner together, and the conversation flowed. Jen was very at ease talking about a range of subjects. Then we turned in early since halfway through the next day the climbing would begin.

We walked through the villages of Santa Catalina de Somoza; El Ganso, home to the infamous Cowboy Bar; and, after the first climb, into the home of the singing monks in Rabanal, where Jen and I stopped for a late lunch. Then came more climbing to the ancient pilgrim village of Foncebadón. The village was in transition, and the ruins were at the beginning stages of revival. We were almost up the mountain, and after dinner, I stood out on the escarpment under a canopy of millions of stars. You could feel the altitude and the spirits of those who had gone before us. The air was chilly to the bone as I gazed at the distant lights of Astorga to the east. I finally hustled back to the bunk room, though I felt like I could have stayed out all night.

Jen was hurting the next morning. She had a few blisters, but mostly it was bad ankles that were slowing her down. We completed the last of the climb to Cruz de Ferro, engaging in the usual solemn ceremonies, and started to head down. Jen told me to go on. She was thinking of taking two days off at the bottom of the mountain. She had friends who lived in Ponferrada, where she could heal. We promised to keep in touch, and maybe if I slowed down and her recovery was complete, she might catch up to me. We both liked the idea of walking into Santiago together.

I sped down the high mountain paths, surrounded by snowcapped peaks. This section would always be one of my favorite places in the world. In the one-building village of Manjarín, I met an old man, Tomas, who claimed he was the last of the Knights Templar warrior priests. I made a mental note to stay overnight with Tomas on a future Camino. I also met Nancy from my home state of Pennsylvania, who was constantly on the move, living sometimes in a flat in London, and at other times in an ashram in India. She walked with a big bear of a man named Gaetano, who was born in Italy but now lived in Germany. Over the next few days, I ran into them daily, including in Molinaseca, Villafranca del Bierzo, and on the next mountain on the scenic alternative route of Pradela. During that time, we formed an alliance and decided to walk together into the holy city. This meant I was only lonely for a few miles, from when I left Jen until I met Nancy and Gaetano. Such are the wonderful ways of pilgrimage.

During this time, I also had some interaction with two lighthearted, entertaining women from Germany. Janine hailed from Hamburg and Stephanie from Stuttgart. Eventually, we all met up at the base of the next big climb, in the little village of Las Herrerías. Our

Camino family now numbered five as I looked forward to exploring Galicia with this stimulating group of pilgrims.

The climb up O Cebreiro is the second-toughest climb on the traditional Frances route, the hardest being up and over the Pyrenees on the first day. But when you have a group as lively as I did, the miles fly by. In Fonfría, we were gifted with a beautiful, sunny day, so we all hung out our clothes on wash lines in a meadow belonging to the albergue. Two years earlier, I was in the midst of a blizzard there. The dirt road we crossed to get to our wash had a lot of traffic; however, it was all cows shepherded by wizened old farmers and spirited dogs. This was the most fun I ever had doing wash.

We descended off the mountain with views in all directions of the pastoral land of Galicia. The vistas kept coming at us. Our quintet bounded down in a state of entrancement. The trail split in Triacastela, and we chose to go left toward the monastery in Samos, where we took a tour with the monks of their chocolate and whiskey making facilities. Except for Nancy, we confessed to the monks that we all had chocolate addictions, and not back home — only here on Camino. At least it was less dangerous than a whiskey addiction, though we heard from other pilgrims that the monks' whiskey was superb. The next morning, we walked the road into Sarria. It saved us four kilometers, but it was off and onto the shoulder, which made for frustrating walking even though traffic was light.

Heading into the last five days of our pilgrimage, we began to jell as a group and rolled on like a well-oiled machine. Each day, I walked for a spell with a different member of the gang and started to form short word sketches in my memory. From Barbadelo to Ferreiros, I observed and learned things about Nancy. "Mata Ji — Mother Beloved" was a term of endearment Nancy's daughter used to address her in correspondence. But on, Camino she was not our mother. She never came off like that. On the contrary, she became like a kid again on the trails and backroads of northern Spain. She was, to me, an example of a non-showy spiritual soul, someone who possesses a spirituality on the inside that burns like the botafumeiro incense burner pilgrims witness during Mass in the cathedral in the city of St. James.

From Portomarín to Eirexe, I walked with the big German bear, Gaetano. From the moment I met him and for days later, he had trouble getting my name right. At various times, he called me Phil, or Bill, or Bub, or Junior, finally settling on "not a son-of-a-bitch." We often talked about music, reciting lyrics as the rest of the gang tried to guess the song title and band or artist. That part of Gaetano's memory was totally intact, rarely missing a beat. He told us he was an Italian mountain man disguised as a German motorcycle dude and one of the leaders of "The Sons of Anarchy — German Division." Gaetano also promised to reveal to us his back tattoo, Gandalf with staff in one hand and lantern in the other, upon completing our pilgrimage in front of the cathedral in Santiago.

Janine was a triathlete who was afraid she would be the first pilgrim to walk to Santiago and actually gain weight, the result of her obsession with Spanish chocolate. I walked with her from Palais de Rei to Melide. Her face projected a certain radiance, a brightness enhanced by her smile and more often by infectious laughter – laughter that soon had everyone in our pilgrim family laughing, that we all missed when she was the first to depart for home after we reached Santiago. All this came with an acerbic wit, one that made you want to hone your own so as not to be caught off guard by Janine.

In Melide, we sampled the world famous pulpo — octopus fried in olive oil — delving into the chewy goodness of the suction-cup like tentacles, all enhanced by the vino blanco, the white wine specialty of Galicia. This made walking hundreds of kilometers worthwhile.

I walked out of Melide with Stephanie through Boente, Castañeda, and Arzúa. Stephanie was the living embodiment of the strong and silent-type cliche. But underneath all the quiet was an intelligence and strength she employed only when the circumstances dictated. Stephanie remained in your memory for a long time.

***

On our second-to-last evening, we had a rousing time with the Russian family that owned an albergue in a resort in Salceda. They were new to the business and tried a bit too hard to please us. We were easy to please, though. Real pilgrims appreciated the smallest of accoutrements. I got a kick out of the Russian son trying to woo Janine and Stefanie. He was way out of his league, yet he didn't have a clue.

The next day, the rain came down in buckets. I have an indelible vision stamped in my memory of the four members of my wonderful family ensconced in their full storm regalia – ponchos on, hoods up, joking around, splashing and playing in the muddy puddles like children, all the time with big smiles on their dripping faces and a sense of the divine in their hearts. This was what I would tell someone who asked me to define pilgrimage.

On our last night before the end of the journey, it got a little quiet. We all felt the weight of the goodbyes that were soon to be part of our journeys. We set our alarms for two in the morning so we could view the Milky Way from the clear skies on top of Monte do Gozo. That put us in the right frame of mind to enter the third-holiest city in the Christian religion.

Finally, we passed through the Portal of Santiago and then turned left onto the Praza do Obradoiro. It was now time for the revelation of what had been promised to us: Gaetano's back tattoo. It definitely lived up to all the hype. I recognized it as part of the artwork on a Led Zeppelin album. Then came Mass, the botafumeiro incense burner, the celebratory parties, and the long goodbyes. We all feared we would never see each other again, but in the hearts of true pilgrims there existed the eternal hope that one day we would walk together again somewhere in the wild, wide world.

***

One day before I left Spain, I got a text from Jen. She had indeed recovered and had progressed westward, always two days behind me. I was so proud of her, and she asked me to walk out a kilometer or two so we could then fulfill our wishes to walk into the holy city together. It was pouring rain that early afternoon as I walked out to meet her. She soon came chugging along with a deep determination in her stride and a look of pure joy on her face. She was walking with a new friend, Wendi from Colorado, who had helped lift Jen's spirits toward the fulfillment of a glorious finish. I almost had trouble keeping up with them, so fierce was their pace.

As we entered the Praza do Obradoiro, I backed off and let Jen and Wendi have those last triumphant steps both together and alone. I had had my celebratory entrance. Now, they had theirs.

We had one more night to party together before I returned to my much-missed loved ones and Jen spread her wings to travel to the rest of the world. I continued to receive dispatches from the frontlines of her life, from the Annapurna circuit in the Himalayas to surfing in Portugal and western Australia to trekking in Peru and to too many more places to mention. That would be Jen's book. I am excited to read it one day.

Chapter 25

Death and Beauty on the Camino Del Norte

"In her soft wind I will whisper
In her warm sun I will glisten
Till we see her once again
In a world without end."

— Crowded House, "She Goes On"

I first became intrigued with northern Spain during my previous Caminos, when others told me tales of stunning scenery and challenging topography in the far north of the country, where another ancient pilgrimage route lay called the Camino del Norte. Following the northern Atlantic Coast and surrounded by the snowcapped mountains of Cantabria and Asturias, snow that lingered well into late spring, this path fascinated me. With each story I heard, it became a vision and called to me. In fact, it became an obsession, just as other exotic and demanding places have worked their magic on my psyche since I was a wee lad. The time had now come to travel upon the earth of this dramatic landscape.

***

All this travel — driving to the airport, flying across the Atlantic Ocean, and taking ground transportation to my destination — energizes me. It gives me blocks of waiting, contemplation and meditation, lead time for my mental and spiritual faculties. As I learned over 108,000 miles of walking, long treks on foot are so much more than the physical aspect. With the gentle rhythm of motorized transport, I go into a deep state of introspection. I unearth memories, the particulars of the current adventure, and the promise of future journeys. And going deeper, I contemplate what got me to this point in my life, the journey of my life, the travails, and the epiphanies. I review and prayerfully thank all the souls who helped get me to this point, to this journey I am on and once again the journey of my life.

***

After a long train ride north, my daughter Amberly and I finally arrived in Irun, Spain, at 11 at night. From the station, it was a short walk toward the dome of the Church of San Gabriel and Santa Gema, our point of orientation here on the border with France. After checking into our room, I walked around Irun a bit to further orient myself and to dissipate some of the jet lag (and because I was excited to be back in Spain). Our pension was above a bar, so we had a red wine nightcap and then headed off to sleep.

We originally planned to take a day off in Irun so we could walk east over the bridge to explore the beaches of Hendaye, France. Hemingway often visited Hendaye in the 1920s, frequenting the Atlantic Ocean cafes on his way to the bullfights in Pamplona or to go trout fishing near Burguete, both of which lie on the path of the Camino Frances south of Irun. However, we now decided to sweat off the jet lag by climbing the mountain to Santuario de Guadalupe, about 4 kilometers on the Camino del Norte. This move would shorten days one and two to 17 kilometers and 10 kilometers, respectively, and break up a long, hilly beginning.

It was cloudy and overcast, threatening rain, when we started climbing the mountain. The views of Hondarribia overlooking the Bay of Txingudi and on into France were still quite wonderful even with the mist on my eyeglasses. The threat of rain gave us reason to skip the wide-open spaces and muddy climbs of the Purgatorio Route and stick to the dirt road that wound slightly south of the ridgeline. Our cloudy vista was now due south to the beginnings of the snowy Pyrenees Mountains, which evoked many memories of climbing over the rugged range. It soon started raining lightly.

Four hours of walking brought us to the steep descent into Pasaia. The rain came down harder as we carefully navigated the stone steps, all the time gaping at the channel cutting in from the ocean and splitting the town in two with a narrow gorge. It was our introduction to the majesty of the Camino del Norte.

We ate a late lunch at a bar along the channel and asked around for lodging. The good thing was we were given a recommendation for a pension with a scenic view. The hard part was having to climb back up to the cliff. But when we saw the little habitation sitting on the hillside, with a front porch hanging out over the bay, we forgot the rain, jet lag, lack of sleep, and our tired legs and reveled in the fact that once more we were among the landscapes of high adventure.

We slept in the next morning because we knew that we only had 10 kilometers to walk that day. The sun finally beckoned us to start. Our day included two twisting descents, a small ferry ride across the channel in which a burly Basque man used a pole to push us across, and one steep ascent. That ascent was compounded by a European footrace that came charging down the narrow trail toward us. There was scant room to move to the side so the runners could continue their torrid pace. Once we had achieved the height of land, we flowed along stone wall outcroppings, which gave us vistas of the ocean that ended at the northern horizon. The Camino del Norte continued to enthrall.

We had walked inland a few paces when a vista opened, revealing the splendor of San Sebastián. This view is a highlight of the Camino del Norte and one of the most stunning I have ever witnessed. You see the grid of the city and the twin horseshoe-shaped beaches the resort is known for, all bordered to the south by a ring of peaks dusted by snow. We descended into all that splendor, waded into the ocean, then began a search for our new travel spirits, who were beginning their Camino with us the next day.

San Sebastián lends itself quite easily to the neural state of sensory overload. I couldn't take it all in — too much exhilaration. Being on pilgrimage does this to me once or twice each day, even in rough weather. This is what I have chased all my life, and I was deep within it once more.

***

Laura and Dave hailed from Boulder, Colorado, and had always been intrigued by my Camino posts. My oldest daughter went to high school with Laura, and I had actually stayed at her apartment twice during road trips west while Laura was still in law school. She met Dave while he got his engineering degree from Penn State. I occasionally bumped into them at one of my hometown bars while they were back in Pennsylvania visiting their parents, and during one such visit, I regaled them with the stories told to me about the wonders of the Norte. Soon, they started to hear the Sirens calling them to adventure.

Unlike in Greek mythology, wherein the boats would crash against the rocks of the shoreline, we had to keep from being blown off the rocks into the Spanish Atlantic. But for now, all was sunny and mild as the four of us met up at a crowded outdoor bar jutting out on a spit of land smack in the middle of San Sebastián's two crescent-shaped beaches. In this magnificent setting, in one of the most beautiful cities of the world, began an adventuresome comradeship that would last for years to come.

Later that evening, we strolled the city streets, enchanted as dusk settled on the ocean horizon. The streetlights and cathedral lights cast a glow. Tomorrow we once again would return to the nitty-gritty, boots-in-the-dust life of pilgrimage with a steep climb out of the western edge of San Sebastián. I savored the present contentment while simultaneously looking forward to the work and sweat of tomorrow. I live and celebrate equally in both spheres. Both bring about a vitality I have chased all my life. Both scenarios were why I went on pilgrimage.

The next morning, we took one last look at San Sebastián and entered an alpine environment consisting of fog, drizzle, fenced-off farm animals, undulating trails, and dirt roads. Then came a rocky descent into Orio, where we stopped for lunch. The small-town cafe was crowded with pilgrims and older townsmen. In limited Spanish, I conversed with the locals to find out that not much was happening in Orio beyond the area surrounding this bar/cafe. Of course, in Spain all cafes and restaurants are also bars, even early in the morning. It was always interesting to watch the joyful interactions of people in this kind of setting, especially at the end of the day in the plazas where huge crowds gathered every night.

After another climb, we soon came within view of the ocean again, knowing that it would be a presence for the next two days. In full sunshine, we walked along the edges of a series of cliffs with long drops into crashing waves. This was another distinguishing feature of the Camino del Norte. We were so mesmerized that we barely noticed that Zarautz Beach loomed beyond and down another set of steps.

Zarautz turned out to be one of the gems of the North Way, a place I could live for a spell, which would include the town to the north, Getaria. On the morning of day four, we followed the shores of the Atlantic for five kilometers, along a promenade, and into Getaria. Those five kilometers were some of the most appealing of any Camino I've walked, where only the waves occasionally crashing into the seawall could break a rapturous spell and bring me back to a cold, wet reality.

A small beach, a stark seaside cathedral, and tight, meandering cobbled streets welcomed walkers as they entered the village. The mix of bicyclists and walkers included pilgrims, tourists, and locals. We stopped at an outdoor cafe for a mid-morning snack and coffee, sat in the warm sunshine, and soaked in the wonderful vibe of the present.

The future vibe was a leg- and lung-straining climb to more cliffs and sea vistas and, at one point, a traffic jam of sheep driven by a shepherd to heavenly fields. Next came a steep descent to the oceanside village of Zumaia, and then we were back on the rollercoaster path with another steep ascent and more walking, as if floating along cliffs. Along such topography, the pilgrim tires from the sensual bombardment as much as the physicality of the rolling hills. The body tires, but the mind and spirit are full of elation.

***

After the overnight in Deba, we broke from the shoreline for a rugged climb of mountains with heavily wooded areas. I had a very queasy stomach all morning, and it finally let loose as I barely made it to the side of the path. Amberly chuckled as a group of pilgrims appeared seconds after my gastric explosion. We had rarely seen other walkers for days, but of course they had to appear right at that moment.

Amberly's giggle was infectious, and I just laughed it off, too. Such was life on pilgrimage. It would eventually happen to everybody at least once.

We overnighted in Gernika, the city fascist air force bombing raids destroyed during the Spanish Civil War in the 1930s. The destruction was the focus of a Pablo Picasso painting hanging in the Museo Nacional Centro de Arte Reina Sofía in Madrid. Leaving the city the next day, we passed a tile recreation of Piccaso's painting and then climbed steeply to the ridge. In the early afternoon, we walked into another gem of the Norte, the city of Bilbao. We had not seen the ocean for two days, and it would be another one until it appeared again.

Amberly flew home the next day to go back to her job in the hospital. I spent the next day in the Frank Gehry-designed Guggenheim Museum, a divine abode of art from around the world, including rusty, industrial metal pieces towering above you that you can walk around and through like a maze. I also enjoyed some time with two friends from England, Heather, a driver for part of my Walk Across America 17 years earlier, and her husband, Wataru, who flew down for an evening.

The city was a feast for the senses as I walked past dizzying, tilting skyscrapers and futuristic cable bridges that contrasted with the plazas and the cobbled, narrow alleys of traditional Spain. Vivid colors of graffiti art decorated the bridges, and many great musicians of all genres recorded live albums there during outdoor festivals. Bilbao was unlike any city I had seen before, a Basque tour de force.

The epicurean pleasures of Bilbao were a wonderful respite from the rigors of the Camino del Norte. But it was now time to get back to the ocean, the mountains, and the path. We had been renewed in grace but were called to the further mind-expanding spirit of the Way.

It took a while to walk out of the city. I was alone, at least until the next day, when Laura and Dave would re-join me. After reaching Portugalete, the Camino's yellow arrows led me onto a bicycle trail, which dramatically deposited me onto the beach at La Arena. Surfers filled a few beachside cafes, while some in wet suits ventured out into the cold Atlantic. Heading a kilometer across the beach brought me to the enclave of Pobeña. Cliffs extended out into the water. To the south were a few conical mountain spires. It was a bit surrealistic.

I was so enthralled that I decided to stay the night in a tavern/pension that also had a washer/dryer. (The albergue was seasonal and not yet open.) Before dinner, I climbed 250 cement steps to the top of the cliffs, where the trail continued for seven kilometers right on the edge with the raging waves crashing several hundred feet below. This is where I would head tomorrow morning.

After dinner later that night, I put on my headlamp, bundled up, and tackled the steps again. Up on the cliffs there now existed an otherworldly realm. Other than a few lights in La Arena, and distant ones inland, it was pure darkness. I could hear the waves but not see them except when the just-risen crescent moon caught their dancing crests. I thought the climb had affected my breathing until I realized that the stimuli of sound, touch, and even minimal sight literally had taken my breath away. I tried to record it and send it to my wife back home but then regretted it. I didn't want her to miss me. I didn't want her to get scared that I was all alone in the dark. But most of all, I didn't want her to be jealous of me being on the beach when she was not. Too late, though. I had already sent it. And, yes, she was all three.

The next morning, I headed up the steps for the third time. This time, I noticed cows and horses roaming the meadows even higher up. After walking along the cliffs for more than an hour, I came to realize this was the greatest stretch of path I had ever been on.

I met Laura and Dave in the small, ancient town of Ontón, where we continued into Mioño. Laura and I sat outside a bar/cafe decorated in festive, tropical regalia, while Dave went inside to order. Laura was usually very talkative, speaking on a multitude of wide-ranging issues. At this moment, she stared off wistfully, seemingly lost in a pensive mood. I photographed her among the tropical decor, her gaze looking toward our future path of more ocean-splashed cliffs. It was a great photo of the exquisite face of a pilgrim who had now returned to her pilgrimage.

The cliffs and ocean continued for 10 kilometers on a less-defined, muddy path, eventually exiting onto the eastern end of a gorgeous, expansive seaside promenade. Off in the distance stood a gothic castle/cathedral, a focal point of another jewel of the Norte, the city of Castro Urdiales. It seemed like you could touch the city, but it took another half hour of walking to get there. That night, we dined on seafood at one of many outdoor restaurants and strolled out in the dying light past the castle. Storm clouds hastened the evening, and the majestic scene made us feel like we were characters from "Game of Thrones."

In the second half of the next day, we went inland and up and over a mountain, through a pastoral setting of cattle, sheep, and horses. We stayed in the town of Hazas, where we met several pilgrims from different parts of the world. In the morning, we entered a raging system of storms as we descended to the ocean in Laredo. The cutting wind and slashing rain made the next two days a challenge. My umbrella was useless in such conditions, causing me to rely on a thin, plastic raincoat as my backup. We were exposed to all the furies of the storm as we walked along the Calle San Francisco promenade, which led to a beach where a small ferry waited to take us across a sizable bay, heavy with choppy waves. Both Laura and I, susceptible to seasickness, dreaded the passage. Steady Dave enjoyed it all, standing with an uncovered head and staring into the maelstrom. It actually wasn't too bad, and after landing, Laura and I caught up to Dave's enthrall just for having survived.

The Norte has several boat passages throughout its 800 kilometers. It is the most visually stunning yet energy-burning challenge of the Caminos. We were about to experience both of the Norte's extreme features a few kilometers beyond.

The rain and wind continued right to the base of Alto de Brusco, and then the sun broke through, teaming up with the wind to further redden our faces. The muddy climb tested us as we slipped and slid, and as we neared the top, a malevolent black cloud enveloped the sun. The wind roared, threatening to blow us off the ledge and into the raging Atlantic hundreds of feet below us. We crouched low, grabbing for the stunted shrubbery as a counter to the push of the wind. We finally turned up the hill, off trail, to get away from the edge. Fighting through a forest of small trees, we descended to a fenced-in sheep meadow. Ah, our heart rates returned to normal as we crossed to the fence on the other side. With about 10 steps to go, we were rushed by a large dog who guarded the sheep. We sprinted for the fence and fell over to the safe side.

The sun returned as we descended to a beach, which in a few miles led us to the town of Noja. We checked into an empty albergue and headed to the bar below to drink away the trauma of another hell-raising day on the Way of the North.

In the week and a half I spent walking with Laura and Dave, I noticed something every day. Dave was a very handsome man, but Laura took it to another dimension. She had the exquisite and elegant face of a leading lady from mid-century European cinema. Early in our adventure, I was determined to take an unflattering picture of Laura. I tried my darndest but couldn't even get close. Now in the bar in Noja, after she drank two tankards of beer following our harrowing, hair-raising day, Laura was setting herself up to be photographed as a creature from the wilds of northern Spain. Her hair was primitive, and her face was burned from a combination of wind, sun, and fear. Her eyes spoke of survival. And now she displayed the effects of an ongoing alcohol bender. The chance of getting an unflattering photo slowly evolved. I quickly reeled off several angled shots. It was now or never. I checked and rechecked the photos. It wasn't happening. Sure, she looked primal, in a "don't you freaking mess with me" kind of way. But the beauty was all there, even enhanced. In those shots, Laura displayed the face of Mother Nature.

It continued raining the next day as we walked into the town of Güemes. We were all thankful for having a rather uneventful day, at least compared to the day before. We felt excited to stay overnight at what was known among pilgrims as the greatest albergue on any Camino. Father Ernesto had travelled the world before settling in northern Spain to build a house of worship and comfort for travelers. I got a little ahead of Dave and Laura and was into my usual groove when I noticed two figures standing on a hill. After I climbed up, I met Father Ernesto and his current cook, who hailed from South Africa. They welcomed me with open arms that made people feel as if they were the most important pilgrims in the world. They did this to everyone who walked there. The vibe was so addictive that pilgrims either stayed for a few weeks or returned the next year to volunteer as hospitaleros.

Jeff was a chef, so it was perfect for him to interrupt his walk on the Norte to volunteer to cook. We had not seen a lot of pilgrims during the last few days, but this refuge was crowded. After a spiritual service and a tour of Father Ernesto's travels displayed in a museum, we sat down to a wonderful communal meal. Most pilgrims spoke several languages, and we heard ones from around the world that night. We stayed up late, emptying several bottles of wine from La Rioja with Jeff. He told us that as he and Father Ernesto watched me walk toward them and up the hill earlier that day, Father Ernesto had commented that they were witnessing the art of a real walker and seeker, someone who had done so all his life and would continue to do so. I knew that deep in my soul, but hearing about someone else saying it substantiated that I was truly on the right path.

On our last day together, we walked into the beautiful city of Santander. Laura and Dave's two weeks were coming to an end, and they would fly home from there. My friends from the walk across France, Carlo and Rebecca, would accompany me to the city of Gijón. The changing of the guard happened the next morning at a breakfast with all five of us. I had grown very close to Laura and Dave, but I would not be lonely. Carlo from Belgium and Rebecca from Los Angeles were proven pilgrims and were sure to pick up the mantle.

Entering my third week, I felt strong and absolutely loved the pilgrim life. The Norte was different from my previous Caminos in France and Portugal. It was lonelier and a little less spiritual, at least in terms of open churches and evening Mass. But there was no doubt that the mix of mountains and sea was unparalleled, and that continued as we moved deeper into the Spanish region of Cantabria. So would the physical challenge of the landscape and the elements.

We had a long walk to Santillana del Mar, a small, charming town with cobbled streets in a fairytale setting. Just outside the town was the ancient Cave of Altamira, which Steely Dan sung about in a song of the same name. We moved back and forth from inland dirt roads over timeworn bridges that led to ocean beaches and back again. In the town of Comillas, we saw outstanding and colorful examples of Gaudi architecture, the colors becoming more pronounced because of the cloudy, drizzly skies. Next came San Vicente de la Barquera for lunch, where a castle sat by the sea. I planned to one day return to this town, from which there is a three-day Camino through the Picos de Europa mountains to the Monastery of Santo Toribio De Liébana. Displayed at this church is a large wooden piece of the one true cross of Jesus.

Soon we crossed into the region called Asturias, a wild place of even bigger mountains and windswept shorelines and cliffs. Rebecca and Carlo had keen senses of humor that expanded exponentially when they were on pilgrimage together. The three of us had not seen each other since walking out of Le Puy-en-Velay, France, two springs earlier. But we fell right back into our friendship, all of us discovering that friendships form at an accelerated rate while walking on Camino.

We also started to pick up other ragtag pilgrims from distant places. Things flowed along on the northern road to Santiago.

We overnighted in the gorgeous seaside resort city of Llanes. The weather conditions were always alternating between drizzle and downpour, and they stayed windy. Torrential downpours accompanied us into the village of Nueva, where we stayed at a pension run by a charming older Spanish couple. That evening, we went to a bar across the street that amazingly enough had really good Wi-Fi for such an out-of-the-way place.

Before dessert arrived, I received a text from my family letting me know that my mom was very sick and had been transferred from the nursing home to the hospital. One hour later, my phone rang. No one ever called me out there, so I knew this was not going to be good. It was my youngest daughter telling me that my mom had passed on into the next world.

I spent my last night on Camino crying and going through photos. After the bar closed, I no longer had an internet connection. Rebecca and Carlo were wonderful with their comforting presence, and they also decided to head home. We agreed to meet back at this spot the next year.

The next day, I took a series of trains to Madrid, from which I flew home in time for the funeral. My mom always worried about me being in far-flung places with all my medical problems. She also made me promise that if she died while I was away, I would try my best to return home for the funeral. She wanted me to give the eulogy. I was now keeping that promise.

I took a long walk in areas known to my mom the day before the funeral. That afternoon, I composed the eulogy, which had a blend of praise and humor. She would have wanted laughter to ring in the church. After the funeral, I decided to take a four-day solo backpacking trip into the Grand Canyon of Pennsylvania. It would help me put my mom's death into perspective.

***

I left the car at a state forest picnic area and started walking north. Pine Creek, which is as big as a river, would be my companion for all four days. The walking would be simple and easy. I didn't want diversions so I could concentrate on confronting the death of my mom. I remembered her being a wonderful mother-in-law to my wife, who she accepted immediately. They became traveling buddies on journeys to the Jersey Shore and comforted each other when I was gone on dangerous expeditions. Both understood the necessity of my endeavors; however, both also agreed that sometimes I was a little obsessive when it came to adventures and snakes. My mom would often lament about me, "Why couldn't you be more like your brothers? Why couldn't you be more like the other kids?" Of course, by the time of her death, she had long understood and accepted that I needed adventures as a hedge against the medical challenges I faced daily.

I threw in a few climbs on offshoot trails to mix up the terrain and give me a break from the continuing mix of grieving for and celebrating my mom's life. The first climb came near the end of the day as I followed Naval Run from where it empties into the Pine Creek to where it intersects the Black Forest Trail. Then I climbed many switchbacks to the top of one of my favorite places in the world, Hemlock Mountain. This was a fitting place to continue my rolling epitaph. Though my mom never visited this spot, she was present many times as I set out to walk here, and she was present when I returned. She was present here now, in my state of reverence, here upon the throne of the mountain gods.

During my second afternoon and my third morning, I climbed to the top of another astonishing vista at Gillespie Point. Starting from the tiny village of Blackwell, this mountain was visible from the approach out of Cedar Run. Its conical peak used to be an outlier, but with the extension of the Mid-State Trail, which passed close by, it soon would have some foot traffic. From the summit, I could see seven miles to the west, to where I had walked from. Twenty miles north, as the crow flies, was the town of Wellsboro, where my mom had vacationed with my family. She had been a wonderful grandmother to both of my daughters. The memories continued to pour forth from my ever-expanding memory, like I was watching a documentary film of the life of Anna Mae Scheidt.

On the last day of my walk, I confronted a reality that I had been blocking from my consciousness. Both my parents had now moved on to the next world. I was the oldest son. I was next in line. I had always wrestled with my own mortality, ever since I had been diagnosed with Type 1 diabetes 43 years earlier. I had occasionally thought, in times of deep duress, of the threat of a diminished life, so the idea was always present. But over the last many years, I had risen above those notions of morbidity. This rise from the muck of despair had happened with the help of my friends and family. My mom had played a big part in that rise. Though she had now passed on from this life, she would continue to be part of my existence, my rise, and the continuation of my life force upon this hallowed earth.

Chapter 26

A Return to the Way of the North

*"Wrap yourself around
The tree of life and the dance of the infinity."*

— Tori Amos, "The Beekeeper"

I was flying over the Atlantic Ocean, heading back to Madrid and thinking about my mom. It was just shy of a year since she had passed on, and I was returning to the place where the news of her death reached me, the Spanish town Nueva. In the past year, as life went on, the memory of her life faded ever so slowly. For the next five weeks, though, it would return to me, in bits and pieces, and in mighty, lashing tidal waves. My holy pilgrimage would be a meditation on the life of one of God's servants, my mom.

I would be alone for big swaths, and I also would have my kindred spirits to guide me for portions. When loneliness threatened, I would be rescued. My dear friends Laura and Dave would meet me in Pamplona. They were with me on the Norte a week before my mom died. Then in Gijón on the Atlantic Coast of Asturias, near where we were at the time of death the previous year, mighty souls Carlo and

Rebecca would return. I could not have chosen better pilgrims than these four, but I didn't have to. They volunteered.

The plan was to start walking from the Basque city of Pamplona to Léon, take the San Salvador trail north to Oviedo, and then take the connector to the Norte. I would then complete the Norte to Santiago. Weather or health variables could alter that plan, but I could easily adjust any portion.

I exited the train looking forward to the sensual fiesta that welcomes a pilgrim in Pamplona. This was the fourth time in five years that I had the pleasure to be there. And it was "Two Euros Tapas and Cerveza Thursday." Once again, I picked the perfect jumping-off point for my Camino.

I checked into my albergue and then strolled into Plaza del Castillo, where I drank a beer in Café Iruña, a haunt of Ernest Hemingway. I was still chasing his ghost. Laura and Dave arrived after dark looking a little worn around the edges after a number of connections and layovers. An evening in the madness of a Thursday night in Pamplona could wash the jet lag out of anyone, though, and indeed it did.

Our first day on the Camino de Santiago involved an easy 11 kilometers walking out of the city, through Cizur Menor, and right to the base of the next day's climb, stopping short in the very small village of Zariquiegui. There was only one other pilgrim at the albergue where the hospitalero cooked an evening meal for us, and there had been no others at our albergue in Pamplona since it was still very early in the season. The next morning, we went up and over the windmill mountain, where the path of the wind meets that of the stars.

I always wondered about staying overnight in the majestic village on a hill of Cirauqui. As dramatic as it looked entering and leaving, though, there was not much happening in the village itself, just one albergue, one small store, and one very old church. But tonight, things were happening. Eight other pilgrims checked in, the most fascinating being a young Italian artist named Eleonora. Dave, Laura, and I were entertained by the dynamic dual nature of her being a mature, fearless solo walker far from home and her teenage stories of boys she had met and left entranced along the Camino. In fact, the next day she walked back 10 kilometers to where we had come from to reconnect with a boy she realized she should not have left behind.

This time, I arrived at the outdoor wine fountain at Monastery of Santa Maria de Irache in the afternoon. As I did five years before, most pilgrims arrive there in the morning after overnighting in Estella. This day, though, we could drink slowly and let the afternoon sun and breeze wrap themselves around us as we lay in the grass in the park. If anyone dozed off for a spell, the first sight he would see upon awakening was the passage of pilgrims in front of the monastery. Other than the neon-colored quick-dry shirts worn by some modern pilgrims, waking up could have felt like you had time-travelled to the 16th century.

It took a half mile to get rolling again. I loved the tranquil smiles on the faces of my comrades, Laura and Dave, smiles that actually grew bigger an hour later as we came in sight of the castle ruins above the hilltop village Villamayor de Monjardín, where we slept that night. We were fully into the pilgrimage mindset, with all the concerns of home and worldly travails slowly evaporating into the celestial sky. We had become pilgrims once again.

Dusty dirt roads and a clear blue sky took us a long way into Los Arcos. The only modern intrusions were a lunch cart at the halfway point and the need to extract money from a bank machine in the village. We then moved on to our overnight stay in Torres del Río (River Towers), where we met up with Elenora again. She regaled us with more tales of her wanderings and introduced us to her companion, who was not the boy she had searched for back in Cirauqui. Later, we discussed the book she was reading, Carlos Castaneda's "A Separate Reality: Further Conversations with Don Juan," stories of the southwestern American desert, a place to which many artists like Elenora are drawn. I had read most of Castenada's books and was especially intrigued to see Elenora's copy in Italian.

Laura and Dave had one more day of walking, which took us through the bustling city of Viana and then on to the even bigger city of Logroño. As a sendoff to my kindred spirits, we stayed in a monastery, where we took part in a pilgrim Mass, met a rough-looking walker who smelled of onions, and found a little hole-in-a-wall restaurant that served only mushrooms. We felt as if we had discovered a new delicacy. Thank goodness it was not a restaurant that served only onions!

In the morning, a group hug sent me on my now solitary journey. It could be quite lonely for the next two to three weeks until I reached the Norte again. Of course, there was always the chance I would meet many fascinating characters along the Way, maybe some as fascinating as Laura and Dave.

***

Beautiful park trails took me out of Logrono and then around a lake where I met a cyclist from southern Spain who was attending college in Germany. He pushed his bike around the lake with me so we could talk. Of course, he was fluent in four languages. It no longer surprised me like it did in my first couple of years in Europe. Back then, I was amazed, especially since, as my daughters tell me, I struggle with my own language.

Days later on the dirt roads of the vineyards of Rioja, I walked with Lena from Germany and Henrik from Denmark. They had met on the Camino a year before and had now come back again to walk it together. I would see them sporadically for the next week in Azofra, Granon, and Belarado.

It was a lonely, cold day's walk heading to Santo Domingo de la Calzada. The wind off the snow-covered peaks seemed to find a way into every opening in my clothes, leaving me chilled and shivering. I noticed someone up ahead taking pictures of the early spring mountains, and I asked her if she wanted to be in that photo. She nodded, and after a few shots, she asked, "Shall I take a photo of you with your camera?" She ended up taking one of the best photos I have of myself, since I don't consider myself very photogenic. That set the tone for the next couple of days as Elizabeth and I walked, talked, and laughed together. She was from South Korea but used her English name when she traveled. She had chosen Elizabeth from reading Jane Austen books. While dancing through an all-day pouring rain, Elizabeth showed an interest in American pop culture, so to take our minds off the cold and rain, I gave her a rousing pop culture tutorial. This was something I knew well, and she complimented my thoughts with her own insightful take on things. It got us all the way to Tosantos.

While enjoying a late afternoon snack, I said a sad goodbye to Elizabeth. She wanted to move further on, and as I explained to her, I was on a different Camino. I wanted to stay at all the places I had not stayed at the first time I walked this way. It was an in-between Camino physically, mentally, and spiritually. I sought the spaces between, from when I had still had an earthly mother to now, a space and time where I was a motherless child.

    I moved over the northern Spanish topography slowly but steadily, past the monastery of San Juan de Ortega, through the village of Agés and the gothic city of Burgos, and then onto the sparse, mystical deserts of the central Camino. The epiphanies would surely present themselves over the next eight days. Epiphanies cannot be conjured up or counted on. All you can do is put yourself into the right frame of mind. More often than not, I can put myself in that state of mind, so even when the epiphanies do not show up, my mind is already in a state of reverence. We can't all be St. Paul, receiving a knock-down epiphany on the road to Damascus. What I did receive, over the next couple of days, was an amazing Camino family. The Meseta turned out not to be lonely in the least.

    I dropped down from out of the sky into the first Meseta town, Hornillos del Camino. At an albergue, I met Lyndsey from England and Andrea from Budapest. Along with a few other people, we had dinner together. Earlier, we lounged in a grassy courtyard after hanging out our wash to dry. We had the usual Camino discussion at the table that lasted long enough for me to be all tight in the joints and muscles when I finally pushed myself up.

    The next day, I encountered more of the same landscapes as the day before. The only village in the 20 kilometers was the almost ghost town of Hontanas. That night, we added Paulina from Mexico to our gang. Before dinner, Andrea and I climbed to the top of the hill above the town of Castrojeriz. On top sat the semi-ruins of an ancient castle, so prominently located that you could see it for many kilometers in all directions. Andrea even walked a bit to the south to an abbey where nuns made wooden cross necklaces for pilgrims. Andrea had a lot of energy to spare, and she needed it because the next day the only feature visible on the horizon was a cloud-encircled dome like a mound with a trail winding its way to the top. That's the direction we were heading, to the top of Alto de Mostelares. Andrea chugged up right behind me, with Lyndsey and Paulina a way's back. The clouds parted, giving us a 360-degree vista.

    That night at the albergue in Frómista, the last two members of our gang of six were introduced. Marja was from Finland, and Mercedes came from Spain. All spoke very good English. Mine was so-so.

For dinner, I went off on my own and ran into a father-daughter team. They were originally from Belgium, but Bee had moved to central France a few years previously. They walked two weeks every year, piecing together sections of different Caminos. They liked to talk about politics, something I had not done much of on this Camino, though I could hold my own. We had a spirited conversation and then hugged goodbye. This was the last night for them this year.

The next day, my family and I walked to Carrión de los Condes, followed by a day on an 18-kilometers stretch of lonely dirt road to dusty Calzadilla de la Cueza. In Sahagún and Calzada del Coto, the family formed into a cohesive unit. I learned a bit more about each of my sisters on the isolated stretches of an old Roman road leading to Reliegos, the only blip on the radar being the small village of Calzadilla de los Hermanillos. Along that road, I learned that Paulina was a sweet soul with the face of an angel and badly blistered feet. She displayed true grit and tenacity to keep going, though I finally got her to see a doctor in León. Marja was calm and serene, a pillar of quiet strength who looked like she could have walked to Santiago without stopping. Of course, she would then have missed the rest of her sisters, and me, her one brother. Andrea was effervescent, bubbling over with high spirits accompanied by a wild laugh. Linsey from England had a very dry sense of humor, bright eyes, and an engaging smile that made even the physically hardest days a breezy walk in the park. Mercedes displayed a magnificent and illustrious beauty that shined through in any kind of weather.

We had two more days to reach León. One of the high spots of any of my Caminos happened with my gang of sisters in Bar La Torre (Bar Elvis) in Reliegos. The bar is one of the features of the Meseta. The building has a ramshackle exterior in the middle of a ramshackle town. The interior is a dirt floor. The bathroom is a hole in the ground in the backyard surrounded by a weathered shower curtain. What the place lacks in infrastructure it makes up for in ambience. The interior walls are covered in thousands of messages from pilgrims from around the world. The music, on repeat, was Cuban dance music by the Buena Vista Social Club. The owner, Elvis, sang "Chan Chan" with a cigarette in his mouth while also using a straight razor blade to slice thin pieces of ham onto a paper plate on the dirt floor, with ashes from the cigarette mixing with the meat. Those plates were specially prepared for us pilgrims.

For most of the evening, it seemed that we could not stop laughing. We laughed while we danced with the villagers, laughed as we tried to eat thinly sliced ham, and laugh as we tried not to have to use the bathroom. Andrea was always loud, so of course when we brought up the volume, she took it up another notch. I did notice that it was all locals in the bar, and we were the only pilgrims. We wondered if this happened every night. Luckily, we were all a bit dehydrated from the long walk, so no one had to use the bathroom. Eventually, things wound down and we left to find our way through the streetlight-less town. Even after we were in our bunks, we couldn't stifle the laughter. Every time it quieted, someone would start up again, and the rest would follow. It was truly a night for the ages.

My sisters would follow the Camino Frances to Santiago without their brother. I had to go north to the Camino del Norte, to where I had gotten the news of my mother's demise, and then continue, also to Santiago, but along the cliffs of the Atlantic Ocean. We had one last Camino dinner in León in front of the grand Cathedral and one last hug, tears appearing as the grand finale. When anyone asks me for an example of a Camino family, I tell them this story, of my wonderful Camino sisters.

***

I found out that lingering winter snows were clogging up the San Salvador trail, making it hard to find the route through the Asturias mountains. I was advised not to go alone, so instead I took the train to Gijón, a fascinating seaside city, and walked east, back to where I stopped last year. Upon arriving, I turned and walked back to Gijón, where I waited for Carlo and Rebecca to arrive from Belgium and Los Angeles. It was the beginning of Holy Week, Semana Santa, so I attended an afternoon Mass complete with palms and an outpouring of acceptance from the rest of the devout inhabitants of Gijón.

In the late afternoon, I sat in the sun at an outdoor cafe with a view of the cathedral behind me and the waves of the Atlantic Ocean in front. My solo time of grieving my mom was coming to an end. It was now exactly a year ago that she had passed. The still-earthbound spirits of Carlo and Rebecca would now carry me west to Santiago de Compostela.

We left the vistas of the sea behind but knew the mighty Atlantic would appear on a regular basis. I had walked with Carlo and

Rebecca across France a few years earlier and then through the Cantabrian coast the previous year. Both overflowed with heart and soul, and I left behind any lingering loneliness from the last week.

During the first few days, we walked through the broad plazas of Avilés, the hills out of Salinas, the castle ruins of Muros de Nalón, and the scenic church of El Pito, which we photographed at sunrise. The ocean was always near but not always seen. Then a path would wind down from the dirt road, taking us to a cliffside vista, sometimes all the way to the shoreline, and then right back up. The sea was way too turbulent and the rocky shore too jagged for us to walk on the beach. This would happen a couple times daily, making the walk exhilarating but also quite exhausting. We all slept very well.

This western part of the Camino del Norte was not heavily used. Most walkers took the mountainous route of the Camino Primitivo. I have hiked in mountains all over North America, but rarely can you walk for days on a wild ocean such as in this part of Spain. That informed my decision to stay on the Norte. There were very few pilgrims, albergues were far apart, and most churches were not open or had Mass. We stayed overnight in lots of pensions. At one rest stop, we sat against a wire fence and ate a snack. When I got up to move on, the wires caught the back of my walking shorts, ripping them right off me. They were starting to get thin anyway.

Further on, Rebecca heard the Siren call and craved the warmth of Málaga in southern Spain. She decamped from us in the resort city of Luarca. Carlo and I carried on, two buddies who we felt were born to walk together. We soon approached the point where the Norte heads into the Galician hills. In the seaside resort of Figueres, we ate lunch while watching a surf competition. As we left, we met Robert from Germany, who walked with us to the city of Ribadeo. He was an avid Camino trekker and also competed in triathlons and ultramarathons. We would have plenty to discuss. He fit in easily and became our third brother for a few days. We were all too tired to catch a ride out to see the world famous colored arches just offshore in the Atlantic. It was a shame, but we had seen plenty of sea and rock.

Robert walked with us as far as Vilalba and was with us when we met our next Camino sister. On his last day, we walked on wooded trails through a remote part of the Norte. Toward late morning, we noticed a sign for a stone cabin albergue. It was just off the trail and small, sleeping only 20. As we walked in looking for a possible second breakfast, we noticed a woman washing dishes in the communal kitchen. I felt a driving energy swirling around her. She smiled, introduced herself as Sabine from Germany, and her mate, who had just walked in from the bunk rooms, as Barry from Atlanta, Georgia. He said they were slacking by getting up late and were still packing to leave.

    We sat at a big wooden table in the dining room, and they joined us to engage in pilgrimage chatter. We learned that Sabine was an art teacher in Heidelberg, and Barry was a professor in Munich. When the discussion turned to my many visitations to Native American reservations and the spirituality I found from the medicine men and women, the shamans, and even the landscapes, I saw Sabine perk up. Then she started asking probing questions. Later, as Carlo, Robert, and I started walking, we were all in agreement that something positive was vibing from Sabine. She seemed to be a force of nature. We struggled to articulate it, maybe a seismic shift, sunspot activity, something cosmic. I sensed and told my comrades that she "knows things." Later, after I knew her better, she admitted she had told Barry the same thing about me.

    We didn't see Sabine and Barry for the rest of the day. Robert soon headed back home to Germany, where he would run a race that weekend. The following day was windy with a notable chill in the air. Carlo and I ate lunch in a lovely park near Pedrouzos with our jackets on and hoods up. The cold winds spun up dust devils that added some grit to our bocadillos. Carlo and I laughed at how woeful the situation seemed on the outside, yet the next day we agreed that it was one of the best lunches we ever ate.

    Toward late afternoon, we walked into Baamonde. The towns on the inland parts of the Norte were rather bland, balanced by the subtle beauty of the woodsy trails connecting them. We met a young couple from France walking in the opposite direction. Back in the albergue lounge, I heard stories of their past, present, and future. They had been on pilgrimage for a year and had no plans to stop for the next year or two. I was intrigued, and when I started asking questions and helping with reconnaissance for what they were heading toward, a woman with her face buried in a book started adding to my questions and suggestions. Upon closer inspection, I realized it was Sabine.

    In the morning, Carlo and I ate breakfast in a diner filled with both locals and pilgrims. Our heads were down as we concentrated on our food, and we didn't see the woman walk up to us. She slammed a book on the table, and I looked up to see Sabine again. She looked piercingly into my eyes and exclaimed in a hard German accent, "You look like someone who knows the wolf book." The black cover had gold lettering that read, "Women Who Run with the Wolves: Myths and Stories of the Wild Woman Archetype," by Clarissa Pinkola Estés, Ph.D. Indeed, I knew it well. It was one of my favorite books. In fact, I buy copies in bulk and have given many copies to recent high school and college grads, both women and men. Most of these men would meet many women who run with wolves, and this book would guide them. What I wanted to know was how would Sabine know how deeply important this book was to me? She answered me with, "It was a hunch or something. I sorta knew, oh I definitely knew." This began a legendary friendship that would last for years, extend beyond the boundaries of countries, and continue although an ocean lay between us. We would go on to know that I was her big brother, and she was my little sister. In the next week, it was a wonder to see it all play out.

The three of us continued westward through San Breixo de Parga and Seixon de Arriba. Sabine and I dug deeper into the "wolf book." The author lived in the southwestern United States desert, but her ancestors hailed from northern Mexico. She was a cantadora, a teller of tales, following a long line of storytellers that included not only her mother and grandmother but also Mexican poets, psychologists, and novelists. One of the seven archetypes in my slideshow was "Women Who Run with the Wolves," and that segment included all the strong women I had met during my travels or who had accompanied me, including my daughters, wife, and mother. I knew Sabine would soon become part of that slideshow, and yet I had known her for only two days.

Our path took us up to the three-building mountain town of Miraz. Two of those buildings were albergues, and one was a restaurant. Our conversations continued as we all lounged in the yard of the British albergue, and Sabine and I traded journals so we could write down suggestions for music, books, and movies. It was a very eclectic listing. We also met a French woman who had just graduated from medical school and was contemplating her specialty. Once again, I pressed her to choose endocrinology. We ate dinner on the restaurant's porch, during which three herds of cows passed by on the dirt road, driven by old farmers and wives or sometimes a couple of dogs.

That night, I announced that my alarm would go off at two in the morning, and if anyone was interested, they were welcome to join me to view the Milky Way outside. I knew it would be cold and that there would be no ambient light. A few expressed interest but as usual, most did not roll their tired bodies from the warmth of their beds. Only one person was curious enough to join me. Of course, it was Sabine. She knew already that she was part of that cosmos. To not view it would go against her nature.

We wrapped blankets around us and followed the beams of my headlight to a pasture, careful not to step in any cow pies. A frozen stream of breath poured out of our mouths. When I turned off my headlight, it felt like the Milky Way dropped out of the sky and fell on us. I had viewed it many times in my life, including a few times on Camino, but never had it seemed so dazzling. Occasionally, shooting stars dropped from the sky, giving off the illusion that you could feel the milky wetness. We stood out there for half an hour, though time had no duration. The show was so bright that we could walk back to the albergue without turning on my headlight. We were no longer foreigners. We were now part of the earth and sky.

Our pilgrimage continued west, and it would be four more days until we entered the holy city. Walking on top of the mountain was glorious. Sabine told me that days before we met, as she walked high on a mountain pass, she came across an old woman, a possible shamanic figure, who proclaimed that Sabine was "amplified aliveness." I agreed with that. I just wish I would have thought of it.

Sabine and I continued to delve into the "wolf book." Estes writes that "the comprehension of this Wild Woman nature is not a religion, but a practice. It is a psychology in its truest sense ... a knowing of the soul." Further, during a retelling of the story of the "Bone Woman Myth," Estes says, "The old woman stands between the worlds of rationality and mythos. This land between the worlds. There is speculation that the immune system of the body is rooted in this mysterious psychic land, and also the mystical as well as all archetypal images and urges." I have been immunocompromised all my life. I live with autoimmune disease. But I rise above it daily. When I read this part of the book, it scrambled my cells, and my being evolved further. It was wonderful to now have sister Sabine to share this with.

For a change of pace, Sabine and Carlo took out their phones at rest breaks and viewed each other's paintings using the language of artists: shadows and light, composition, and color as a language. I listened and learned. I so loved these two kindred spirits. One time they did this at another wonderfully woodsy albergue off the beaten path. As they sat at a picnic table analyzing each other's art, I noticed a basketball hoop and net on the side of a barn. I went into the albergue and procured a basketball from the hospitalero. For the next half hour, I shot hoops while simultaneously receiving a tutorial on the value and nature of art. Where else could this happen except on a pilgrimage?

We started seeing more pilgrim activity as we got closer to the linkup with the usually crowded Camino Frances route. In Sobrado, there is an ancient, magnificent cathedral that prepares you for the further magnificence to come in Santiago de Compostela. We stayed in the monastery in Sobrado and had a few chuckles when we checked in with the aged British monk as he flirted with Carlo, causing Carlo's face to flush. We all did our wash and hung it on the line in the sunny courtyard. When we woke up the next day, we realized we had forgotten to bring in our wash. We would have to hang the now dew-laden clothing from our packs to dry it. This is a common pilgrimage trope. What we discovered though was that both Carlo's and Sabine's underwear were gone. Mine was not. We speculated that the flirting monk stole Carlo's, but why Sabine's? And why not my underwear? I was a little letdown but soon got over it.

The weather turned unseasonably warm as we got closer to the holy city. The much-larger crowds broke our cozy idyl but also invited new chances for a communion with new souls. On arrival in Santiago, I once more felt the rearranging of my molecules. This experience never got old. And now I was there with two of my favorite people in the world.

***

The celebrations in Santiago are a big part of a pilgrimage. This time, they were even more special because I ran into Lyndsey from England, with whom I had walked weeks earlier along with the four other women. Then I was surprised to see Gaetano, the big German bear, whom I had walked into Santiago with two years earlier. He had just walked up the Camino Portuguese from Lisbon. Then we also ran into the French doctor we had met only a week ago but had not seen since. The festivities were thus ratcheted up a notch or two.

    The celebrations are quite lovely and necessary yet sometimes bittersweet. One still longs to be back "out there" but also begins to feel the ritual of returning home. What I have learned is that you must take your Camino home with you. You must live your life like you are still "out there among the eternities." It is hard at times to do this, but what one finds, and which is quite noticeable to those around you, is that the Camino glow is palpable. You have found the Holy Grail; now you must bring it back to share that magic with all the creatures surrounding you. If not, it is as if you had never gone.

    I took an ocean shoreline train to Porto, Portugal, from which I would fly home. While observing the passing scene, I noticed yellow arrows. I had heard a rumor that this Camino existed, and now I realized it was true. I said the names of the villages out loud like an incantation as we passed, almost willing myself to one day walk into them. And that's when I made my decision: I would return here next year and walk the Portuguese Coastal Camino. This was an amazing sleight of hand. With fresh memories of the Camino I just completed, I already started planning my next one. Such are the wonders of life, especially my life. I inched closer to the window and whispered, "I shall return."

Chapter 27

Obrigado, Merci, and Gracias

"Isis, oh, Isis, you mystical child
What drives me to you is what drives me insane
I still can remember the way that you smiled
On the fifth day of May in the drizzlin' rain."

— Bob Dylan, "Isis"

Eleven months after witnessing the signs and arrows along the Portuguese coast from the windows of a train, I kept my vow to walk that path. The strange happenings and eerie prophecy of this year's adventure began while I was still in the Newark, New Jersey, airport, waiting to embark. My buddy and this year's walking partner was supposedly flying out of Philadelphia. Bryce was to meet me in Porto, Portugal, so it surprised the heck out of me when he yelled across the terminal just minutes before boarding. He had made a mistake in booking his flight and that morning had to hustle a ride all the way up to Newark. This set the tone for the entire adventure as we hugged, laughed, and boarded, not even fazed by the turn of events. We expected stuff like this to happen.

We experienced a lot of turbulence on the flight over the Atlantic. The winds gusted as we started to land in Porto and one hit us as we touched down, sending us careening and the wings dipping close to the runway. The genius pilot righted us, and then another gust hit us from the opposite direction, sending us, with wing dipping, toward the runway on the other side. Once again, the pilot corrected us. Everyone on the plane thought we were going to die and became sick with a deep nausea. We exited rubber-legged, Bryce and I looking at each other with the goofy smiles of survivors who just cheated death.

Bryce, though only 25, was a seasoned traveler. He was the son of writers and adventurers Cindy Ross and Todd Gladfelter. After they had hiked the entire Appalachian Trail and the Pacific Crest Trail, Cindy and Todd produced daughter Sierra, followed two years later by Bryce. So at age 2, Bryce and his 4-year-old sister rode a llama from Canada to Mexico on the Continental Divide Trail on the spine of the Rocky Mountains. Since that time, he traveled the world with his family to the Andes of South America, made the Annapurna Trek in the Himalayas, bicycled and floated the Irrawaddy River from Yangon to Mandalay in Myanmar, among countless other adventures.

Even though I had been friends with his family for all of Bryce's life, our adventures rarely crossed paths. While studying at the Tyler School of Art and Architecture at Temple University in Philadelphia, he worked for me for several summers. During those long, hot, hard-working days we planned a hundred future trips together. Here we were, finally, on the precipice of a grand endeavor.

Bryce and his family had once spent two days in a freezing airplane hangar in Moscow while waiting for a transfer to an Aeroflot Airlines flight to China. He was totally accustomed to the kind of airplane contingencies we had experienced. We took a cab downtown, and thus I was back for the third time in four years to my favorite city in the world. Porto felt like home to me, and I especially liked to see my friends experience it for the first time. Even though Bryce had been almost everywhere, I now saw Porto through his eyes as he took in all the enchanting mix of hip and ancient, sacred and profane that was the feature of the second-largest city in Portugal. The following day, we would walk six miles along the Douro River, west to the shores of the Atlantic Ocean, turn, and head north along the beach, arriving two weeks later in Santiago de Compostela.

Early on during the first day, there existed a sense of change in the air. The grand weather, almost unseasonably warm with blue skies, was shifting. There was a subtle hastening of the wind and wisps of possible storm clouds to the north. While that could be ominous, we also had a sense of something big happening, something good, even beyond all the goodness that normally exists on pilgrimage.

While arriving and existing in Porto is fantastic, leaving Porto on the Coastal Camino route is pure heaven. You keep turning around to see another phase of the disappearing city with its primeval towers, the bridges over the river, and its outdoor riverside markets. After six kilometers, you begin to see the first of the thousands of ocean waves you will take in over the next week and a half.

The storms touched down, and stinging rain lashed our faces over the next two days. The grand ocean paths made it easier to glide through the wetness. Again and again, a foreshadowing of something provocative coming in a future town continued to drive us forward like the Holy Grail. We sang U2's "I Still Haven't Found What I'm Looking For" as we walked through Vila do Conde, Esposende, and Marinhas.

In Viana do Castelo, we slept in an albergue in the cathedral and we engaged with a bunch of other pilgrims for the first time. We went to Mass in another church that evening and noticed an orange, glowing, mosque-like building on top of the seaside mountain. The next day, the rains returned, and we sought shelter in a cafe playing videos of Britney Spears singing in Portuguese. The language barrier did nothing to stem our enjoyment because we knew all the words to Britney's songs. Bryce and I laughed at what our mutual friends back home would say if they knew we were putting off the miles to watch just one more video, and another after that, and so on into the late afternoon. We ended up walking in the dark during the early portion of the evening with our headlamps.

In Caminha, we were supposed to take a ferry across a long channel passage. Because of the high winds and very choppy waters, we learned that it was too dangerous to cross that day. Instead of waiting, we took the train inland to Valença on the central route I had walked before. Walking through the walls of a fortress, continuing across a long footbridge, and crossing into Spain in the beautiful city of Tui with Amberly was one of my most cherished memories. After the train, Bryce and I also followed that route, which featured a castle on a peak in hilly Tui. After grabbing lunch in one of my favorite albergues, Ideas Peregrinas, we took the night train back to the coastal route. Though we had missed the dramatic crossing of the bay, and the route we took was tiring into the night, it had still been a captivating day.

We were back on the beach, this time with pleasant weather conditions, as the miles flew by. We walked through Mougas and Baiona and eventually entered the cosmopolitan shipyard city of Vigo. Just inland was a suspension bridge reminiscent of the Golden Gate Bridge. We followed a woodland path for 10 miles the next day with jumping deer, goats, and a waterfall. That bridge would be in our view for the next day and half.

That constant driving feeling of anticipation, a mystical precognition of some sort, followed us into Redondela. Bryce got a haircut in town, trading his wild appearance for one more presentable to what lay ahead. I had gotten sheared before leaving home, which was now almost a week and a half ago. I already felt presentable to what lay ahead. The next day's trail took us over rivers and bays on long stone bridges through Arcade, Pontesampio, and O Pobo/Santa Maria. We still hadn't found what we were looking for.

The afternoon of our ninth day of walking took us into the biggest city since Porto. As we entered Pontevedra, there was a big albergue that drew large crowds of pilgrims. We had decided to look for shelter further into the old town center, where we had planned to attend Mass at Igrexa da Virxe Peregrina, an archaic, rounded cathedral. However, as we passed that first albergue, something told us to stop in. Maybe this was what we were waiting for. We walked into the checkout area, and I suddenly remembered that maybe we could find information about the new anagogic trail called the Variante Espiritual. We needed some sort of map or guidebook. A woman with shining black hair who had her back to us was speaking in Spanish to the hospitalero, and I thought I heard the words "Variante Espiritual." She stopped mid-sentence, turned around, and gave Bryce and I one of the brightest smiles we have ever seen. She told us her name was Cristina and then told the hospitalero to take care of us. I asked about the Variante. Cristina grabbed my arm and, joyfully, in broken English, told us that she also was thinking about doing that trail. She suggested we should walk together. It was a demanding, rarely used, remote trail. I jokingly asked her if she was sure she wanted to walk with two crazy Americano pilgrims. She giggled with delight and let out a sentence of what sounded like a mix of Spanish and English assurances that she knew what she was doing. We agreed to meet at the entrance to the Variante the next morning.

As we left the Albergue grounds to head downtown, Bryce and I simultaneously turned to each other and said, "Was she what we have been anticipating this entire trip?" As a more mature elder statesman, I counselled caution. "My dear Bryce, we must not let our emotions run wild with our lives. Yes, Cristina did snap, crackle, and pop with a kind of vitality that one does not find in the average person one meets. There is definitely something going on. But my advice is to follow the rule of three. If two more situations present themselves in the next few days, then her energy is something we have truly been waiting for. We run the risk of never seeing her again. But if it was meant to be, then it will happen. We will leave fate and the magic of the Camino to decide."

After checking into our lodging, we ate at a small bar with the owners, a comical older couple. We liked them immensely, so we planned to eat breakfast there the next morning. Over dinner, Bryce voiced his concern about following my rule of three. He was a bit nervous. I didn't help by going on about the Father, Son, and Holy Ghost of the Trinity, or some other arcane religious tie-ins, and even how in stand-up comedy there is the rule of three. As we walked to the cathedral, he kept questioning this chance we were taking. We climbed the stairs and entered the holy portal, and my explanations suddenly became pointless. There she was, waiting for Mass to begin, and upon seeing us, that smile appeared again. Cristina, in all her radiant splendor, had passed rule number two.

It was raining steadily the next morning as we exited Pontevedra over a lengthy bridge spanning the Rio Lérez and traveled two miles to the entrance to the Variante Espiritual. Most pilgrims keep going straight on the main Camino Portuguese to Santiago de Compostela. Our route on the new trail would take us one day longer. The rain became a drizzle as we prepared to climb. We rounded a bend, and there she was again, putting on her bright yellow poncho. She flashed that smile, lighting up the fog. Cristina had achieved the Camino rule of three. From this time forward, Cristina, Bryce, and I would soon be eternal, endearing friends. The magic of the Camino had revealed itself.

While walking up and down forested hillsides, we learned that Cristina was from the region of Andalusia in southern Spain and now lived in Madrid, where she was going to university and teaching. Her major was musical performance/theatrical arts, and she also was a choreographer. She would not have had to tell us any of that, because in just a few miles of walking she displayed all her talents. Upon exiting the monastery at Poio, with sheets of rain bearing down upon us, Cristina danced an expressive flamenco, visually enhanced by her yellow poncho. She had a kind of buoyancy, which served to rescue our floundering spirits from drowning.

Throughout the first day of the Variante, the weather changed hourly. It cleared somewhat along the shores of an Atlantic bay in Combarro, and then the sun shined brightly during the long, steep climb to a mountain platform vista of the ocean. There were some problems with markings because of logging, so we had to be vigilant while walking along the ridge. This was a very remote area.

More of Cristina was revealed along the way. We learned that her pack was heavy because she carried some big books. She also carried a blow dryer, which we made fun of her for. She just shook her head and wagged a finger at us. None of this slowed her down. Though small, Cristina was a steady, rhythmic walker. Her laugh was infectious, as we learned that she studied English by watching Woody Allen movies, even some of his lesser-known ones. Then the conversations advanced to other American movies, beginning a trading-off of movie dialogue as mirth ensued. It would have sounded strange to other pilgrims, but we saw no other pilgrims for the full three days.

The rain came down hard as we entered the village of Armenteira. We hustled to find the albergue, though that didn't keep Cristina from dancing a jig in front of the stone arches of the monastery. We were delighted to find a brand new albergue and rang the number, and soon a wonderful hospitalero arrived, gave us the keys, and pointed to a bar a quarter-mile down the street that served pilgrim meals.

Now came the task of drying out. Bryce and I could no longer laugh at Cristina for carrying a hair dryer. It was lightweight and not for her hair: it was very effective for drying socks. Once again, Cristina got the last laugh.

We got totally soaked in an antediluvian deluge as we walked to the bar. There the conversation flowed, enhanced by red wine, and continued for hours back at the ultra-modern albergue. We traded lists of books, movies, and music by writing in each other's journals. Those lists were diverse and enlightening. We had become old friends in only one day.

The following morning, we walked through pure enchantment. Ruta de la Piedra y del Agua (Route of the Stone and the Water) consists of four miles of waterfalls, stone ruins, and footbridges. It is another of the many highlights of the Variante Espiritual, especially that day as the storms brought the falls to torrent level. It was beyond beautiful. At another tavern stop, where we ate outside, I got out my spiky football and rolled my bare feet back and forth on it to ease the soreness. Cristina wasn't grossed out. She was a real pilgrim.

Later in the afternoon, we finished the day by walking along the ocean right into the town of Vilanova de Arousa. This was the boat dock where, the next morning, we would float up a channel past 20 Stations of the Cross made of cement, all the way to Padrón. This is the same route that a stone boat had sailed from the Holy Land with the remains of St. James, who was then carried on foot to Santiago de Compostela. We stayed at another new albergue with a modern kitchen, so Cristina told us that she would cook us an Andalusian specialty. The hospitalero told us the market was too far to walk to but that we could use a bunch of children's bicycles, stored at the albergue, to get there. It was like a Keystone Cops movie. Bryce and I were way too big for our bikes, and Cristina was too small for hers. Some of the rims were bent, and some of the tires were half-flat. We could not stop laughing the entire three blocks to the Supermercado. Yes, it was only three blocks. We could have walked there faster. The entire junket was so absurd that we could not stop laughing about it the rest of the night.

We had stayed up way too late, drank way too much Rioja wine, and had both deep and whimsical conversations. Bryce and I continued to be dazzled by Cristina's elan, her verve and sparkle, but especially by the joyfulness of her enthusiasm, which translates from the Greek "entheos" – "having a god within."

We learned that the boat needed eight paying customers to make the run. We were the only three to show up, so we decided instead to take the train up to Padrón on the Central Portuguese Camino route. Padrón was celebrating Holy Week with festivals everywhere. Now came the tearful goodbye between us and Cristina. She had to continue by train to Santiago that day since she was scheduled to sing there at night. The next morning, she had to return to university. It was tempting to ride along with her to hear her sing, but Bryce and I had a day and a half of walking still to complete. Right before she boarded the train, we all hugged goodbye. An overhead screen in the station had music videos playing, and Camilla Cabello's "Havana" flashed on. We suddenly broke into a song and dance, practically inserting ourselves into the video. The finale tailed off with our whoops and howls of laughter, a quite fitting way of saying adios to some of the best three days of adventure I have ever experienced.

***

Bryce and I entered the Praza do Obradoiro in front of that stately cathedral in Santiago de Compostela with an ebullience that never grows old. This was Bryce's second arrival. Years earlier, when he was a wee lad, he had bicycled with his family from France to Santiago. This was my sixth arrival. No matter how many times you arrive, though, it rearranges your molecules every time. We had walked the last mile with Chris from Australia. I traded information, hoping to walk with him sometime in the future. Bryce hustled home the next day, but we stayed up late into the night composing and performing a music video with Bryce rapping and me announcing, in a deep radio voice, slogans, passages, and names of places we walked through. At the end of each verse, we sang "Santiago de Compostela" to the chorus of "Havana." Then we sent the video to Cristina, and right before Bryce headed home, we heard the singsong laughter of Cristina in a return message. It felt like we had never parted.

I hung around Santiago for a day, took in the Semana Santa parades and concerts with some German pilgrims we had met at the albergue the night before, and ate a few bowls of Caldo Gallego soup. Then I boarded a train, riding for 10 hours through the night over the border and into France. I planned to walk along the beaches from Hendaye to Saint-Jean-de-Luz and Biarritz and back. This was Hemingway country again. I was afraid of a letdown after the last two weeks, but once I saw the big waves among stone formations, my passion returned. I would only be alone for a few days. Then nine other pilgrim friends from around the world would join me to recreate the first two weeks of my walk on the majestic Camino del Norte.

***

Seven of us set off on the climb up into the mountains along this wild stretch of Northern Spain on Easter. There would be some terra incognita on the route even though I had walked here two years earlier. Since the weather was perfect, we chose the Purgatorio route this time, with its steep climbs and balds with 360-degree views of the bay of Hondarribia, the beaches of France, and the foothills of the Pyrenees. As soon as your heart rate returns to normal, you are gripped by the magnificence of the entire scene. This was a spectacular place for a reunion of pilgrims.

I had met Sheryl, Glenn, Carlo, and Jenny during my first Camino in 2013. The following year, we all walked across France together, and a few years had passed since I had seen almost everyone. Carlo, however, had walked with me on the Norte the year my mom died and then again the following year when we returned to complete the Norte into Santiago. Since Carlo had cut his walk short when I quickly returned home to present my mom's eulogy and then rejoined me the following year, I vowed to walk with him this year for two weeks to Santander.

Jenny had met Dominique at the tail end of our walk in France. They continued to walk together over the next few years, eventually getting married and maintaining homes in both France and Australia. Dominique's steady pace and sharp sense of humor were on full display every day. I knew he needed that fast walk to keep up with mighty Jenny. He claimed it was uncivil to begin the day without a croissant.

Denise, meanwhile, was friends with Sheryl and Glenn and like them was also from North Carolina. She had a mystical sensibility about her enhanced by her dark-haired beauty. She worked in banking finance, and Sheryl told me Denise had vast skills and brilliance in those endeavors. I would witness all these pilgrims experiencing the wonders of the Camino del Norte for the first time.

One week later, we entered Bilbao. I started to feel a bit homesick for my family, but my daughter Amberly was due to fly into the city the next day. Knowing that family was on the way, it was a bit perplexing that I had this dour mood. Everyone noticed it, too, but being pilgrims meant that they understood the wide range of emotions sure to make their way into one's psyche. I decided to turn in early, skipping the communal meal the rest of the gang was excited about.

I knew Bilbao was a gem of a city, so I finally kicked my butt out the pension door, crossed a few of the marvelous bridges, and entered the old city, looking for a place to eat dinner. I poked my head into a cellar-like stone restaurant. If in doubt, always go with something unique. I entered and to my surprise, the whole gang was sitting in a back corner with way too many empty wine bottles on the table. In a large city, it was uncanny for me to have picked this place. They started questioning each other as to who had sent me a text with the address, but it was all serendipity. My prescient nature was still working.

It turned out to be a wonderful meal of gourmet seafood specially made by the chef. More empty bottles of wine were soon stacked by the old ones. Yes, I was still a bit homesick, but when one is on pilgrimage, your Camino family is your present family. They are there to boost you up and vice versa. This was another example of Camino magic. When the night ended, my blues had dissipated into the starry skies above joyous Bilbao.

Amberly arrived around two in the afternoon. She had returned home from here two years ago, so she was already open to the wizardry of Bilbao. We walked off her jet lag all around the city. The next day, I was thrilled to show her the further charms of the Camino del Norte. We approached the beaches of La Arena and Pobeña at the end of our walking day. Amberly, still a bit jet lagged, was a little grumpy about having to climb 300 stairs at the end of a long day, but I knew what was up there. I had been places since last proclaiming that these next five miles were the most scenic I'd ever walked on. Once up, she agreed, and for me, they remained so. I couldn't talk Amberly into going up the stairs at night, but that was okay. That had been my personal, solitary experience the year before.

The next morning, we went up the steps once more and then headed out to Ontón. This time, there were goats and cows right on the path, even on the narrow ledge above the Atlantic, on the outside of the split-rail fence. It could not have been easy for them to get out there. Soon, Amberly was coming out of her jet-lagged state and was back into her fast pace, two steps for my one. I had slowed down a bit since entering my 60s. Then we moved onto the promenade of Castro Urdiales and into the city. We secured an ultra-modern pension one block off the beach, right across the street from a great little bar. We washed our clothes at a laundromat, though we bought too many soap pods. Even the chores and maintenance were fun on pilgrimage, and doubly so with Amberly there.

Castro Urdiales lights up at night, creating a jubilant atmosphere and mood. We ate outside at a table on the dock where the barkeep told us a big rainstorm was coming that evening. We had to get an early start to catch the rest of the crew, who were just ahead of us.

Amberly knew and loved almost everyone in my Camino family. She had walked with them across France back in 2014. Now she was meeting Denise and Dave for the first time. Dave, a good friend of Carlos back in Belgium, had joined us a week earlier in Markina-Xemein. We caught up to them in the town of Laredo. It was as windy and rainy as two years ago. I probably wouldn't recognize many places on the Norte if I ever returned in sunny weather conditions. We walked out onto the four-mile promenade and were met by a full force of elements. The upcoming ferry to Santoña was on my mind. Amberly also gets very nauseous from motion, and today, like two years earlier, there would be lots of motion in these inlet waters. Another pilgrim told us the last ferry would leave the pier at noon. It was 11:45, and we were about a mile and a half from there, so I used my 60 years of fast walking experience, stepped up the pace, and got to the ferry right at noon only to find out that the ferry runs all afternoon.

We rolled on into Noja on cold, beautiful beaches while wearing most of our clothing. The next day took us to the famous albergue in Güemes run by Father Ernesto, who was off traveling somewhere else in the world. The experience for my team was still one of deep spirituality, though not so much in the three-tiered bunk room where 10 of us were crammed in along with our drying clothes. I wondered, once again, how this albergue could be so full if we had not seen many pilgrims along the way.

On our last full day of walking, we headed toward Santander, following the resplendent coastline one last time. Several stairways led down to beaches dappled by light waves. It was the first spectacular sendoff we received. The second was the long, gentle ferry ride over the bay to the downtown of the third and last of the sendoffs, the ancient yet urban elegance of Santander.

The Norte is breathtaking both in beauty and in the calories expended to walk its ups and downs. You are always rewarded for the effort. What the Norte lacks when compared to the Camino Frances is a lot of other pilgrims from around the world and a deeper sense of piety with fewer cathedrals and Masses. It does include a lot of blacktop roads, though after having walked around most of the United States on blacktop, it does not bother me. The Norte is not better or worse than the Frances. It is just different.

Carlos and Dave joined Amberly and I for the train ride back to Madrid. Together we could celebrate one last night, which was fitting since Carlos had officially completed the Camino del Norte in three stages over three years. He was a very stalwart pilgrim, and during the last six years, our mutual respect for each other as true pilgrims had increased. There would be many more miles to share in the future.

I was very excited that a planned get-together at La Pentola Mágica restaurant with my Variante Espiritual buddy Cristina would happen on our last night in Madrid. It would be cool for Dave, Carlos, and Amberly to meet the wonderfulness of Cristina. As expected, they too were dazzled by her charm and energy. When we left the gathering, Carlos and Dave wanted us to take a tour of gay bars with them. We were very tired and had an early flight the next morning, so we turned down their offer. We have since regretted that decision. Carlos texted us the next day to tell us the first bar was mostly older queens with a lot of ABBA coming out of the sound system. The second bar had a much younger crowd, several of whom took off their shirts.

I flew home worn out yet euphoric. I had walked three Caminos in three countries. I had walked with old friends and my daughter and had met new friends. Each year, I had felt as if I lived the experience of a lifetime. Already looking ahead, I was thrilled to begin planning the next big adventure.

Chapter 28

Following in the Footsteps of Myself

"Speak to me heart
All things renew
Hearts will mend
Round the bend
Paths that cross, cross again
Paths that cross, will cross again."

— Patti Smith, "Paths That Cross"

For weeks leading up to my spring 2019 liftoff and continuing on the flight to Madrid, it felt like something strange was happening. It could be a foretelling of a planetary shift, a doomsday scenario, or just a subtle reminder to enjoy and value the adventure I was about to set off on. This adventure did not loom large compared to what had gone before. Why would I return to the Camino Frances, the main pilgrims' path to Santiago? I completed it twice in the last seven years. When there are so many paths and challenges and adventures in the world, or even just in Europe — hell even just in Spain — why go again for a third time? Something told me this would be the last time I would go for a while. Was I going to die, get sick and feeble, or have an accident and lose mobility? I did not know, and so I put all that to the far corners of my brain and embraced the beauty of the people, landscapes, and visions I know I can find on this path. The rest of the world could wait. This is where I wanted to be at this moment in time. "Be here now" — that's what I was going to do.

Laura and Dave were back. In the pantheon of returning actors in the comedic drama of my life, they were, as the Greeks say, "Zoi," forces of life. They would walk with me from Logroño to Burgos. That first week would set me up to carry on alone all the way to Santiago de Compostela. Laura and Dave's high spirits would accompany me the rest of the way, even though their earthly bodies would have to return home.

We met at the airport in Madrid and took the afternoon bus north to Logroño. After checking into our room, we hit the streets in search of the taste sensation of Logroño, mushrooms at Bar Soriano. We found this place two years ago. The only thing on the menu was mushrooms grilled in butter. It's amazing how explosive the taste sensation is. What was different this year was that Bar Soriano had been discovered. The streets leading up to the small serving counter were packed with a mix of locals, tourists, and pilgrims. After receiving their orders, patrons ate standing up at tables in the closed middle of the street. It was worth the wait. The mushrooms were as grand as last time.

Before setting out on the Way to Santiago, we had a simple meditation in the magnificence of Iglesia de Santiago del Real. I felt the excitement of sharing with Laura and Dave the wonders of the province of La Rioja. I had come to love the wine made there. We made it an easy first day to the village of Navarrete, surrounded by snowy mountains and vineyards. We spent the balmy day lounging in front of a cafe, petting the village cats, and attended Mass. We loved talking to the bar owners, who made us feel like we had always lived there. It was only day one and already the Camino was seeping into our souls.

We advanced west to more vineyards and mountains, skirting Ventosa, climbing Alto de San Antón, and then sleeping in Nájera. All traces of jet lag and weariness had long gone. In Santo Domingo de la Calzada, I attended Mass with about 10 classy, elderly Spanish women bedecked in fur coats. After the service, I asked them in broken Spanish where their husbands were. Did they not attend church, too? They motioned me to follow them and lead me to the corner bar. Inside were the men of the town, including my walking partner, Dave, and one woman, Laura. I guess in our pilgrim group of three, Dave and Laura were the old men, and I was the old lady. All I needed was a classy fur coat.

As we left Belorado in the morning, the skies portended storms. A few kilometers later as we walked through Villambistia, the wind-driven rain pelted us with a hint of sleet mixed in. My backpacking umbrella was useless in the wind. We scrambled to put on our storm gear under a porch in Espinosa del Camino. Nothing was open in any of these villages, and our only hope ahead was Villafranca Montes de Oca. After that, it would be a long slog up a mountain and through a 12-kilometer stretch of wilderness leading to Monasterio de San Juan de Ortega. Thank God the bar/restaurant at Casa rural la Alpargatería was open and hopping with pilgrim festivities. Everyone on Camino was seeking sanctuary from the storm.

Most of the tables were crowded, but two pilgrims motioned us over, and we squeezed in. The father and son, Alan and Stephen, were from Ireland, and immediately we knew we were at the right table. We fell into an easy and amusing flow with them as the afternoon slipped by. At this point, we knew we weren't going into that long stretch of trail above us in the still-raging maelstrom. Most procured rooms right there, others searched around, and one guy even jumped into a bus and headed to Burgos. That night, we again got together with Alan and Stephen and felt like old friends already. I felt confident enough with them to share the quest I had been on for a few years now to take an unflattering photo of Laura. I even showed them the one from that hair-raising day on the Norte when, after drinking two tankards of beer, a sun- and wind-burned Laura still photographed like a model. The Irish told me to surrender. They didn't think it was going to happen either, as Laura blushed. You can't ignore what is.

Everything cleared the next day as we decided to do a long day into the city of Burgos. Laura and Dave decided that they would leave the city and head to warmer climes in Seville, so it would be lonely for me once again. I would miss their grace and light.

On my own, I dove into the Spanish Meseta that called me to face the challenge of its austere, windswept emptiness. But I also knew from previous walks through here that the Meseta helped screw your head on tighter. I walked a bit with Shirley from Puerto Rico but marched into Hontanas alone.

As far as towns in this part of Spain went, none exemplified the Spanish desert like Hontanas. I searched for a place to sleep but found nothing other than wisps of dust spinning down empty streets. A monk opened the door to the monastery and motioned me in to where they had 20 bunks in a side room for pilgrims. It, too, was dusty, and the light filtered in in shafts. It was as cold inside as out, and I had only a thin silk sleep sack. I was going to have to sleep in all my clothes. Soon a burly Irishmen entered, and he smiled when I told him of my anticipated cold night. He got out a softball-sized sack and told me, "You gotta get yourself one of these." He pulled out a goose-down quilt and shook it a few times as it puffed up. It looked luxurious. I made a note in my journal. This guy had good instincts.

I told him that I didn't see anywhere to eat or drink in Hontanas, and he said, "Oh, we'll find something." We hit the town and found a rough-looking shack on a dead-end side street. He thought it had to be a bar, but I was less certain. We knocked and, sure enough, it was indeed a bar with a bunch of locals drinking and playing cards. The bartender even made us egg sandwiches but said he would close at eight that night. We walked back to the monastery as my buddy told me that an Irishman will always be able to find a bar.

A thin German man entered the monastery a little after eight o'clock. He introduced himself as Willi and said he was 80 and had walked half his age in kilometers that day. He was hungry, but I told him everything was closed. I gave him a banana and a Clif Bar, and he was very thankful. The following night, I ran into him in Itero de la Vega, where he paid for my meal and handed me a banana from the market. The Camino spirit was alive and well.

I reconnected and had dinner with Alan and Stephen from Ireland in Frómista. They told me I had to make it to León by Saturday because there was going to be a major rugby match between Ireland and Spain that day. I thought they meant live in a stadium, but Stephen said, "Oh no, it's going to be televised in an Irish bar."

"I didn't know there were any Irish bars in León," I said.

They laughed, and Alan gave me the address of one. The next morning, I started walking with a French kid on the alternative creek trail out of Población de Campos. We had a good discussion on several subjects and decided to cook in the albergue at the abbey in Carrión de los Condes. The nuns asked us to attend an early Mass, so we walked a few blocks with them. There was even a mystical-looking nun dressed in a hijab. We walked back with them after the service and invited them to eat dinner with us, but they said that they go to sleep at eight and rise at four in the morning. That's why Mass was so early.

***

    I spent most of the next five days alone, which allowed me to face some trauma issues I had struggled with lately. Only five months earlier, Amberly and I had entered the Fall Classic 50-mile bike race. It was our third time tackling this hilly, challenging race, and our fourth race of this season. The morning of the race, it was drizzling but warm. There were lots of slippery, leaf-strewn corners. On our first descent, about 20 miles in, we encountered a thick, pervading mist. As we attained speed, Amberly screamed that her brakes were not working because of the wetness (I had disc brakes, which worked despite the weather). In a split second, I noticed an intersection at the bottom of the hill. I pictured her going through that and getting hit by a car, so I forced her into a hedge-filled bank, hoping it would slow her descent. Initially it did, until she hit a hidden rock that threw her from her bike onto the road. I swear she bounced as she hit the blacktop, and other racers swerved to avoid running over her.

    Amberly groaned as I stopped and ran up to her. Other racers stood guard and redirected bike traffic. I immediately asked if she could feel her legs and she nodded. The pain was in her shoulder. Someone had called an ambulance, which soon arrived. And this is where the amazing little girl that her mother and I had raised showed what she was made of. She was in deep pain, but first she asked about her bike, which was totaled, and joked with the EMTs. As they loaded her in the ambulance, she told me to throw her bike into the field, ride on and finish the race, and then come to the hospital. She knew she was going to the hospital she worked at, so she would know most of the nurses in the ICU and would need to go for a bunch of tests anyway.

    I did a quick check, and my blood glucose was 300. After calling my wife, and in a state of trauma and determination, I completed the last 30 miles in what was, for me, a record time and then headed directly to the hospital, only 10 minutes away. I arrived right as Amberly came out of her initial tests. She had broken her collarbone, torn part of her liver and one kidney, and had bad scrapes on one arm and leg. Her now-crushed helmet had saved her. She would recover for many weeks, which was why she had not joined me on my next Camino.

I still dealt with the trauma of seeing Amberly's body bounce off the road during her accident. I had nightmares of her continuing through that intersection and getting hit. Obviously my trauma was not as heightened as what Amberly experienced, but it was enough to creep into my life, especially on that year's walk since I was alone most of the time.

In León, I stayed with the young family that owned León Hostel, right around the corner from the cathedral. I had mailed a package of my medical supplies to the hostel, just like I had before. Back then, the wife of the family was pregnant, and this time, I got to meet the now almost 2-year-old boy. The next morning, I was a bit low when my buddy Gabriel called from home to let me know that his mother had passed away from cancer. She was only in her early 60s. I figured it was going to be a long, lonely walk through the last of the stark meseta.

As the last of the industrial surroundings of León started to fade, I began walking with Nini from Taiwan. She had balloons tied to her pack, and she was so light on her feet that I thought she would float away on the windy dirt roads. When I laid my burdens on Nini, she made a plan that would help alleviate them. She had that same buoyancy other pilgrims on Camino carry. During a visit to the modern-looking La Virgen del Camino, I felt some of my burden lift. Later, I heard stories about Nini that confirmed what I initially thought: she indeed was a Camino angel.

As I approached Astorga, I started walking with a young German boy named Martin. He was a quiet but a strong walker as the last of the Spanish meseta fell away under our feet. Together we had a reunion with Stephen and Alan, the Irish father and son, who said the rugby match in León had not gone well for Ireland. Together, we walked into the walled city and had a great meal together.

Martin and I planned to sleep at the albergue on top of the mountain, just beyond Cruz de Ferro in Manjarín. I really wanted to sit around the fire, late into the night, and have a dialogue with Thomas, the last of the Knights Templar. But both Martin and I agreed that the conditions of the sleeping quarters needed tons of work. Once again, I promised myself that I would stay there on a future Camino.

It was very late as we headed to El Acebo on the most perilous descent on the Camino. We arrived as the darkness descended and were both very tired after a long day. I was glad to have Martin as a kindred spirit on that most treacherous stretch on the Way.

The following day, Martin and I entered Ponferrada with a Japanese woman named Sayo. After that, I lost track of them, but I did run into Nini again at an albergue built into a rock at Villafranca del Bierzo. On the remaining walk into Santiago, I was alone most of the way, up and over O Cebreiro and down into the valley at Triacastela. There, for the first time, I took the main route, trading the monastery at San Xil for the monastery at Samos. This route was very steep and not as pleasant as the softer trails on the other path, and the monastery looked deserted. I didn't mind. I had my own monastery in my consciousness, in my own being.

***

I had dinner one night with Jill from France, a retired Lufthansa pilot, and we walked all day together into Sarria and on to just before Portomarín. Jill went on, as I wanted to stay in places I had not stayed in during my other two walks through there. That put me five kilometers away from Jill each night, but we did run into each other in Santiago. I walked the last 100 kilometers alone, preparing myself for what was on the horizon when I got home — something I could not have had any notion of, other than that low-level feeling that swirled about during my Camino and for the next year. That feeling constantly reminded me to live from day to day and to immerse myself in the beauties of the world I passed through, somehow, someway. I knew I would not come back to Spain or Europe for a few years, so I would need a bit of spirit to send me home.

I visited Cristina from the Variante Espiritual in Madrid. We had three hours in our favorite restaurant to talk about walking, books, adventures, music, movies, and pilgrimage paths. Cristina was her usual self, a high-speed vector of energy. We could have talked all night, but I had an early-morning flight to catch. We walked together to the Metro and hugged goodbye, planning to walk together the next year but somehow feeling that we would not see each other for many years to come.

Chapter 29

The Camino of the Imagination — The COVID-19 Pandemic

*"I come down from the misty mountain
I got lost on the human highway
Take my head, refreshing fountain
Take my eyes from what they've seen
Take my head and change my mind
How could people get so unkind?"*

— Neil Young, "Human Highway"

I was five days away from flying to Madrid. After landing, I planned to hang out in the city; spend a day or two with Cristina; visit the Picasso, Miró, and Dalí paintings at the Museo Nacional Centro de Arte Reina Sofía; and then hop a train to Santiago de Compostela. I would take a day to walk all around the city and then start my unique pilgrimage. I would walk south, following the blue arrows instead of the yellow, which come north. The blue arrows would lead me, in 30 days, to Fatima, Portugal, the site where the Virgin Mary appeared numerous times to three shepherd children in the early 1900s. Since the time of that miracle, millions of pilgrims had walked, bicycled, and driven to Fatima, where a huge cathedral rises from the village. The route would be unique because even though I had walked the Camino Portuguese, this time it would be in the opposite direction. Also unique would be a new variante that would lead me west to Fatima. I was fit and trained, packed and prepared, and in a spiritual frame of mind, because I would walk most days alone.

Around this time, there was a lot of news about a SARS-type virus that had possibly originated in China and was spreading dangerously fast. It was named COVID-19 and considered lethal. After it spread into Europe, I knew I would have to put my trip on hold until the autumn or possibly the next year. I managed to get my flight refunded from United Airlines and canceled the early lodging I had booked. Though I was dejected, I realized there was now a good possibility that COVID-19 could turn into a worldwide pandemic.

***

Two months before the pandemic began, my youngest daughter got married. The ceremony and reception took place in the historic Hotel Bethlehem. We had prepared for the possibility of winter storms by holding everything at one location, including blocking off rooms for travelers from near and far. On the weekend of the early January wedding, we broke records for the warmest weekend in history for that time of year. The entire city was still decorated for Christmas, including the wedding venue. Crowds were sitting outside at restaurant, bars, and cafe tables. The scene reminded me of Europe. The morning of the wedding, I took a five-mile walk along the trails paralleling the Lehigh River in a T-shirt, shorts, and headband as the sweat poured forth.

One amazing feature of the Hotel Bethlehem is a gallery of hundreds of photos of people who have stayed overnight there, including famous politicians, movie stars, athletes, musicians, and more. They line the walls and columns in the 1920s-era bar. There were a few rouges represented, including notorious politicians from the early 1970s. My favorites were Amelia Earhart, Muhammad Ali, Kurt Vonnegut, and the Grateful Dead. The Dalai Lama slept there when he gave a presentation and workshop Adrienne and I attended at Lehigh University. When we booked our rooms, I requested the same one the Dalai Lama slept in. I figured it would put me in a peaceful mood for the wedding proceedings.

I cried during the wedding ceremony because it was my youngest daughter, but I also added some levity when I was asked to read a Tahoe Native American prayer. Standing up front with the wedding party, I acted like I couldn't find the paper in my pockets. I pulled out a fortune cookie and read the fortune, then acted like I found the piece of paper and started reading it, but it was a grocery store list. Finally, I found the prayer in another tuxedo pocket and solemnly recited it. A family friend, Chip, officiated the ceremony and was a pro at providing the perfect mix of the sacred and whimsical.

The reception was a festive affair with the Paris-like ballroom, still decorated for the holidays, as one of the features (the other, of course, being the glowing faces of bride Amberly and her groom, Steve). There was much imbibing of alcohol, which sped through the bloodstream thanks to the spirited dancing. My wife's dress of choice and style of hair had her looking like Jane Fonda. We all felt the obscene winter heat as we sweated through our expensive couture apparel. Big sister Adrienne and her cousin Allison sang a hilarious tribute to Amberly and Steve, adding their own lyrics to the Barry Manilow song "Copacabana."

Then it was time for me to keep the promise that I made to the girls when they were little, during those fun, crazy snowy days. I had kept that promise when I sang at Adrienne's wedding 10 years earlier, so it was now time to sing to Amberly. I chose the song "Waltz for Debby" written by jazz pianist Bill Evans for his daughter but sung on record by Tony Bennett. I had practiced for half a year because I'm not a singer, but I pulled it off, a cappella, and brought forth tears from Amberly, Steve, and a few from my wife and myself. That's all that mattered.

The reception eventually spilled onto the streets of downtown Bethlehem, the city now becoming part of the jubilant affair, and then into the various late-night bars. None of us needed shawls or coats as we finally returned, through the balmy January morning, to our rooms in the hotel where famous guests had one time slept and snored, including the Dalai Lama.

***

Two months after the wedding, the COVID-19 pandemic came upon us. We went into lockdown, and everything closed except businesses and establishments necessary for day-to-day survival. My family and I took all the precautions and figured we were at low risk for contracting the virus. Our one worry was about my father-in-law, who lived in a nursing home. He was 95 but otherwise in decent shape. It must have been horrifying for him, however, to suddenly have no visitors, no group programs, and no cafeteria time with his table mates. All the staff entered his room dressed in head-to-toe hazmat suits with shields covering their faces. It looked like something out of an apocalyptic sci-fi movie. This was how the pandemic moved across the landscapes of thousands of hospitals and nursing homes.

My wife and I had plenty of activities to keep us entertained. Nancy was retired for a year at that point, and I was semi-retired and could hope to make up some lost hours when the pandemic restrictions eased. Amberly worked in a medical setting, but eventually she could counsel patients online. Her husband could work out of his home office as well. Adrienne and her husband already worked out of their home, and my grandson started attending kindergarten online. Considering the fates of many people around us, in the country and around the world, we were relatively safe. The death count started to mount as we moved from March to April.

I normally had a pretty good immune system, but if I did contract the virus, I would have an against-the-odds battle because of my age (upper 60s) and my three pre-existing conditions. Of lesser concern, though still psychologically and spiritually significant, was my loss of taking a yearly pilgrimage — not the travel, or the festivity, or the discovery of new things around me or inside of me but instead the movement across the route of the ancients. The rhythm of life. Adventure as a metaphor for the journey of life itself. I would now have to use all my creative faculties to make, amid the strictures of a deadly virus, something resembling the Camino de Santiago experience.

One saving grace of the pandemic was that you could still go outside if you stayed away from people or crowds. My wife and I started taking three walks a day, two or three miles at a pop, mostly through the deserted town sidewalks and the equally deserted Kutztown University campus. The morning walk was different from the afternoon walk, and the third one happened either at dusk or in the dark with the streetlights glowing. We took the same route, but it looked different every time. We started noticing the smallest details that deviated from the previous walk. A security car parked in an alcove, a grove of trees that had turned green from the previous night's rain, the temperature change of the heavily chlorinated fountain water in which I soaked my headband to cool off. The weather changed constantly, and that alone made each walk uniquely interesting.

My wife and I found out that we could spend huge swaths of time together and not get belligerent. During somewhat normal times, we would split the day almost evenly between being alone and together. Now we hung out together all the time like we had in our youth. However, we still read entirely different books, and that continued as usual. We had totally different literary and philosophical tastes, and never the twain shall meet.

***

One Saturday, though it could have been any day of the week because they were the same, I decided to walk six laps of our route in one day, totaling 15 miles (the same distance I averaged on Camino). That would take us past six church towers and included a walk into and out of a labyrinth in a cemetery behind one of the churches. I even laid down in front of the 60- to 80-foot church steeples and photographed them to make them look taller. I had painted and repaired a few of them over the last 45 years. Everything would be in place for a Camino-like experience, and indeed it worked. With an assist from my big ol' imagination, I came home from the last mile and looked for the menu del dia, the cheap but satisfying pilgrims' menu found in Spain. That night I missed the Camino just a little bit less.

I noticed on social media that many pilgrims around the world walked virtual Caminos, and I could follow along almost as if I had walked or broken bread with them that day. I planned my next virtual Camino. A water tank and a few transmission towers rise behind Kutztown, and to get to them, I had to climb two switchbacks. It used to be a dirt road that my family and I hiked a couple times each week, but people built houses there over the years, adding blacktop roads and street lights. To this day, we climb it at least one or two times a week as part of our cardio-vascular training. As a Camino approached, I would wear my pack up to the top, slowly adding weight each week until I neared the weight I would have overseas.

Reaching the top provided the hard-breathing pilgrim a nearly 360-degree view of the immediate world. I could see the tower above

Topton five miles southeast; Deka Battery, one of my long-term sponsors, to the south; and at night, the faint lights of the cities of Reading to the west and Allentown to the east. Spread out beneath ran the borough of Kutztown's streets, zigging and zagging save for Main Street, which runs straight and true from the pine trees of the park to the other end of town, through the fountain and flowers of the university. The memories of the miles that my feet alone have left on those streets would pile up higher than the buildings, clogging up traffic far into the hinterlands.

My idea was to walk six laps from my house, up and back, totaling 18 miles. Each climb up would be one of the six summits pilgrims crest on a 500-mile walk across the Camino de Santiago. The first simulated climb was up and over the Pyrenees, from France to Spain, and the sixth and last simulated climb would be the Galacian summit of O Cebreiro. The effort of the climbs was stimulating and left a sheen of sweat on my skin that the winds at the apex dried. It was just another day in the building of the substitute Camino to assuage my longing.

On a Sunday in June, my daughter, son-in-law, and I masked up and participated in a march to remember those killed by unjust police actions, including George Floyd and Breonna Taylor. For me, it was a call to end systemic racism in police forces. I was proud of our town for coming out to march in large numbers. Main Street was closed to traffic and instead lined with walkers holding signs. All the speakers were inspiring, including Kutztown Mayor James F. Schlegel. We all kneeled for nine minutes to simulate, to just a tiny degree, what George Floyd went through as an officer watched him die with a knee on his neck. The march happened sensibly during the pandemic with many precautions, and as far as I know, nobody got COVID, and there was no violence.

During these homebound days, I luxuriated in my memories of past Caminos by spilling my guts as a guest on four Camino podcasts. I talked with Bradley from England on the "El Camino de Santiago Pilgrims' Podcast"; on Dan's "My Camino" podcast, which is broadcast from Australia; and with Dave from Oregon on "The Camino Podcast." Years earlier, I had spoken with Brendan from Spain twice on the podcast "Project Camino," one of which took place live from a courtyard in Santiago de Compostela with the ringing of the cathedral bells occasionally accompanying us. These wonderful hosts took me back to the Camino in spirit and alleviated my yearning for pilgrimage. I even met some new pilgrims through the interviews on these podcasts, including Vivek from India and Melanie from Germany. I plan to walk with these two pilgrims at some point. The magic of the Way still permeates through my life.

Simulation three was more of a mythical quest, but it still had Camino qualities to it. It involved my wife and I setting out on a 12-mile journey like Guinevere and Sir Galahad to the distant town of Topton, on paths and dirt roads where there were cathedral towers and castles, a domed mosque on a distant hill, and a mythical river we had to cross like entering the underworld. We encountered strange beasts along the way, including a snake, horse, fox, and magical dog named Princess Daisy. We survived the trek and returned to Kutztown with an empty water bottle that we pretended was the Holy Grail.

Another activity that helped me to get through the pandemic, and prepared me for writing these very memoirs, was writing word sketches of some of the wonderful pilgrims I met along the Camino over those seven glorious years. I posted them on Facebook and Instagram, thereby receiving some valuable feedback from readers. Some forms of those word sketches eventually made their way into the book.

***

My family experienced death during the first May of the pandemic. My father-in-law died after battling COVID-19 for two weeks. He was 94 and had proclaimed to anyone within earshot, during the years preceding his death, that he was making a definitive run to reach triple figures age-wise. He only missed it by five years, and a few days. Had he not gotten COVID, he may have pulled it off.

My father-in-law was the last of our parents to pass on to the next world. He had beaten cancer, had new knees, and had worked hard all his life. He died in his nursing home bed after spending almost two weeks in the hospital. He had made a valiant recovery, but the virus had weakened him so much that the fight drained from his body. None of us were allowed in since the nursing home was rife with COVID cases. Irvin died alone, although he hopefully could somehow still appreciate his drive-through funeral that many friends attended and his last ride on the back of a wagon, which was pulled by a tractor driven by his great-grandson from the funeral home to the cemetery at Zion's Union Maxatawny Church five miles away.

As of this writing, the pandemic has not yet ended. The family patriarch has passed on to the next world, but a new life appears. My second grandchild, Felix Stephen, was born to Amberly in September in a rough-and-tumble delivery. Amberly had a great pregnancy, but then her blood pressure spiked, and she was diagnosed with preeclampsia. The doctors induced her, and tiny Felix made his grand entrance four weeks early at 4 pounds, 12 ounces. His mom recovered slowly, but Felix avoided the neonatal intensive care unit, and the family went home a few days later. The extended family, including me, took him for his first walk that weekend, his first miles of many to come.

His birth was a grand adventure, just like my first grandchild's had been. Nothing in this family gets done the easy way. But both my grandsons have in their spirit a sense of the journeys to come. You may ask how I would know this when they are so young. I may not know a lot, but I know a sense of adventure. I know it well, and I can detect it in others, even the newly born. I now look forward to being part of those adventures with Miles and Felix. It's time to get out the maps, again.

Chapter 30

My Magnum Opus — From the Black Madonnas of Southern France to the End of the Earth

*"There's just this human heart
That's built with this human flaw
What was your question
Love is the answer."*

— St. Vincent, "All My Stars Aligned"

In autumn 2023, I plan to walk a long pilgrimage. One of the reasons for this grand undertaking is to celebrate 50 years of living with Type 1 diabetes — celebrating not only surviving this affliction but also thriving despite it. I plan to honor one of the biggest factors in that thriving — movement across the landscapes. I plan to invite all my friends from around the world who have been on past adventures with me to walk a section. I predict a moving, ceremonial hullabaloo will ensue.

The grand finale, the swan song, the epilogue, the magnum opus. All the adventures I took prepared me for this, and in fact it's not too melodramatic to say that everything that happened in my life readied me for this pilgrimage. It ultimately will be in parts a vagabondage, a walkabout, an adventure, an expedition, an odyssey, a sojourn, a wandering, a peregrination. If I were to die along the way, it could even be a transmigration of the soul. But in the end, this walk of over 1,600 kilometers/1,000 miles, covering two countries, would, in its simplest form, be a true pilgrimage.

Before setting out, one could pick out the spiritual highlights: a pre-walk Mass in the French city Toulouse and amid the medieval fortress of Carcassonne. Both locations were known for the Black Madonnas in the cathedrals. Then, we will go by train to the beginning of the walk in the mythical city of Cahors, encircled by the river Lot. The first morning, we will ascend on foot out of Cahors and head to the hilltop villages of Lascabanes and Lauzerte, culminating in a Mass with the monks at the cathedral of Moissac.

The highlights will continue: a night spent in the monasteries in Aire-sur-l'Adour, Lectoure, and La Romieu. A visit to a 16th-century church in Pimbo. A monumental climb out of France and into Spain, from the transformative village of Saint-Jean-Pied-de-Port over the Pyrenees Mountains to the cathedral of Roncesvalles. The holy fiesta of Pamplona. The climb to Alto del Perdón, where the path of the stars meets that of the wind. The Knights Templar octagonal Church of St. Mary of Eunate. The hallowed blessing of the wine at Monastery of Irache. The high-on-a-hill villages of Cirauqui, Villamayor de Monjardin, and Navarrete. More blessing of the wine in La Rioja. The Iglesia de San Juan, where we will experience a communitas pilgrim meal. The climb to the Montes de Oca and monastery for Mass at San Juan de Ortega.

After the Gothic city of Burgos and Mass in one of the most beautiful cathedrals in the world, then will come an eight-day, sometimes solo, mystical journey across the Meseta, the Spanish desert. Out of that starkness will appear the monastery of Carrión de los Condes and, days later, the monastery of Sahagún. Next will come the city León with its sophisticated and cosmopolitan brand of mysticism and the holy walled city Astorga, with a Gaudi-designed castle and cathedral. More spiritual highlights will follow, like breaking bread with the singing monks at Refugio Gaucelmo in the mountain town Rabanal del Camino. The sacred cross at Cruz de Ferro, where you leave a stone from back home and your burdens behind. Then a descent out of the clouds and snowy peaks to a village from another time, Molinaseca. The stunning Knights Templar castle at Ponferrada. The village of wine and rivers, Villafranca del Bierzo. Two massive climbs up to O Cebreiro, the Galician summit, where a village from another century and a simple cathedral stand guard. The woods and hills of Samos leading one to a mind-bending vista of the holy monastery. A walk through what seems like a hundred Galician villages and then the triumphant yet humbling entrance, through the Portal de Camino, into the third-holiest city in Christianity, Santiago de Compostela – St. James in a Field of Stars.

The pilgrimage will not end here as most do. West to the Atlantic Ocean, first to the fishing village of Muxia, then along the seaside cliffs to Finisterre, which the ancients believed was the end of the earth! That is the route of my magnum opus. The question one cannot help but ask is, what will this walk reveal to me, if I am truly open to receiving that sublime and divine message?

But by now, I know a pilgrimage is not a list or a series of experiences to be piled one upon the other, items to be checked off. The goal is the path. Walking is meditation. Walking is a celebration. Walking is the prayer. Walking is what is holy. The walking is the Mass, the bread and wine you carry with you in your pack and in your heart. The goal is the path. Adelante y mas alla — onward and beyond. Ultreia et suseia — beyond upwards. Buen Camino — good way, good journey. We will hear all those greetings on a daily basis from many pilgrims from around the world. And we, too, will proclaim those greetings to all we encounter during that holy pilgrimage, during my magnum opus. Even as I write this, the training and preparations have begun.

Chapter 31

Walking My Way into the Next World

"There's a pale sky in the east, all the stars are in the west
Oh, here's to all the dreamers, may our open hearts find rest
The wing and the wheel are gonna carry us along
And we'll have memories for company, long after the songs are gone."

— Nanci Griffith, "The Wing & the Wheel"

I learned many things from the Native American medicine men and women I was blessed to talk with during my travels. In different forms and embodiments, they enlightened me with the belief that death is not an end, only a changing of worlds. I figure I have about 13 years left to live if I'm lucky, which puts me at 80 years old. I already have beaten the odds two doctors gave me during my diagnosis with Type 1 diabetes at age 18: I would only live to be 55 to 60. Why have 80 as a goal? One of my heroes was actress Mary Tyler Moore, who also had Type 1 diabetes for most of her life. She, too, lived a full and amazing life and was physically active as a dancer, training to the very end. Mary Tyler Moore passed on to the next world at 80. I think I can make it to 80, maybe even a bit beyond, because Mary Tyler Moore is my spirit guide.

Documentary filmmaker Werner Herzog never takes the paved road, always the dirt track, adding that he has probably, from mid-puberty, been trying very hard to die a grand, poetic death. My diagnosis at 18 initially caused, in my psyche, a sense of "a diminished life." Of course, that didn't last long. Figuratively, I took the bull by the horns, and that was 40 years before I visited Madrid and Pamplona. I created and lived the life I have shared here. But I still have 13 years to create, design, prepare, train, and implement the rest of my life. In other words, it's time to get out the maps again. My magnum opus doesn't have to be my coda, my postscript.

I always found this passage from the book "Almanac of the Dead" by Native American author Leslie Marmon Silko to be a comfort when contemplating death: "Calabazas had begun to notice that he did not sleep as much as he once had, and he identified that characteristic with old age. As the human soul approached death, it got more and more restless and more and more energy for wandering, a preparation for all eternity where the old people believed no one would rest or sleep but would range over the earth and between the moon and stars, traveling on winds and clouds, in constant motion with ocean tides, migrations of birds and animals, pulsing within all life and all beings ever created."

I always was an ebullient, joyous soul. The setbacks put dents in that joyfulness but did not depreciate me. The biggest reason is that I had what the French call a "raison d'être" — a justification for existence. I knew all that in my youth before my many health problems began. How did I come to think like that, to begin to know it? I have no idea. Mark Twain wrote, "The two most important days in your life are the day that you are born, and the day you find out why." I was fortunate — I knew why at a very early age, and that carried me through the coming hard times.

A few years before my mom died, she told me, "I'm sorry you had to fight most of your life to survive. But thank God you were the one to carry the burdens. Your brothers would have struggled more, maybe not handled it as well. I've always felt it was your destiny."

Lying on his deathbed, Henry David Thoreau was said to have suddenly sat up and said his last two words, "Moose" and "Indians." He was probably remembering a canoe trip upriver into Maine that he and his brother took a few years before. This points to the possibility that family and adventures, especially when the two are combined, are what you might well remember most as you lay dying, which brings me to a passage of Thoreau's from "Walden": "I went to the woods because I wished to live deliberately, to front only the essential facts of life, and see if I could not learn what it had to teach, and not, when I came to die, discover that I had not lived."

Someone once told me that it's much easier to enter heaven if you have a lot of scars to show St. Peter, or whoever is tending the gate that day. If that is true, then I have nothing to worry about. I'll get in on the full ticket, which includes unlimited turns on all the amusement park rides and free Netflix for the rest of eternity. My poor body has many visible scars showing outside my clothing, and a bunch more under it. Plus, I wonder if psychological scars count, and if they are even able to be counted, those cracks in the psyche that trauma causes. Two of my favorite authors have written some perceptive ruminations about the scars of life. Author Michael Ondaatje wrote these lines in his book, "The English Patient": "We die containing a richness of lovers and tribes, tastes we have swallowed, bodies we have plunged into and swum up as if rivers of wisdom, characters we have climbed into as if trees, fears we have hidden in as if caves. I wish for all this to be marked on by body when I am dead." To further illuminate this theme, I give you a quote from Argentine writer Jorge Luis Borges: "A man sets out to draw the world. As the years go by, he peoples a space with images of provinces, kingdoms, mountains, bays, ships, islands, fishes, rooms, instruments, stars, horses, and individuals. A short time before he dies, he discovers that the patient labyrinth of lines traces the lineaments of his own face."

What exactly will our consciousness be like in heaven, the next world, the afterlife, the eternal sunshine of the spotless mind? Religion, spirituality, psychology, philosophy, and quantum physics have tried and sometimes may have shed a bit of light on the possibilities, although surely not enough to ease our apprehensive souls. Living life to the fullest leaves less time and space in an average day for those worries to creep in. At least, that's what works for me. Maybe this, in its ultimate form, is what the book that I have written was for me: both the living of these experiences and the documenting of them. It may ease my way through death and on into the next world. Or maybe not. I'll have to wait and see. When it does happen, it will be part of my continuing adventure. Stay tuned. An insider's view of the afterlife would most certainly be a bestseller. Until then, I'll end with a quote from Dag Hammarskjöld: "Do not seek death. Death will find you. But seek the road which makes death a fulfilment." Amen!